CW00404426

A Treasure Trove of Quotations for Speakers, Writers and Raconteurs

John Andrew

Copyright © John Andrew 2014
This book is sold subject to the condition that it shall not, by way of trade or
otherwise, be lent, resold, hired out, or otherwise circulated without the
publisher's prior consent in any form of binding or cover other than that in
which it is published and without a similar condition including this condition
being imposed on the subsequent publisher.
The moral right of John Andrew has been asserted.
ISBN: 1495203700
ISBN-13: 978-1495203701

CONTENTS

ABILITY

1. The greatest ability is dependability.
- *anon.*

2. Natural abilities are like natural plants, they need pruning by study.
- **Francis Bacon:** *Essays*, 1625.

3. Knowing what you cannot do is more important than knowing what you can do.
- **Lucille Ball:** *The Real Story of Lucille Ball* by Eleanor Harris, 1954.

4. Natural ability without education has more often raised a man to glory and virtue, than education without natural ability.
- **Marcus Tullius Cicero:** *Oration in defence of a poet accused of not being a Roman citizen,* **circa** 62 BC.

5. If money is your hope for independence you will never have it. The only real security that a man can have in this world is a reserve of knowledge, experience and ability.
- **Henry Ford:** *The Toastmaster's Treasure Chest* compiled by H.V. Prochnow and H.V. Prochnow Jr. 1979.

6. To be sure, we have inherited abilities, but our development we owe to thousands of influences coming from the world around us from which we appropriate what we can and what is suitable to us.
- **Johann Wolfgang von Goethe**: *Conversations with Eckermann*, 1828.

7. Compared to what we ought to be, we are only half awake. We are making use of only a small part of our mental and physical resources. Stating the thing broadly, the human individual thus lives far within his limits. He possesses powers of various sorts which he habitually fails to use.
- **William James**: *The Principles of Psychology*, 1890.

8. We judge ourselves by what we feel capable of doing, while others judge us by what we have already done.
- **Henry Wadsworth Longfellow:** *Kavanagh: a Tale*, 1849.

9 Competence, like truth, beauty and contact lenses, is in the eye of the beholder.
- **Laurence J. Peter:** *The Peter Principle: Why Things Always Go Wrong*, 1969.

10. Able people can do more.
- *Chinese Proverb*.

11. If you think that others do not rate your abilities as highly as you do yourself, do not be too sure that it is they who are mistaken.
- **Bertrand Russell:** *The Conquest of Happiness*,1930.

12. A man must not deny his manifest abilities, for that is to evade his obligations.
- **Robert Louis Stevenson:** *The Merry Men and Other Tales and Fables*, 1887.

13. I know of no more encouraging fact than the unquestioned ability of man to elevate his life by conscious endeavour.
- **Henry David Thoreau:** *Walden*, 1854.

14. The world cares very little what you or I know, but it does care a great deal about what you or I are able to do.
- **Booker T. Washington:** *The Boston Globe, 31ˢᵗ July, 1903*.

15. Intelligence is quickness to apprehend as distinct from ability which is capacity to act wisely on the thing apprehended.
- **Alfred North Whitehead:** *Dialogues of Alfred North Whitehead*, 1953.

16. Don't measure yourself by what you have accomplished, but by what you should have accomplished with your ability.
- **John R. Wooden.**

17. You are the only one who can use your ability. It is an awesome responsibility.
- **Zig Ziglar:** *Zig Ziglar's Little Book of Big Quotes*, 1990.

ABSENCE

18. Absence makes the heart grow fonder.
- **Thomas Haynes Bayly**: *Isle of Beauty* from *Collected Works*, 1844.

19. I was court martialled in my absence, and sentenced to death in my absence, so I said they could shoot me in my absence.
- **Brendan Behan**: *The Hostage*.

20. Even though I am not physically present, I am with you in spirit.
- **The Bible**: *1st Corinthians 5: 3a, NIV*.

21. Love reckons hours for months, and days for years; every little absence is an age.
- **John Dryden**: *Amphitryon*, 1678.

22. Absence sharpens love, presence strengthens it.
- **Thomas Fuller**: *Gnomologia: Adages and Proverbs*, 1732.

23. The joy of life is variety; the tenderest love requires to be renewed by intervals of absence.
- **Samuel Johnson**: *The Idler* – Essays, 1758 - 1760.

24. Sometimes, when only one person is missing, the world seems depopulated.
- **Alphonse de Lamartine**: *Poetic Meditations*, 1820.

25. Absence diminishes small loves and increases great ones, as the wind blows out the candle and fans the bonfire.
- **Francois, Duc de La Rochefoucauld**: *Maxims*, 1665.

26. Absences are a good influence in love and keep it bright and delicate.
- **Robert Louis Stevenson**: *Virginibus Puerisque*, 1881.

ACCOUNTANT

27. When the accountant husband proposed, he said, "I'd like to make a joint income tax return with you."
- **anon.**

28. The company accountant is shy and retiring. He's shy of a quarter of a million dollars. That's why he is retiring.
- **Milton Berle:** *Milton Berle's Private Joke File*, 1989.

29. An accountant is a man who is always dealing in numbers, but who doesn't count much when his wife is around.
- **Evan Esar:** *20,000 Quips & Quotes*. 1968.

30. Never ask of money spent, / Where the spender thinks it went. / Nobody was ever meant / To remember or invent / What he did with every cent.
- **Robert Frost:** *The Hardship of Accounting* in *The Poetry of Robert Frost* edited by E.C. Lathem, 1969.

31. Our accounting department is the office that has the little red box on the wall saying, "In case of emergency, break glass." And inside are two tickets to Brazil.
- **Robert Orben:** *Quotable Business* by Louis E. Boone, 1999.

32. Old accountants never die, they just lose their balance.
- **Mark Ortman:** *The Teacher's Book of Wit*. 1996.

33. I have no use for bodyguards, but I have a very special use for two highly trained certified public accountants.
- **Elvis Presley:** *Quotable Business* by Louis E. Boone, 1999.

34. In filling out an income tax return, let an accountant instead of your conscience, be your guide.
- **Will Rogers:** *20,000 Quips & Quotes* by Evan Esar.

ACHIEVEMENT

35. Better to try something and fail than to try nothing and succeed.
- *anon*.

36. The man who claims a thing cannot be done is invariably correct for he will never do it.
- *anon*.

37. According to a 20th century myth, the bumble bee's body weight in relation to its wing span is such that, aerodynamically, the bumble bee is incapable of flight. However, no one has told the bumble bee this, consequently, the bumble bee flies.
- *anon*.

38. If you think you can, you can. And if you think you can't, you're right.
- **Mary Kay Ash:** *New York Times, October 20th, 1985*.

39. Wha does the utmost that he can / Will whiles do mair. NB Scots: wha = who: whiles = at times: mair = more.
- **Robert Burns:** *The Poems and Songs of Robert Burns: Harvard Classic 6* edited by Charles Eliot, 1909.

40.If we attend continually and promptly to the little we can do, we shall ere long be surprised to find how little remains that we cannot do.
- **Samuel Butler:** *Geary's Guide to the World's Great Aphorists* by James Geary. 2007.

41. Every achievement is a servitude. It drives us to a higher achievement.
- **Albert Camus**.

42. Whatever is worth doing at all, is worth doing well.
- **Lord Chesterfield:** *Letters to His Son*, March 10th, 1746.

43. The greatest achievement of the human spirit is to live up to one's opportunities and make the most of one's resources.
- **Luc de Clapiers, Marquis de Vauvenargues:** *Reflections and Maxims*,1746.

44. The difficult we do immediately; the impossible takes a little longer.
- *It has been suggested that this is an unofficial motto of the Seabees*, **The Construction Battalions (cbs) of the United States Navy.**

45. No great deal is done by falterers who ask for certainty.
- **George Eliot:** *The Spanish Gypsy*, 1868.

46. No great thing is created suddenly.
- **Epictetus:** *Discourses*, **circa** 108 AD.

47. For a man to achieve all that is demanded of him he must regard himself as greater than he is.
- **Johann Wolfgang von Goethe:** *Art and Antiquity*.

48. Somebody said that it couldn't be done / But he with a chuckle replied / That "maybe it couldn't," but he would be one /Who wouldn't say so till he tried./ So he buckled right in with a trace of a grin /On his face. If he worried he hid it/ He started to sing as he tackled the thing / That couldn't be done, and he did it!
- **Edgar Albert Guest**; *Collected Verses of Edgar A. Guest.* 1945.

49. My mother drew a distinction between achievement and success. She said that achievement is the knowledge that you have studied and worked hard and done the best that is in you. Success is being praised by others, and that's nice too, but not as important or satisfying. Always aim for achievement and forget about success.
- **Helen Hayes.**

50. Back of every achievement is a proud wife and a surprised mother-in-law.
- **Brooks Hays:** *The New York Herald Tribune, 2nd December, 1961.*

51. We never do anything well till we cease to think about the manner of doing it.
- **William Hazlitt:** *On Prejudice*, 1821.

52. Nothing will ever be attempted if all possible objections must first be overcome.
- **Samuel Johnson:** *The History of Rasselas*. 1759.

53. It is most mortifying for a man to consider what he has done, compared to what he might have done.
- **Samuel Johnson:** *The Life Of Samuel Johnson* by James Boswell, 1791.

54. We judge ourselves by what we feel we are capable of doing, while others judge us by what we have already done.
- **Henry Wadsworth Longfellow:** *Kavanagh: A Novel*. 1849.

55. If we are ever in doubt about what to do, it is a good rule to ask ourselves what we shall wish on the morrow that we had done.
- **John Lubbock**.

56. Small deeds done are better that great deeds planned.
- **Peter Marshall:** *The Prayers of Peter Marshall*, 1954.

57. Achievement, I have heard it said, is largely the product of steadily raising one's level of aspiration and expectation.
- **Jack Nicklaus:** *My Story*. 1997.

58. Anybody can do just about anything with himself that he really wants to and make up his mind to do. We are capable of greater things than we realize.
- **Norman Vincent Peale:** *Have a Great Day – Every Day*, 1984.

59. Get good counsel before you begin, and when you have decided, act promptly.
- **Sallust:** *The Conspiracy of Catiline*, 42-43 BC.

60. He that is overcautious will accomplish little.
- **Johann Christoph Friedrich von Schiller:** *William Tell, Act 3, Scene 1* 1804.

61. The reason why so little is done, is generally because so little is attempted.
- **Samuel Smiles:** *Self – Help*, 1859.

62. Nothing ever comes to me that is worth having, except as the result of hard work.
- **Booker T. Washington:** *Up From Slavery*, 1901.

63. Out of the strain of Doing / Into the peace of the Done.
- **Julia Louise Woodruff:** *Sunday at Home.* 1910.

ACTION

64. We have too many high sounding words, and too few actions that correspond with them.
- **Abigail Adams:** *in a letter to her husband, John Adams, 1774.*

65. Man was made for action and for bustle too, I believe.
- **Abigail Adams:** *in a letter to her sister, Mary Smith Cranch, 1784.*

66. I judge by deeds, not words.
- **Aeschylus:** *Prometheus Bound.* **circa** 415 BC.

67. Simple, sincere people seldom speak of their piety. It shows itself in acts rather than in words, and has more influence than homilies or protestations.
- **Louisa May Alcott:** *Little Women,* 1869.

68. For purposes of action nothing is more useful than narrowness of thought combined with energy of will.
- **Henri Frederic Amiel:** *Journal Intime,* 1882.

69. I do not regret the things I've done, but those I did not do.
- ***anon.***

70. Actions can be more eloquent than words.
 - ***anon.***

71. We acquire a particular quality by constantly acting in a certain way. We become just by performing just actions, temperate by performing temperate actions, brave by performing brave actions.
- **Aristotle:** *Nicomachean Ethics,* 4th century BC.

72. Think like a man of action, and act like a man of thought.
- **Henri Bergson:** *Forbes Magazine, 1989.*

73. Action springs not from thought, but from a readiness for responsibility.
- **Dietrich Bonhoeffer:** *Letters and Papers from Prison*, 1953.

74. The method of the enterprising is to plan with audacity and execute with vigour.
- **Christian Nestell Bovee:** *Intuitions and Summaries of Thought*, 1862.

75. However many holy words you read, however many you speak, what good will they do you if you do not act upon them?
- **Buddha:** *The Dhammapada: Wisdom of the Buddha*, **circa** 483 BC.

76. Talk that does not end in any kind of action is better suppressed altogether.
- **Thomas Carlyle:** *Inaugural Address on being installed as Rector of Edinburgh University, 1860.*

77. Deliberate with caution, but act with decision; and yield with graciousness, or oppose with firmness.
- **Charles Caleb Colton:** *Lacon,* or *Many Things in Few Words: Addressed to Those Who Think,* 1826, edited by George J. Barbour, 2001.

78. The superior man is modest in his speech, but exceeds in his actions.
- **Confucius:** *The Analects,* 5th century BC.

79. I have long since come to believe that people never mean half of what they say, and that it is best to disregard their talk and judge only their actions.
- **Dorothy Day:** *The Long Loneliness: The Autobiography of Dorothy Day.* 1952.

80. Thought is the seed of action.
- **Ralph Waldo Emerson:** *Essays,* 1841.

81. Good thoughts are no better than good dreams unless they be executed.
- **Ralph Waldo Emerson:** *Nature,* 1836.

82. Let's plunge ourselves into the roar of time, the whirl of accident; may pain and pleasure, success and failure, shift as they will – it's only action that can make a man.
- **Johann Wolfgang von Goethe:** *Faust,* 1806.

83. If you rest, you rust.
- **Helen Hayes:** *My Life in Three Acts,* 1990.

84. When the iron is hot, strike.
- **John Heywood:** *Proverbs,* 1546.

85. That action is best, which procures the greatest happiness for the greatest number.
- **Francis Hutcheson:** *Inquiry Concerning Moral Good & Evil.* 1725.

86. The great end of life is not knowledge, but action.
- **T. H. Huxley:** *Aphorisms & Reflections* from *The Works of T. H. Huxley* selected by Henrietta Huxley, 1907.

87. The actions of men are the best interpreters of their thoughts.
- **John Locke:** *An Essay Concerning Human Understanding,* 1690.

88. Action without thought is shooting without aim.
- ***American Proverb.***

89. Don't be afraid to take a big step if one is necessary. You can't cross a chasm in two small steps.
- ***Chinese Proverb.***

90. Love of bustle is not industry.
- **Seneca:** *Epistles,* 1st century AD.

91. What a man believes may be ascertained, not from his creed, but from the assumptions on which he habitually acts.
- **George Bernard Shaw:** *Maxims For Revolutionists,* 1903.

92. Fortune cannot aid those who do nothing.
- **Sophocles:** *Fragments,* 5th cent. BC.

93. It is the mark of a good action that it appears inevitable in retrospect.
- **Robert Louis Stevenson, *attributed.***

ADVERSITY

94. He knows not his own strength that has not met adversity.
- **Francis Bacon:** *Essays*, 1625.

95. Affliction comes to us, not to make us sad, but sober; not to make us sorry, but wise; not to make us despondent, but by its darkness to refresh us as the night refreshes the day; not to impoverish us, but enrich us.
- **Henry Ward Beecher**.

96. Adversity has the same effect on a man that severe training has for the pugilist: it reduces him to his fighting weight.
- **Josh Billings:** *Geary's Guide to the World's Great Aphorists* by James Geary, 2009.

97. If we had no Winter, the Spring would not be so pleasant; if we did not sometimes taste of adversity, prosperity would not be so welcome.
- **Anne Bradstreet:** *Meditations Divine and Moral*, 1664.

98. Adversity is more supportable with equanimity by most people than any great prosperity.
- **Samuel Butler:** *The Way of All Flesh*, 1903.

99. Adversity is sometimes hard upon a man, but for one man who can stand prosperity, there are a hundred that will stand adversity.
- **Thomas Carlyle:** *Heroes and Hero Worship*, 1841.

100. Friendship makes prosperity brighter, while it lightens adversity by sharing its anxieties.
- **Marcus Tullius Cicero:** *On Friendship*.

101. Constant success shows us but one side of the world. Adversity brings out the reverse of the picture.
- **Charles Caleb Colton:** *Lacon*, or *Many Things in Few Words*, 1826, edited by George J. Barbour, 2001.

102. The finest friendships have been formed in mutual adversity, as iron is most strongly united in the fiercest flame.
 - *ibid.*

103. Adversity can strengthen us if it does not go on too long.
- **Mason Cooley:** *City Aphorisms, 9ᵗʰ Selection*, 1992.

104. Adversity has the effect of eliciting talents, which in prosperous circumstances would have lain dormant.
- **Horace:** *Satires*, 35 BC.

105. I'll say this for adversity: people seem to be able to stand it, and that's more than I can say for prosperity.
- **Kin Hubbard:** *The Dictionary of Humorous Quotations* edited by Evan Esar, 1949.

106. He knows not his own strength that has not met adversity.
- **Ben Jonson.**

107. It is often better to have a great deal of harm happen to you than a little; a great deal may rouse you to remove what a little one will only accustom you to endure.
- **Grenville Kleiser.**

108. Into each life some rain must fall, / Some days must be dark and dreary.
- **Henry Wadsworth Longfellow:** *The Rainy Day*, 1842.

109. Let us be of good cheer, however, remembering that the misfortunes hardest to bear are those which never come.
- **James Russell Lowell:** *Democracy and Other Addresses*, 1887.

110. One time or another we all face adversity's chilling wind. One man flees from it, and like an unresisting kite, falls to the ground. Another yields no retreating inch, and the wind that would destroy him lifts him as readily to the heights. We are not measured by the trials we meet, only those we overcome.
- **David McKay:** *Ensign Magazine, May, 1961.*

111. The old proverb says, "Take it as a blessing or take it as a test; whatever happens, happens for the best." And as it happens, adversities may sometimes contain their own blessings.
- **Dan Millman:** *The Twelve Gateways to Personal Growth*, 1990.

112. Smooth seas do not make skilful sailors.
- *African Proverb.*

113. The gem cannot be polished without friction, nor man perfected without trials.
- *Chinese Proverb.*

114. Fire is the test of gold; adversity of strong men.
- **Seneca:** *Moral Essays.* 1st century AD.

115. If all our misfortunes were laid in one common heap, whence every one must take an equal portion, most people would be content to take their own and depart.
- **Solon.**

116. Prosperity makes friends, adversity tries them.
- **Syrus:** *Maxims.*1st century BC.

117. Many who seem to be struggling with adversity are happy; many amid great affluence, are utterly miserable.
- **Tacitus.**

118. The manner in which one endures what must be endured is more important than the thing that must be endured.
- **Harry S. Truman:** *Plain Speaking: an Oral Biography of Harry S. Truman* by Merle Miller, 1973.

119. You learn the most from life's hardest knocks.
- **Conway Twitty:** *The Book of Country Music Wisdom* edited by Criswell Freeman, 1994.

120. People never fail to amaze me. They face the unimaginable with a shot of grace and a rush of adrenaline; they steel their nerves. They summon their cool or anger or faith or whatever it takes to pull them through, and they go on to live another day.
- **Oprah Winfrey:** *O Magazine, April, 2007.*

ADVERTISING

121. The great art in writing advertisements is the finding out a proper method to catch the reader's eye; without which a good thing may pass over unobserved.
- **Joseph Addison:** *The Tatler No 224.*

122. Advertising is the art of making whole lies out of half truths.
- ***anon.***

123. The codfish lays 10,000 eggs, / The homely hen just one; / The codfish never cackles / To tell you that she's done. / And so we scorn the codfish, / And the homely hen we prize. / Which demonstrates to you and me / That it pays to advertise.
- **anon:** Lighten *Up! Bk Two* edited by Bruce Lansky, 1999.

124. Advertising helps raise the standard of living by raising the standard of longing.
- **Jacob M. Braude:** *Braude's Handbook of Stories for Toastmasters and Speakers,* 1957.

125. Doing business without advertising is like winking at a girl in the dark. You know what you're doing, but nobody else does.
- **Steuart Henderson Brit:** *The New York Herald Tribune, 30ᵗʰ October, 1956.*

126. The very first law of advertising is to avoid the concrete promise and cultivate the delightfully vague.
- **Stuart Chase:** *The Life and Writings of Stuart Chase: Volume 8.* edited by Richard Vangermeer, 2005.

127. A car dealer was asked if advertising was effective. "Yes, it brings quick results," he replied. "Once we ran an ad that our watchdog was missing and offered a reward for his return." "Did you get him back?" "No, but that very night three cars were stolen!"
- **Sam Ewing:** *Reader's Digest, August, 1992.*

128. Good advertising for a bad product is hucksterism. Good advertising for a good product is honesty. Bad advertising for a good product is incompetence. Bad advertising for a bad product is sweet justice.
- **Brett Feinstein**. NB "Hucksterism" is an American word derived from "huckster", a person who uses aggressive techniques.

129. Our society's values are being corrupted by advertising's insistence on the equation: youth equals popularity, popularity equals success, success equals happiness.
- **John Fisher:** *The Plot to Make You Buy*, 1968.

130. Advertising may be described as the science of arresting human intelligence long enough to get money from it.
- **Stephen Leacock:** *Garden of Folly*, 1924.

131. You can fool all the people all of the time if the advertising is right and the budget is big enough.
- **Joseph E**. **Levine:** *New York Times, 1987.*

132. Advertising is a valuable economic factor because it is the cheapest way of selling goods, particularly if the goods are worthless.
- **Sinclair Lewis:** *The New York Times, 18th April, 1943.*

133. History will see advertising as one of the real evil things of our time. It is stimulating people constantly to want things, want this, want that.
- **Malcolm Muggeridge:** *attributed*

134. Ads are the cave art of the twentieth century.
- **Marshall McLuhan:** *Culture is Our Business*, 1970.

135. I don't know why they call them unmentionables when you can't pick up a magazine without seeing a full page of them!
- **Robert Orben:** *2,000 Sure-Fire Jokes for Speakers*, 1986.

136. Advertising is the art of convincing people to spend money they don't have for something they don't need.
- **Will Rogers**.

137. Let advertisers spend the same amount of money improving their product that they do on advertising, and they wouldn't have to advertise it.
- *ibid.*

138. Many a small thing has been made large by the right kind of advertising.
- **Mark Twain:** *A Connecticut Yankee in King Arthur's Court*, 1889.

139. Half the money I spend on advertising is wasted, the trouble is I don't know which half.
- **John Wanamaker:** *Confessions of an Advertising Man* by David Ogilvy, 1963.

ADVICE

140. There is nothing which we receive with so much reluctance as advice.
- **Joseph Addison:** *The Spectator, 17th October, 1712.*

141. Unsought advice is freely given / By those who want to give it away /But the best advice you could have / Is don't listen to what they say.
- *anon.*

142. Don't be troubled if the temptation to give advice is irresistible; the ability to ignore it is universal.
- *anon.*

143. The getting is easy, / The giving is nice; / The taking's the tough part / About advice.
- **Richard Armour:** *An Armoury of Light Verse,* 1963.

144. I don't give advice. I can't tell anybody what to do. Instead, I say this is what we know about this problem at this time, and here are the consequences of these actions.
- **Joyce Brothers**.

145. P.S. I know this letter has been filled with advice - all unsolicited. Take what you want and throw the rest away. As George Bernard Shaw said, "Advice is like kissing: it costs nothing and is a pleasant thing to do".
- **H. Jackson Brown Jr:** *P.S. I Love You,* 1990.

146. Advice is judged by results, not by intentions.
- **Cicero:** *Maxims,* 1st cent. BC.

147. We ask advice, but we mean approbation.
- **Charles Caleb Colton:** *Lacon. Or Many Things in Few Words* edited by George J. Barbour, 2001.

148. Perhaps one of the only positive pieces of advice that I was ever given was that supplied by an old courtier who observed: 'Only two rules really count. Never miss an opportunity to relieve yourself; never miss a chance to sit down and rest your feet'.
- **Edward VII:** *Dictionary of Quotations*.

149. Sound advice can often be ninety-nine per cent sound and one per cent advice.
- **Sam Ewing:** *Wall Street Journal, 3rd March, 1993*.

150. If you can tell the difference between good advice and bad advice, you don't need advice.
- **Leopold Fechtner:** *5,000 One-And-Two-Line Jokes*, 1973.

151. Advice is what we ask for when we already know the answer but wish we didn't.
- **Erica Jong:** *How To Save Your Own Life*, 1977.

152. Write down the advice of him who loves you, though you like it not at present.
- ***English Proverb***.

153. Nothing is given so profusely as advice.
- **Francois, Duc de La Rochefoucauld:** *Maxims*, 1665.

154. Old men are fond of giving good advice to console themselves for their inability to give bad examples.
- ***ibid***.

155. There is nothing more hateful than bad advice.
- **Sophocles:** *Electra*, 406 BC.

156. Many receive advice, few profit by it.
- **Publilius Syrus:** *Maxims*, 1st century BC.

157. Listen to advice, but follow your heart.
- **Conway Twitty:** *The Book of Country Music Wisdom* edited by Criswell Freeman, 1994.

AGE

158. You can live to be a hundred if you give up all the things that make you want to live to be a hundred.
- **Woody Allen:** *Geary's Guide to the World's Great Aphorists* by James Geary, 2007.

159. To know how to grow old is the master-work of wisdom, and one of the most difficult chapters in the great art of living.
- **Henri Frederic Amiel:** *Journal Intime,* 1882.

160. No pleasure is worth giving up for the sake of two more years in a geriatric home in Weston-super-Mare.
- **Kingsley Amis:** *The Times, 21ˢᵗ June, 1994.*

161. You're getting old when you get the same sensation from a rocking chair that you once got on a roller coaster.
- ***anon.***

162. One of the nice things about old age is that you can whistle while you brush your teeth.
- ***anon.***

163. Old people, I have discovered, take old age in different ways. Some accept it as inevitable and are tolerant of it. Some ignore it, pretending it isn't there. Some are aware of it, but only in others. Some fight it, snarl at it, curse it. Still others, believe it or not, enjoy it.
- **Richard Armour:** *Going Like Sixty: A Lighthearted Look at the Years,* 1974.

164. Of late I appear / To have reached that stage / When people look old / Who are only my age.
- ***ibid.***

165. Age appears to be best in four things: Old wood best to burn, old wine to drink, old friends to trust, and old authors to read.

- **Francis Bacon:** *Apophthegms*, 1625. NB An apophthegm is a short cryptic remark containing some general or accepted truth.

166. The secret of staying young is to live honestly, eat slowly, and lie about your age.
- **Lucille Ball:** *Uncommon Scold* by Abby Adams, 1989.

167. If I had known what fun it is to be 83, I would have done it long ago.
- **Tony Benn:** *Quotes of the Day, The Press and Journal, 9th April, 2008.*

168. Age is strictly a case of mind over matter. If you don't mind it doesn't matter.
- **Jack Benny:** *New York Times, 15th February, 1974.*

169. You know you're getting older .....
A. when your actions creak louder than your words.
– Milton Berle.
B. when it takes you more time to recover than it did to tire you out.
- ibid.
C. when you're sitting in a rocking chair and you can't get it started.
- ibid.
D. when the candles cost more than the cake.
- **Bob Hope.**
E. when the gleam in your eye is just the sun on your bifocals.
- **H.Youngman.**

170. Grow old along with me! / The best is yet to be.
- **Robert Browning:** *Rabbi Ben Ezra*, 1864.

171. Age is something that doesn't matter, unless you are a cheese.
- **Luis Bunuel:** *My Last Sigh: The Autobiography of Luis Bunuel*, 1983.

172. There's many a good tune played on an old fiddle.
- **Samuel Butler:** *The Way of All Flesh*, 1903.

173. Old age isn't so bad when you consider the alternative.
- **Maurice Chevalier:** *New York Times, 9th October, 1960.*

174. I find four causes of the apparent misery of old age: first, it withdraws us from active accomplishments; second, it renders the body less powerful; third, it deprives us of almost all forms of enjoyment; fourth, it stands not far from death.

- **Marcus Tullius Cicero:** *On Old Age*, *circa* 44 BC.

175. Old age is really not so bad, may you come to know the condition.
- *ibid.*

176. No one is so old that he does not think he could live another year.
- *ibid.*

177. Like everyone else who makes the mistake of getting older, I begin each day with coffee and the obituaries.
- **Bill Cosby:** *Time Flies*, 1987.

178. Regrets are the natural property of grey hairs.
- **C. Dickens:** *Martin Chuzzlewit.*

179. I'm at an age when my back goes out more than I do.
- **Phyllis Diller.**

180. In youth we learn; in age we understand.
- **Marie von Ebner-Eschenbach:** *Aphorisms*, 1905.

181. Sixty is a wonderful age, especially if you're seventy.
- **Sam Ewing:** *Mature Living Magazine, February, 1999.*

182. After 45, your get up and go has got up and gone!
- **Leopold Fechtner:** *5,000 One-And-Two-Line Jokes*, 1973.

183. This question of ageing is a strange business. Have you ever gone upstairs or into another room of your house and wondered why you were there? What is even more worrying is when you dial someone's number, then can't remember who you are phoning and why. I've certainly tried to answer the phone by lifting up the TV remote control. Funnily enough, saying "hello" into it doesn't help....... It's not that I'm all that old. I would tell you how old I am but unfortunately I've forgotten.
- **Ron Ferguson:** *The Press and Journal 26/10/10.*

184. I don't need you to remind me of my age. I have a bladder to do that for me.
- **Stephen Fry:** as his creation, Professor Donald Trefusis, whose radio essays featured in the BBC Radio 4 series *Loose Ends.*

185. When people say I'm 70 I say that's a confounded lie. I'm twice 35, that's all, twice 35.
- **Sir Alfred Hitchcock:** *Halliwell's Who's Who in the Movies, 1999.*

186. The best part of the art of living is to know how to grow old gracefully.
- **Eric Hoffer:** *The Passionate State of Mind and Other Aphorisms*, 1954.

187. I don't like the fact that I have to get older so fast, but I like the fact that I'm ageing so well.
- **Dustin Hoffman:** *Halliwell's Who's Who in the Movies, 1999.*

188. Age is only a number. However, in my case, it is rather a large number.
- **Bob Hope:** *Bob Hope: My Life in Jokes*, 2003.

189. I do the same things I did when I was fifty-five. I just take a nap after each one now.
- *ibid.*

190. You're not old until you are eighty... that is the new theory and with that comes the belief that old age has been postponed... not indefinitely but certainly for longer than before.
- **Annie Hulley:** *How to Spend Your Kids Inheritance: All You Need to Know to Manage a Successful Retirement*, 2006.

191. Nothing makes one old so quickly as the ever-present thought that one is growing old.
- **Georg Christoph Lichtenberg:** *Notebook* K. 1789 – 1793.

192. Age Is a State of Mind.
- **Joan Lunden:** Chapter title in *Wake-Up Calls: Making the Most of Every Day Regardless of What Life Throws at You*, 2001.

193. Age is not particularly interesting. Anyone can get old. All you have to do is live long enough.
- **Groucho Marx:** *Groucho and Me,* 1959.

194. The older I grow, the more I distrust the familiar doctrine that age brings wisdom.
- **H. L. Mencken:** *Prejudices, Third Series,* 1922.

195. What's a geriatric ? - a German footballer scoring three goals.
- **Bob Monkhouse.**

196. Growing old is compulsory – growing up is optional.
- **Bob Monkhouse.**

197. Old age has one consolation; it doesn't last forever.
- **Mitch Murray:** *Mitch Murray's One-Liners for Speeches on Special Occasions,* 1997.

198. The best way to tell a woman's age is in a low whisper.
- *ibid.*

199. When a man has a birthday, he may take a day off. When a woman has a birthday, she'll take five *years* off.
- *ibid.*

200. When you're fifty you start thinking about things you haven't thought of before. I used to think getting old was about vanity – but actually it's about losing people you love.
- **Joyce Carol Oates:** *The Guardian, 18th August, 1989.*

201. *You know you are getting old when...*
A. You sink your teeth into a steak and they stay there.
B. You begin to act your age instead of your urge.
C. You're not inclined to exercise anything but caution.
- **Mark Ortman:** *The Teacher's Book of Wit,* 1996.

202. I believe in ageing gracefully – and, of course, buying as many anti-ageing creams as possible.
- **Sarah Jessica Parker:** *The Press and Journal, 18/7/08.*

203. I didn't get old on purpose, it just happened. If you are lucky, it could happen to you.
- **Andy Rooney:** *60 Minutes, CBS's TV Show.*

204. One of the blessings of age is to learn not to part on a note of sharpness, to treasure the moments spent with those we love, and to make them whenever possible good to remember, for time is short.
- **Eleanor Roosevelt:** *My Day: The Best of Eleanor Roosevelt's Acclaimed Newspaper Columns* edited by David Emblidge, 2001.

205. Getting old has its advantages. I can no longer read the bathroom scales.
- **Brad Schreiber:** *Laugh Twice and Call Me in the Morning. The Best Quotes and Cartoons to Cure What Ails You* selected by Bruce Lansky, 1999.

206. Old Age is an incurable disease.
- **Seneca:** *Epistles,* 1ˢᵗ century AD.

207. Age is a very high price to pay for maturity.
- **Tom Stoppard**.

208. I enjoy talking with very old people. They have gone before us on a road which we, too, may have to travel, and I think we do well to learn from them what it is like.
- **Socrates:** *Ageing Well* by George E. Vaillant, 2002.

209. Nobody loves life like an old man.
- **Sophocles:** *Fragments*, 5ᵗʰ century BC.

210. Inside every older person, there's a younger person wondering what happened.
- **Gloria Swanson:** *Swanson on Swanson* 1980.

211. Nobody grows old merely by living a number of years. We grow old by deserting our ideals.
- **Samuel Ullman:** *Youth*

212. Thirty-five is a very attractive age. London society is full of women.... who have, of their own free choice, remained thirty-five for years.
- **Oscar Wilde:** *The Importance of Being Ernest; A Trivial Comedy for Serious People, Act 3*, 1895.

AIR TRAVEL

213. It can hardly be a coincidence that no language on earth has ever produced the expression: "as pretty as an airport."
- **Douglas Adams:** *The Long Dark Tea-Time of the Soul*, 1988.

214. It's a small world, once you've made the long trip to the airport.
 - ***anon.***

215. Our new faster-than-sound jet planes are wonderful. You can eat dinner in London and get indigestion in New York.
- ***anon.***

216. This book is dedicated to Wilbur and Orville Wright, without whom air sickness would still be just a dream.
- **Dave Barry:** *The Only Travel Guide You'll Ever Need*, 1991.

217. I had arrived at the airport one hour early so that in accordance with airline procedures, I could stand around.
- **Dave Barry:** *Dave Barry is Not Taking This Sitting Down*, 2000.

218. Air travel will be much safer when they eliminate the car ride between the city and the airport.
- **Jacob M. Braude:** *Braude's Treasury of Wit and Humour For All Occasions*, 1991.

219. Thanks to modern air travel we can now be sick in countries we never even knew existed before.
- **Leopold Fechtner:** *Encyclopaedia of Ad-Libs, Crazy Jokes, Insults and Wisecracks*, 1977.

220. Uncle, whose inventive brains / Kept evolving aeroplanes, /Fell from an enormous height / Upon my garden lawn last night. /Flying is a fatal sport, / Uncle wrecked the tennis court.
- **Harry Graham:** *Ruthless Rhymes for Heartless Homes*, 1899.

221. Boy, the Concorde travels fast. It's like being shot out of a cannon – first class. It's so fast they don't have time to lose your luggage.
- **Bob Hope:** *My Life in Jokes*, 2003.

222. I like terra firma; the more firma , the less terra..
- **George S. Kaufman**.

223. I feel about airplanes the way I feel about diets. It seems to me that they are wonderful things for other people to go on.
- **Jean Kerr:** *The Snake Has All the Lines*, 1960.

224. When strapped into an airplane seat, I wonder where to put my feet.
And as the plane soars through the sky, I wonder how the thing can fly.
And when I use the airplane john, I wonder who it's flushing on.
And when we're finally on the ground, I wonder where my bags are bound.
And when I'm in the parking lot, I wonder why my car is not
- **Bruce Lansky:** *What I Think About When Travelling* in *Lighten Up*. 1999.

225. Airplanes are invariably scheduled to depart at such times as 7.54; 9.21 or 11.37 This extreme specificity has the effect on the novice of instilling in him the twin beliefs that he will be arriving at 10.08; 1.43 or 4.22, and that he should get to the airport in time. These beliefs are not only erroneous but actually unhealthy.
- **Fran Lebowitz:** *Social Studies*, 1981.

226. On a plane you can pick up more and better people than on any other public conveyance since the stage coach.
- **Anita Loos**.

227. Modern air travel means less time spent in transit. That time is now spent in transit lounges.
- **P. J. O'Rourke:** *Holidays in Hell*, 1988.

228. After all the passengers were belted in, and the aircraft reached its flight path of thirty-two thousand feet, through the loudspeakers came this message:
"Good morning, ladies and gentlemen. Thank you for flying Eagle Airlines. We shall be flying at a height of thirty two thousand feet. Our present ground speed is six hundred and thirty miles per hour. So lean back and relax, read, take a nap. This plane, the JX-802, is the latest, most modern model. It is the safest aircraft anywhere in the world. All

our operations are governed by the finest computers, which guarantee that nothing can go wrong... nothing can go wrong... nothing can go wrong... nothing can go wrong... "
- **Leo Rosten:** *Leo Rosten's Book of Laughter,* 1985.

229. You know the oxygen masks on airplanes? I don't think there's really any oxygen. I think they're just to muffle the screams.
- **Rita Rudner.**

230. The scientific theory I like best is that the rings of Saturn are composed entirely of lost airline baggage.
- **Mark Russell.**

231. You define a good flight by negatives: you don't get high jacked, you don't crash, you didn't throw up, you weren't late, you weren't nauseated by the food. So you are grateful.
- **Paul Theroux:** *The Old Patagonian Express: By Train Though the Americas,* 1979.

ALCOHOL

232. In the order named, these are the hardest to control: Wine, Women, and Song.
- **Franklin Pierce Adams:** *The Treasury of Humorous Quotations* edited by Evan Esar, 1955.

233. If on my theme I rightly think, / There are five reasons why men drink:/ Good wine; a friend; because I'm dry; / Or lest I should be by and by;/Or – any other reason why.
- **Henry Aldrich:** *Five Reasons for Drinking,* 1705.

234. The first thing in a man's personality that dissolves in alcohol is dignity.
- ***anon.***

235. A hangover is the wrath of grapes.
- ***anon.***

236. The horse and the mule live 30 years / And nothing know of wine and beers./ The goat and sheep at 20 die, / And never taste of scotch and rye. / The cow drinks water by the ton / And at 18 is almost done. /The dog at 15 cashes in / Without the aid of rum and gin... . /All animals are strictly dry, / They sinless live and quickly die. /But sinful, ginful rum-soaked men / Survive for three score years and ten, / And some of them, a very few, / Stay pickled till they're 92.
- ***anon:*** *Lighten Up! 100 Funny Little Poems, Bk 2* edited by Bruce Lansky, 1999.

237. Before we pursue this delicate subject further it might be wise to define intoxication. If you wake up in bed with your hat on, it's my guess you may have been addled on retirement.
- **Tallulah Bankhead:** *Tallulah,* 1952.

238. Without question, the greatest invention in the history of mankind is beer. Oh, I grant you that the wheel was also a fine invention, but the

wheel does not go nearly as well with pizza.
- **Dave Barry:** *Dave Barry Turns Forty*, 1990.

239. Drinking makes such fools of people, and people are such fools to begin with that it's compounding a felony.
- **Robert Benchley.**

240. I have a friend who swears the Bible condones getting plastered. He quotes the verse: "He who sins should be stoned!"
- **Milton Berle:** *Milton Berle's Private Joke File*, 1989.

241. He makes grass grow for the cattle, and plants for man to cultivate – bringing forth food from the earth; wine that gladdens the heart of man... and bread that sustains his heart.
- **The Bible:** *Psalm 104: 14 & 15. NIV.*

242. To insist on drinking before driving is to put the quart before the hearse.
- **Jacob M. Braude:** *Braude's Handbook of Stories for Toastmasters and Speakers*, 1957.

243. No animal invented anything so bad as drunkenness, nor so good as drink.
- **G. K. Chesterton:** *All Things Considered*, 1915.

244. No one can ever say that I ever failed to display a meet and proper appreciation of the virtues of alcohol.
- **Sir Winston Churchill:** *The Wit and Wisdom of Winston Churchill* by James C. Humes, 1994.

245. Alcohol postpones anxiety, then multiplies it.
- **Mason Cooley:** *City Aphorisms, Eighth Selection*, 1991.

246. There's nothing like drinking / So pleasant on this side of the grave, /It keeps the unhappy from thinking, / And makes e'en the valiant more brave.
- **Charles Dibden:** *Humour in American Song* by Arthur Loesser, 1942.

247. Alcohol is necessary for a man so that he can have a good opinion of himself.
- **Finley Peter Dunne:** *Dooley on Alcohol, Chicago Tribune, 26th April, 1914.*

248. Alcohol will kill anything that's alive, and preserve anything that's dead.
- **Bob Dylan:** *Quotes of the Day, The Press and Journal, 2nd January, 2008.*

249. I knew I was drunk. I felt sophisticated and couldn't pronounce it.
- **Leopold Fechtner:** *5,000 One-And-Two-Line Jokes,* 1973.

250. I'm watching my drinking, I only visit pubs that have mirrors.
- *ibid.*

251. He has a profound respect for old age, especially when it's bottled.
- **Gene Fowler:** Hollywood film editor, commenting on W.C. Fields.

252. Let schoolmasters puzzle their brain,
With grammar, and nonsense, and learning,
Good liquor I stoutly maintain,
Gives genius a better discerning.
- **Oliver Goldsmith:** *She Stoops to Conquer,* 1771.

253. There's alcohol in plant and tree,
 It must be nature's plan that there should be in fair degree
 Some alcohol in man.
- **A. P. Herbert:** *Number Nine,* 1951.

254. If you are young and drink a great deal it will spoil your health, slow your mind, make you fat – in other words, turn you into an adult.
- **P. J. O'Rourke:** *Modern Manners,* 1983.

255. Alcohol kills brain cells, but it's very selective. It only kills the brain cells that contain good sense, shame, embarrassment, and restraint.
- **P. J. O'Rourke:** *The Bachelor Home Companion,* 1993.

256. Since my leaving drinking of wine, I do find myself much better, and do mind my business better, and do spend less money, and less time in idle company.
- **Samuel Pepys:** *Diary ,* 26th January, 1662.

257. An alcoholic spends his life committing suicide on the instalment plan.
- **Laurence J. Peter:** *Well Said, Well Spoken* by D. Ramsey, 2001.

258. 'Tis not the drinking that is to be blamed, but the excess.
- **John Selden:** *Table Talk,* 1689.

259. O God, that men should put an enemy in their mouths to steal away their brains.
- **William Shakespeare:** *Othello, Act 2, Scene 3,* 1604.

260. Drinking and driving can cause liquor mortis to set in.
- **James A. Simpson:** *More Holy Wit,* 1990.

261. 'Twas an evening in October, I'll confess I wasn't sober, / I was carting home a load with manly pride, / When my feet began to stutter and I fell into the gutter, / And a pig came up and lay down by my side. / Then I lay there in the gutter and my heart was all a-flutter, / Till a lady, passing by, did chance to say,/ "You can tell a man that boozes by the company he chooses,"/ Then the pig got up and slowly walked away.
- **Clarke Van Ness:** *The Famous Pig Song,* quoted in *Clarke's Comedy Song Folio.* 1935.

AMBITION

262. The ambition of many women is to be weighed and found wanting.
- ***anon***.

263. Ambition is like a treadmill; it knows no limits; you no sooner get to the end of it than you begin again.
- **Josh Billings**.

264. Ah, but a man's reach should exceed his grasp,/Or what's a heaven for?
- **Robert Browning:** *Andrea del Sarto*, in *Men and Women*, 1855.

265. Hitch your wagon to a star.
- **Ralph Waldo Emerson:** *Society and Solitude*, 1870.

266. Most men become successful and famous, not through ambition, but through ability and character.
- **William Feather:** *The Business of Life*, 1949.

267. My ambition is to marry a rich girl who is too proud to let her husband work.
- **Leopold Fechtner:** *5,000 One-And-Two-Line Jokes*, 1973.

268. What is my loftiest ambition? I've always wanted to throw an egg into an electric fan.
- **Oliver Herford:** *The Treasury of Humorous Quotations* edited by Evan Esar, 1955.

269. Ambition is an uncomfortable companion... He creates a discontent with present surroundings and achievements; he is never satisfied but always pressing forward to better things in the future.
- **Lyndon B. Johnson:** *College Newspaper*, 1929.

270. Most people would succeed in small things if they were not troubled with great ambitions.
- **Henry Wadsworth Longfellow:** *Driftwood, Table Talk,* 1857.

271. Many people seem to think that ambition is a quality born within us; that it is not susceptible to improvement; that it is something thrust upon us which will take care of itself. But it is a passion that responds very quickly to cultivation, and it requires constant care and education, just as the faculty for music or art does, or it will atrophy.
- **Orison Swell Marden:** *Pushing to the Front,* 1894.

272. We pay a price for everything we get or take in this world, and although ambitions are well worth having, they are not to be cheaply won, but exact their dues of work and self-denial, anxiety and discouragement.
- **Lucy Maud Montgomery:** *Anne of Green Gables,* 1908.

273. Most of us find some of our ambitions are nipped in the budget.
- **Herbert V. Prochnow & Herbert V. Herbert Jr,** *The Public Speaker's Source Book.*

274. Better to light one candle than to curse the darkness.
- ***Chinese Proverb.***

275. I charge thee, fling away ambition:/ By that sin fell the angels.
- **William Shakespeare:** *King Henry V111, Act 3, Scene 2 ,* 1612.

276. Wouldn't it be great if we grew up to be what we wanted to be? The world would be full of nurses, firemen, and ballerinas.
- **Lily Tomlin:** *Saturday Night Live, 25th November, 1975.*

277. Keep away from people who try to belittle your ambitions. Small people always do that, but the really great make you believe that you, too, can become great.
 - **Mark Twain.**

278. There is a loftier ambition than merely to stand high in the world. It is to stoop down and lift mankind a little higher.
- **Henry Van Dyke.**

AMERICA AND THE AMERICANS

279. Americans have more food to eat than any other people on earth, and more diets to keep them from eating it.
- *anon.*

280. Americans have the highest yearning power of any people on earth.
- *anon.*

281. The Constitution of the United States of America, Article V, Section 1: "There shall be a National Anthem containing incomprehensible words and a high note that normal humans cannot hit without risk of hernia."
- **Dave Barry**: *Dave Barry Hits Below the Belt*, 2001.

282. America is an outstandingly dangerous place. Consider this: every year in New Hampshire a dozen or more people are killed crashing their cars into moose. Now correct me if I am wrong, but this is not something that is likely to happen to you on the way home from Sainsbury's.
- **Bill Bryson:** *Notes From A Big Country*, 1998.

283. Americans are broad-minded. They'll accept the fact that a person can be an alcoholic, a dope fiend, a wife beater and even a newspaperman, but if a man doesn't drive, there's something wrong with him.
- **Art Buchwald:** *Have I Ever Lied To You?* 1968.

284. The way things are going, aside from wheat and auto parts, America's biggest export is now the Oscar.
- **Billy Crystal:** *Hosting the Annual Academy Awards in Los Angeles, 1997.*

285. Disneyland: The biggest people trap ever built by a mouse.
- **Halliwell's Filmgoers Companion**, edited by John Walker, 1993.

286. More die in the United States of too much food than of too little.
- **John Kenneth Galbraith:** *The Affluent Society*, 1958.

287. America is one of the finest countries anyone ever stole.
- **Bobcat Goldthwart.**

288. In the average (American) home television is watched for five hours and fifty minutes a day... the equivalent of twelve full weeks out of the year in front of that one eyed monster. The only activity that occupies more time in the home is sleeping – and some would observe that the two pastimes are synonymous.
- **John Macy Jr:** *To Irrigate a Wasteland: The Struggle to Shape a Public Television System in the United States*, 1974.

289. There are two ghastly things about living in America: the President and American television.
- **Mariam Margoyles:** *BBC Radio Times, 26th November, 2005.*

290. It was decided almost two hundred years ago that English should be the language spoken in the United States. It is not known, however, why this decision has not been carried out.
- **George Mikes:** *How To Scrape Skies*, 1955.

291. The Americans are extremely gadget minded people and American gadgets have a peculiar characteristic: they work.
- *ibid.*

292. Americans... still believe in an America where anything's possible – they just don't think their leaders do.
- **Barack Obama**: *in a fund raising letter, September, 2006.*

293. America is the world's policeman all right – a big, dumb, mick flatfoot in the middle of the one thing cops dread most, a "domestic disturbance."
- **P. J. O'Rourke:** *Give War A Chance*, 1992.

294. Individual success for the average person is a rather new concept in history, and an argument could be made that the United States was the first to bring it into the world scene... Europe has no tradition of ordinary people becoming successful. America has little else.
- **Barbara Sher:** *It's Only Too Late If You Don't Start Now: How to Create Your Second Life at Any Time*, 1998.

295. In America any boy may become President, and I suppose it's just one of the risks he takes.
- **Adlai Stevenson:** *in a speech given in Indianapolis, 26th September, 1952.*

296. They're completely barbaric... but they make the best chocolate chip cookies in the galaxy.
- **Bob Thaves:** in a cartoon showing two alien creatures from outer space heading towards America.

297. There are some circles in America where it seems to be more socially acceptable to carry a hand-gun than a packet of cigarettes.
- **Katharine Whitehorn:** *The Observer, 30th October, 1988.*

298. Americans... often seem to be so overwhelmed by their children that they'll do anything for them except stay married to the co-producer.
- **Katharine Whitehorn:** *Saga Magazine.*

299. Like so many substantial citizens of America, he had married young and kept on marrying, springing from blonde to blonde like the chamois of the Alps, leaping from crag to crag.
- **P. G. Wodehouse:** *Summer Moonshine,* 1938.

300. Americans are getting stronger. Twenty years ago it took two people to carry ten dollars worth of groceries. Today a five year old does it.
- **Henny Youngman:** *How Do You Like Me So Far?* 1963.

301. The three great American vices seem to be efficiency, punctuality, and the desire for achievement and success. They are the things that make the Americans so unhappy and so nervous.
- **Lin Yutang:** *The Importance of Living,* 1937.

302. Anger is one letter short of danger.
- *anon.*

303. The trouble with letting off steam is it only gets you into more hot water.
- *anon.*

304. Anyone can become angry – that is easy. But to be angry with the right person, to the right degree, at the right time, for the right purpose, and in the right way – that is not easy.
- **Aristotle:** *Nicomachean Ethics, **circa** 350 BC.*

305.. How much more grievous are the consequences of anger than the causes of it.
- **Marcus Aurelius:** *Meditations,* **circa** 180 AD

306. A fool gives full vent to his anger, but a wise man keeps himself under control.
- **The Bible:** *Proverbs 29: 11, NIV.*

307. Do not let the sun go down while you are still angry.
- **The Bible:** *Ephesians 4: 26, NIV.*

308. A man is never in worse company than when he flies into a rage and is beside himself.
- **Jacob M. Braude:** *Braude's Treasury of Wit and Humour For All Occasions,* 1991.

309. Anger repressed can poison a relationship as surely as the cruellest words.
- **Joyce Brothers:** *When Your Husband's Affection Cools* in *Good Housekeeping Magazine, May, 1972.*

310. Beware of the anger of the mouth, / Master your words, / Let them serve truth.
- **Buddha:** *Dhammapada: The Wisdom of the Buddha,* **circa** 483 BC.

311. The intoxication of anger, like that of the grape, shows us to others, but hides us from ourselves.
- **Charles Caleb Colton:** *Lacon,* or *Many Things In Few Words,* 1826, edited by George J. Barbour, 2001.

312. Never go to bed angry, stay up and fight.
- **Phyllis Diller:** *Phyllis Diller's Housekeeping Hints,* 1966.

313. When you're angry, take a lesson from space exploration – always count down before blasting off.
- **Sam Ewing:** *The Sun, 20ᵗʰ July.*

314. This makes me so sore it gets my dandruff up.
- **Samuel Goldwyn:** *Quotations For Our Time* by Laurence Peter, 1977.

ANGER

315. One can overcome the forces of negative emotions, like anger and hatred, by cultivating their counter forces, like love and compassion.
- **Tenzin Gyatso**.

316. Anger is a brief madness.
- **Horace:** *Epistles*, ***circa*** 20 BC.

317. Anger is a wind which blows out the lamp of the mind.
- **Robert G. Ingersoll**.

318. The best remedy for a short temper is a long walk.
- **Joseph Joubert**.

319. Anger is a signal and one worth listening to.
- **Harriet Lerner:** *The Dance of Anger*, 1984.

320. Speak when you are angry, and you will make the best speech you'll ever regret.
- **Laurence J. Peter:** *Quotations For Our Time*, 1977.

321. Anger is often more hurtful than the injury that caused it.
- ***English Proverb***.

322. People who fly into a rage always make a bad landing.
- **Will Rogers**.

323. I've learned that when you harbour bitterness, happiness will dock elsewhere.
- **Andy Rooney:** *60 Minutes, CBS Television Show*.

324. It is a waste of energy to be angry with a man who behaves badly, just as it is to be angry with a car that won't go.
- **Bertrand Russell:** *Conquest of Happiness*, 1930.

325. The greatest remedy for anger is delay.
- **Seneca:** *On Anger. circa* 41 AD.

326. Anger, if not restrained, is frequently more hurtful to us than the injury that provoked it.
- *ibid.*

327. Do not plunge thyself too far in anger.
- **William Shakespeare:** *All's Well That Ends Well, Act 2, Scene 3,* 1623.

328. Anger kills both laughter and joy; what greater foe is there than anger?
- **Tiruvalluvar.**

329. Flying off the handle sometimes causes hammers and humans to loose their heads, as well as their effectiveness.
- **William ArthurWard.**

ANIMALS

330. A house is not a home without a pet.
- ***anon***.

331. I am a bunny rabbit, / Sitting in me hutch, /
I like to sit up this end, / I don't care for that end, much. /
I'm glad tomorrow's Thursday, / 'Cause with a bit of luck, /
As far as I remember, / That's the day they pass the buck.
- **Pam Ayres:** *The Bunny Poem* in *Some of Me Poetry*, 1976.

332. Frankly, I prefer to spend my time with animals than with people. Animals are truthful and spontaneous. If an animal doesn't like you, he won't come to you.
- **Brigitte Bardot:** *The Sunday Times Magazine, 9ᵗʰ April, 2006.*

333. A man is rated the highest animal, at least among all animals who returned the questionnaire.
- **Robert Brault**. NB This writer's web site, www.robertbrault.com, is well worth a visit.

334. I believe in animal's rights and high among them is the right to the gentle stroke of a human hand.
- **Robert Brault**.

335. I am not a vegetarian because I love animals; I am a vegetarian because I hate plants.
- **A**. **Whitney Brown:** *The Big Picture*, 1991.

336. All animals, except man, know that the principal business of life is to enjoy it.
- **Samuel Butler:** *The Way Of All Flesh*, 1903.

337. The dodo never had a chance. He seems to have been invented for the sole purpose of becoming extinct, and that is all he was good for.
- **Will Cuppy:** *How To Become Extinct*, 1941.

338. If it's true that men are such beasts, this must account for the fact that most women are animal lovers.
 - **Doris Day**.

339. Animals are such agreeable friends, they ask no questions, they pass no criticism.
- **George Eliot:** *Scenes of Clerical Life,* 1857.

340. The only thing that separates us from the animals is our ability to accessorize.
- Olympia Dukakis as Clairee Belcher in the **1989 Film**: *Steel Magnolias.*

341. I think animal testing is a terrible idea, they get all nervous and give wrong answers.
- **Stephen Fry:** *A Bit of Fry and Laurie,* (a British television comedy series), 1989 – 1995.

342. I hope to make people realize how totally helpless animals are, how dependent on us, trusting as a child must that we will be kind and take care of their needs... (they) are an obligation put on us, a responsibility which we have no right to neglect, nor to violate by cruelty.
- **James Herriot:** *A Television interview.*

343. The fretful little bunny rabbit
 Has one peculiar nervous habit.
 It seems wherever bunny goes
 A fitful twitch afflicts her nose.
 Well, you'd be twitching too, my dear,
 If you were pregnant every year.
- **Bob Mc Kenty:** *Light – A Quarterly of Light Verse, Summer 1999 Issue.*

344. There was once a little boy trying to persuade his granddad to take him to the circus. But his granddad wasn't having any because he thought he was too old for that sort of thing But the little boy said:"It's different now, Granddad. A girl dressed in nothing but her beautiful hair comes into the ring riding a lovely white horse." So his Granddad said: "Right, in that case we'll go. It's 30 years since a saw a white horse."
- **Eric Morecambe and Ernie Wise:** *Bring Me Sunshine,* 1979.

345. The cow is of the bovine ilk;
 One end is moo, the other, milk.
- **Ogden Nash:** *The Cow* in *Free Wheeling,* 1931.

346. There is one respect in which brutes show real wisdom when compared with us - I mean their quiet, placid enjoyment of the present moment.
- **Arthur Schopenhauer:** *On the Suffering of the World,* 1850.

347. So, naturalists, observe, a flea hath smaller fleas that on him prey;
And they have smaller still to bite 'em, and so proceed *ad infinitum.*
- **Jonathan Swift:** *On Poetry: A Rhapsody,* 1733.

348. Two cows were watching as a milk float passed. On the float's side was written, "Homogenized, Pasteurized, with Vitamin A added." One cow remarked, "Kind of makes you feel inadequate, doesn't it?"
- **Pat Williams:** *Winning With One-Liners,* 2002.

APOLOGIES AND EXCUSES

349. Any excuse will serve a tyrant.
- The moral of **Aesop's Fable**: *The Wolf and the Lamb*.
NB Online collection of Aesop's Fables available on www.aesopfables.com

350. We are all manufacturers – some make good, others make trouble, and still others make excuses.
 - ***anon***.

351. Excuses are tools of the incompetent, and those who specialize in them seldom go far.
- ***anon***.

352. An apology is a good way to have the last word.
- ***anon***.

353. Very sorry can't come. Lie follows by post.
- **Lord Charles Beresford**.
NB This was a telegram sent to the Prince of Wales declining a dinner invitation.

354. Ninety-nine per cent of the failures come from people who have the habit of making excuses.
- **George Washington Carver:** *The Reader's Digest, 1985*

355. There are two kinds of people in the world: those who make excuses and those who get results. An excuse person will find any excuse for why a job was not done, and a results person will find any reason why it can be done.
- **Alan Cohen:** *A Deep Breath of Life: Daily Inspiration for Health-Centred Living,* 1996.

356. Excuses change nothing, but make everyone feel better.
 - **Mason Cooley:** *City Aphorisms, Second Selection,* 1985.

357. Never apologize. It's a sign of weakness. - John Wayne as Captain Nathan Brittles in the **1949 RKO Film:** *She Wore a Yellow Ribbon.*

358. The most profitless thing to manufacture is excuses.
- **B. C. Forbes:** *Forbes Epigrams or 1,000 Thoughts on Life,* 1922.

359. He that is good for making excuses is seldom good for anything else.
- **Benjamin Franklin:** *The Treasury of Humorous Quotations.*

360. Bad excuses are worse than none.
- **Thomas Fuller:** *Gnomologia,* 1732.

361. Several excuses are always less convincing than one.
- **Aldous Huxley:** *Point Counter Point,* 1928.

362. I attribute my success to this: I never gave or took an excuse.
- **Florence Nightingale.**

363. An excuse is worse and more terrible than a lie, for an excuse is a lie guarded.
- **Alexander Pope.**

364. Accusing the times is but excusing ourselves.
- *English Proverb.*

365. If you don't want to do something, one excuse is as good as another.
- *Yiddish Proverb.*

366. We have more ability than will power, and it is often an excuse to ourselves that we imagine that things are impossible.
- **Francois, Duc de La Rochefoucauld:** *Maxims,* 1665.

367. It is better to offer no excuse than a bad one.
- **George Washington.**

368. It is a good rule in life never to apologize. The right sort of people do not want apologies, and the wrong sort take a mean advantage of them.
- **P. G. Wodehouse:** *The Man Upstairs,* 1914.

APPEARANCE

369. Appearances often are deceiving.
- The moral of **Aesop's Fable:** *The Wolf in Sheep's Clothing.*

370. Use a make-up table with everything close at hand and don't rush, otherwise you'll look like a patch work quilt.
- **Lucille Ball:** *Family Weekly, July, 1975.*

371. Man looks at the outward appearance, but the Lord looks at the heart.
- **The Bible:** *1ˢᵗ Samuel 16: 7, NIV.*

372. Stop judging by mere appearance, and make a right judgement.
- **The Bible:** *John 7: 24, NIV.*

373. Before you try to keep up with the Jones, be sure they're not trying to keep up with you.
- **Erma Bombeck.**

374. The young man in front of me... had the sort of face that makes you realize God does have a sense of humour.
- **Bill Bryson:** *Neither Here Nor There: Travels in Europe,* 1991.

375. Things are seldom what they seem,
Skim milk masquerades as cream.
- **Sir W. S. Gilbert:** *HMS Pinafore, Act 2,* 1878.

376. A hair in the head is worth two in the brush.
- **Oliver Herford:** *The Altogether New Cynic's Calendar,* 1907.

377. For attractive lips, speak words of kindness.
- **Sam Levinson:** *In One Era And Out The Next,* 1973.

378. I've been fat all my life and I expect to die fat. But I'm not fat inside, I'm a little darting thing with quick movements to match my

quick mind.
- **Miriam Margoyles**.

379. Sure, deck your limbs in pants;
Yours are the limbs, my sweeting.
You look divine as you advance -
Have you seen yourself retreating?
 - **Ogden Nash**: *What's The Use?* in *Free Wheeling*, 1931.

380. Some people in looks take so much pride,
They don't think much of what's inside,
Well, as for me, I know my face
Can ne'er be made a thing of grace.
And so I rather think I'll see
How I can fix the inside o' me
So people'll say, "He looks like sin
But ain't he beautiful within."
- **Herbert V. Prochnow & Herbert V. Prochnow Jr**: *Jokes, Quotes and One- Liners, Vol 2,* 1992.

381. Men of all professions affect such an air and appearance as to seem to be what they wish to be believed to be – so that one might say the whole world is made up of nothing but appearances.
- **Francois, Duc de La Rochefoucauld**: *Maxims,* 1665.

382. Were we to take as much pains to be what we ought, as we do to disguise what we are, we might appear like ourselves without being at the trouble of any disguise at all.
- *ibid.*

383. She wears her clothes as if they were thrown on her with a pitchfork.
- **Jonathan Swift**: *Polite Conversation Dialogue 1,* 1738.

384. Clothes make the man. Naked people have little or no influence on society.
- **Mark Twain**: *Mark Twain's Notebook,* 1935.

ARGUMENT

385. When a man's argument is weak he generally uses stronger words.
- *anon.*

386. The husband who apologises always has the last word in an argument with his wife.
- *anon.*

387. I can win an argument on any topic, against any opponent. People know this, and steer clear of me at parties. Often, as a sign of their great respect, they don't even invite me.
- **Dave Barry:** *Miami Herald.*

388. My wife was too beautiful for words, but not for arguments.
- **John Barrymore:** *The Treasury of Humorous Quotations* edited by Evan Esar, 1955.

389. There's two theories to arguin' with a woman. Neither one works.
- **Texas Bix Bender:** *Don't Squat with Your Spurs On,* 1992.

390. The argument became so heated that the woman next door sent for the fire brigade.
- **Nicolas Bentley:** *The Treasury of Humorous Quotations* edited by Evan Esar, 1955.

391. Argument is generally a waste of time and trouble. It is better to present one's opinion and leave it to stick or not as it may happen. If sound, it will probably in the end stick, and the sticking is the main thing.
- **Samuel Butler:** *The Note-Books of Samuel Butler,* 1912.

392. After an argument, silence may mean acceptance – or the continuation of resistance by other means.
- **Mason Cooley:** *City Aphorisms,* 1993.

393. When confronted by two courses of action, I jot down on a piece of paper all the arguments in favour of each one – then, on the opposite side, I write the arguments against each one. Then by weighing the arguments pro and con and cancelling them out one against the other, I take the course indicated by what remains.
- **Benjamin Franklin**.

394. Truth springs from arguments among friends.
- **David Hume**.

395. Argument should be polite as well as logical.
 - **Alphonse de Lamartine**.

396. If you have learned how to disagree without being disagreeable, then you have discovered the secret of getting along – whether it be business, family relations, or life itself.
 - **Bernard Meltzer**.

397. When the girlfriend and I get in an argument, I begin to believe in flying saucers... and plates, pots, mugs.
- **Robert Paul**.

398. Discussion is an exchange of knowledge, argument is an exchange of ignorance.
- **Robert Quillen**.

399. When men argue with their wives, words often flail them.
 - **James A.Simpson:** *The Laugh Shall Be First,* 1998.

400. Arguments only confirm people in their own opinion.
- **Booth Tarkington**.

ART AND ARTISTS

401. A pretty young artist from Warsaw,
Displayed a great deal of her torso.
A crowd soon collected,
But no one objected,
Indeed, some were in favour of more so!
- **anon:** *Milton Berle's Private Joke File,* 1989.

402. Painting: the art of protecting flat surfaces from the weather and exposing them to the critic.
- **Ambrose Bierce:** *The Devil's Dictionary,* 1911.

403. Abstract art is a product of the untalented, sold by the unprincipled, to the utterly bewildered.
- **Al Capp:** *The National Observer, 1ˢᵗ July, 1963.*

404. The Bayeux Tapestry is accepted as an authority on many details of life and the fine points of history in the eleventh century. For instance, the horses in those days had green legs, blue bodies, yellow manes, and red heads, while the people were all double-jointed and quite different from what we generally think of as human beings.
- **Will Cuppy:** *The Decline and Fall of Practically Everybody,* 1950.

405. I finished a sculpture today,
I made it from soup tins and clay.
I put it outside,
To show off with pride,
But the garbage men took it away.
- **Norma Dixon:** *Lighten Up! Bk 2,* edited by Bruce Lansky, 1991.

406. An abstract painting is like a woman: you'll never get to like it if you try to understand it.
- **Evan Esar:** *20,000 Quips and Quotes,* 1968.

407. A highbrow is the kind of person who looks at a sausage and thinks of Picasso.
- **Sir A. P. Herbert:** *Is Highbrow Libellous?* in *Uncommon Law*, 1935.

408. Sculpture is what you bump into when you back up to look at a painting.
- **Des MacHale:** *Wit, Wit, Wit*, 2002.

409. If people knew how hard I had to work to gain my mastery, it would not seem so wonderful at all.
- **Michelangelo:** *Happiness is Everything* by Chris Crawford, 2000. NB Michelangelo was to explain his motivation when he said: "Art is a jealous mistress; she requires the whole man."

410. Said Hamlet to Ophelia,
I'll draw a sketch of thee.
What kind of pencil shall I use?
2B or not 2B.
- **Spike Milligan:** *A Silly Poem.*

411. Modern art is when you buy a picture to cover a hole in the wall — and then decide the hole is better.
- **Robert Orben:** *2,000 Sure-Fire Jokes for Speakers*, 1986.

412. The art museum in my home town just acquired an early Rembrandt. A very early Rembrandt. It's done in crayons.
- **Robert Orben:** *2,400 Jokes to Brighten Your Speeches*, 1984,

413. Looking at modern art is like trying to follow the plot in a bowl of alphabet soup.
- **Herbert V. Prochnow and Herbert V. Prochnow Jr:** *The Public Speaker's Source Book*, 1977.

414. Modern artists sign their names at the bottoms of paintings so that we'll know how to hang them.
- **Pat Williams:** *Winning with One-Liners*, 2002.

415. Someone asked Picasso how one could tell the importance of a painting. "Is it the style, the history, or is it the master who painted it?" they asked the master. Picasso replied, "They are all very important, but for a painting to be truly important, it must first be expensive."
- *ibid.*

ATHEISM

416. To be an atheist requires an infinitely greater measure of faith than to receive all the great truths which atheism would deny.
- **Joseph Addison:** *The Spectator, 8th March, 1711.*

417. Atheism is not always the antithesis of religion, especially if it betrays deep interest in the goings-on of religion. People are often called atheists, and often call themselves so, for no other reason than that they do not believe in a generally approved definition of God.
 - **Gordon W. Allport:** *The Individual and His Religion*, 1951.

418. A little philosophy inclines man's mind to atheism, but depth in philosophy brings men's minds about to religion.
- **Francis Bacon:** *Essays,* 1625.

419. I had rather believe all the fables in the legends and the Talmud and the Alcoran than that this universal frame is without a mind.
- *ibid.*

420. I am a daylight athiest.
- **Brendan Behan:** *Sacred Monsters* by Daniel Farson.

421. They now have a special Dial-a-Prayer number for atheists. You call it and nobody answers!
- **Milton Berle:** *Milton Berle's Private Joke File*, 1989.

422. The fool says in his heart, "There is no God."
- **The Bible:** *Psalm 14: 1, NIV.*

423. I have heard an atheist defined as a man who has no invisible means of support.
- **John Buchan:** *Canadian Occasions: Speeches and Addresses.* 1940.

424. I am an atheist, thank God.
- **Luis Bunuel:** *My Last Sigh: The Autobiography of Luis Bunuel.* 1983.

425. If there were no God, there would be no atheists.
- **G. K. Chesterton:** *Where All Roads Lead.* 1922.

426. There are no atheists in the foxholes.
- **William Thomas Cummings:** *I Saw the Fall of the Philippines by* Col.P. Romula, 1942.

427. Agnosticism is a perfectly respectable and tenable philosophical position; it is not dogmatic and makes no pronouncements about the ultimate truths of the universe. It remains open to evidence and persuasion; lacking faith, it nevertheless does not deride faith. Atheism, on the other hand, is as unyielding and dogmatic about religious belief as true believers are about heathens. It tries to use reason to demolish a structure that is not built upon reason.
- **Sydney J. Harris:** *Pieces of Eight*, 1984.

428. To admit there is no god is to provide free license to pillage and rape with clear conscience.
- **Eli Khamarov:** *Surviving on Planet Reebok.*

429. There's something in every atheist, itching to believe, and something in every believer, itching to doubt.
- **Mignon McLaughlin:** *The Second Neurotic's Notebook,* 1966.

430. The best reply to an atheist is to give him a good dinner and ask him if he believes there is a cook.
- **Louis Nizer.**

431. The modern atheist is always angered when he hears anything said about God and religion. He would be incapable of such resentment if God were only a myth.
- **Fulton Sheen:** *Peace of Soul,*1949

432. I once thought of becoming an atheist, but I changed my mind; no paid holidays.
- **Henny Youngman:** *The Best Little Book of One-Liners*, 1992.

ATTITUDE

433. It's difficult in times like these: ideals, dreams and cherished hopes rise within us, only to be crushed by grim reality. It's a wonder I haven't abandoned all my ideals, they seem so absurd and impractical. Yet I cling to them because I still believe, in spite of everything, that people are truly good at heart. I simply can't build my hopes on a foundation of confusion, misery, and death... and yet ... I think... this cruelty will end, and that peace and tranquillity will return again.
- **Anne Frank:** *The Diary of a Young Girl*, 1967.

434. We who lived in concentration camps can remember the men who walked through the huts comforting others, giving away their last piece of bread. They may have been few in number, but they offer sufficient proof that everything can be taken away from a man but one thing: the last of the human freedoms - to choose one's attitude in any given set of circumstances, to choose one's own way.
- **Viktor Frankl:** *Man's Search for Meaning*, 1946.

435. Ability is what you're capable of doing. Motivation determines what you do. Attitude determines how well you do it.
- **Lou Holtz**.

436. Human beings, by changing the inner attitudes of their minds, can change the outer aspects of their lives.
- **William James**.

437. The greatest discovery of any generation is that human beings can alter their lives by altering their attitudes.
- **William James**.

438. It is our attitude at the beginning of a difficult task which, more than anything else, will affect its successful outcome.
- **William James**.

439. A positive attitude is something everyone can work on, and everyone can learn how to employ it... it shapes your life and determines the quality of your life.
- **Joan Lunden:** in a *Cable News Network Chat Show, 17th October, 2000.*

440. The greatest day in your life and mine is when we take total responsibility for our attitude. That's the day we truly grow up.
- **John C. Maxwell:** *Developing the Leader Within You,* 1979.

441. A strong positive mental attitude will create more miracles than any wonder drug.
- **Patricia Neal.**

BABIES

442. A baby is an alimentary canal with a loud voice at one end and no responsibility at the other.
- *anon*.

443. A baby is born with a need to be loved and never outgrows it.
- *anon*.

444. His mother's eyes, /His father's chin, /His auntie's nose, /His uncle's grin, / His great-aunt's hair, /His grandma's ears, /His grandpa's mouth, /So it appears/ Poor little tot, /Well may he moan, /He hasn't much, / To call his own.
- **Richard Armour:** *Copy* in *An Armoury of Light Verse*, 1964.

445. Baby's room should be close enough to your room so that you can hear baby cry, unless you want to get some sleep, in which case baby's room should be in Peru.
- **Dave Barry:** *Dave Barry's Babies and Other Hazards of Sex*, 1984.

446. I got so much food spit back in my face when my kids were small, I put wind shield wipers on my glasses.
- **Erma Bombeck:** *Motherhood*, 1983.

447. "From the day your baby is born,"counselled a famous scholar, "you must teach him to do without things. Children today love luxury too much. They have execrable manners, flaunt authority, have no respect for their elders. They no longer rise when their parents or teachers enter the room. What kind of awful creatures will they be when they grow up?
- **Bennett Cerf:** *The Laugh's On Me*, 1959. NB Cerf here recalls what Socrates said shortly before his death in 399 BC.

448. There are three reasons for breast feeding: the milk is always at the right temperature; it comes in attractive containers; and the cat can't get it.
- **Irena Chalmers**.

449. Parents can become boring talking on and on about their new baby. It all ends, however, when the parents have to change the subject.
- **Sam Ewing:** *The Saturday Evening Post, August, 2002.*

450. A baby is a full time job for three adults. Nobody tells you that when you're pregnant, (or you'd probably jump off a bridge)... Nobody tells you how all consuming it is to be a mother.
- **Erica Jong:** *Fear of Fifty,* 1994.

451. Training babies is mostly a matter of pot luck.
- **Bob Monkhouse:** *Just Say a Few Words,* 1988.

452. A baby's like a new car. It has two lung power, free squealing, streamlined body, changeable seat covers and an easily flooded carburettor.
- ***ibid***

453. Good work, Mary. We all knew you had it in you.
- **Dorothy Parker:** in a telegram to a friend who had given birth after a well publicised pregnancy.

454. A baby is God's opinion that life should go on.
- **Carl Sandburg:** *Remembrance Rock,* 1948.

455. Babies need social interactions with loving adults who talk with them, listen to their babblings, name objects for them, and give them opportunities to explore their worlds.
- **Sandra Scarr:** *Mother Care / Other Care,* 1984.

456. The more people have studied different methods of bringing up children the more they have come to the conclusion that what good mothers and fathers instinctively feel like doing for their babies is the best after all.
- **Benjamin Spock:** *The Common Sense Book of Baby and Child Care,* 1946.

457. Every newborn child is a reminder that God has not yet lost faith in humankind.
- **Rabindranath Tagore:** *Gitanjali: Song Offerings,* 1910.

458. Adam and Eve had many advantages, but the principle one was that they escaped teething.
- **Mark Twain:** *Pudd'nhead Wilson,* 1894.

459. A baby is an inestimable blessing and bother.
- **Mark Twain**: *in a letter, 1876.*

460. People who say, "I slept like a baby," usually never had one.
- **Pat Williams:** *Winning With One-Liners,* 2002.

BACHELORS

461. Not all men are fools – some are bachelors.
- **Joey Adams**: *Joey Adams' Encyclopedia of Humour,* 1968.

462. A bachelor is a man who is completely dedicated to life, liberty and the happiness of pursuit.
- ***anon.***

463. A bachelor is a fellow who doesn't think the bonds of matrimony are a good investment.
- **Jacob M. Braude:** *Braude's Handbook of Stories for Toastmasters and Speakers,* 1957.

464. A bachelor is a chap who believes it's much better to have loved and lost than to have to get up for the 2 a.m. feeding.
- ***ibid.***

465. A confirmed bachelor is a man with no wife expectancy.
- **Jacob M. Braude:** *Braude's Treasury of Wit and Humour for all Occasions,* 1991.

466. I would be married, but I'd have no wife,/I would be married to a single life.
- **Richard Crashaw:** *On Marriage,* 1646.

467. Do not let your bachelor ways crystallize so that you can't soften them when you come to have a wife and a family of your own.
- **Rutherford Birchard Hayes:** *in a letter to his son, 20th March, 1890.*

468. I said, "Dad, should I marry a girl who can take a joke?"
He said, "Son, that's the only kind you'll get."
- **Bob Monkhouse:** *Just Say A Few Words,* 1988.

469. We are a select group without personal obligation, social encumbrance, or any socks that match.
- **P. J. O'Rourke:** *The Bachelor Home Companion,* 1987.

470. Bachelor cooking is a matter of attitude. If you think of it as setting fire to things and making a mess, it's fun. It's not so much fun if you think of it as dinner.
- *ibid.*

471. Bachelor: One who treats all women as sequels.
- **Leo Rosten:** *Leo Rosten's Book of Laughter,* 1985.

472. A Bachelor of Arts is one who makes love to a lot of women, and yet has the art to remain a bachelor.
- **Helen Rowland:** *A Guide to Men,* 1922.

473. Marrying an old bachelor is like buying second hand furniture.
- **Helen Rowland:** *Reflections of a Bachelor Girl,* 1909.

474. A bachelor never quite gets over the idea that he is a thing of beauty and a boy for ever.
- **Helen Rowland:** *A Guide to Men,* 1922.

475. One drawback of being a bachelor is doing the dishes and making the bed and knowing that you're going to have to do the same thing again next month.
- **Pat Williams:** *Winning with One-Liners, 2002.*

476. A bachelor is a guy who leans towards women – but not far enough to loose his balance.
- **Earl Wilson**.

BEAUTY

477. You can only perceive real beauty in a person as they get older.
- **Anouk Aimee:** *The Guardian, August, 1988.*

478. Natural beauty takes at least two hours in front of a mirror.
- **Pamela Anderson:** *Reader's Digest, March, 2007.*

479. It's beauty that captures your attention; personality captures your heart.
- ***anon.***

480. Beauty is one of the rare things that do not lead to doubt of God.
- **Jean Anouilh:** *Becket,* 1962.

481. Beauty is the gift of God.
- **Aristotle:** *Lives of Eminent Philosophers* by Diogenes Laertius, 4th cent BC.

482. A man complained, "My wife is still as beautiful as she used to be. It just takes her a little longer now."
- **Milton Berle:** *Milton Berle's Private Joke File,* 1989.

483. Charm is deceptive, and beauty is fleeting.
- **The Bible:** *Proverbs chapter 31: 30, NIV.*

484. Character contributes to beauty. It fortifies a woman as her youth fades.
- **Jacqueline Bisset:** *Los Angeles Times, 1974.*

485. There is no cosmetic for beauty like happiness.
- **Countess of Blessington:** *Desultory Thoughts and Reflections,* 1839.

486. Earth's crammed with heaven, / And every common bush afire with God; / But only he who sees takes off his shoes;/ The rest sit round it and pluck blackberries.
- **Elizabeth Barrett Browning:** *Aurora Leigh,* 1806.

487. As a white candle in a holy place / So is the beauty of an aged face.
- **Joseph Campbell.**

488. Beauty that dies the soonest has the longest life; because it cannot keep itself for a day, we keep it forever. Because it can have existence only in memory, we give it immortality there.
- **Bertha Damon:** *A Sense of Humus,* 1943.

489. Old as I am, for ladies' love unfit,
The power of beauty I remember yet.
- **John Dryden:** *Fables Ancient and Modern,* 1700.

490. The most beautiful thing we can experience is the mysterious.
- **Albert Einstein:** *What I Believe,* 1930.

491. Her face, figure, and voice makes you stop, look, and listen.
- **Leopold Fechtner:** *5,000 One-And-Two-Line Jokes,* 1973.

492. Think of all the beauty still left around you and be happy.
- **Anne Frank:** *The Diary of a Young Girl,* 1967.

493. There is certainly no absolute standard of beauty. That precisely is what makes its pursuit so interesting.
- **John Kenneth Galbraith:** *New York Times Magazine, September, 1960.*

494. Beauty is in the eye of the beholder.
- **Margaret Wolfe Hungerford.** NB Mrs Hungerford is credited as the first writer to coin this phrase in *Molly Bawn,* 1878.

495. A thing of beauty is a joy forever; it's loveliness increases; it will never pass into nothingness.
- **John Keats:** *Endymion,* 1818.

496. The beauty of a woman is not in the clothes she wears,
The figure she carries or the way she combs her hair.
The beauty of a woman must be seen in her eyes,
Because that is the doorway to her heart, the place where love resides.
- **Sam Levenson:** *Time Tested Beauty Tips,* an extract from the poem Levenson wrote for his grandchild. NB The complete version of the poem is available on the Internet at:
www.robinsweb.com/inspiration/beauty_tips.html

497. Beauty in a woman's face, like sweetness in a woman's lips, is a matter of taste.
 - **Mary Wilson Little:** *The Treasury of Humorous Quotations edited by* Evan Esar, 1955.

498. Every girl should use what Mother Nature gave her before Father Time takes it away.
 - **Laurence J. Peter:** *Quotations For Our Time*, 1977.

 499. Beauty is a short-lived tyranny.
- **Socrates:** 4th century BC.

 500. She got her good looks from her father. He's a plastic surgeon.
- **Henny Youngman:** *The Best Little Book of One-Liners*, 1992.

BEHAVIOUR

501. A person who is nice to you, but rude to the waiter, is not a nice person.
- **Dave Barry**; *Dave Barry Turns 50*, 1998.

502. Do to others as you would have them do to you.
 - **The Bible**; *Luke 6: 31, NIV.*

503. Don't criticize, condemn or complain.... Be a good listener. Encourage others to talk about themselves.
- **Dale Carnegie**; *How To Win Friends And Influence People*, 1936.

504. Etiquette means behaving yourself a little better than is absolutely essential.
- **Will Cuppy**.

505. Let nothing be done in your life which will cause you fear if it becomes known to your neighbour.
- **Epicurus**; 3rd century BC.

506. By the time most men learn how to behave themselves, they are too old to do anything else
- **Leopold Fechtne**; *5,000 One-and-Two-Line Jokes*, 1973.

507. Treat people as if they were what they ought to be, and you help them to become what they are capable of being.
 - **Johann Wolfgang von Goethe**.

 508. Behaviour is a mirror in which everyone shows his image.
Johan Wolfgang von Goethe; *Maxims and Reflections* translated by Elizabeth Stopp, 1998.

509. Beginning today, treat everyone you meet as if you were going to be dead by midnight. Extend to them all the care, kindness and understanding you can muster, and do it with no thought of any reward.

Your life will never be the same again.
- **Og Mandino**; *The Greatest Miracle in the World*, 1977.

510. Treat people better than they treat you.
- **John C. Maxwell**; *There's No Such Thing as "Business Ethics,"* 2003.

511. Be nice to people on your way up because you'll meet 'em on the way down.
- **Wilson Mizner:** *The Legendary Mizners* by Alva Johnson, 1953.

512. Some people seem as if they can never have been children, and others seem as if they could never be anything else.
- **George D. Prentice**.

BELIEFS

513. There is nothing that can help you understand your beliefs more than trying to explain them to an inquisitive child.
- *anon*.

514. A belief is not merely an idea the mind possesses; it is an idea that possesses the mind.
- **Robert Bolton**.

515. People readily believe what they want to believe.
- **Julius Caesar:** *The Gallic War, Book 3, Chapter 18.*

516. Alice laughed, "There's no use trying," she said, "one can't believe impossible things."
"I dare say you haven't had much practice," said the Queen. "When I was younger, I always did it for half an hour a day. Why, sometimes I've believed as many as six impossible things before breakfast."
- **Lewis Carrol**; *Alice in Wonderland*, 1865.

517. One does not have to believe everything one hears.
- **Marcus Tullius Cicero**; *Concerning Divination*, **circa** 44BC.

518. He does not believe that does not live according to his belief.
- **Thomas Fuller**; *Gnomologia: Adages and Proverbs*, 1732.

519. Beliefs must be lived in for a good while before they can accommodate themselves to the soul's wants, and wear loose enough to be comfortable.
- **Oliver Wendell Holmes**; *Elsie Venner*, 1859.

520. To make our influence felt we must live our faith, we must practice what we believe.
- **William George Jordan**; *Majesty of Calmness*, 1900.

521. The test of all beliefs is their practical effect on life.
- **Helen Keller**; *Optimism.*

 522. If you don't have solid beliefs you cannot build a stable life. Beliefs are like the foundations of a building; they are the foundations to build your lives upon.
 - **Alfred A. Montapert.**

523. I never cease to being dumbfounded by the unbelievable things people believe.
- **Leo Rosten**; *Quotations for Our Time* by Laurence J. Peter, 1977.

524. The old believe everything; the middle-aged suspect everything; the young know everything.
 - **Oscar Wilde**; *Epigrams of Oscar* by Alvin Redman, 1952.

BIRDS

525. I value my garden more for being full of blackbirds than of cherries, and very frankly give them fruit for their songs.
- **Joseph Addison:** *The Spectator.*

526. Song birds are appreciated at any time, but the stork is welcome only when he has been invited.
- ***anon***.

527. My wife does bird imitations. She always watches me like a hawk.
- **Leopold Fechtner**; *5,000 One-And-Two-Line Jokes,* 1973.

528. Alas! My child, where is the pen
That can do justice to the hen?
Like Royalty, she goes her way,
Laying foundations every day,
Though not public buildings, yet
For custard, cake and omelette.
- **Oliver Herford.**

529. There was an old man with a beard, / Who said, "It is just as I feared! /Two owls and a hen / Four larks and a wren
Have all built their nests in my beard!"
- **Edward Lear:** *A Book of Nonsense,* 1861.

530. "Have you got a cold!" said the Heron
To another he met in a moat.
"Naw," said the other big heron,
"It's just a frog in ma throat!"
- **Walter McCorrisken:** *The Heron* in *Hairy Knees and Heather Hills,* 1995.

531. A wonderful bird is the pelican,
His bill will hold more than his belican.
He can take in his beak
Food enough for a week;

But I'm damned if I see how the helican.

- **Dixon Lanire Merritt**. NB This limerick, which Merritt wrote in 1910, has often been attributed incorrectly to Ogden Nash.

532. The ostrich roams the great Sahara,
Its mouth is wide, its neck is narra.
It has such long and lofty legs,
I'm glad it sits to lay it eggs.

- **Ogden Nash:** *The Ostrich* in *Selected Poetry of Ogden Nash,* 1956.

BIRTH

533. When I was born I was so surprised I didn't talk for a year and a half.
- **Gracie Allen.**

534. Monday's child is fair of face,
Tuesday's child is full of grace,
Wednesday's child is full of woe,
Thursday's child has far to go,
Friday's child is loving and giving,
Saturday's child works hard for a living,
But the child born on the Sabbath day
Is happy and wise and good and gay.
- *anon.*

535. I have a horror of ending up like the woman in the old joke who was asked by her child where he came from and after she explained all the technical processes in a well chosen vocabulary, he looked at her intently and said, "I just wondered. Mike came from Hartford, Connecticut."
- **Erma Bombeck:** *Forever Erma*, 1996.

536. Birth dates and bathroom scales tell me more truth than I want to know.
- **Mason Cooley:** *City Aphorisms, Fourth Selection*, 1987.

537. My father said the day I was born was a red letter day. He received final demands for the gas, electricity, rates and half a dozen assorted h.p. items.
- **Tommy Cooper:** *Just Like That!* 1975.

538. Birth is the sudden opening of a window through which you look out upon a stupendous prospect. For what has happened? A miracle. You have exchanged nothing for the possibility of everything.
- **William M. Dixon.**

539. Although it is generally known I think it's about time to announce that I was born at a very early age.
- **Groucho Marx:** *Groucho and Me*, 1959.

540. To my embarrassment I was born in bed with a lady.
 - **Wilson Mizner:** *Rogue's Progress: The Fabulous Adventures of Wilson Mizner* by John Burke, 1975.

541. We hear of the chap frantically phoning 999 and blurting out that he needs help as his wife has gone into labour and the contractions are only five minutes apart.
"Is this her first child ?" the operator asks, trying to be helpful.
"Don't be an idiot," he shouts back, "of course it isn't. It's her husband."
- **Tom Shields:** *Tom Shields Takes the Fifth*, with Ken Smith, 2002

BIRTHDAY MILESTONES

542. You've had too many birthdays when the only thing you want for your birthday is not to be reminded of it.
- ***anon.***

543. I have my eighty-seventh birthday coming up and people ask me what I'd most appreciate getting. I'll tell you: a paternity suit.
- **George Burns:** *Age Happens – The Best Quotes and Cartoons About Growing Older* selected by Bruce Lansky, 1996.

544. Life begins at forty, but so does fallen arches, rheumatism, faulty eyesight, and the tendency to tell a story to the same person, three or four times.
- **William Feather.**

545. Life begins at forty, but you will miss a lot of fun if you wait that long.
- **Leopold Fechtner:** *5,000 One-and-Two-Line Jokes*, 1973.

546. She may very well pass for forty three In the dusk with the light behind her.
- **Sir W. S. Gilbert:** *Trial by Jury*, 1875.

547. To be 70 years young is sometimes far more cheerful and hopeful than to be 40 years old.
- **Oliver Wendell Holmes:** *in a letter to the poet Julia Ward Howe on her 70th birthday.*

548. Everyone if getting older, even young people. But if you feel you are past it, then consider Mick Jagger, Paul McCartney, Twiggy, David Bowie, Cliff Richard, Elton John, Cilla Black, Barbara Streisand, Steven Spielberg, Raquel Welch, Alex Ferguson to name but a few.... are all past it too. Life begins at 50 and you better believe it.
- **Annie Hulley:** *How to Spend Your Kids Inheritance: All You Need Know to Manage a Successful Retirement*, 2006.

549. To be seventy years old is like climbing the Alps. You reach a snow-crowned summit, and see behind you the deep valley stretching miles and miles away, and before you other summits higher and whiter, which you may have strength to climb, or may not. Then you sit down and meditate and wonder which it will be.
- **Henry Wadsworth Longfellow:** *in a letter written on March 13th, 1877, two weeks after his 70th birthday.*

550. I cross the forty year mark with severe hay fever, but otherwise in prime condition.
- **H. L. Mencken:** *in a letter, 1920.*

551. I have a bone to pick with Fate,
Come here and tell me girly,
Do you think my mind is maturing late,
Or simply rotted early ?
- **Ogden Nash:** *Lines on Facing 40* in *Selected Poetry of Ogden Nash*, 1995.

552. When a man has a birthday he takes a day off. When a woman has a birthday, she takes at least three years off.
- **Joan Rivers.**

553. I have always felt that a woman has the right to treat the subject of her age with ambiguity until, perhaps, she passes into the realm of over ninety. Then it is better she be candid with herself and with the world.
- **Helena Rubinstein:** *My Life For Beauty*, 1966.

554. I think the reason I want to run away from home is that the person who lives there is turning forty.
- **Barbara Sher:** quoting a client in *It's Only Too Late If You Don't Start Now.*

555. It is a bore, I admit, to be past seventy, for you are left for execution and are daily expecting the death warrant.
- **Sydney Smith:** *The Letters of Sydney Smith* edited by N. C. Smith, 1953.

556. She's no chicken, she's on the wrong side of thirty, if she be a day.
- **Jonathan Swift:** *Polite Conversation, Dialogue 1*, 1738.

557. Women deserve to have more than twelve years between the ages of twenty-eight and forty.
- **James Thurber:** *Time Magazine, 1960.*

558. When I was five-and-thirty, I thought that I was old,
My waist no longer sylph-like, my hair no longer gold.
'Twas useless to console me, or offer me champagne,
For I was five-and-thirty, and death was on my brain.
When I was five-and-forty, my heart was full of fears.
When I was five-and-fifty, I would not count the years.
But there've been subtle changes in Nature's paradigm -
Now I am five-and-sixty, and I've got lots of time.
 - **Gail White:** *Song of a Rolling Stone* in *Mezzo Cammin,* the web journal of
formal poetry by women.

559. My grandmother is over eighty and still doesn't need glasses, (she)
drinks right out of the bottle.
- **Henny Youngman**.

BLONDES

560. **Q:** What do you call an intelligent blonde?
A: A golden retriever.
- *anon*.

561. She was a brunette by birth but a blonde by habit.
- **Arthur "Bugs" Baer**.

562. She was what we used to call a suicide blonde – dyed by her own hand.
- **Saul Bellow**.

563. Gentlemen Prefer Blondes.
- The title of the **1953 Film** from the novel by Anita Loos, starring Jane Russell and Marilyn Monroe.

564. Blondes make the best victims. They're like virgin snow that show up the bloody footprints.
- **Sir Alfred Hitchcock:** *in a TV Interview, February, 1977*.

565. "Whatever happened to that skinny blonde your husband was once married to?" "I dyed my hair," replied the lady.
- **Robert Morley:** *Robert Morley's Book of Bricks*, 1978.

566. I'm not offended by dumb blonde jokes because I know I'm not dumb. I also know I'm not blonde.
- **Dolly Parton**.

BOOKS

567. Books are the legacy... which are delivered down from generation to generation, as presents to the posterity of those who are yet unborn.
- **Joseph Addison:** *The Spectator, No 166.*

568. That is a good book which is opened with expectation and closed with profit.
- **Amos Bronson Alcott:** *Table Talk,* 1877.

569. Book lovers never go to bed alone.
- ***anon.***

570. Some books are to be tasted, others to be swallowed, and some few to be chewed and digested.
 - **Francis Bacon:** *Essays, Of Studies,* 1625.

571. Of making many books there is no end.
 - **The Bible:** Ecclesiastes *12: 12a, NIV.*

572. All that mankind has done, thought, gained or been.... . is lying as in magic preservation in the pages of books.
 -**Thomas Carlyle:** *The Speaker's Treasury of Stories for all Occasions* by Herbert V. Prochnow, 1953.

573. One of the great battles we face today is to persuade our children away from computer games towards what can only be described as worth-while books.
- **Charles, Prince of Wales:** *in a speech, July, 2001.*

574. A room without books is like a body without a soul.
- **Marcus Tullius Cicero.**

575. Books, like friends, should be few and well chosen. Like friends too, we should return to them again and again for, like true friends, they will never fail us – never cease to instruct – never cloy.
- **Charles Caleb Colton:** *Lacon, or Many Things in Few Words,*1826, edited by George J. Barbour, 2001.

576. A LIBRARY, to modify the famous metaphor of Socrates, should be the delivery room for the birth of ideas.
- **Norman Cousins:** quoted in the American Library Association's *Bulletin, October, 1954.*

577. The reading of all good books is indeed like a conversation with the noblest men of past centuries who were the authors of them, nay a carefully studied conversation, in which they reveal to us none but the best of their thoughts.
- **Rene Descartes:** *Discourses on Method,* 1638.

578. Books are the quietest and most constant of friends; they are the most accessible and wisest of counsellors, and the most patient of teachers.
- **Charles W. Eliot**: *The Happy Life* in *The Durable Satisfactions of Life,* 1910.

579. Books... will open your eyes, and your ears, and your curiosity, and turn you inside out or outside in.
- **Ralph Waldo Emerson**: *Journals.*

580. If a small book is a booklet, is a small toy a toilet?
- **Leopold Fechtner**.

581. Whatever the future for the book, writing will never die. The distinguished American essayist Joan Didion has said: "We tell stories in order to live." Good writing helps us to see the world anew, helps us to live more fully.
- **Ron Ferguson:** *Don't write off books – reports of their death are premature* in *The Press and Journal, 30th August, 2011.*

582. A well composed book is a magic carpet on which we are wafted to a world that we cannot enter any other way.
 - **Caroline Gordon**.

583. From your parents you learn love and laughter and how to put one foot before the other. But when books are opened you discover you

have wings.
- **Helen Hayes:** *On Reflection*, 1968.(Her second book of memoirs).

584. A book burrows into your life in a very profound way because the experience of reading is not passive.
- **Erica Jong:** *O Magazine, 2003.*

585. I love to lose myself in other men's minds.
- **Charles Lamb**: *Detached Thoughts on Books and Reading* in *Last Essays of Elia*, 1833.

586. To me, nothing can be more important than giving children books. It is better to be giving books to children than drug treatment when they're 15 years old. Did it ever occur to anyone that if you put nice libraries in public schools you wouldn't have to put them in prisons?
- **Fran Lebowitz**: *NY Times, 1994.*

587. The crime of book purging is that it involves a rejection of the word. For the word is never absolute truth, but only man's frail and human effort to approach the truth. To reject the word is to reject the human search.
- **Max Lerner:** *The New York Post, 1953.* (Commenting on the McCarthy book burnings)

588. From the moment I picked up your book until I laid it down I was convulsed with laughter. Someday I intend reading it.
- **Groucho Marx:** *in a book blurb.*

589. A book tight shut is but a block of paper.
- ***Chinese Proverb.***

590. A book store is one of the only pieces of evidence we have that people are still thinking.
- **Jerry Seinfeld:** *Jerry Seinfeld Live on Broadway, 1998.*

591. A good book is the best of friends, the same today and forever.
- **Martin FarquharTupper:** *Proverbial Philosophy: A Book of Thoughts and Arguments, Originally Treated,* 1849.

592. When I am King, they shall not have bread and shelter only, but also teaching out of books, for a full belly is little worth where the mind is starved.
- **Mark Twain:** *The Prince and the Pauper,* 1881.

593. I was in a used book store the other day and found "How To Hug." I thought it was a romantic how-to book, but when I got it home I discovered that it was volume six of the World Book Encyclopedia.
- **Pat Williams:** *Winning With One-Liners*, 2002.

594. I loved books so much as a child. They were my outlet to the world.
- **Oprah Winfrey:** *in an interview in Chicago, 1991.*

BORES

595. Bore: a person who talks when you wish him to listen.
- **Ambrose Bierce:** *The Devil's Dictionary.* 1911.

596. Society is now one polished horde, Formed of two mighty tribes, the *bores* and the *bored*.
- **Lord Byron:** *Don Juan*, 1824.

597. Bore: one who has the power of speech but not the capacity for conversation.
- **Benjamin Disraeli.**

598. Life is never boring but some people choose to be bored. The concept of boredom entails an inability to use up present moments in a personally fulfilling way.
- **Wayne Dyer.**

599. Talk about others and you're a gossip; talk about yourself and you're a bore.
- **Sam Ewing:** *The Sun, 7ᵗʰ September, 1999.*

600. Boredom is nothing but the experience of a paralysis of our productive powers.
- **Erich Fromm:** *The Sane Society,* 1955.

601. A bore is a man who deprives you of solitude without providing you with company.
- **Giovanni Vincenzo Gravina.** *Italian Man of Letters*, 1664 – 1718.

602. Sheer silliness does not make one a bore. A great deal of hard work or innate ability is needed in addition.
- **George Mikes:** *Wisdom for Others*, 1950.

603. A bore is a fellow talker who can change the subject to his topic of conversation faster than you can change back to yours.
- **Laurence J. Peter:** *Quotations For Our Time*, 1977.

604. The secret of being a bore is to tell everything.
- **Francois, Duc de La Rochefoucauld:** *Maxims*, 1665.

605. A bore is a man who, when you ask him how he is, tells you.
- **Bert Leston Taylor:** *The So-Called Human Race*, 1922.

606. A healthy male adult bore consumes each year one and a half times his own weight in other people's patience.
- **John Updike:** *Confessions of a Wild Bore* in *Assorted Prose,* 1965.

THE BRAIN

607. Before putting your mouth in gear ensure your brain is engaged.
- *anon.*

608. A brain is no stronger than its weakest think.
- *anon.*

609. Brain: n. An apparatus with which we think we think.
- **Ambrose Bierce:** *The Devil's Dictionary*, 1911.

610. Aristotle was famous for knowing everything. He taught that the brain exists merely to cool the blood and is not involved in the process of thinking. This is true only of certain persons.
- **Will Cuppy:** *The Decline and Fall of Practically Everybody*, 1950.

611. The brain is like a TV set; when it goes blank, it's a good idea to turn off the sound.
- **Sam Ewing:** *The Wall Street Journal, 1997.*

612. This is my simple religion,
There is no need for temples;
No need for complicated philosophy,
Our own brain, our own heart is our temple;
The philosophy is kindness.
 - **Tenzin Gyatso:** 14th Dalai Lama.

613. Thinking is a brain exercise - and no faculty grows save as it is exercised.
- **Elbert Hubbard:** *A Message to Garcia*, 1899.

614. The human brain is a wonderful thing. It starts working the moment you are born, and never stops until you stand up to speak in public.
- **Sir George Jessel**. CP Robert Frost's statement:
"The brain is a wonderful organ; it starts working the moment you get

up in the morning, and does not stop until you get into the office."

615. I'm a Bear of Very Little Brain, and long words Bother me.
- **A. A. Milne:** *Winnie the Pooh*, 1926.

616. We are an intelligent species and the use of our intelligence quite properly gives us pleasure. In this respect the brain is like a muscle. When it is in use we feel very good.
- **Carl Sagan:** *Broca's Brain: Reflections on the Romance of Science*. 1974.

BUREAUCRACY

617. Bureaucracy is a giant mechanism operated by pygmies.
- **Honore de Balzac:** *Bureaucracy*, 1824.

618. Bureaucrats are the only people in the world who can say absolutely nothing and mean it.
- **James H. Boren**.

619. Guidelines for bureaucrats: when in doubt, mumble: when in trouble, delegate: when in charge, ponder.
- **James H. Boren:** *New York Times, 8th November, 1970*.

620. I am fed up with being told what not to eat, drink or smoke. I am fed up with speed cameras and health-and-safety regulations. We are being ruled by hysterical and hypochondriac bureaucrats.
- **Kenneth Clarke:** *Quotes of the Year, Press & Journal, 28th December, 2006*.

621. The purpose of bureaucracy is to compensate for incompetence and lack of discipline – a problem that largely goes away if you have the right people in the first place.
- **Jim Collins:** *Good to Great: Why Some Companies Make the Leap... and Others Don't*. 2001.

622. Man makes or mars an organisation.
- **B.C Forbes**.
NB This quotation appeared in the first issue of "Forbes Magazine" which B.C Forbes founded in 1917 and edited till his death in 1954.

623. It never pays to deal with the flyweights of the world. They take too much pleasure in thwarting you at every turn.
- **Sue Grafton:** *"H" is for Homicide, 1991*.

624. Bureaucracy destroys initiative. There is little that bureaucrats hate more than innovation, especially innovation that produces better results than the old routines. Improvements always make those at the top of the

heap look inept.
- **Frank Herbert:** *Heretics of Dune,* 1987.

625. The only thing that saves us from bureaucracy is its inefficiency.
- **Eugene McCarthy:** *Time Magazine, 12th February, 1979.*

626. Bureaucracy defends the status quo long past the time when the quo has lost its status.
- **Laurence J. Peter:** *Quotations For Our Time,* 1977.

627. Give people, including yourself, clear permission to make mistakes, and to fix the problems. Since nobody's perfect, mistakes should be allowed, cover-ups shouldn't. Cover-ups create twice the trouble.
- **Price Pritchett:** *The Ethics of Excellence,* 1993.

628. Everybody makes honest mistakes, but there's no such thing as an honest cover-up.
- *ibid.*

629. If you are going to sin, sin against God, not the bureaucracy. God will forgive you, but the bureaucracy won't.
- **Admiral Hyman G. Rickover:** *The New York Times, 3rd November, 1986.*

BUSINESS

630. Pay peanuts and you get monkeys.
- *anon*.

631. Business by no means forbids pleasures; on the contrary, they reciprocally season each other; and I will venture to affirm that no man enjoys either in perfection that does not join both.
- **Lord Chesterfield:** *Letters to His Son* , 26th February, 1754.

632. Few people do business well who do nothing else.
- **Lord Chesterfield:** *Letters to His Son,* 7th August, 1749.

633. In the business world an executive knows something about everything, a technician knows everything about something, and the switchboard operator knows everything.
- **Harold Coffin:** *The Peter Pyramid,* by Laurence J. Peter, 1986.

634. A man should never neglect his family for business.
- **Walt Disney:** *The Quotable Walt Disney* by Dave Smith., 2001.

635. Wherever you see a successful business, someone once made a courageous decision.
- **Peter Drucker.**

636. Business was originated to produce happiness, not to pile up millions.
- **B. C. Forbes:** *Forbes Magazine.*

637. No one can possibly achieve real and lasting success or "get rich" in business by being a conformist.
 - **J. Paul Getty:** *International Herald Tribune, January, 1961.*

638. In the end, all business operations can be reduced to three words: people, product, and profits. People come first.
- **Lee Iacocca.**

639. A satisfied customer is the best business strategy of all.
- **Michael Leboeuf**.

640. I think that business practices would improve immeasurably if they were guided by "feminine" principles – qualities like love and care and intuition.
- **Dame Anita Roddick:** *Body and Soul: Profits with Principle,* 1991.

641. I am still looking for the modern equivalent of those Quakers who ran successful businesses, made money because they offered honest products and treated their people decently... This business creed, sadly, seems long forgotten.
- *ibid*.

642. Perpetual devotion to what a man calls his business, is only to be sustained by perpetual neglect of many other things.
- **R. L. Stevenson:** *Virginibus Puerisque,* 1881.

CARS

643. There once was a man with a very fine car/ Which no one had seen go very far/ When asked to explain he would sadly reply:/ "You can't understand it, and neither can I. / Ten years ago she was tuned and they greased her, / And I fill her with petrol every Christmas and Easter."
- *anon*.

644. Never drive faster than your guardian angel can fly.
- *anon*.

645. He passed a car without a fuss. He passed a cart of hay. He tried to pass a swerving bus, and then he passed away.
- *anon: Passport to Paradise*, quoted in *Lighten Up! Bk 2*, edited by Bruce Lansky, 1999.

646. Where Bishop Patrick crossed the street / An "X" now marks the spot./ The light of God was with him, / But the traffic light was not.
- **E.Y. Harburg:** *Lead Kindly Light*, in *Lighten Up! Bk 2*, by Bruce Lansky.

647. If I must tangle fenders – please, / That other driver – I hope he's / A person calm and gentle spoken, / Not too upset, what ever's broken, / A man of easygoing sort, / With temper long instead of short, / Considerate, and quite forgiving, / A listener and not a speaker, / One shorter, slighter, somewhat weaker / On whom the dove of peace has hovered, / A gentleman – and fully covered.
- **Richard Armour:** *Prayer of a Motorist*, in *An Armoury of Light Verse*,1964

648. What fools indeed we mortals are
To lavish care upon a car,
With ne'er a bit of time to see
About our own machinery.
- **John Kendrick Bangs**.

649. Signs that you might be losing it. When you drive your car, you notice that people yell at you a lot. Often these are lying on your bonnet.
- **Dave Barry**: *Dave Barry Turns Fifty*, 1998.

650. The one thing that unites all human beings, regardless of age, gender, religion, economic status or ethnic background, is that, deep down inside, we ALL believe we are above-average drivers.
- *ibid.*

651. I have a baby car. It goes everywhere with a rattle!
- **Milton Berle**: *Milton Berle's Private Joke File*, 1998.

652. The best way to stop the noise in your car is to let her drive.
- *ibid.*

653. Car designers are just going to have to come up with an automobile that outlasts the payments.
- **Erma Bombeck**.

654. Have you ever noticed that when you're drivin', anyone going slower than you is an idiot? And anyone goin' faster than you is a maniac?
- **George Carlin**: *Napalm and Silly Putty*, 2001.

655. The curfew tolls the knell of party day;
The line of cars winds slowly o'er the lea.
Our friend jay-walked his absent-minded way
And left the world most unexpectantly.
- **Bennet Cerf:** quoting what certain Duke University students thought Thomas Gray might have written in his *Elegy Written in a Country Churchyard* were he alive today.

656. I have always considered that the substitution of the internal combustion engine for the horse marked a very gloomy milestone in the progress of mankind.
- **Sir Winston Churchill**: *The Wit and Wisdom of Winston Churchill* edited by James C. Humes, 1994.

657. You know, somebody actually complimented me on my driving today. They left a little note on the windscreen, it said, "Parking Fine." So that was nice.
- **Tommy Cooper**.

658. Auto accidents are less often caused by tyres that are loose than by drivers that are tight.
- **Evan Esar**: *Esar's Comic Dictionary of Wit and Humour.* 1943.

659. Most auto accidents occur on Saturday and Sunday; it's a great life if you don't weekend.
- ***ibid.***

660. The car was invented as a convenient place to sit out traffic jams.
- **Evan Esar:** *20,000 Quips and Quotes,* 1968.

661. Nothing improves your driving like being followed by a police car.
- **Sam Ewing**: *The Sun, 19th October, 1999.*

662. Travelling on motorways at night is like Russian roulette – you never know which drivers are loaded.
- **Sam Ewing**: *The Sun, 20th July, 1999.*

663. I was trying to get a new car for my wife but nobody would swap.
- **Leopold Fechtne**: *5,000 One-And-Two-Line Jokes,* 1973.

664. The automobile has not merely taken over the street, it has dissolved the living tissue of the city. Its appetite for space is absolutely insatiable; moving and parked, it devours urban land, leaving the buildings as mere islands of habitable space in a sea of dangerous and ugly traffic.
- **James Marston Fitch:** *The New York Times, 1st May, 1960.*

665. I taught my daughter how to drive, / She finally got it right; / She goes on green and stops on red - / And brakes when I turn white.
- **Charles Ghigna:** *Driving Lesson.* in *Lighten Up!* edited by Bruce Lansky.

666. That morning,when my wife eloped/ With James, our chauffeur, how I moped/What tragedies in life there are!/ I'm dashed if I can start the car!
- **Harry Graham:** *Ruthless Rhymes for Heartless Homes,* 1901.

667. The car has become an article of dress without which we feel uncertain, unclad and incomplete... (it) has become the carapace, the protective and aggressive shell of urban and suburban man.
- **Marshall McLuhan:** *Understanding Media: The Extensions of Man,* 1964.
NB Carapace is the hard upper shell of a tortoise.

668. I wanted to become a mechanic, but my father told me I wasn't motorvated enough.
- **Robert Paul**.

669. The car to watch is the car behind the car in front of you.
- **Herbert V. Prochnow & Herbert V. Prochnow Jr:** *The Public Speaker's Source Book, 1977.*

670. It is the overtakers who keep the undertakers busy;
Sayings of the Week, the Observer, 22nd December, 1963, quoted in *Cassell's Humorous Quotations* by **Nigel Rees**, 2001.

671. Another way to solve the traffic problems of this country is to pass a law that only paid-for cars be allowed to use the highways. That would turn our boulevards into children's playgrounds overnight.
- **Will Rogers:** *The Best of Will Rogers* edited by Bryan Sterling, 1979.

672. Be a patient pedestrian, otherwise you will become a pedestrian patient.
- **Robert C. Savage**: *Life Lessons: An Inspirational Instruction Book*, 1993.

673. Everything in life is somewhere else, and you get there in a car.
- **E. B. White**: *One Man's Meat*, 1943.

674. Why do they call it "Rush Hour" when nothing moves.
- **Robin Williams:** as Mork from Ork in *The Mork and Mindy Show*.

675. I took my car down to see what I could get for a trade-in. One dealer took a look at it and offered me a ball-point pen.
- **Henny Youngman**: *How Do You Like Me So Far?* 1963.

676. I just bought a little Italian car. It's called a Mafia. There's a hood under the hood.
- *ibid*.

677. A woman driver hit a guy and knocked him six feet in the air. Then she sued him for leaving the scene of the accident.
- *ibid*.

CATS

678. Cats Have No Masters... Just Friends.
- **Karen Anderson**: *Book Title*. 2004.

679. In ancient times cats were worshipped as gods. They have never forgotten.
- *anon.*

680. Kittens are wide-eyed, soft and sweet / With needles in jaws and feet.
- **Pam Brown**.

681. Work – other people's work – is an intolerable idea to a cat. Can you picture cats herding sheep or agreeing to pull a cart?
- **Louis J. Camuti**.

682. Independence is the most important single attribute of a cat's personality... but independence doesn't preclude active relationship with humans... Cats have the uncanny knack of knowing... which human is a soft touch, and which one isn't.
- **Louis J. Camuti**: *Knowing Cats, An Anthology For. Unsentimental Cat Lovers* edited by Alan Harvey, 1977.

683. Cats were put into this world to disprove the dogma that all things were created to serve man.
- **Francois-Rene de Chateaubriand**.

684. Cats are nice to have when you're lonely.
- The view expressed by the owner of Garfield in the Cartoon Series created by **Jim Davis**.

685. It is a curious truth that many cats enjoy warmer, more convivial, even affectionate relationships with humans than they could ever do with fellow felines.
- **Bruce Fogle**:*The Cat's Mind :Understanding Your Cat's Behaviour*, 1991

686. You call to a dog and a dog will break its neck to get to you. Dogs just want to please. Call to a cat and its attitude is, "What's in it for me?"
- **Lewis Grizzard**.

687. Women and cats do as they please. Men and dogs had better get used to it.
- **Robert Heinlein:** *Time Enough For Love,* 1973.

688. Never try to out-stubborn a cat.
- **Robert Heinlein:** *The Notebooks of Lazarus Long,* 1978.

689. The cat is a wild animal that inhabits the homes of humans.
 - **Konrad Lorenz:** *Man Meets Dog* translated by Marjorie Kerr Wilson, 2002.

690. Cats regard people as warm-blooded furniture.
- **Jacquelyne Mitchard**.

691. When I play with my cat, who knows but she regards me more as a plaything than I do her.
- **Michel de Montaigne:** *Essays,* 1580 – 1588.

692. There are two means of refuge from the miseries of life – music and cats.
- **Albert Schweitzer**.

693. Now I am not a cat man, but a dog man, and all felines can tell this at a glance – a sharp, vindictive glance.
- **James Thurber:** *Lanterns and Lances,* 1980.

694. A home without a cat – and a well-fed, well-petted, and properly revered cat - may be a perfect home, perhaps, but how can it prove title?
- Mark Twain: ***Pudd'nhead Wilson,*** **1894**.

CHANGE

695. Change is inevitable, except from a vending machine.
- ***anon.***

696. You can learn from people, and educate others, but the only one you can change is yourself.
- ***anon.***

697. Any change, even a change for the better, is always accompanied by drawbacks and discomforts.
- **Arnold Bennett**.

698. The only person who likes change is a wet baby.
- **Roy Blitzer**.

699. You do not notice changes in what is always before you.
- **Colette:** *My Apprenticeships and Music Hall Sidelights*, 1957.

700. Don't fear change – embrace it.
- **Anthony J.D'Angelo:** *The College Blue Book:A Few Thoughts, Reflections And Reminders On How To Get The Most Out Of College And Life, 1995.*

701. It is not the strongest of the species that survives, nor the most intelligent, but rather the ones most responsive to change.
- **Charles Darwin:** *On the Origin of the Species*. 1859.

702. In the struggle for survival, the fittest win out at the expense of their rivals because they succeed in adapting themselves best to their environment.
- ***ibid.***

703. It is not necessary to change. Survival is not mandatory.
- **W. Edwards Deming**.

704. Change is inevitable in a progressive country.
- **Benjamin Disraeli:** *in a speech in Edinburgh, 29ᵗʰ October, 1867.*

705. One must never lose time in vainly regretting the past or complaining against the changes which cause us discomfort, for change is the very essence of life.
 - **Anatole France:** *Penguin Island,* 1909.

706. People are very open-minded about new things – as long as they're exactly like the old ones.
- **Charles Kettering**.

707. The world hates change, yet it is the only thing that has brought progress.
- ***ibid***

708. If you want to change the way people respond to you, change the way you respond to people.
- **Timothy Leary:** *Changing My Mind, Among Others,* 1982.

709. I cannot say whether things will get better if we change: what I can say is they must change if they are to get better.
- **Georg Christoph Lichtenberg:** *Notebook,* 1806.

710. Whether it's a breakup, a job change, or a loss of your health or a loved one, you need to learn to change what you can, (and) accept what you can't.
 - **Joan Lunden:** *A Bend in the Road is Not the End of the Road: Ten Positive Principles For Dealing With Change;* 1998.

711. I have learned at first hand that simply **wanting** to make changes in your life is not enough. However, once you are clear abount your vision and are committed to working towards achieving it, the path to reaching your goals reveals itself with new opportunities and possibilities.
- **Mignon McLaughlin:** *The Second Neurotic's Notebook,* 1966.

712. It ought to be remembered that there is nothing more difficult to take in hand, more perilous to conduct, or more uncertain in its success than to take the lead in the introduction of a new order of things.
 - **Niccolo Machiavelli:** *The Prince,* 1513.

713. God grant me the serenity to accept the things I cannot change, courage to change the things I can, and wisdom to know the difference.

- **Reinhold Niebuhr:** *The Serenity Prayer,* **circa** 1942.

714. If you want things to be different, perhaps the answer is to become different yourself.
- **Norman Vincent Peale:** *Positive Thinking Every Day*, 1993..

715. You must take personal responsibility. You cannot change the circumstances, the seasons or the wind, but you can change yourself.
- **Jim Rohn**. American entrepreneur, author and motivational speaker, 1930 – 2009.

716. Change is not only likely, it's inevitable.
- **Barbara Sher:** *I Could Do Anything If I Only Knew What it Was*, 1994.

717. Failure is not fatal but failure to change might be.
- **John R. Wooden:** *A Lifetimes of Observations On and Off the Court* with Steve Jamison, 1997.

CHARACTER

718. A man is literally *what he thinks*, his character being the complete sum of all his thoughts.
- **James Allen:** *As a Man Thinketh*, 1918.

719. Happiness is not the end of life, character is.
- **Henry Ward Beecher**: *Life Thoughts*, 1858.

720. The three events which cause us to think most seriously and to feel most profoundly and which make the most decided influence upon the character, are unsuccessful love, thwarted ambition, and the approach of death.
- **Christian Nestell Bovee:** *Thoughts, Feelings and Fancies*, 1857.

721. A pat on the back develops character, if administered young enough, often enough, and low enough.
- **Jacob M. Braude:** *Braude's Handbook of Stories for Toastmasters and Speakers*, 1979.

722. Our character is what we do when we think no one is looking.
 - **H. Jackson Brown Jr:** *P. S. I Love You*, 1990.

723. Don't *say* things. What you *are* stands over you the while, and thunders so that I cannot hear what you say to the contrary.
- **Ralph Waldo Emerson:** *Letters and Social Aims*, 1876.

724. Wealth stays with us a little moment, if at all; only our characters are steadfast, not our gold.
 - **Euripides:** 5th century BC.

725. A man's character is determined by how hard he fights for what he believes in.
- Dialogue from the **1943 Film:***The Iron Major*. NB This biopic was based on the life of Frank Cavanaugh, an American football coach who was blinded for a time in action in the first world war. He recovered from his

injuries and won his nickname: "The Iron Major."

726. Do your best every time because by doing a thing well you build something valuable into yourself.
- **Henry Ford:** *Theosaphat Magazine, February, 1930.*

727. The final forming of a person's character lies in their own hands.
- **Anne Frank:** *The Diary of a Young Girl,* 1947.

728. Talent develops in quiet places, character in the full current of human life.
- **Johann Wolfgang von Goethe:** *Torquato Tasso, Act 1, Scene 2,* 1790.

729. Character is the result of two things, mental attitude and the way we spend our time. It is what we think and what we do that makes us what we are.
- **Elbert Hubbard:** *Love, Life and Work,* 1906.

730. No matter how full a reservoir of maxims one may possess, and no matter how good one's sentiments may be, if one has not taken advantage of every concrete opportunity to act, one's character may remain entirely unaffected for the better. With mere good intentions, hell is proverbially paved.
- **William James:** *The Principles of Psychology,* 1890.

731. Every man has three characters – that which he exhibits, that which he has, and that which he thinks he has.
- **Alphonse Karr:** *Les Guepes, 1849.*

732. Character cannot be developed in ease and quiet. Only through experience of trial and suffering can the soul be strengthened, vision cleared, ambition inspired, and success achieved.
- **Helen Keller:** *Helen Keller's Journal,* 1938.

733. By constant self-discipline and self-control you can develop greatness of character.
- **Grenville Kleiser.**

734. A person reveals his character by nothing so clearly as the joke he resents.
- **Georg Christoph Lichtenberg:** *Notebook K.* 1789 – 1793.

735. Character, rather than education, is a man's greatest need and a man's greatest safeguard, because character is far superior to, far higher than, the intellect.
- **Vince Lombardi:** *The Essential Vince Lombardi*, 2002.

736. Character is what emerges from all the little things you were too busy to do yesterday, but did anyway.
 - **Mignon McLaughlin:** *The Second Neurotic's Notebook*, 1966.

737. Character consists of what you do on the third or fourth tries.
- **James A. Michenor:** *Chesapeake*, 1978.

738. Character is much easier kept than recovered.
 - **Thomas Paine:** *The American Crisis*, 1776.

739. Character is long-standing habit.
 - **Plutarch:** *On Moral Values*, **circa** 100 AD.

740. Only a man's character is the real criterion of worth.
- **Eleanor Roosevelt:** *My Day* , 22nd August, 1944.

741. No laws, however stringent, can make the idle industrious, the thriftless provident or the drunken sober.
- **Samuel Smiles**: *Self – Help*, 1859.

742. Character, not circumstances, makes the man.
- **Booker T. Washington:** *in a speech in New York, September, 1896.*

CHILDHOOD

743. The habits we form from childhood make no small difference, but rather they make all the difference.
- **Aristotle:** 4th century BC.

744. Childhood: n. The period of human life intermediate between the idiocy of infancy and the folly of youth – two removes from the sin of manhood and three from the remorse of age.
- **Ambrose Bierce:** *The Devil's Dictionary.*

745. One of the luckiest things that can happen to you in life is, I think, to have a happy childhood.
- **Agatha Christie:** *Wit and Wisdom from the Peanut Butter Gang* compiled and edited by H. Jackson Brown Jr., 1994.

746. My childhood should have taught me lessons for my own parenthood but it didn't because parenting can be learned only by people who have no children.
- **Bill Cosby:** *Childhood,* 1991.

747. He who can't remember his own childhood is a poor educator.
- **Marie von Ebner-Eschenbach:** *Aphorisms,* 1905.

748. I cannot think of any need in childhood as strong as the need for a father's protection.
- **Sigmund Freud:** *Civilization and Its Discontents,* 1930.

749. There is always one moment in childhood when the door opens and lets the future in.
- **Graham Green:** *The Power and the Glory,* 1958.

750. The four stages of man are infancy, childhood, adolescence and obsolescence.
- **Art Linkletter:** *A Child's Garden of Misinformation,* 1965.

751. *Childhood:* that wonderful time when all you had to do to loose weight was to bathe.
 - *Leo Rosten's Book of Laughter,* by **Leo Rosten**, 1978.

752. The childhood shows the man, / As morning shows the day.
- **John Milton:** *Paradise Regained, Bk IV*, 1671.

753. Childhood is for spoiling adulthood.
- **Bill Watterson:** Calvin's views in *The Days Are Just Packed,* 1993.

CHILDREN

754. Our children have an adult's right to make their own choices and have the responsibility of living with the consequences. If we make their problems ours, they avoid that responsibility, and we are faced with problems we can't and shouldn't solve.
- **Jane Adams:** *I'm Still Your Mother: How to Get Along With Your Grown-Up Children For the Rest of Your Life*, 1994.

755. Children have more need of models than of critics.
- **Carolyn Coats**.

756. In the little world in which children have their existence... there is nothing so finely perceived, and so finely felt, as injustice.
- **Charles Dickens:** *Great Expectations*, 1861.

757. Cleanliness may be next to godliness, but with young kids it is next to impossible.
- **Sam Ewing**: *The Sun, 24ᵗʰ August, 1999.*

758. You can tell a child is growing up when he stops asking where he came from and starts refusing to tell you where he is going.
- **Leopold Fechtner:** *5,000 One-And-Two-Line Jokes*, 1979.

759. When children are doing nothing they are doing mischief.
- **Henry Fielding:** *The History of Tom Jones*, 1749.

760. As parents, our most important role is to recognize, honour, and then nurture our child's natural and unique growth process. We are not required in any way to mould them into who we think they should be. Yet we are responsible to support them wisely in ways that draw out their individual gifts and strengths.
- **John Gray:** *Children Are From Heaven: Positive Parenting Skills for Raising Cooperative, Confident, and Compassionate Children*, 1999.

761. It is not giving children more that spoils them; it is giving them

more to avoid confrontation.
- *ibid.*

762. Children allowed to develop at their own speed will usually win the race of life.
- **Fred G. Gosman**: *How to be a Happy Parent in Spite of Your Children,* 1995.

763. The beauty of "spacing" children many years apart lies in the fact that parents have time to learn the mistakes that were made with the older ones – which permits them to make exactly the opposite mistakes with the younger ones.
- **Sydney J. Harris:** *Leaving the Surface,* 1968.

764. If from infancy you treat children as gods they are liable in adulthood to act as devils.
- **P. D. James:** *The Children of Men,* 1992.

765. Nothing you do for children is ever wasted. They seem not to notice us, hovering, averting our eyes, and they seldom offer thanks, but what we do for them is never wasted.
- **Garrison Keillor:** *Leaving Home,* 1987.

766. In the final analysis it is not what you do for your children, but what you have taught them to do for themselves that will make them successful human beings.
- **Ann Landers**: *Ann Landers Says That Truth is Stranger,* 1968.

767. The real question isn't whether or not you love your kids, but how well you are able to demonstrate your love and caring so that your children really feel loved.
- **Stephanie E. Marston:** *Love: Quotes and Passages From the Heart* edited by B.C. Aronson, 2007.

768. If children live with encouragement, they learn confidence... If children live with acceptance, they learn to love.
- **Dorothy L. Nolte**: *Children Learn What They Live* 1972. NB For the complete version of this poem type in the poem's title into your Search Engine panel.

769. What children hear at home soon flies abroad.
- ***English Proverb.***

770. It is important to remember that many of our youngest kids need to learn to respect themselves. You learn your worth from the way you are treated.
- **Anna Quinlen:** *New York Times, 6th January, 1993.*

771. I hope to leave my children a sense of empathy and pity and a will to right social wrongs.
- **Dame Anita Roddick:** *The Sunday Express, 9th June, 1991.*

772. Could I climb the highest place in Athens, I would lift my voice and proclaim: "Fellow citizens, why do you turn and scrape every stone to gather wealth, and take so little care of your children, to whom one day you must relinquish it all."
- **Socrates:** *The Strong Family* by Charles R. Swindoll, 1991.

773. Children nowadays are tyrants. They contradict their parents, gobble their food, and tyrannise their teachers.
- **Socrates:** 5th century BC.

774. Each day of our lives we make deposits in the memory banks of our children.
- **Charles R. Swindoll:** *The Strong Family: Growing Wise in Family Life.*

775. Familiarity breeds contempt – and children.
- **Mark Twain:** *Mark Twain's Notebook* edited by Albert Bigelow Paine, 1935.

CHOICE

776. All through life we must keep choosing... as we look back, it is to wonder what would have happened if we had gone the other way when the road forked.
- *anon*.

777. It's your choice how you climb a tree – you could sit on an acorn, make friends with a big bird, or get off your butt and make the effort.
- *anon*

778. I shall be telling this with a sigh / Somewhere ages and ages hence; / Two roads converge in a wood, and I - / Took the one less travelled by, / And that has made all the difference.
- **Robert Frost**: *The Road Not Taken* from *Mountain Interval*, 1916.

779. When you have to make a choice and don't make it, that is in itself a choice.
- **William James:** *The Treasury of Humorous Quotations* edited by Evan Esar, 1955.

780. I believe that we are solely responsible for our choices, and we have to accept the consequences of every deed, word, and thought throughout our lifetime.
- **Elizabeth Kubler-Ross**.

781. It is the ability to choose which makes us human.
- **Madeleine L'Engle:** *Walking on Water: Reflections on Faith and Art*. 1980.

782. He who does anything because it is the custom, makes no choice.
- **John Stuart Mill:** *On Liberty*, 1859.

783. One's philosophy is not best expressed in words; it is expressed in the choices one makes... and the choices we make are ultimately our responsibility.
- **Eleanor Roosevelt**, *My Day*. NB *My Day* was the daily newspaper

column written by Mrs Roosevelt from 1935 – 1962.

784. It is our choices... that show what we truly are, far more than our abilities.
- **J. K. Rowling**: *Harry Potter and the Chamber of Secrets,* 1999.

785. Where to elect there is but one, / 'Tis Hobson's choice, - take that or none.
- **Thomas Ward:** *England's Reformation – A Poem in Four Cantos,* 1710. NB Thomas Hobson was a Cambridge carrier, who, in order to rotate the use of his horses, stipulated that customers must take the horse nearest the door, failing that they had no other choice.

786. When you choose to be pleasant and positive in the way you treat others, you have also chosen, in most cases, how you are going to be treated by them.
- **Zig Ziglar:** *Zig Ziglar's Little Book of Big Quotes,* 1990.

CHRISTIANITY

787. The Christian ideal has not been tried and found wanting; it has been found difficult and left untried.
 - **G. K. Chesterton:** *What's Wrong With the World,* 1910.

788. I want to take the word Christianity back to Christ himself... I go back to that great Spirit which contemplated a sacrifice for the whole of humanity... and I thank God for it.
- **Julia Ward Howe:** *What is Religion?* 1893.

789. Christianity has taught us to care. Caring is the greatest thing, caring matters most.
- **Friedrich von Hugel:** *Letter to his niece,* quoted in *Chambers Dictionary of Quotations,* 1996.

790. Christianity is the highest perfection of humanity.
- **Samuel Johnson:** *Letters of Samuel Johnson* edited by R. W. Chapman, 1963.

791. Christianity will go. It will vanish and shrink. I needn't argue with that; I'm right and I will be proved right.
- **John Lennon:** *London Evening Standard, 4th March, 1966.*

792. We are told that Christ was killed for us, that His death has washed out our sins, and that by dying He has disabled death itself. That is the formula. That is Christianity. That is what has to be believed.
 - **C. S. Lewis:** *Mere Christianity,* 1952.

793. Reality, in fact, is always something you couldn't have guessed. That's one of the reasons I believe Christianity. It's a religion you couldn't have guessed.
 - ***ibid.***

794. I believe in Christianity as I believe that the sun has risen. Not only because I see it, but because by it I see everything else.
- **C. S. Lewis:** *Is Theology Poetry ? - a talk given in Oxford in 1944.*

795. I doubt if there is in the world a single problem, whether social, political, or economic, which would not find ready solution if men and nations would rule their lives according to the plain teaching of the Sermon on the Mount.
- **Franklin D. Roosevelt:** *The Age of Roosevelt* by Arthur M. Schlesinger. 1957.

796. The essence of Christianity is the appeal to the life of Christ as a revelation of the nature of God and of his agency in the world.
- **Alfred North Whitehead:** *Adventures of Ideas*, 1933.

CHRISTMAS

797. Christmas is a time when everybody wants his past forgotten and his present remembered.
- *anon.*

798. O for the good old days when people would stop Christmas shopping when they ran out of money.
- *anon.*

799. I have always thought of Christmas time, when it comes around... as a good time, a kind, forgiving, charitable, pleasant time.
- **Charles Dickens:** *A Christmas Carol.* 1843.

800. The day after Christmas, and out in the yard Two snowmen in shorts are fighting hard. And why are they fighting? That's easy to say, the day after Christmas is Boxing Day.
- **Richard Edwards:** *Nonsense Christmas Rhymes,* 2002.

801. Whoever said, "Talk is cheap," never heard children tell what they want for Christmas.
- **Sam Ewing:** *The National Enquirer, 24th November, 1966.*

802. The best of all gifts around any Christmas tree: the presence of a happy family all wrapped up in each other.
- **Burton Hillis:** *Better Homes and Gardens.*

803. When the Bishop of Chester said there should be a religious message on Christmas stamps, *Punch* suggested, "Lord Deliver Us."
- **Bob Monkhouse:** *Just Say a Few Words.* 1988.

804. In a survey, the top three stresses for men were: a fighter pilot in battle, an actor delivering a monologue and Christmas shopping an hour before closing.
- **Liam Neeson:** *Newsweek,* quoted in *Reader's Digest, December, 2005.*

805. Too soon I learned the bitter truth: There isn't any Santa Claus, Each Yuletide mocks my touching trust; the give and let give is my plea, It's Christmas Day for some, but just December twenty-fifth for me.
- **Dorothy Parker:** *The Uncollected Dorothy Parker*, 1999.

806. Last Christmas my sister, Geri, gave me a lovely cloth calendar. It only took me five hours to sew in a Doctor's appointment.
 - **Robert Paul**.

807. Love came down at Christmas, / Love all lovely, Love Divine; / Love was born at Christmas, / Star and angels gave the sign.
- **Christina Rossetti:** *Time Flies: A Reading Diary*, 1885.

CITIES

808. A great city, a great solitude.
- ***anon.***

809. Every city is a living body.
- **St. Augustine:** *City of God,* 413 – 426.

810. We shall defend every village, every town, and every city. The vast mass of London itself, fought street by street, could easily devour an entire hostile army; and we would rather see London laid in ruins and ashes than that it should be tamely and abjectly enslaved.
- **Sir Winston Churchill:** *BBC Radio Broadcast, 14th July, 1940.*

811. If you would be known, and not know, vegetate in a village; if you would know, and not be known, live in a city.
- **Charles Caleb Colton:** *Lacon, or Many Things in Few Words,* 1826, edited by George J. Barbour, 2001.

812. The cities drain the country of the best part of its population; the flower of youth, of both sexes, goes into the towns.
- **Ralph Waldo Emerson:** *Nature.*

813. Our cities with their swollen populations and cliff dwelling high-rise buildings are breeding places for loneliness.
- **Allan Fromme:** *The Ability to Love,* 1966.

814. Suburbs... have become the heirs to their cities' problems. They have pollution, high taxes, crime. People thought they would escape all these things in the suburbs. But like the people of Boccaccio's *Decameron,* they ran away from the plague and took it with them.
- **Charles Haar:** *The New York Times, 16th March, 1980.*

815. Cities are expanding at an alarming rate.
- **Penny Kemp and Derek Wall:** *A Green Manifesto for the 1990's,* 1990.

816. Kindness is a virtue neither modern nor urban. One almost unlearns it in a city.
- **Phyllis McGinley:** *The Province of the Heart,* 1957.

817. Clearly, then, the city is not a concrete jungle, it is a human zoo.
- **Desmond Morris:** *The Human Zoo,* 1969.

818. We live in a lovely little suburb. It's just two miles beyond our income.
 - **Robert Orben:** *2,400 Jokes to Brighten Your Speeches,* 1984.

819. City life: millions of people being lonesome together.
- **Henry David Thoreau.**

COMMITMENT

820. To say yes, you have to sweat and roll up your sleeves and plunge both hands into life up to the elbows.
- **Jean Anouilh:** *Antigone*, 1944.

821. Consider the postage stamp;its usefulness consists in the ability to stick to one thing till it gets there.
- **Josh Billings**.

822. The die is cast.
- According to the Roman historian Suetonius.these words were said by **Julius Caesar:** In crossing the river Rubicon in 49 BC Caesar was committing himself to the conquest of Gaul. "To cross the Rubicon" has come to mean, in our idiom, "to make an irrevocable commitment."

823. There is only one way to create meaning in life; and that, friends, is through commitment. Only through commitment do people achieve an identity and a meaning and a purpose in life.
- **Tony Campolo:** *You Can Make a Difference*, 1984.

824. Whatever I have tried to do in life, I have tried with all my heart to do well; that whatever I have devoted myself to, I have devoted myself to completely; that in great aims and in small, I have always been thoroughly in earnest.
 - **Charles Dickens:** *David Copperfield*, 1850.

825. Give us clear vision that we may know where to stand and what to stand for - because unless we stand for something, we shall fall for anything.
- **Peter Marshall:** *The Prayers of Peter Marshall*, 1955.

826. The relationship between commitment and doubt is by no means an antagonistic one. Commitment is healthiest when it is not without doubt but in spite of doubt.
- **Rollo May:** *The Courage to Create*, 1975.

827. The notion of looking on at life has always been hateful to me... I must participate.
- **Antoine de Saint-Exupery:** *Flight to Arras*, 1942.

828. When you have bacon and eggs for breakfast the chicken makes a contribution, but the pig makes a commitment.
- **Fred Shero**.

829. Commitment means that it is possible for a man to yield the nerve centre of his consent to a purpose or cause, a movement or an ideal, which may be more important to him whether he lives or dies.
- **Howard Thurman:** *Disciplines of the Spirit*, 1963.

COMMITTEES

830. Committee - a group of men who individually can do nothing but as a group decide that nothing can be done.
- **Fred Allen**.

831. If I had to identify, in one word, the reason why the human race has not achieved, and never will achieve, its full potential, that word would be "meetings".
- **Dave Barry:** *Dave Barry Turns Fifty,* 1999.

832. A committee is a group that keeps minutes and loses hours.
- **Milton Berle**.

833. A member of the committee slapped a name tag over my left bosom. "What shall we name the other one?" I smiled. She was not amused.
- **Erma Bombeck:** *A Marriage Made in Heaven,* 1994.

834. Nothing is impossible until it is taken to a committee.
- **James H. Boren**.

835. A committee is a cul-de-sac down which ideas are lured and then quietly strangled.
- **Sir Barnett Cocks**.

836. What is a committee? A group of the unwilling, picked from the unfit, to do the unnecessary.
- **Richard Harkness**.

837. A committee is a thing that takes a week to do what one good man can do in an hour.
 - **Elbert Hubbard**.

838. If you want to kill any idea in the world, get a committee working on it.
- **Charles F. Kettering**.

839. To kill time, a committee meeting is the perfect weapon.
- **Laurence J. Peter:** *Quotations For Our Time,* 1977.

840. To get something done, a committee should consist of no more than three men, two of them absent.
- *ibid.*

841. We all have heard the saying, which is true as well as witty,
That a camel is a horse that was designed by a committee.
- **Allan Sherman:** *A Gift of Laughter,* 1965.

842. Any committee that is the slightest use is composed of people who are too busy to want to sit on it for a second longer than they have to.
- **Katherine Whitehorn:** *Are You Sitting Comfortably?* in *Observations,*1970

COMMON SENSE

843. What we all have so much of, and can't understand why everybody else doesn't have any.
- **Milton Berle:** *Milton Berle's Private Joke File*, 1989.

844. Common Sense is the knack of seeing things as they are, and doing things as they ought to be done.
- **Josh Billings**.

845. Common sense always speaks too late... (it) tells you you ought to have had your brakes relined last week before you smashed a front end this week.
- **Raymond Chandler:** *Playback*, 1989.

846. Common sense in an uncommon degree is what the world calls wisdom.
- **Samuel Taylor Coleridge**.

847. Common sense is the best distributed thing in the world, for we all think we possess a good share of it.
- **Rene Descartes:** *Discourse on the Method*, 1637.

848. Common sense is genius dressed in its working clothes.
- **Ralph Waldo Emerson**: *Letters and Biographical Sketches*, 1883.

849. Nothing astonishes men so much as common sense and plain dealing.
- **Ralph Waldo Emerson:** *Essays, First Series*, 1841.

850. There is nobody so irritating as somebody with less intelligence and more sense than you have.
- **Don Herold**.

851. A handful of common sense is worth a bushel of learning.
- ***Spanish Proverb***.

852. If a man has common sense, he has all the sense there is.
- **Sam Rayburn**.

853. Common sense is instinct. Enough of it is genius.
- **George Bernard Shaw:** *Androcles and the Lion*, 1916.

854. Good health and common sense are two of life's greatest blessings.
 - **Publius Syrus:** 1st century BC.

855. Common sense is not so common.
- **Voltaire**: *Philosophical Dictionary*, 1764.

COMPUTERS

856. Hardware is the part of the computer that can be kicked. If all you can do is swear at it, then it must be software.
- ***anon***.

857. Computers will never replace man entirely until they learn to laugh at the boss's jokes.
- ***anon***

858. I am not the only person who uses his computer mainly for the purpose of diddling with his computer.
 - **Dave Barry:** *Miami Herald, 1994.*

859. In the Computer Revolution everything changes way too fast for the human brain to comprehend. That is why only 14 year olds really understand what is going on.
- **Dave Barry:** *Dave Barry in Cyberspace,* 1996.

860. They've finally come up with the perfect office computer. If it makes a mistake, it blames another computer.
- **Milton Berle**: *Milton Berle's Private Joke File,* 1989.

861. Computers are incredibly fast, accurate, and stupid. Human beings are incredibly slow, inaccurate and brilliant. Together they are powerful beyond imagination.
- **Albert Einstein**.

862. Computers will never take the place of books. You can't stand on a floppy disc to reach a high shelf.
 - **Sam Ewing:** *National Enquirer, July, 1994.*

863. Computers are like bikinis – they save people a lot of guesswork.
- **Sam Ewing:** *The Sun, 25ᵗʰ May, 1999.*

864. If it's in the computer, they believe anything.
- Jessica, Jonah's friend, in the **1993 Film**: *Sleepless in Seattle*, written by Nora Ephron **et al**.

865. Home computers are being called upon to perform many new functions, including the consumption of homework formerly eaten by the dog.
- **Doug Larson**.

866. No more will I retype a page / to change a single line; / though erring may be human, / deleting is divine.
- **Leslie Danford Perkins**: *On Using My First Computer*, quoted in *Lighten Up, Book Two* edited by Bruce Lansky, 1999.

867. The new computers do everything but think, which we must admit makes them almost human.
- **Herbert V. Prochnow & Herbert V. Prochnow Jr**: *The Public Speaker's Source Book, 1977*.

868. Computers make it easier to do a lot of things, but most of the things they make it easier to do don't need to be done.
- **Andy Rooney**: *60 Minutes, CBS*.

869. The fastest thing a computer does is become outdated.
- *ibid*.

870. A Glasgow father is watching over his young daughter's shoulder as she sets up an Email account on the family computer. She reaches the point where she has to put in a password and the message on the screen says that it has to have at least four characters. So, after thinking about it, she types in "snowwhite bartsimpsonshrekwoodie".
- **Tom Shields and Ken Smith**: *Tom Shields Takes the Fifth*, 2002.

871. Why is it drug addicts and computer aficionados are both called users?
- **Clifford Stoll**: *Silicon Snake Oil*, 1995.

CONVERSATION

872. It is all right to hold a conversation, but you should let go of it now and then.
- **Richard Armour:** *Reader's Digest, August, 1985.*

873. My idea of good company is the company of clever, well-informed people who have a great deal of conversation.
- **Jane Austen:** *Persuasion,* 1817.

874. Let your conversation be always full of grace, seasoned with salt.
- **The Bible:** *Colossians 4: 6a, NIV.*

875. A gossip is someone who talks to you about others; a bore is someone who talks to you about himself; and a brilliant conversationalist is one who talks to you about yourself.
- **Lisa Kirk.**

876. The great gift in conversation lies less in displaying talent ourselves than in drawing it out of others. He who leaves your company pleased with himself and his own cleverness is perfectly well pleased with you.
- **Jean de La Bruyere:** *The Morals and Manners of the Seventeenth Century: Being The Characters of La Bruyere,* 1688.

877. Polite conversation is rarely either.
- **Fran Lebowitz:** *Social Studies,* 1981.

878. There is no conversation more boring than the one where everybody agrees.
- **Michel de Montaigne:** *Essays,* 1595.

879. What a delicate and rare and gracious art is the art of conversation.
- **Christopher Morley:** The essay *What Men Live By,* in *Mince Pie,* 1919.

880. Beware of the conversationalist who adds, "In other words." He is merely starting afresh.
- **Robert Morley:** *Observer, 6th December, 1964.*

881. The real art of conversation is not only to say the right thing at the right place, but to leave unsaid the wrong thing at the tempting moment.
- **Lady Dorothy Nevill:** *The Remembrances of Lady Dorothy Nevill,* 1907.

882. Ideal conversation must be an exchange of thought, and not, as many of those who worry most about their shortcomings believe, an eloquent exhibition of wit or oratory.
- **Emily Post:** *Etiquette,* 1922.

883. Sidney Smith said of Macaulay, "He once talked too much; but now he has occasional flashes of silence that make his conversation perfectly delightful."
- **Herbert V. Prochnow:** *The Speaker's Treasury of Stories for all Occasions.*

884. To listen closely and reply well is the highest perfection we are able to attain in the art of conversation.
- **Francois, Duc de La Rochefoucauld:** *Maxims.*

885. Silences make the real conversations between friends. Not the saying but they never needing to say is what counts.
- **Margaret Lee Runbeck:** *Answer Without Ceasing,* 1949.

886. When you enter into conversation with a man, the first thing you should consider is whether he had a greater inclination to hear you, or that you should hear him.
- **Sir Richard Steele:** *The Spectator, April, 1711.*

887. And surely one of the best rules in conversation is never to say a thing which any of the company can reasonably wish had been left unsaid.
- **Jonathan Swift:** *Hints Toward an Essay on Conversation,* 1713.

888. He had a good memory, and a tongue tied in the middle. This is a combination which gives immortality to conversation.
- **Mark Twain:** *Roughing It,* 1872.

889. Lettuce is like conversation; it must be fresh and crisp, and so sparkling that you scarcely notice the bitter in it.
- **Charles Dudley Warner.**

COOKS AND COOKING

890. I got a wife that dresses to kill – and cooks the same way.
- **Joey Adams:** *Joey Adams' Encyclopedia of Humour,* 1969.

891. I cook with wine, sometimes I even add it to the food!
- *anon.*

892. The only concession we have made to automation was a smoke alarm. It told me when our dinner was ready.
- **Erma Bombeck:** *A Marriage Made In Heaven,* 1993.

893. Every time my wife has an accident in the kitchen I get it for dinner.
- **Leopold Fechtner:** *5,000 One-And-Two-Line Jokes,* 1979.

894. I'm not saying my wife is a bad cook, but my doctor advised me to eat out more.
- *ibid.*

895. Cooking is like love. It should be entered into with abandon, or not at all.
- **Harriet Van Horne:** *Vogue Magazine, October, 1956.*

896. The most indispensable ingredient of all good home cooking: love for those you are cooking for.
- **Sophia Loren.**

897. We may live without poetry, music and art;
We may live without conscience and live without heart;
We may live without friends, we may live without books;
But civilized man can not live without cooks.
- **Owen Meredith.**

898. Restaurant staff, tiring of abusive customers, took it upon themselves to strike back. Several years ago a notice appeared in a

Channel Islands restaurant: "If you like home cooking – stay home."
More chilling, was the warning spotted in a northern cafe: "Complaints
to the cook can be hazardous to your health."
- **Derek Nimmo:** *Table Talk*, 1990.

899. A good cook is like a sorceress who dispenses happiness.
- **Elsa Schiaparelli:** From her autobiography, *Shocking Life*, 1954.

900. For those who cannot even boil an egg, we recommend the
cookbook published by St. Ninian's Church Woman's Guild of
Stonehouse. The ingredients for Kay Nichol's fail-safe recipe are: "One
or more eggs, the Methodist Hymn Book and a pan of boiling water".
The method is simplicity itself: for a hard-boiled egg, sing all the verses
of 'Onward Christian Soldiers'; for medium-boiled omit one verse, and
for soft-boiled sing only two verses.
- **Tom Shields:** *Tom Shields Free At Last*, 1997.

COSMETICS

901. **A**. Cosmetics are a powerful form of chemical warfare used by women in the battle of the sexes.
 B. Beauty always comes from within – within jars, tubes and compacts
 C. Many women are as pretty as they used to be, but it takes them much longer.
 D. It always takes a woman longer to make up her face than her mind.
- ***anon***: *20,00 Quips and Quotes* by Evan Esar, 1968.

902. Use a make-up table with everything close at hand and don't rush, otherwise you'll look like a patchwork quilt.
- **Lucille Ball:** *Family Weekly, 6th July, 1975.*

903. Most women are not as young as they are painted.
- **Max Beerbohm:** *A Defence of Cosmetics.* NB This satirical essay, written in 1894, appeared in the first issue of the quarterly magazine, *The Yellow Book.*

904. There is no cosmetic for beauty like happiness.
- **Marguerite**, **Countess of Blessington**.

905. Cosmetics may improve on Mother Nature, but they can never fool Father Time.
 - **Sam Ewing:** *The National Enquirer, November, 1994.*

906. Cosmetics keep people from reading between the lines.
- **Sam Ewing:** *The Sun, 7th September, 1999.*

907. A girl whose cheeks are covered in paint
Has an advantage with me over one whose ain't.
- **Ogden Nash:** *Biological Reflection* in *Hard Lines,* 1931.

908. Cosmetics is a boon to every woman, but a girl's best beauty aid is still a near-sighted man.
- **Yoko Ono**.

909. I was going to have cosmetic surgery until I noticed that the doctor's office was full of portraits by Picasso.
- **Rita Rudner**.

910. Taking joy in life is a woman's best cosmetic.
- **Rosalind Russell**.

911. God hath given you one face, / And you make yourselves another.
 - **William Shakespeare:** *Hamlet, Act 3m Scene 1*. (Hamlet to Ophelia)

COURAGE AND COWARDICE

912. Until the day of his death, no man can be sure of his courage.
- **Jean Anouilh:** *Becket,* 1959.

913. Coward: n. One who in a perilous emergency thinks with his legs.
- **Ambrose Bierce:** *The Devil's Dictionary,* 1911.

914. All of us have moments in our lives that test our courage. Taking children into a house with a white carpet is one of them.
- **Erma Bombeck**.

915. To know what is right and not to do it is the worst cowardice.
- **Confucius:** *Analects*, 5th century BC.

916. You can't test courage cautiously.
- **Annie Dillard:** *Pilgrim at Tinker Creek*. 1974.

917. Unless you have courage, a courage that keeps you growing, always growing, no matter what happens, there is no certainty of success. It really is an endurance race.
- **Henry Ford:** *Theosophist Magazine, February, 1930.*

918. Courage is contagious. When a brave man takes a stand, the spines of others are stiffened.
- **Billy Graham:** *Reader's Digest, July, 1964.*

919. Oh courage... oh yes! If we only had that, then life might be liveable, in spite of everything.
 - **Henrik Ibsen:** *Hedda Gabler,* 1890.

920. Do not dare not to dare.
- **C. S. Lewis:** *The Chronicles of Narnia,* 1950.

921. Courage is the ladder on which all the other virtues mount.
- **Clare Boothe Luce:** *Reader's Digest, 1979.*

922. To sin by silence when we should protest makes cowards of men.
- **Abraham Lincoln**.

923. Courage can't see around corners, but goes round them anyway.
- **Mignon McLaughlin:** *The Neurotics Notebook*, 1960.

924. The only courage that matters is the kind that gets you from one moment to the next.
- **Mignon McLaughlin:** *The Second Neurotic's Notebook*, 1966.

925. The opposite of courage in our society is not cowardice, it is conformity.
- **Rollo May:** *Man's Search For Himself*, 1953.

926. Courage is not a virtue of value among other personal values like love or fidelity. It is the foundation that underlies and gives reality to all other virtues and personal values.
- **Rollo May:** *The Courage to Create*, 1975.

927. The acorn becomes an oak by means of automatic growth; no commitment is necessary... But a man or woman becomes fully human only by his or her choices and his or her commitment to them. People attain worth and dignity by the multitude of decisions they make from day to day. These decisions require courage.
- *ibid.*

928. Courage is fear holding on a minute longer.
- **George Patton**.

929. You gain strength, courage and confidence by every experience in which you really stop to look fear in the face. You are able to say to yourself, "I lived through this horror. I can take the next thing that comes along."
- **Eleanor Roosevelt:** *You Learn by Living: Eleven Keys for a More Fulfilling Life*, 1960.

930. Sometimes even to live is an act of courage.
- **Seneca:** *Epistles*, 1st century, BC.

931. Cowards die many times before their deaths;
The valiant never taste of death but once.
- **William Shakespeare:** *Julius Caesar, Act 2, Sc 2*, 1599.

932. A great deal of talent is lost in the world for want of courage. Every day sends to their graves obscure men whose timidity prevented them from making a first effort.
- **Sydney Smith**.

933. Fortune never helps the faint hearted.
- **Sophocles:** *Fragments*, 5th century BC.

934. Courage is resistance to fear, mastery of fear – not absence of fear.
- **Mark Twain:** *Pudd'nhead Wilson's Calendar*, 1894.

935. Courage is being scared to death but saddling up anyway.
 - **John Wayne:** *Reader's Digest, September, 1970.*

COURTSHIP

936. Those marriages generally abound most with love and constancy that are preceded by a long courtship.
- **Joseph Addison:** *The Spectator, 1711.*

937. You don't need scores of suitors, you only need one, if he's the right one.
- **Louisa May Alcott:** *Little Women,* 1868.

938. The only thing he ever takes out on a moonlit night is his upper plate.
- **Fred Allen:** *The Treasury of Humorous Quotations* edited by Evan Esar, English edition edited by Nicolas Bentley, 1955.

939. Courtship – a man pursuing a woman until she catches him.
- ***anon.***

940. I came, I saw, I conquered.
- **Julius Caesar:** Widely considered to be one of the greatest military leaders of all time he is reputed to have written this statement in a report he made after a successful campaign.

941. Courtship to marriage, as a very witty prologue to a very dull play.
- **William Congreve:** *The Old Bachelor: A Comedy,* 1693.

942. When I in my Love's shadow sit, / I do not miss the sun one bit. / When she is near, my arms can hold / All that's worth having in this world.
- **W. H. Davies:** *Charms.* NB The text of this poem and others by Davies is available on the Internet at:
www.theotherpages.org/poems/davies

943. Faint heart never won fair lady.
- ***English Proverb.***

944. He that would the daughter win, must with the mother first begin.
- *ibid.*

945. Courting and wooing bring dallying and doing.
- *ibid.*

946. A man who would woo a fair maid, / Should 'prentice himself to the trade; / And study all day, / In methodical way, / How to flatter, cajole and persuade.
- **Sir William Gilbert:** *The Yeomen of the Guard,* 1888.

947. The surest way to hit a woman's heart is to take aim kneeling.
- **Douglas W. Jerrold:** *Specimens of Douglas Jerrold's Wit,* 1858.

948. The time I've lost in wooing, / In watching and pursuing. / The light that lies / In woman's eyes / Has been my heart's undoing.
- **Thomas Moore.**

949. An object in possession seldom retains the same charm that it had in pursuit.
- **Pliny the Younger:** *Epistles,* early 2nd century AD.

950. They dream in Courtship, but in Wedlock wake.
- **Alexander Pope:** *Poetical Miscellanies,* 1714.

951. The hardest task of a girl's life nowadays is to prove to a man that his intentions are serious.
- **Helen Rowland:** *A Guide to Men,* 1922.

952. Love sought is good, but given unsought is better.
- **William Shakespeare:** *Twelfth Night. Act 3, Sc 1,* 1602.

953. You think that you are Ann's suitor, that you are the pursuer and she the pursued, that it is your part to woo, to persuade, to prevail, to overcome. Fool, it is you who are pursued, the marked-down quarry, the destined prey.
- **George Bernard Shaw:** *Man and Superman,* 1903.

CRIME

954. The annual cost of crime to the British tax payer is at present colossal – but we *do* get a lot of crime for our money!
 - ***anon***.

955. The toilets at a local police station have been stolen. Police say they have nothing to go on.
- **Ronnie Barker**: *The Two Ronnies*.(BBC TV Show)

956. Labour is the party of law and order in Britain today. Tough on crime and tough on the causes of crime.
- **Tony Blair**: *in a speech. 1993.*

 957. There are too many scumbags out there who are allowed to get away with it. The more they escape any form of justice, the more they feel they can cause hurt and damage. Victims feel helpless and lose the will to leave their homes... I am not saying that there was no crime or violence around when I was growing up., . . But I can't remember old people terrified to go out.
- **Michael Caine:** *Saga Magazine, November, 2009.*

958. An art thief is a man who takes pictures.
- **George Carlin:** *Napalm*, 2001.

959. Thieves respect property. They merely wish the property to become their property that they may more perfectly respect it.
- **G. K. Chesterton:** *The Man Who Was Thursday*, 1908.

960. We believe this to be the work of thieves, and I'll tell you why. The whole pattern is very reminiscent of past robberies where we have found thieves to be involved. The tell-tale loss of property – that's one of the signs to look for.
- **Peter Cook:** *Beyond the Fringe*. NB *Beyond the Fringe* was a satirical stage revue written and performed in the 1960's by Peter Cook, Dudley Moore, Alan Bennett and Jonathan Miller

961. Police arrested two kids yesterday, one was drinking battery acid, and the other one was eating fireworks. They charged one and let the other off.
- **Tommy Cooper**.

962. A cement mixer collided with a prison van on the Kingston bypass. Motorists are asked to be on the lookout for 16 hardened criminals.
- **Ronnie Corbett:** *The Two Ronnies*. (BBC Television show: 1971 - 1987)

963. My children never, never steal!
To know their offspring is a thief
Will often make a father feel
Annoyed and cause a mother grief;
So never steal, but, when you do,
Be sure there's no one watching you.
- **Harry Graham:** *Ruthless Rhymes for Heartless Homes*, 1901.

964. He who profits by crime commits it
- **Seneca:** *Medea*, 1st century AD.

965. The scene is a Glasgow court where the accused is vehemently denying a charge of shoplifting. The problem, as is so often the case, is that the prosecution have a video tape which shows quite clearly the accused in the act of purloining the goods in question.
The accused watches the video which, incontrovertibly, has footage of himself stuffing the items up his jumper. He appears despondent.
Suddenly he cheers up considerably, and even leaps to his feet in elation.
"Look," he cries. "I put the stuff back."
"Naw, son, we're rewinding the tape," says the court officer.
- **Tom Shields:** *Tom Shields Goes Forth*, 2000.

966. He who helps the guilty, shares the crime.
- **Publilius Syrus:** *Maxims*, 1st century BC.

967. He was given ten years for something he didn't do. He didn't run fast enough.
- **Pat Williams:** *Winning With One-Liners*, 2002.

968. We had gay burglars the other night. They broke in and rearranged the furniture
- **Robin Williams**.

DANCE

969. I have no desire to prove anything by it. I have never used it as an outlook or a means of expressing myself. I just dance.
- **Fred Astaire:** *Steps in Time: An Autobiography,* 1959.

970. Our parents sent us to ballroom-dancing classes, but it would have been equally cost effective for them to simply set fire to their money.
- **Dave Barry:** *Dave Barry is Not Making This Up,* 1995.

971. Custom has made dancing sometimes necessary for a young man; therefore mind it while you learn it, that you may learn to do it well, and not be ridiculous though it is a ridiculous act.
- **Lord Chesterfield:** *Letters to His Son.*

972. No sane man will dance.
- **Marcus Tullius Cicero:** 1st century BC.

973. Dancing and running shake up the chemistry of happiness.
- **Mason Cooley:** *City Aphorisms, Third Selection,* 1986.

974. A very merry, dancing, drinking,
Laughing, quaffing, and unthinking time.
- **John Dryden:** *The Secular Masque* in *Poetry, Prose, and Plays,* 1952.

975. In all there were seven brothers. That's how I learned to dance – waiting for my turn of the bathroom.
- **Bob Hope:** *Bob Hope, My Life in Jokes,* 2003.

976. At 14, I discovered girls. At that time, dancing was the only way you could put your arm around the girl. Dancing was courtship. Only later did I discover that you dance joy. You dance love. You dance dreams.
- **Gene Kelly.**

977. Dancing is a wonderful training for girls, it's the first way you learn to guess what a man is going to do before he does it.
- **Christopher Morley**: *Kitty Foyle,* 1940.

978. I was dancing with my girl friend and mentioned it was a nice floor. She said, "Why don't you get off my feet and try it then?"
- **Chic Murray**: *The Chic Murray Bumper Fun Book* by Andrew Yule, 1991.

979. If I could have said it, I shouldn't have had to dance it.
- Reputed to have been the answer given by **Anna Pavlova** when asked what was the meaning of one of her dances.

980. Let us read and let us dance - two amusements that will never do any harm to the world.
- **Voltaire:** The Readers Digest *Quotable Quotes,* 1998.

DEATH

981. Death leaves a heartache no one can heal,
Love leaves a memory no one can steal.
- **anon**. NB This epitaph was taken from a tombstone in an Irish cemetery.

982. I get up each morning and dust off my wits,
Then pick up the paper and read the "o-bits".
If my name isn't there, then I know I'm not dead.
I eat a good breakfast and go back to bed.
- **anon**: *Age Happens* in *The Best Quotes and Cartoons About Growing Older* selected by Bruce Lansky, 1996.

983. Death is not the end. There remains the litigation over the estate.
- **Ambrose Bierce:** *Age Happens* by Bruce Lansky, 1996.

984. If I have said goodbye to stream and wood, / To the wide ocean and the green-clad hill, / I know that He who made this world so good, / Has somewhere made a heaven better still. / This I bear witness with my latest breath, / Knowing the love of God, I fear not death.
- **Major Malcolm Boyd**, 7th Battalion, the Green Howards. NB Major Boyd was killed in action at the Battle of Normandy, June, 1944. The quotation above comes from a short, hand-written poem found in his Bible after his death. The full text of this poem is available on the Internet at: **www.poeticexpressions.co.uk** under "Life" and "If I should never."

985. A ship sails and I stand watching till she fades on the horizon and someone at my side says, "She is gone" Gone where? Gone from my sight, that is all.
She is just as large now as when I last saw her. Her diminished size and total loss from my sight is in me, not in her. And just at the moment when someone at my side says she is gone there are others who are watching her coming over their horizon and other voices take up a glad shout, "There she comes!"

That is what dying is - a horizon; and a horizon is just the limit of our sight.
- **Charles Henry Brent:** *What is Dying?* 1904.

986. The strangest man in the parish was the old Colonel who lived near the church. He confessed to the Vicar that he thought the reason for his longevity was that every morning he sprinkled gunpowder on his cornflakes instead of sugar. He was well into his nineties when he died. He left a widow and three sons, and a very large crater where the crematorium used to stand.
- **Ronald Brown:** *Bishop's Brew:An Anthology of Clerical Humour*, 1991.

987. To live in hearts we leave behind is not to die.
 - **Thomas Campbell:** *Hallowed Ground* in *The Poetical Works of Thomas Campbell* (Bibliobazaar Reproduction), 2009.

988. I am ready to meet my Maker. Whether my Maker is prepared for the ordeal of meeting me is another matter.
- **Sir Winston Churchill:** This was Churchhill's answer to a journalist who asked him if he feared death.

989. Death is not the enemy; living in constant fear of it is.
- **Norman Cousins:** *The Healing Heart*, 1983.

990. Our dead are never dead to us until we have forgotten them.
- **George Eliot:** *Adam Bede*, 1859.
Compare the question and answer given by the Mexican novelist, Laura Esquivel, in her 1996 novel: *The Law of Love:* "When do the dead die ? When they are forgotten."

991. Every man dies, not every man really lives.
- Mel Gibson in his role as William Wallace in the **1995 Film**: *Braveheart*.

992. In this world nothing is certain but death and taxes.
- **Benjamin Franklin:** *in a letter*, 1789.

993. Methinks, by most, 'twill be confess'd
That Death is never quite a welcome guest.
- **Johann Wolfgang von Goethe:** *Faust, 1832.*

994. I have a certainty about eternity that is a wonderful thing, and I thank God for giving me that certainty. I do not fear death. I may fear a little about the process but not death itself, because I think the moment

that my spirit leaves my body I will be in the presence of the Lord.
- **Billy Graham:** *Newsweek, August 14th, 2006.*

995. Death can stretch out at any time and take you. It does not ask permission.
 - **Kelsey Grammer:** *Saga Magazine, October, 2008.*

996. If I should die before the rest of you / Break not a flower nor inscribe a stone / Nor, when I'm gone, speak in Sunday voice, / But be the usual selves that I have known. / Weep if you must / Parting is hell. / But life goes on, / So sing as well.
- **Joyce Grenfell:** *If I Should Die*
NB:1. This poem is available on the Internet at: www.poeticexpressions.co.uk
under "Grief" and "If I Should Die" This website leads to a collection of web pages well worth a visit.
NB:2 A wealth of material for use at funeral services is available on the Internet at: http//www.lastingpost.com/pa/pa_readings_db.php

997. Do not seek death, / Death will find you, / But seek the road which makes death a fulfilment.
- **Dag Hammarskjold:** *Markings*, 1964.

998. You can shed tears that she is gone, or you can smile because she has lived. You can close your ears and pray that she will come back, or you can open your eyes and see all that she has left. Your heart can be empty because you can't see her, or you can be full of the love that you shared. You can turn your back on tomorrow and live yesterday, or you can be happy for tomorrow because of yesterday. You can remember her and only that she is gone, or you can cherish her memory and let it live on. You can cry and close your mind, be empty and turn your back, or you can do what she would want: smile, open your eyes, love and go on.
- **David Harkins:** *She is Gone*, 1981. NB. This poem and information on how it came to be written is available on the Internet at: www.poeticexpressions.co.uk under "Grief" and "She is Gone."

999. Someone should tell us, right at the start of our lives, that we are dying. Then we might live life to the limit of every minute of every day. Do it, I say, whatever you want to do, do it now! There are only so many tomorrows.
- **Michael Landon:** Expressed days before he died of cancer on 1st July,1991

1,000. As I have accompanied the dying to the threshold over the last twenty years, it has become painfully clear how often death takes people unawares. Even those who had months or even years of illness to prepare themselves often lamented how completely unprepared they were for their death.

- **Stephen Levine**: *A Year to Live: How to Live This Year as if it Were Your Last,* 1997.

1,001. If you were going to die soon and had only one phone call you could make, who would you call and what would you say? And why are you waiting?

- **Stephen Levine**.

1,002. As life runs on, the road grows strange / With faces new, and near the end / The milestones into headstones change, / 'Neath every one a friend.

- **J . R. Lowell**: *Sixty-Eighth Birthday,* 1889.

1,003. Death is unavoidable, life can pass you by.

- **Theo Mestrum**: *Geary's Guide to the World's Great Aphorists* by James Geary, 2007.

1,004. I'm rather relaxed about death. From quite an early age I've regarded it as part of the deal, the unwritten guarantee that comes with your birth certificate.

- **Bob Monkhouse. 1,005**.

1,005. When it is over, I don't want to wonder if I have made of my life something particular and real. I don't want to find myself sighing and frightened or full of argument. I don't want to end up simply having visited the world.

- **Mary Oliver:** *When Death Comes*. NB: Some of Mary Oliver's poems – including *When Death Comes* – are available on the Internet at :
www.famouspoetsandpoems,com/poets/mary_oliver.

1,006. Death is nature's way of telling you to slow down.

- **Terry Pratchett:** *Strata*.

1,007. Say not in grief. "He is no more," but live in thankfulness that he was.

- **Hebrew Proverb**.

1,008. Death is nothing at all, I have only slipped away into the next room. I am I and you are you. Whatever we were to each other that we are still. Why should I be out of mind because I am out of sight. I am waiting for you for an interval, somewhere very near. Just around the corner. All is well.
- **Canon Henry Scott-Holland:** *Death is nothing at all,* 1910. NB The full text of this poem is available on the Internet at:
 www.poeticexpressions.co.uk under "Grief"and "Death is nothing at all".

1,009. Won't you tell me please that life is eternal
And love is immortal and death is only a horizon.
Life is eternal as we move into the light
And a horizon is nothing save the limit of our sight.
- **Carly Simon**: *Life is Eternal,* from her 1990 Album, *Have You Seen Me Lately?*

1,010. Death is not extinguishing the light; it is putting out the lamp because dawn has come.
 - **Rabindranath Tagore**: *Gitanjali: Song Offerings,* 1912.

1,011. You can't take it with you. If you could, hearses would come with roof racks.
- **Pat Williams**: *Winning With One-Liners,* 2002.

DEBT

1,012. Consider carefully what action you would take were your best friend to say, "If you would lend me £100 I would be everlastingly in your debt."
- *anon*.

1,013. You'll quickly land in the mire of debt if you try to keep up with your neighbours who are already there.
- *anon*.

1,014. There are a number of different roads that lead to happiness, however, if you steer clear of debt, you need never know what these are.
- *anon*.

1,015. If you must borrow money, borrow it from a pessimist – he'll not expect it back.
- *anon*.

1,016. Many people are always in debt because they can't do without the things they don't need.
- **Sam Ewing:** *Mature Living, September, 1998*.

1,017. If there's anyone listening to whom I owe money, I'm prepared to forget it if you are.
- **Errol Flynn:** *on Australian radio,* quoted in *The Penguin Dictionary of Modern Humorous Quotations* edited by Fred Metcalf, 1986.

1,018. Debt... is the worst poverty.
- **Thomas Fuller:** *Gnomologia: Adages and Proverbs*, 1732.

1,019. In the midst of life we are in debt.
- **Oliver Herford:** *The Altogether New Cynic's Calendar*, 1907.

1,020. I'm not sure just what the unpardonable sin is, but I believe it is a disposition to evade the payment of small bills.
- **Elbert Hubbard**: *The Notebooks of Elbert Hubbard*, 1927.

1,021. Free from debt is free from care.
- *Chinese Proverb*.

1,022. A debt is still unpaid, even if forgotten.
- *Irish Proverb*.

1,023. Neither a borrower nor a lender be; for loan oft loses both itself and friend.
- **William Shakespeare:** Polonius to Laertes in *Hamlet*, 1601.

1,024. The first step in debt is like the first step in falsehood, involving the necessity of going on in the same course, debt following debt, as lie follows lie.
- **Samuel Smiles:** *Self – Help*, 1859.

1,025. What can be added to the happiness of a man who is in health, out of debt, and has a clear conscience.
- **Adam Smith**.

1,026. This would be a much better world if more married couples were as deeply in love as they are in debt.
- **Earl Wilson**.

DECISIONS

1,027. The man who insists upon seeing with perfect clearness before he decides, never decides. Accept life and you must accept regret.
- **Henri-Frederic Amiel:** *Journal Intime*, 1882.

1,028. A wise man makes his own decisions; an ignorant man follows public opinion.
- ***anon***.

1,029. Good decisions come from experience, and experience comes from bad decisions.
- ***anon***.

1,030. Your life is the sum result of all the choices you make, both consciously and unconsciously. If you can control the process of choosing, you can take control of all aspects of your life.
- **Robert F. Bennett**.

1,031. When you come to a fork in the road, take it.
- **Yogi Berra:** *The Yogi Book: I Really Didn't Say Everything I Said*, 1998.

1,032. Our most important decisions are made while we are thinking about something else.
- **Mason Cooley:** *City Aphorisms, Second Selection*, 1985.

1,033. Most of my decisions in life seem absent-minded but inevitable.
- **Mason Cooley:** *City Aphorisms, Twelfth Selection*, 1993.

1,034. When it is not necessary to make a decision, it is necessary not to make a decision.
- **Lord Falkland**.

1,035. No trumpets sound when the important decisions of your life are made.
- **Agnes de Mille**.

1,036. Maturity involves being honest and true to oneself, making decisions based on a conscious internal process, assuming responsibility for one's decisions, having healthy relationships with others and developing one's true gifts.
- **Mary Pipher:** *Reviving Ophelia: Saving the Selves of Adolescent Girls*, 1994.

1,037. In a moment of decision the best thing you can do is the right thing. The worst thing you can do is nothing.
- **Theodore Roosevelt:** *Geary's Guide to the World's Great Aphorists* by James Geary, 2007.

DEFINITIONS

1,038. <u>Straight actress</u>: 36, 36, 36.
- *anon*.

1,039. <u>Marital freedom</u>: The liberty that allows a husband to do exactly that which his wife pleases.
- *anon*.

1,040. <u>Pedestrian</u>:
(A) Someone who thought there were a couple of gallons left in the tank.
- *anon*.
(B) A parent who didn't think the family had any need of two cars.
- *anon*.

1,041. <u>Shin</u>: A part of one's anatomy designed to find furniture in the dark.
- *anon*

1,042. <u>Bigamist</u>: A man who makes the same mistake twice.
- *anon*.

1,043. <u>A will</u>: A dead give away.
- *anon*.

1,044. <u>Darling</u>: The popular form of address used in addressing a person of the opposite sex whose name you cannot call to mind.
- *anon*.

1,045. <u>Bankruptcy</u>: When you plan on early retirement but your company beats you to it.
- **Milton Berle:** *Milton Berle's Private Joke File.*

1,046. <u>A definition</u> is the enclosing a wilderness of an idea within a wall of words.
- **Samuel Butler:** *Notebooks*, 1912.

1,047. <u>Acquaintance</u>: A person we know well enough to borrow from, but not well enough to lend to.
- **Evan Esar:** *A Dictionary of Humorous Quotations.* 1949'

1,048. <u>Vacation</u>: Two weeks on the sunny sands – and the rest of the year on the financial rocks.
- **Sam Ewing:** *The Sun, February, 1999.*

1,049. <u>Mixed emotions</u>: Watching your mother-in-law drive off a cliff in your new car.
- **Leopold Fechtner:** *5,000 One-And-Two-Line Jokes*, 1979.

1,050. <u>Christmas</u>: The time when father owes best.
- ***The Public Speaker's Source Book*** by Herbert V Prochnow **et al**, 1977.

1,051. An Italian dictionary contains the word <u>*Lollobrigidian*</u>. It is defined as 'a landscape with prominent hills'.
The Guinness Book of Film Facts and Feats by Patrick Robertson, 1980.

1,052. <u>Good clean fun</u>: A couple taking a bath together.
- **Henny Youngman**; *Henny Youngman's 400 Travelling Salesman's Jokes.*

DEMOCRACY

1,053. As the happiness of the people is the sole end of government, so the consent of the people is the only foundation of it.
 - **John Adams:** *Wit and Wisdom of the American Presidents* edited by Joslyn Pine, 2001.

1,054. Democracy arose from men thinking that if they are equal in any respect they are equal in all respects.
- **Aristotle**: *Politics*, 4th century BC.

1,055. Democracy means despair of ever finding any heroes to govern you, and contentedly putting up with the want of them.
- **Thomas Carlyle:** *Past and Present*, 1843.

1,056. Democracy, as has been said of Christianity, has never really been tried.
- **Stuart Chase**: *The Life and Writings of Stuart Chase* edited by Richard Vangermeersch, 2005.

1,057. No one pretends that democracy is perfect or all wise. Indeed, it has been said that democracy is the worst form of government except all those other forms that have been tried from time to time.
- **Sir Winston Churchill:** *in a speech in the House of Commons, 11th November, 1947.*

1,058. At the bottom of all the tributes paid to democracy, is the little man walking into the booth, with a little pencil, making a little cross on a little bit of paper.
- **Sir Winston Churchill:** *The Wit and Wisdom of Winston Churchill* edited by James C. Humes, 1995.

1,059. Democracy is based upon the conviction that there are extraordinary possibilities in ordinary people.
 - **Harry Emerson Fosdick:** *Inciting Democracy: A Practical Proposal for Creating a Good Society* by Randy Schutt, 2001.

1,060. The death of democracy is not likely to be by assassination from ambush. It will be a slow extinction from apathy, indifference, and undernourishment.
- **Robert Maynard Hutchins:** *The Great Book of the Western World* in *Encyclopedia Britannica,* 1954.

1,061. The ideal for a well-functioning democratic state is like the ideal for a gentleman's well-cut suit – it is not noticed.
- **Arthur Koestler:** *New York Times, 14th February, 1943.*

1,062. I have cherished the idea of a democratic and free society... if needs be, it is an ideal for which I am prepared to die.
- **Nelson Mandela:** *in a speech, February, 1990.*

1,063. The tyranny of a prince in an oligarchy is not so dangerous to the public welfare as the apathy of a citizen in a democracy.
- **Charles de Secondat, Baron de Montesquieu:** *The Spirit of the Laws.*

1,064. Democracy may not prove in the long run to be as efficient as other forms of government, but it has one saving grace: it allows us to know and say that it isn't.
- **Bill Moyers.**

1,065. The chief defect of a democracy is that only the political party out of office knows how to run the government.
- **Laurence J. Peter,** *attributed.*

1,066. Democracy is a form of government that substitutes election by the incompetent many for appointment by the corrupt few.
- **George Bernard Shaw:** *Major Barbara,* 1905.

1,067. No government is perfect. One of the chief virtues of a democracy however, is that its defects are always visible, and under democratic processes can be pointed out and corrected.
- **Harry S. Truman:** *in a speech before the American Senate, 12th March, 1947.*

DETERMINATION

1,068. People of mediocre ability sometimes achieve outstanding success because they don't know when to quit. Most men succeed because they are determined to.
- **George E. Allen**.

1,069. What this power is I cannot say; all I know is that it exists and it becomes available only when a man is in the state of mind in which he knows exactly what he wants and is fully determined not to quit until he finds it.
- **Alexander Graham Bell**.

1,070. Courage,determination, and hard work are all very nice, but not so nice as an oil well in the back yard.
- **Mason Cooley**: *City Aphorisms, Second Selection,* 1985.

1,071. We shall defend our island, whatever the cost may be. We shall fight on the beaches, we shall fight on the landing grounds, we shall fight in the fields and in the streets, we shall fight in the hills, we shall never surrender.
- **Sir Winston Churchill:** *in a speech, 4th June, 1940.* NB This speech was delivered on the last day of the evacuation of 338,226 Allied soldiers from Dunkirk.

1,072. Everyone has his superstitions. One of mine has always been when I started to go anywhere, or to do anything, never to turn back or to stop until the thing intended was accomplished.
- **Ulysses S. Grant:** *Braude's Handbook of Stories for Toastmasters and Speakers* by Jacob Braude, 1957.

1,073. You can do what you want to do, accomplish what you want to accomplish, attain any reasonable objective you may have in mind – not all of a sudden, perhaps not in one swift and sweeping act of achievement – but you can do it gradually, day by day and play by play, if you want to do it, if you work to do it, over a sufficiently long period of time.
- **William E. Holler**.

1,074. Man has his will, but woman has her way.
- **Oliver Wendell Holmes:** *The Public Speaker's Source Book* by Herbert V. Prochnow and Herbert V. Procknow Jr,.1977.

1,075. Always bear in mind that your own resolution to succeed is more important than any other one thing.
- **Abraham Lincoln:** *Collected Works of Abraham Lincoln* edited by Roy P. Basler, 1953. NB The extract above is the concluding sentence of a letter Lincoln sent to a young man who had applied for a post in his law office.

1,076. You've got to get up every morning with determination if you're going to get to bed with satisfaction.
- **George Horace Lorimer**.

1,077. I do not recall that I ever became discouraged over anything that I set out to accomplish. I have begun everything with the idea that I could succeed, and I never had much patience with the multitude of people who are always ready to explain why one cannot succeed.
- **Booker T. Washington:** Quoted in his autobiography, *Up From Slavery*, 1901.

DIETING

1,078. A person on a diet goes to great lengths to avoid great widths.
- *anon.*

1,079. Consider your diet as the penalty for exceeding the feed limit.
- *anon.*

1,080. A dieter's ambition is to be weighed and found wanting.
- *anon.*

1,081. Inside many of us is a thin person struggling to get out, but they can usually be sedated with a few pieces of chocolate cake.
- *anon*

1,082. She who overindulges / Turns her curves into bulges.
- **Richard Armour:** *Form Fitting* in *An Armoury of Light Verse,* 1964.

1,083. A. He went on a crash diet – that's why he looks a wreck!
B. A husband and wife were waiting for their prescription at a chemists. Seeing a scale, they walked over and the lady got on. A moment later a card came out. It said, "You are warmhearted, lovable, understanding, and an excellent cook." Peeking over his wife's shoulder, the husband said, "It didn't get your weight right either."
- **Milton Berle.**

1,084. Diets are for people who are thick and tired of it.
- **Jacob M. Braude:** *Braude's Treasury of Wit & Humor for all Occasions, Revised Edition,* 1991.

1,085. My wife... recently put me on a diet after suggesting, (a little unkindly, if you ask me), that I was beginning to look something Richard Branson would try to get airborne.
- **Bill Bryson:** *Notes from a Big Country,* 1998.

1,086. Betty Hutton knew an actress who got rid of 215 pounds of excessive, flabby fat in ninety days. She divorced him.
- **Bennett Cerf:** *The Laugh's On Me.*

1,087. Until I am ready to loose weight, I cannot see how fat I am.
- **Mason Cooley:** *City Aphorisms, Tenth Selection, New York,* 1992.

1,088. At the end of every diet, the path curves back towards the trough.
- **Mason Cooley:** *City Aphorisms, Fourth Selection,* 1987.

1,089. My wife is always on a diet. She's on one now – eats nothing but bananas and coconuts, coconuts and bananas. She hasn't lost any weight, but you ought to see her climbing trees!
- **Tommy Cooper:** *The Very Best of Tommy Cooper, Volume 2,* 2005.

1,090. My husband lost a lot of weight in a new diet, and I resent it. The formula is simple, he just doesn't eat when I'm talking.
- A friend of **Dick Enberg** quoted in *Dick Enberg's Humorous Quotes for All Occasions,* 2000.

1.091. Diet and exercise can help overweight people to break the pound barrier.
- **Sam Ewing:** *Mature Living, January, 1999.*

1,092. It's not the minutes we spend at the table that put on weight. It's the seconds.
- **Sam Ewing:** *Mature Living, September, 1995.*

1.093. More diets originate in clothing stores than in doctor's offices.
- **Sam Ewing:** *Mature Living, November, 1999.*

1,094. People who say they are going on a diet are just wishful shrinkers.
- **Leopold Fechtner:** *5,000 One-And-Two-Line Jokes,* 1979.

1,095. If you cheat on a diet you gain in the end.
- *ibid.*

1.096. Stay slim and die later.
- **Malcolm Forbes:** *The Further Sayings of Chairman Malcolm,* 1986.

1,097. To lengthen thy life, lessen thy meals.
- **Benjamin Franklin:** *Poor Richard's Almanack,* 1739.

1,098. Eat to live, and not live to eat.
- *ibid*.

1,099. We sneak another midnight snack
And think no one will know it;
But those who don't count calories
Have figures that will show it.
- **Charles Ghigna**: *Laugh Twice and Call Me in the Morning: The Best Quotes and Cartoons to Cure what Ails You* selected by Bruce Lansky, 1999.

1,100. The papers are full of endless diets just when I am in need of comfort food.
- **Sandra Howard**: *Quotes of the Day* in *The Press and Journal, 9 / 1/ 07*

1,101. I feel about airplanes the way I feel about diets. It seems to me that they are wonderful things for other people to go on.
- **Jean Kerr:** *The Snake Has All the Lines*, 1959.

1,102. If you have formed the habit of checking on every new diet that comes along, you will find that, mercifully, they all blur together, leaving you with only one definite piece of information. French-fried potatoes are out.
- **Jean Kerr:** *Please Don't Eat the Daisies*, 1960.

1,103. If you wish to grow thinner, diminish your dinner,
And take to light claret instead of pale ale;
Look down with an utter contempt upon butter,
And never touch bread till it's toasted – or stale.
- **Henry S. Leigh:** *A Day For Wishing* in *Carols of Cockayne*, 1874.

1,104. An apple a day keeps the doctor away; an onion a day keeps everyone away.
- **Wolfgang Mieder:** *A Dictionary of American Proverbs*, 1992.

1,105. How easy for those who do not bulge./To not overindulge!
- **Ogden Nash:** *A Necessary Dirge* in *I'm a Stranger Here Myself*, 1938.

1,106. Have you noticed when you go on a diet, the first thing you loose is your temper?
- **Robert Orben:** *2,000 Sure-Fire Jokes for Speakers*, 1971.

1,107. When dieting, avoid all sweets,
No matter if they're yummy;

They may melt inside your mouth -
But they firm up on your tummy!
- **Robert Orben:** *2,400 Jokes to Brighten Your Speeches,* 1984.

1,108. I went on that Drinking Man's Diet, and I wanna tell you, it's great. Lost six pounds and three weekends!
- **Robert Orben:** *2,000 New Laughs for Speakers: The Ad-Libber's Handbook,* 1978.

1,109. I've been on every diet in the world. The best one is the BBC diet: Buy Bigger Clothes.
- **Gary Owens:** *Dick Enberg's Humorous Quotes for All Occasions.* 2000.

1,110. I tried every diet in the book. I tried some that weren't in the book. I tried eating the book. It tasted better than most of the diets.
 - **Dolly Parton:** *Dolly: My Life and Other Unfinished Business,* 1995.

1,111. You dig your grave with your teeth.
 - ***English Proverb.***

1,112. Many a woman who goes on a diet finds that she is a poor loser.
- **Herbert V. Prochnow and Herbert V. Prochnow Jr:** *The Public Speaker's Source Book,* 1977.

1,113. The following notice appeared in a church newsletter: 'Weight watchers will meet at 6.30 pm. Please use the large double door on the North side.'
- **James Simpson:** *The Laugh Shall be First,* 1998.

1,114. The conclusions are what most people trying to lose weight don't want to hear - the only way to lose weight is to eat better and exercise more.
 - A reader's review of *Don't Eat This Book: Fast Food and the Supersizing of America* by **Morgan Spurlock**, 2005.

1,115. You know that it's time to diet when your doctor tells you that that mysterious rash on your stomach is steering wheel burn.
- **Pat Williams:** *Winning With One-Liners,* 2002.

DIVORCE

1,116. Statistics show that 100% of all divorces start with marriage.
- *anon*.

1,117. Maintenance payments often enables a woman who lived unhappily married to live happily unmarried.
- *anon*.

1,118. My wife Mary and I have been married for 47 years and not once have we had an argument serious enough to consider divorce. Murder, yes, but divorce, never!
- **Jack Benny**.

1,119. The obvious effect of frivolous divorce will be frivolous marriages. If people can be separated for no reason they will feel it all the easier to be united for no reason.
- **G. K. Chesterton**: *The Superstition of Divorce*, 1920.

1,120. So many persons think divorce a panacea for every ill, who find out, when they try it, that the remedy is worse than the disease.
- **Dorothy Dix:** *Dorothy Dix. Her Book*, 1926.

1,121. I want a divorce because everything my wife says, does and cooks disagrees with me.
- **Leopold Fechtner:** *5,000 One-And-Two-Line Jokes*, 1979.

1,122. My wife is suing for divorce and she's asking for custody of the money.
- *ibid*.

1,123. Conrad Hilton was very generous to me in the divorce settlement. He gave me 5,000 Gideon Bibles.
- **Zsa Zsa Gabor**.

1,124. People are silly to have a "friendly divorce" - if you can be friends, you've already got more than most married couples have.
- **Sydney J. Harris:** *Pieces of Eight*, 1975.

1,125. My wife would divorce me tomorrow if she could find a way to do it without making me happy.
- **Bob Monkhouse:** *Just Say a Few Words*, 1988.

1,126 ... most marriages end in divorce due to unrealistic idealized expectations of marriage. But marriage can survive by remembering that it's not what happens to us but our attitude toward it that makes a difference in our lives together. By committing to shared beliefs, values, and supporting one another we can get through life's battles together.
- Publisher's blurb on *A Very Good Marriage* by **Tom Mullen**, 2001.

1.127. I no longer believe... that a marriage is a failure if it doesn't last forever. It may be a tragedy, but it is not necessarily a failure. And when a marriage does last for ever with love alive, it is a miracle.
 - **Peggy O'Mara:** *Mothering Magazine, Autumn, 1989.*

1,128. So this fella is arrested for running out on his wife, but there's a difference of opinion on what he should be charged with. She claims it's desertion and he says it should be leaving the scene of an accident!
- **Robert Orben:** *2,000 Sure-Fire Jokes for Speakers*, 1971.

1,129. Nowadays love is a matter of chance, matrimony a matter of money and divorce a matter of course.
- **Helen Rowland:** *Reflections of a Bachelor Girl*, 1903.

1,130. When two people decide to get a divorce, it isn't a sign that they "don't understand" one another, but a sign that they have, at last, begun to.
 - **Helen Rowland:** *A Guide to Men*, 1922.

1,131. Marrying a divorced man is ecologically responsible. In a world where there are more women than men, it pays to recycle.
- **Rita Rudner:** *Rita Rudner's Guide to Men*, 1994.

1,132. My husband and I divorced over religious differences. He thought he was God, and I didn't.
- **T-shirt slogan.**

1,133. Divorce: Going through a change of wife.
 - **Henny Youngman.**

DOCTORS

1,134. Doctor to patient: I have good news and bad news. The good news is that you are not a hypochondriac.
- *anon.*

1,135. When a patient is at death's door, it is the duty of his doctor to pull him through.
 - **anon:** 20,000 *Quips and Quotes* by Evan Esar, 1968.

1,136. A man went to his doctor and said, "Doctor, I can't stop singing, 'The green green grass of home' " and the doctor said, "That sounds like the Tom Jones syndrome."
And the man said, "Is that common?"
"Well," said the doctor, "it's not unusual."
- **Tommy Cooper:** *The Very Best of Tommy Cooper*, 2005.

1,137. I went to the doctor yesterday. I said, "I've got a bad foot, what should I do?" And he said, "Limp."
- **ibid**.

1,138. Each patient carries his own doctor inside him.
- **Norman Cousins:** *Anatomy of an Illness*, 1979.

1,139. Doctors have made great medical progress in the past generation. What used to be an itch is now an allergy.
 - **Leopold Fechtner:** *5,000 One-And-Two-Line Jokes*, 1973.

1,140. I was thinking of becoming a doctor. I have the handwriting for it.
- *ibid*

1,141. Either he's dead or my watch has stopped.
- Groucho Marx as Dr Hackenbush in the **1937 Film:** *A Day at the Races*.

1,142. "Virus" is a Latin word
That doctors won't define
Because they know the message is
"Your guess is good as mine".
  - **Charles Ghigna:** *The Cold Facts* in *Lighten Up!* edited by Bruce Lansky.

1,143. There was an old Fellow of Trinity,
A Doctor well versed in Divinity;
But he took to free-thinking,
And then to deep drinking,
And so had to leave the vicinity.
- **A. C. Hilton.**

1,144. In the days of FDR, doctors were making house calls for five dollars, and were available 24 hours a day. They hadn't learned to play golf yet.
- **Bob Hope:** *Don't Shoot. It's Only Me* with Melville Shavelson, 1990.

1,145. Hundreds of lives were saved when I failed to get into medical school.
- *ibid.*

1,146. Finish last in your league and they call you idiot. Finish last in medical school and they call you Doctor.
- **Abe Lemons.**

1,147. "So you're a naval surgeon,"
The woman spoke in surprise.
"It's great nooadays how doctors
Tend to specialize.
  - **Walter McCorrisken:** *A Naval Surgeon* in *A Wee Dribble of Dross*, 1993.

1,148. I called my acupuncturist and told him I was in terrible pain. He told me to take two safety pins and call him in the morning.
  - **Fred Metcalf:** *Laugh Twice and Call Me in the Morning: The Best Quotes and Cartoons to Cure What Ails You* selected by Bruce Lansky.

1,149. The killing vice of the young doctor is intellectual laziness.
- **Sir William Osler:** *Aequanimitas: With Other Addresses for Medical Students*, 1920.

1,150. The practice of medicine is an art, not a trade; a calling, not a business; a calling in which your heart will be exercised equally with your head.
- *ibid.*

1,151. The middle-aged man shuffled along, bent over at the waist, as his wife helped him into the doctor's waiting room. The doctor's nurse viewed the scene with sympathy. "Arthritis with complications?" she asked. The wife shook her head. "Do-it-yourself," she explained, "with concrete blocks."

- **Herbert V. Prochnow and Herbert V. Prochnow Jr:** *The Public Speaker's Source Book*, 1977.

1,152. A good laugh and a long sleep are the two best cures in the doctor's book.

- ***Irish Proverb***.

1,153. The best doctors in the world are Doctor Diet, Doctor Quiet and Doctor Merryman.

- **Jonathan Swift:** *Polite Conversation. Dialogue 2*, 1738.

DOGS

1,154. Buy one dog and get one flea!
- ***anon*** (Sign seen in a pet shop window)

1,155. The reason a dog has so many friends is that he wags his tail instead of his tongue.
- ***anon.***

1,156. A man may smile and bid you "hail"
Yet wish you to the devil;
But when a good dog wags its tail,
You know he's on the level.
- ***anon.***

1,157. A watchdog is a dog kept to guard your home, usually by sleeping where a burglar would awaken the household by falling over him.
- ***anon.***

1,158. The person always bragging
Of dogs as man's best friend,
Is thinking of their wagging
and not their biting end.
- **Richard Armour:** *An Armoury of Light Verse,* 1942.

1,159. A dog teaches a boy fidelity, perseverance, and to turn round three times before lying down
- **Robert Benchley:** *Chips Off the Old Benchley,* 1949.

1,160. They call their dog "Day Worker" because he does odd jobs about the house.
- **Milton Berle:** *Milton Berle's Private Joke File,* 1989.

1,161. Dogs come when they're called; cats take a message and get back to you.
- **Mary E. Bly:** *Dogs are Better Than Cats,* 1985.

1,162. The great pleasure of a dog is that you may make a fool of yourself with him and not only will he not scold you, but he will make a fool of himself too.
 - **Samuel Butler:** *Notebooks*, 1912.

1,163. If you don't own a dog, at least one, there is not necessarily anything wrong with you, but there may be something wrong with your life.
- **Roger Caras:** *A Celebrations of Dogs*, 1985.

1,164. We derive immeasurable good, uncounted pleasures, enormous security, and many critical lessons about life by owning dogs.
- ***ibid***.

1,165. He looks love at me deep as word e'er spake;
 And from me never crumb nor sup will take.
 But he wags thanks with his most vocal tail.
- **William Croswell Doane**.

1,166. Dogs in Siberia are the fastest in the world because the trees are so far apart.
- **Leopold Fechtner:** *5,000 One-And-Two-Line Jokes*, 1979.

1,167. Properly trained, a man can be the dog's best friend.
- **Corey Ford**.

1,168. A dog is the only exercise machine you cannot decide to skip when you don't feel like it.
- **Carolyn Heilbrun**: *The Last Gift of Time: Life Beyond Sixty*, 1997.

1,169. Let's be honest here, our dogs are the only creatures on earth that love us more than we love ourselves.
- **Val Hennessy**: *Saga Magazine, January, 2007*.

1,170. Nobody can fully understand the meaning of love unless he's owned a dog. A dog can show you more honest affection with a flick of his tail than a man can gather through a lifetime of handshakes.
- **Gene Hill**.

1,171. With so many boys, my father bought us a dachshund so we could all pat him at the same time.
- **Bob Hope**: *My Life in Jokes* with Linda Hope, 2003.

1,172. With the exception of women, there is nothing on earth so agreeable or necessary to the comfort of man as the dog.
- **Edward Jesse**: *Anecdotes of Dogs*, 1846.

1,173. I don't mean to say one word against beagles. They have rights just like other people. But it is a bit of a shock when you bring home a small ball of fluff in a shoebox, and in three weeks it's as long as the sofa.
- **Jean Kerr:** *Please Don't Eat the Daisies*, 1960.

1,174. The truth I do not stretch or shove / When I state that the dog is full of love, / I've also found, by actual test, / A wet dog is the lovingest.
- **Ogden Nash:** *The Dog* in *Everyone But Thee and Me*, 1962.

1,175. I think I've seldom run across a life so far from lawful;
Your manners are a total loss, your morals, something awful,
Perhaps you'll ask, as many do, what I endure your thrall for?
'Twas ever thus - it's such as you that women always fall for.
- **Dorothy Parker:** *To My Dog* in *The Uncollected Dorothy Parker* edited by Stuart Y. Silverstein, 1999.

1,176. My wife cooks liver once a week and serves it lightly peppered; I always sneak it off my plate to feed our German shepherd. My wife cooks liver once a week; she says its very nourishing;
I guess she must be right because our German shepherd's flourishing.
- **Leslie Danford Perkins**.

1,177. The noblest of all dogs is the hot dog; it feeds the hand that bites it.
- **Laurence J. Peter**; *Quotable Trivia* by Nigel Rees, 1985.

1,178. If dogs could talk, it would take a lot of the fun out of owning one.
- **Andy Rooney**; *CBS TV 60 Minutes*.

1,179. No matter how little money and how few possessions you own, having a dog makes you rich.
- **Louis Sabin**; *All About Dogs as Pets*, 1983.

1,180. My goal in life is to become the person my dog thinks I am.
- **Suzanne Somers**; *Halliwell's Who's Who in the Movies* edited by John Walker, 2003.

1,181. Getting a dog is like getting married. It teaches you to be less self-centred, to accept sudden, surprising outbursts of affection, and not to be upset by a few scratches on your ear.
- **Will Stanton**.

1,182. Mother doesn't want a dog,
Mother says they smell,
And never sit when you say sit,
Or even when you yell,
And when you come home late at night
And there is ice and snow,
And you have to go back out because
The dumb dog has to go ...
Mother doesn't want a dog,
She's making a mistake,
Because, more than a dog, I think
She will not want this snake.
- **Judith Viorst**; *Mother Doesn't Want a Dog* in *If I Were in Charge of the World and Other Worries: Poems for Children and their Parents,* 1981. NB This poem, and others by Judith Viorst, is available on the Internet at: **www.poemhunter.com**

1,183. Old dogs, like old shoes, are comfortable. They might be a bit out of shape and a little worn around the edges, but they fit well.
- **Bonnie Wilcox and Chris Walkowicz**; *Old Dogs, Old Friends: Enjoying Your Old Dog.* 1991.

DOUBT

1.184. A belief which leaves no place for doubt is not a belief; it is a superstition.
- **Jose Bergamin**: *The Rocket and the Star*, 1923.

1,185. (The father said), "if you can do anything, take pity on us and help us."
"If you can?" said Jesus, "Everything is possible for him who believes."
Immediately the boy's father exclaimed, "I do believe; help me overcome my unbelief!"
- **The Bible**: *Mark 9: 22 – 24, NIV.*

1,186. Doubt whom you will, but never yourself.
- **Christian Nestell Bovee.**

1,187. What makes a river so restful to people is that it doesn't have any doubt – it is sure to get where it is going, and it doesn't want to go anywhere else.
- **Hal Boyle**: *Help, Help! Another Day!* 1969.

1,188. If you are ever in doubt as to whether or not you should kiss a pretty girl, always give her the benefit of the doubt.
- **Thomas Carlyle, *attributed.***

1,189. Courage overrides self-doubt, but does not end it.
- **Mason Cooley**: *City Aphorisms, Eleventh Selection,* 1993.

1,190. We know accurately only when we know little; with knowledge doubt increases.
- **Johann Wolfgang Von Goethe.**

1,191. Four be the things I'd been better without. Love, curiosity, freckles and doubt.
- **Dorothy Parker:** *Enough Rope: Poems by Dorothy Parker,* 1928.

1,192. Doubt, it seems to me, is the central condition of a human being in the twentieth century.
- **Salman Rushdie**: *The Observer, 19th February, 1989.*

1,193. Doubt thou the stars are fire; doubt that the sun doth move; doubt truth to be a liar; but never doubt I love.
- **William Shakespeare**: *Hamlet, Act 2, Sc 2.*

1,194. Our doubts are traitors, and make us lose the good we oft might win, by fearing to attempt.
- **William Shakespeare:** *Measure for Measure, Act 1.*

1,195. Doubt isn't the opposite of faith; it is an element of faith.
- **Paul Tillich**.

1,196. Faith which does not doubt is dead faith.
- **Miguel de Unamuno**.

DREAMS

1,197. When a dream takes hold of you, what can you do? You can run with it, let it run your life, or let it go and think for the rest of your life about what might have been.
- **Hunter Campbell "Patch" Adams**: *Gesundheit !: Bringing Good Health To You, the Medical System, and Society through Physician Service, Complimentary Therapies, Humour, and Joy* with Maureen Mylander, 1993.

1,198. The greatest achievement was at first and for a time a dream. The oak sleeps in the acorn; The bird waits in the egg; and in the highest vision of the soul a waking angel stirs. Dreams are the seedlings of realities.
- **James Allen**; *As a Man Thinketh*, 1902.

1,199. He who cherishes a beautiful vision, a lofty ideal in his heart, will one day realize it. Columbus cherished a vision of another world, and he discovered it. Copernicus fostered the vision of a multiplicity of worlds and a wider universe, and he revealed it. Buddha beheld the vision of a spiritual world of stainless beauty and perfect peace, and he entered into it.
- *ibid.*

1,200. Dream lofty dreams, and as you dream, so shall you become. Your vision is the promise of what you shall one day be.
- *ibid.*

1,201. When you dream in colour, it's a pigment of your imagination.
- *anon.*

1,202. A dream without action is just a day-dream.
- *anon.*

1,203. Only as far as we seek can we go, only as much as we dream can we be.
- *anon.*

1,204. Dreams do come true, if we only wish hard enough. You can have anything in life if you will sacrifice everything for it.
 - **Sir J. M. Barrie**: *Peter Pan*, 1911.

1,205. The world needs dreamers and the world needs doers. But above all, the world needs dreamers who do.
 - **Sarah Ban Breathnach**: *Simple Abundance*, 1996.

1,206. Last night I dreamed I ate a ten-pound marshmallow, and when I woke up the pillow had gone.
 - **Tommy Cooper**.

1,207. A dream is a wish your heart makes.
- Quoted in **Walt Disney's** 1959 film *Sleeping Beauty*.

1,208. To accomplish great things, we must dream as well as act.
- **Anatole France**.

1,209. Not much happens without a dream, and for something great to happen, there must be a great dream. Behind every great achievement is a dreamer of great dreams. Much more than a dreamer is required to bring it to reality; but the dream must be there first.
- **Robert K. Greenleaf**: *Servant Leadership: A Journey into Legitimate Power and Greatness*, 1977.

1,210. Climb every mountain,
ford every stream,
Follow every rainbow,
till you find your dream.
- **Oscar Hammerstein**: *The Sound of Music*, 1959.

1,211. Hold fast to dreams
For if dreams die
Life is a broken-winged bird
That cannot fly.
- **Langston Hughes**: *The Dream Keeper and Other Poems*, 1932.

1,212. Castles in the air – they are so easy to take refuge in, and so easy to build too.
- **Henrik Ibsen**: *The Master Builder*, 1892.

1,213. Your hopes, dreams, and aspirations are legitimate. They are trying to take you airborne, above the clouds, above the storms, if you only let them.
- **William James**.

1,214. Most people never run far enough on their first wind to find out they've got a second. Give your dreams all you've got and you'll be amazed at the energy that comes out of you.
- **William** James.

1.215. I have a dream that my four children will one day live in a nation where they will not be judged by the colour of their skin but by the content of their character.
- **Martin Luther King**: *in a speech delivered in Washington after a civil rites march, August 28th, 1963.*

1,216. If you want your dreams to come true, don't sleep.
- **Sam Levenson**: *In One Era And Out The Other*, 1973.

1,217. A fulfilling life is different for each person. You have to acknowledge your dreams, and not just wait for life to happen, and opportunities to come knocking at your door.
- **Joan Lunden**: *in answer to a viewer's question on a telephone chat show held on 17th October, 2000.*

1,218. When you write down your dreams they become goals, and then you can take steps towards that goal.
- *ibid*

1,219. A dream is just a dream. A goal is a dream with a plan and a deadline.
- **Harvey MacKay:** *United Features Syndicated Column.*

1,220. Dreams are necessary to life.
- **Anais Nin:** *The Diary of Anais Nin.*

1,221. Dreams pass into the reality of action. From the action stems the dream again; and this interdependence produces the highest form of living.
- *ibid.*

1,222. You see things, and you say, "Why?" But I dream things that never were, and I say, "Why not?"
- **George Bernard Shaw**: *Back to Methuselah*, 1921.

1,223. Dreams are astonishingly important. They keep nagging you because you're supposed to fulfil them.
- **Barbara Sher:** *Live the Life You Love*, 1996.

1,224. As soon as you start to pursue a dream, your life wakes up and everything has meaning.
- **Barbara Sher:** *I Could Do Anything If I Only Knew What It Was*, 1995.

1,225. Talk about a dream; try to make it real.
- **Bruce Springsteen:** *Badlands*, from his 1978 Album, *Darkness on the Edge of Town*.

1,226. I learned this... if one advances confidently in the direction of his dreams, and endeavours to live the life which he had imagined, he will meet with a success unexpected in common hours.
- **Henry David Thoreau:** *Walden*, 1854.

1,227. The key to realizing a dream is to focus not on success but significance – and then even the small steps and little victories along your path will take on greater meaning.
- **Oprah Winfrey:** *O Magazine, September, 2002.*

DUTY

1,228. Our duty is to be useful, not according to our desires but according to our powers.
- **Henri Frederic Amiel:** *Journal Intime,* 1882.

1,229. The scouts' motto is founded on my initials, it is: BE PREPARED, which means you are always to be in a state of readiness in mind and body to do your duty.
 - **Robert Baden-Powell:** *Scouting for Boys,* 1908.

1,230. Responsibility: An obligation, especially to give account of one's actions.
 - *The NIV Thematic Study Bible,* 1996.

1,231. I know of only one duty, and that is to love.
 - **Albert Camus:** *Notebooks, 1935 – 1942.*

1,232. Lay this precept well to heart, which to me was of invaluable service: "Do thy duty which lies nearest thee, which thou knowest to be a duty!" The second duty will already become clearer.
- **Thomas Carlyle:** *Sartor Resartus* – a novel first published as a serial in Fraser's Magazine, 1833 – 1834.

1,233. Duty is whatever opposes inclination.
- **Mason Cooley:** *City Aphorisms,* 1993

1,234. The best way to get rid of your duties is to discharge them.
- **Evan Esar:** *20,000 Quips and Quotes,* 1968.

1,235. Do your duty until it becomes your joy.
 - **Marie von Ebner-Eschenbach:** *Aphorisms,* 1905.

1,236. The reward of one duty is the power to fulfil another.
 - **George Eliot:** *Daniel Deronda,* 1876.

1,237. For duty, duty must be done; / The rule applies to everyone.
- **Sir W. S. Gilbert:** *Ruddigore,* 1887.

1,238. But what is your duty? What the day demands.
- **Johann Wolfgang von Goethe,**

1,239. How can one learn to know oneself? Never by introspection, rather by action. Try to do your duty, and you will know right away what you are like.
- **Johann Wolfgang von Goethe:** *Wilhelm Meister's Travels,* 1829.

1,240. Let us have faith that right makes might, and in that faith let us to the end dare to do our duty as we understand it.
- **Abraham Lincoln:** *in a speech, February 27th, 1860.*

1,241. England expects every man will do his duty.
- **Horatio Nelson:** at the battle of Trafalgar. Quoted in *The Life of Nelson* by Robert Southey, 1813.

1,242. There is no duty we so much underrate as the duty of being happy.
- **Robert Louis Stevenson:** *Virginibus Puerisque,* 1881.

1,243. The first duty of love is to listen.
- **Paul Tillich:** *O Magazine, February,*2004

1,244. Make it a point to do something every day that you don't want to do. This is the golden rule for acquiring the habit of doing your duty without pain.
- **Mark Twain:** *Following the Equator,* 1897.

EDUCATION

1,245. Nothing in education is so astonishing as the amount of ignorance it accumulates in the form of inert facts.
 - **Henry Adams:** *The Education of Henry Adams*, 1918. NB *The Education of Henry Adams* is Henry Adams' autobiography published after his death, for which he won the Pulitzer Prize in 1919.

1,246. Din it in, din it in, children's heads are hollow,
Din it in, din it in, still there's more to follow.
 - ***anon.*** NB Scots: <u>Din</u>: *vb. instil something to be learned by constant repetition.*

1,247. The educated differ from the uneducated as much as the living from the dead.
- **Aristotle:** 4th century BC.

1,248. Education is the best provision for old age.
- **Aristotle**: *Diogenes Laertius' Lives of Eminent Philosophers.*

1,249. The secret of sound education is to get each pupil to learn for himself, instead of instructing him by driving knowledge into him on a stereotyped system.
- **Robert Baden-Powell:** *The Scouter, January, 1912.*

1,250. Education is learning what you didn't even know what you didn't know.
- **Daniel Boorstin:** *Newsweek, 6th July, 1970.*

1,251. Education is a wonderful thing. If you couldn't sign your own name you'd have to pay cash.
- **Rita Mae Brown:** *Starting from Scratch*, 1989.

1,252. Without education we are in a horrible and deadly danger of taking educated people seriously.
- **G. K. Chesterton:** *Illustrated London News, December 2, 1905.*

1,253. I think the growth industry of the future in this country and the world will soon be the continuing education of adults. I think the educated person of the future is somebody who realizes the need to continue to learn. That is the new definition and it is going to change the world we live in and work in.
- **Peter Drucker:** *Managing in a Time of Great Change,* 1995.

1,254. It is not so very important for a person to learn facts. For that he does not really need a college... The value of an education in a liberal college is not learning so many facts but the training of the mind to think something that cannot be learned from text books.
- **Albert Einstein:** *Einstein: His Life and Times* by Philipp Frank, 1947.

1,255. Only the educated are free.
- **Epictetus:** *Discourses,* 2nd century.

1,256. An education isn't how much you have committed to memory, or even how much you know. It's being able to differentiate between what you do know and what you don't. It's knowing where to go to find out what you need to know, and it's knowing how to use the information you get.
- **William Feather:** *Quotable Quotes on Education* by August Kerber, 1967.

1,257. Education's purpose is to replace an empty mind with an open one.
- **Malcolm S. Forbes**: *Forbes Magazine.*

1,258. Nine tenths of education is encouragement.
- **Anatole France:** *The Crime of Sylvestre Bonnard,* 1881.

1,259. Learning is its own exceeding great reward.
- **William Hazlitt**: *The Plain Speaker,* 1826.

1,260. Everyman should have a college education in order to show him how little the thing is really worth.
- **Elbert Hubbard::***A Message to Garcia,* 1899.

1,261. The object of the educational system, taken as a whole, is not to produce hands for industry or to teach the young how to make a living. It is to produce responsible citizens.
- **Robert Maynard Hutchins:** *The University of Utopia,* 1953.

1,262. Perhaps the most valuable result of all education is the ability to make yourself do the thing you have to do, when it ought to be done, whether you like it or not.
- **H. Huxley:** *Aphorisms and Reflections from the Works of T. H. Huxley* selected by Henrietta A. Huxley, 1907.

1,263. Eric: When it came to education, my father wanted me to have all the opportunities he never had.
Ernie: So what did he do?
Eric: He sent me to a girl's school.
- ***The Morecambe and Wise Joke Book***, 1979.

1,264. To repeat what others have said requires education; to challenge it, requires brains.
- **Mary Pettibone Poole:** *A Glass Eye at a Keyhole*, 1938.

1,265. More important than the curriculum is the question of the methodology of teaching and the spirit in which the teaching is given.
- **Bertrand Russell:** *Education and the Good Life*, 1926.

1,266. A good education is the next best thing to a pushy mother.
- **Charles Schultz**; *Inspirational Quotes, Notes and Anecdotes That Honour Teachers and Teaching* by Robert D. Ramsay, 2006.

1,267. Education is what survives when what has been learned has been forgotten.
- **B. F. Skinner:** *New Scientist, May, 1964.*

1,268. Education is a private matter between the person and the world of knowledge and experience, and has little to do with school or college.
- **Lillian Smith:** *Redbook*, an online American magazine for career women.

1,269. Education is the kindling of a flame, not the filling of a vessel.
- **Socrates:** 4th century BC.

1,270. It is only the ignorant who despise education.
- **Publilius Syrus:** *Maxims.*

1,271. Education has produced a vast population able to read but unable to distinguish what is worth reading.
- **G. M. Trevelyan:** *English Social History*, 1944.

1,272. For me, education is about the most important thing because that is what liberated me.

- **Oprah Winfrey:** *in an interview in Chicago, 1991.*

EFFORT

1,273. Get up and put your shoulder to the wheel!
- The moral of **Aesop's Fable:** *Hercules and the Waggoner.*

1,274. On this day I remember words that have stayed with me since my childhood and which matter a great deal to me today, my school motto: "**I will try my utmost**". This is my promise to all of the people of Britain and now let the work of change begin.
- **Gordon Brown** made this statement outside 10 Downing Street immediately after becoming Prime Minister, *BBC News Transcript, 27th June, 2007.*

1,275. Don't be afraid to give your best to what seemingly are small jobs. Every time you conquer one it makes you that much stronger. If you do the little jobs well, the big ones will tend to take care of themselves.
- **Andrew Carnegie,** *attributed.*

1,276. Leave no stone unturned.
- **Euripides**: *Heraclidae.* 5th century BC.

1,277. How hard you try is rooted to how often you try.
- **Doug Hall**: *Jump Start Your Brain,* 1996.

1,278. Effort only fully releases its reward after a person refuses to quit.
- **Napoleon Hill**: *Think and Grow Rich,* 1937.

1,279. Keep the faculty of effort alive in you by a little gratuitous exercise every day. That is, be systematically ascetic or heroic in little unnecessary points, do every day or two something for no other reason than that you would rather not do it, so that when the hour of dire need draws nigh, it may find you not unnerved and untrained to stand the test.
- **William James**: *Talks to Teachers on Psychology,* 1899.

1,280. When we do the best that we can, we never know what miracle is wrought in our life, or in the life of another.
 - **Helen Keller:** *Out Of the Dark,* 1914.

1,281. Despite the success cult, men are most deeply moved not by the reaching of the goal but by the greatness of the effort involved in getting there – or failing to get there
- **Max Lerner**.

1,282. Very few people are capable of sustained effort, and that's the reason why we have comparatively few outstanding successes.
- **John McDonald:** *The Message of a Master,* 1929. NB. This book has been described as "A classic tale of wealth, wisdom and the secret of success achieved through the power of the mind."
Nothing is known about the author.

1,283. Who first consults wisely, then resolves firmly, and then executes his purpose with inflexible perseverance... can advance to eminence in any line.
- **Orison Swett Marden:** *Pushing to the Front,* 1894.

ENGLAND AND THE ENGLISH

1,284. Thirty million, mostly fools.
- **Thomas Carlyle:** is reputed to have said this on being asked what he thought the population of England was.

1.285. It's such a surprise to Eastern eyes to see / That though the English are effete / They're quite impervious to heat.
- **Noel Coward:** *Mad Dogs and Englishmen*, 1930.

1,286. (The Englishman) has been taught at his public school that feeling is bad form. He must not express his joy or sorrow, or even open his mouth too wide when he talks – his pipe might fall out if he did.
- **E. M. Forster:** *Abinger Harvest*, 1936.

1,287. But this idiot is English. Is there any other kind?
- **The Goon Show Episode** entitled: *The Case of the Missing Heir* written by Spike Milligan and Eric Sykes,

1,288. Continental people have sex lives, the English have hot-water bottles.
- **George Mikes:** *How to be an Alien* with Nicholas Bentley, 1973.

1,289. On the continent people have good food; in England people have good table manners.
- *ibid.*

1,290. English humour resembles the Loch Ness monster in that both are famous but there is a strong suspicion that neither exists.
- **George Mikes:** *English Humour for Beginners*, 1983.

1,291. Remember that you are an Englishman and have consequently won first prize in the lottery of life.
- **Cecil Rhodes:** *Dear Me* by Peter Ustinov, 1977.

1,292. It is the proud perpetual boast of the Englishman that he never brags.
- **Dominic Bevan Wyndham-Lewis:** quoted in *The Treasury of Humorous Quotations* edited by Evan Esar, 1955.

1,293. An oft-repeated, but worth repeating story, is that when God was creating the British Isles He started with Scotland and was busy installing beautiful mountains, breath taking glens, salmon-filled rivers and all the rest of the glories that are Scotia, when one of the angels asked Himself if perhaps He was not going over the top in the provision of amenities to Scotland. "Perhaps," He replied, "but wait and see who they are getting as neighbours."
- **Tom Shields:** *Tom Shields' Diary*, 1991.

ENTHUSIASM

1,294. If you can give your son or daughter only one gift, let it be enthusiasm.
- **Bruce Barton.**

1,295. Enthusiasm is the greatest asset in the world, it beats money, power, and influence. Enthusiasm is nothing more or less than faith in action.
- **Henry Chester.**

1,296. With enthusiasm anything is possible.
 - **Arlene Dahl:** quoted in *Halliwell's Who's Who in the Movies*, 2003.

1,297. Ability without enthusiasm is like a rifle without a bullet.
- **Sir Thomas Dewar:** *Wit and Wisdom of Tommy Dewar* edited by Ian Robert Buxton, 2001.

1,298. Nothing great was ever achieved without enthusiasm.
- **Ralph Waldo Emerson:** *Essays, First Series*, 1841.

1,299. Acquire an enthusiasm; you can't be enthusiastic and unhappy at the same time.
- **Evan Esar:** *20,000 Quips and Quotes*, 1968.

1,300. I am convinced that the fortunate individuals who achieve the most in life are invariably activated by enthusiasm.
- **Norman Vincent Peale:** *Enthusiasm.*

1,301. There is real magic in enthusiasm. It spells the difference between mediocrity and accomplishment.
 - *ibid.*

1,302. Those who are fired with an enthusiastic idea and who allow it to take hold and dominate their thoughts, find that new worlds open for them. As long as enthusiasm holds out, so will new opportunities.
- **Norman Vincent Peale:** *Positive Thinking Every Day*, 1993.

1,303. Enthusiasm... the sustaining power of all great actions.
- **Samuel Smiles:** *Self – Help*, 1859.

1,304. What makes a person attractive is their enthusiasm for life.
- **Una Stubbs:** *Life Lessons* in *Saga Magazine, June, 2007*.

1,305. Years may wrinkle the skin, but to give up enthusiasm wrinkles the soul.
- **Samuel Ullman:** *Youth* in *The Silver Treasury: Prose and Verse for Every Mood*, 1935.

ENVY

1,306. Lord, if I cannot have what I want, let me want what I have.
- *anon*.

1,307. As iron is eaten away by rust, so the envious are consumed by their own passion.
- **Antisthenes**.

1,308. Envy and anger shortens a man's life.
- **The Apocrypha:** *Ecclesiasticus 30: 24a, NEB*.

1,309. Love is patient, love is kind. It does not envy, it does not boast, it is not proud.
- **The Bible:** *1st Corinthians 13: 4, NIV*.

1,310. Love looks through a telescope; envy, through a microscope.
- **Josh Billings**.

1,311. He who envies others does not obtain peace of mind.
- **Buddha**.

1,312. Envy is the art of counting the other fellow's blessings instead of your own.
- **Harold Coffin**.

1,313. People may show jealousy, but hide their envy.
- **Mason Cooley:** *City Aphorisms, Eleventh Edition*, 1993.

1,314. Fools may our scorn, not envy raise, / For envy is a kind of praise.
- **John Gay:** *Fables*, 1727.

1,315. Envy is a littleness of soul.
- **William Hazlitt:** *Characteristics*, 1823.

1,316. Envy is the sincerest form of flattery.
- **Herbert V. Prochnow and Herbert V. Prochnow Jr:** *The Public Speaker's Source Book*, 1977.

1,317. Compete, don't envy.
- ***Arab Proverb***.

1,318. Our envy always lasts longer than the happiness of those we envy.
- **Francois, Duc de La Rochefoucauld:** *Maxims*, 1665.

1,319. There is not a passion so strongly rooted in the human soul as envy.
- **Richard Brinsley Sheridan:** *The Critic, Act 1, Scene 1*, 1779.

EPITAPHS

1,320. Don't pity me now, / Don't pity me never; / I'm going to do nothing / For ever and ever.
- **James Agate:** *A Charwoman's Epitaph* in *Ego*, 11/3/33. NB *Ego* is the title of Agate's nine volume autobiography.

1,321. Here lies an atheist, all dressed up and nowhere to go.
- **anon.** NB These words are engraved on a tombstone in a Maryland Cemetery.

1,322. I have gone home.
- **Robert Baden-Powell.** NB The Boy Scout trail sign conveying this message is a circle with a dot in the middle. This sign is engraved on Baden-Powell's simple tombstone on his grave in Kenya.

1,323. Epitaph: a monumental lie.
- **J.M. Braude:** *Treasury of Wit for Occasions.*

1,324. As father Adam first was fool'd, / (A case that's still too common), / Here lies a man a woman ruled, / The devil ruled the woman.
- **Robert Burns:** *Epitaph on a Henspeckled Country Squire.*

1,325. Here lie Willie Michie's banes: / O Satan, when ye tak him, / Gie him the schulin o' your weans, / For clever deils he'll mak them !
- **Robert Burns:** *Epitaph for Mr William Michie, Schoolmaster.* NB Scots: <u>banes</u> = bones: <u>gie</u> = give: <u>weans</u> = young children.

1,326. Lament him, Mauchline husbands a' / He aften did assist ye, / For had ye staid hale weeks awa, / Your wives they ne'er had miss'd ye. / Ye Mauchline bairns, as on ye pass / To school in bands the gither, / O tread ye lightly on his grass - / Perhaps he was your faither!
- **Robert Burns:** *Epitaph for James Smith.*

1,327. *Dorothy Parker:* Excuse my dust.
Jack Benny: Did you hear about my operation?
Robert Benchley: All this is over my head.
Leo Rosten: This is much too deep for me.
 - Suggested **Celebrity Epitaphs:** quoted in *Laugh Twice and Call Me in the Morning* selected by Bruce Lansky, 1999.

1,328. You know what I'm going to have on my gravestone? "She did it the hard way."
 - **Bette Davis**: *on CBS TV, 5ᵗʰ May, 1985.*

1,329. His form was of the manliest beauty, / His heart was kind and soft; / Faithful below he did his duty, / But now he's gone aloft.
 - **Charles Dibdin:** This verse, from a popular song written by Dibdin, is inscribed on his gravestone in a cemetery in Camden Town, London.

1,330. Here lies my wife, Samantha Proctor,
She ketched a cold, but wouldn't doctor,
She could not stay, she had to go -
Praise God from whom all blessings flow.
 - **Evan Esar:** *The Comic Encyclopedia*, 1978.

1,331. To yesterday's companionship and tomorrow's reunion.
- **Rita Hayworth's** epitaph inscribed on her gravestone in Holy Cross cemetery, Culver City, California.

1,332. Epitaph for a dead waiter: "God finally caught his eye."
 - **George Kaufman.**

1,333. Beneath this lavish stone lies / ALOYSIUS XAVIER SMILEY / Buried one beautiful day in May/ He lived the life of Reilly / When Reilly was away.
- Quoted in **Leo Rosten's Book of Laughter** and said to have been inscribed on a tombstone in Dublin.

1,334. Under this stone lies our dog Spot,
Whose only fault he piddled a lot.
A quiet dog and though seldom seen,
We always knew where he had been.
 - **Walter McCorrisken:**(semi-skilled poet), *Hairy Knees and Heather Hills*

1,335. Gone is the collie we loved so dear
To Heaven's loving care.

But though we've lost a collie
At least we've gained a chair.
  - *ibid*

EULOGIES

1,336. The greatest mistake I made was not to die in office.
- **Dean Acheson:** is reputed to have said this after hearing the funeral eulogy of his successor, John Foster Dulles, May,1959.

1,337. Eulogy: n. Praise of a person who has either the advantage of wealth and power, or the consideration to be dead.
- **Ambrose Bierce**.

1,338. I'm always relieved when someone is delivering a eulogy and I realize I'm listening to it.
- **George Carlin:** *Napalm and Silly Putty*, 2001.

1,339. A funeral eulogy is a belated plea for the defence after the evidence is all in.
- **Irvin S. Cobb**.

1,340. The only farewells that politicians handle well are deaths. You can hear some excellent eulogies in the House of Commons.
- **Carol Goar:** *The Toronto Star, December, 1993*.

1,341. What value is life if the kindest things said about oneself are done so at one's eulogy?
- **Eli Khamarov**: *Surviving on Planet Reebok*.

1,342. I read a thing that actually says that speaking in front of a crowd is considered the number one fear of the average person. I found that amazing - number two was death! That means to the average person if you have to be at a funeral, you would rather be in the casket than doing the eulogy.
- **Jerry Seinfeld:** *Seinlanguage*, 1993.

EXAMPLE

1,343. Example has more followers than reason. We unconsciously imitate what pleases us, and approximate to the characters we most admire.
- **Christian Nestell Bovee.**

1,344. We are, in truth, more than half what we are by imitation. The great point is to choose good models and to study them with care
- **Lord Chesterfield**: *Lord Chesterfield's Worldly Wisdom* by George Birkbec Hill, 2008.

1,345. Children have more need of models than of critics.
- **Carolyn Coats:** *Things Your Dad Always Told You But You Didn't Want to Hear,* 1988.

1,346. Setting an example is not the main means of influencing another, it is the only means.
- **Albert Einstein.**

1,347. There's only one thing more contagious than measles, and that's a good example.
- **Evan Esar:** *20,000 Quips and Quotes,* 1968.

1,348. Example is always more efficacious than precept.
- **Samuel Johnson:** *The History of Rasselas,* 1759.

1,349. The first great gift we can bestow on others is a good example.
- **Thomas Morell:** *Braude's Handbook of Stories for Toastmasters and Speakers* by Jacob M. Braude, 1957.

1,350. A good example is the best sermon.
- ***English Proverb.***

1,351. Personal example carries more weight than preaching.
- ***Chinese Proverb***

1,352. Nothing is so contagious as example, and our every really good or bad action inspires a similar one.
- **Francois, Duc de La Rochefoucauld:** *Maxims*.

1,353. To set a lofty example is the richest bequest a man can leave behind.
- **Samuel Smiles:** *Self – Help*, 1859.

1,354. I bid him look into the lives of men as though into a mirror, and from others to take an example for himself.
 - **Terence:** *Adelphoe*, 2nd century BC.

1,355. Few things are harder to put up with than the annoyance of a good example.
 - **Mark Twain:** *Pudd'nhead Wilson*, 1894.

1,356. Example, whether it is good or bad, has a powerful influence.
- **George Washington:** *in a letter, 1780*.

EXCELLENCE

1,357. The sad thing is that excellence makes people nervous.
- **Shana Alexander:** *Neglected Kids – the Bright Ones* in *Life Magazine.*

1,358. Excellence is the result of caring more than others think is wise, risking more than others think is safe, dreaming more than others think is practical, and expecting more than others think is possible.
- ***anon.***

1,359. We are what we repeatedly do. Excellence is not an act but a habit.
- **Aristotle:** *Nicomachean Ethics*, 4th century BC.

1,360. Excellence is doing ordinary things extraordinarily well.
- **John W. Gardner:** *Excellence*, 1961.

EXECUTIVES

1,361. A molehill man is a pseudo-busy executive who comes to work at 9 a.m. and finds a molehill on his desk. He has until 5 p.m. to make this molehill into a mountain. An accomplished molehill man will often have his mountain finished before lunch.
- **Fred Allen:** *Treadmill to Oblivion*, 1954.

1,362. A man knocked at the heavenly gate,
His face was scarred and old.
He stood before the Man of Fate
For admission to the fold.
"What have you done," St. Peter asked,
"To gain admission here?"
"I've been an executive, Sir," he said,
"For many and many a year."
The pearly gates swung open wide;
St.Peter touched the bell.
"Come in and choose your harp," he said,
"You've had your share of hell."
- ***anon:*** quoted in *Braude's Treasury of Wit and Humour for all Occasions* by Jacob M. Braude, 1991.

1,363. Good executives never put off until tomorrow what they can get someone else to do today.
- ***anon.***

1,364. I don't expect executives to be creative, but I do expect them to have courage.
- **Rita Mae Brown:** *Starting From Scratch*, 1988.

1,365. In the business world an executive knows something about everything, a technician knows everything about something, and the switchboard operator knows everything.
- **Harold Coffin:** quoted in *The Peter Pyramid* by Laurence J. Peter, 1986.

1,366. A successful executive is one who delegates all responsibility, shifts all the blame, and appropriates all the credit.
  - **Evan Esar:** *20,000 Quips and Quotes,* 1995.

1,367. There is more credit and satisfaction in being a first rate truck driver than a tenth-rate executive.
- **B.C. Forbes:** *Forbes Magazine.*

1,368. Executives who get there and stay suggest solutions when they present the problems.
- **Malcolm Forbes**: *Forbes Magazine.*

1,369. An executive is a man who can make quick decisions and is sometimes right.
- **Elbert Hubbard:** quoted in *The Forbes Book of Business Quotations.*

1,370. A born executive is someone whose father owns the business.
  - **Mad Magazine:** *Mad:The Half-Wit and Wisdom of Alfred E. Neuman,* 1997

1,371. Big shots are only little shots who keep shooting.
- **Christopher Morley**.

1,372. A businessman is judged by the company he keeps solvent.
  - **Herbert V. Prochnow and Herbert V. Prochnow Jr:** *The Public Speaker's Source Book.* 1977.

EXERCISE

1,373. Some people confine their exercise to jumping to conclusions, running up bills, stretching the truth, bending over backward, lying down on the job, side-stepping responsibility, and pushing their luck.
- ***anon***: quoted in *Braude's Treasury of Wit and Humour For All Occasions*,

1,374. If your dog is fat, you are not getting enough exercise.
- ***anon***.

1,375. My doctor recently told me that jogging could add years to my life, I think he was right. I feel ten years older already.
- **Milton Berle**.

1,376. Exercise is a dirty word. Every time I hear it I wash my mouth out with chocolate.
- **Charlie Brown:** the Peanuts Cartoon character created by Charles M. Schultz.

1,377. I get my exercise being a pallbearer for those of my friends who believe in regular running.
- **Sir Winston Churchill:** *The Wit and Wisdom of Winston Churchill* edited by James C. Humes, 1994.

1,378. The worse curse of human life is the detestable necessity of taking exercise.
- **Wilkie Collins:** *I Say No*, 1884.

1,379. I nauseate walking; 'tis a country diversion – I loathe the country.
- **William Congreve**: *The Way of the World, Act IV. Scene V* , 1700.

1,380. Better to hunt in fields for health unbought, / Than fee the doctor for a nauseous draught. / The wise, for cure, on exercise depend; / God never made His work for man to mend.
- **John Dryden:** *Epistle to John Driden of Chesterton*, 1700.

1,381. Young people think nothing of jogging five miles every morning, and older people don't think much of it either.
- **Sam Ewing:** *The Sun, October, 1999.*

1,382. You're in poor physical shape when weight lifting consists of standing up.
- **Sam Ewing:** *The Sun, 26th October, 1999.*

1,383. Diet and exercise can help overweight people break the pound barrier.
- **Sam Ewing:** *Mature Living, January, 1999.*

1,384. Back in my rummy days, I would tremble and shake for hours upon rising. It was the only exercise I got.
- **W. C. Fields:** as Eustace McGargle in the 1936 Paramount film *Poppy*.

1,385. The older I get, the more I realize the importance of exercising the various dimensions of my body, soul, mind and heart. Taken together, these aspects give me a sense of wholeness. I want to be a whole human being rather than one who limps on one leg because I don't know how to use all of my parts. Intellectual, emotional, and physical activity are not separate entities. Rather, they are dimensions of the same human being.
- **Robert Fulgham:** quoted in *Handbook for the Soul* edited by Richard Carlson, **et al**, 1996.

1,386. Anybody can exercise. But this kind of lethargy takes real discipline.
- **Garfield:** the bone idle cartoon cat created by Jim Davis.

1.387. Keeping fit starts in the mind, so concentrate in keeping that in good order and your body will quickly find its own levels of well-being.
- **Jim Green:** *Your Retirement Master Plan: How to Ensure You Have a Fulfilling and Enjoyable Third Age*, 2006.

1,388. There is no exercise better for the heart than reaching down and lifting people up.
- **John Andrew Holmes:** *Wisdom in Small Doses*, 1927.

1,389. Whenever I feel like exercising, I lie down until that feeling goes away.
- **Robert Maynard Hutchins.**

1,390. Exercise and application produce order in our affairs, health of body, cheerfulness of mind, and these make us precious to our friends.
- **Thomas Jefferson:** *The Family Letters of Thomas Jefferson*, 1966.

1,391. The only athletic sport I ever mastered was backgammon.
Douglas Jerrold.

1,392. The trouble with jogging is that, by the time you realize you're not in shape for it, it's too far to walk back.
- **Franklin P. Jones**

1,393. Most of my exercise has come from strenuously avoiding all forms of physical fitness.
- **Patrick F. McManus:** *Rubber Legs and White Tail-Hairs*, 1988.

1,394. I have always believed that exercise is the key not only to physical health but to peace of mind.
- **Nelson Mandela:** *Long Walk to Freedom*, 1995.

1,395. How do I keep fit? I lay down a lot.
- **Robert Mitchum:** quoted in *Halliwell's Who's Who in the Movies*, 2003.

1,396. Another good reducing exercise is placing the hands against the table's edge and pushing back.
- **Robert Quillen:** quoted in *Quotations For Our Time* compiled by Laurence J. Peter, 1977.

1,397. I feel about exercise the same way I feel about a few other things; that there is nothing wrong with it if it is done in private by consenting adults.
- **Anna Quinlen:** *Living Out Loud*, 1988.

1,398. The first time I see a jogger smiling, I'll consider it.
- **Joan Rivers.**

1,399. Nothing like a night-time stroll to give you ideas.
- **J. K. Rowlings:** *Harry Potter and the Goblet of Fire*, 2000.

1,400. The word "aerobics" came about when the gym instructors got together and said: "If we're going to charge $10 an hour, we can't call it 'Jumping up and down'."
- **Rita Rudner:** *Naked Beneath My Clothes*, 1993.

1,401. Those who think they have no time for bodily exercise will sooner or later have to find time for illness .
- **Edward Stanley, 15ᵗʰ Earl of Derby**.

1,402. The bicycle is just as good company as most husbands and, when it gets old and shabby, a woman can dispose of it and get a new one without shocking the entire community.
- **Ann Louise Strong:** *The Minneapolis Tribune, 1895*

1,403. An early morning walk is a blessing for the whole day.
- **Henry David Thoreau:** *The Journal, 1837 – 1861,* 2009.

1,404. I have never taken any exercise except sleeping and resting, and I never intend to take any. Exercise is loathsome, and it cannot be any benefit when you are tired; and I am always tired.
- **Mark Twain:** *in a speech on his 70ᵗʰ birthday.*

1,405. To get back my youth I would do anything in the world, except take exercise, get up early, or be respectable.
- **Oscar Wilde:** *The Picture of Dorian Gray,* 1891.

1,406. My wife's idea of exercise is to shop faster.
- **Pat Williams:** *Winning With One-Liners,* 2002.

1,407. I don't take enough exercise, but what is the longest-lived animal in the world? The giant tortoise – 120 years old and it hardly moves.
- **Sir Terry Wogan:** quoted in *The Press and Journal Quotes of the Day,*
18ᵗʰ June, 2007.

1,408. In wisdom gathered over time I have found that every experience is a form of exploration.
- **Ansel Adams:** quoted in *Older and Wiser* by Gretchen B. Dianda, 1995.

1,409. Human beings, who are almost unique in having the ability to learn from the experience of others, are also remarkable for their apparent disinclination to do so.
- **Douglas Adams:** *Last Chance to See,* 1991.

1,410. They had been brought up in the School of Hard Knocks.
- **George Ade:** *Knocking the Neighbours,* 1912.

1,411. Experience is what allows you to recognize a mistake when you are about to make it again.
- ***anon.***

1,412. Some people speak from experience. Others – from experience – don't speak.
- ***anon.***

1,413. All experience is a torch to light the way to each new challenge.
- **anon**: *quoted* in *Wake- Up Calls: Making the Most of Every Day Regardless of What Life Throws You* by Joan Lunden, 2001.

1,414. Experience is a good teacher, but she sends in terrific bills.
- **Minna Thomas Antrim:** *Naked Truth and Veiled Allusions*, 1902.

1,415. Good judgement comes from experience, and a lot of that comes from bad judgement.
- **Texas Bix Bender:** *Don't Squat With Yer Spurs On!: A Cowboy's Guide to Life*, 1992.

1,416. Experience is the best of schoolmasters, only the school fees are heavy.
- **Thomas Carlyle:** *Miscellaneous Essays*, 1890.

1,417. We all learn from experience, but some of us have to go to Summer School.
- **Peter De Vries:** *The Tunnel of Love*, 1954.

1,418. Men learn little from others' experience.
- **T. S. Eliot:** *Murder in the Cathedral*, 1938.

1,419. Experience is the name everyone gives to his mistakes.
- **Elbert Hubbard:** *The Note Book of Elbert Hubbard*, 1927.

EXPERIENCE

1,420. Experience is not what happens to a man; it is what a man does with what happens to him.
- **Aldous Huxley:** *Texts and Pretexts,* 1932.

1,421. The only function that one experience can perform is to lead into another experience.
- **William James:** *Essays in Radical Empiricism,* 1912.

1,422. One thorn of experience is worth a whole wilderness of warning.
- **James Russell Lowell:** *Among My Books,* 1870.

1,423. There is only one thing more painful than learning from experience and that is not learning from experience.
- **Archibald MacLeish**.

1,424. I like to think of anything stupid I've done as a "learning experience." It makes me feel less stupid.
- **P. J. O'Rourke:** *Give War a Chance,* 1992.

1,425. Experience is what you get looking for something else.
- **Mary Pettibone Poole:** *A Glass Eye at a Keyhole,* 1938.

1,426. Experience is the father of wisdom, and memory the mother.
- ***English Proverb.***

1,427. Do you know the difference between education and experience? Education is what you get when you read the fine print; experience is what you get when you don't.
- **Pete Seeger:** quoted in *Loose Talk* by L. Botts, 1980.

1,428. The experience gathered from books, though often valuable, is but the nature of learning; whereas the experience gained from actual life is one of the nature of wisdom.
- **Samuel Smiles:** *Self – Help,* 1859.

1,429. A man who carries a cat by the tail learns something he can learn in no other way.
- **Mark Twain:** quoted in *The Friars' Club Encyclopedia of Jokes*, 1997.

1,430. If we could sell our experiences for what they cost us we'd be millionaires.
- **Abigail Van Buren**.

EXPERTS

1,431. An expert is a man who has made all the mistakes which can be made in a very narrow field.
- **Niels Bohr.**

1,432. Too bad that all the people who know how to run the country are busy driving taxi-cabs and cutting hair.
- **George Burns:** *Life Magazine, December, 1979.*

1,433. An expert is one who knows more and more about less and less.
- **Nicholas Murray Butler:** *in a speech, Columbia University, 1901.*

1,434. When a politician is in opposition he is an expert on the means to some end; and when he is in office he is an expert on the obstacles to it.
- **G. K. Chesterton:** quoted in *Geary's Guide to the World's Great Aphorists* by James Geary, 2007.

1,435. The childless experts on child rearing also... bring tears of laughter to my eyes when they say, "I love children because they are so honest." There is not an agent in the CIA or the KGB who knows how to conceal the theft of food, how to fake being asleep, or how to forge a parent's signature like a child.
- **Bill Cosby:** *Fatherhood, 1986.*

1,436. An expert is someone called in at the last minute to share the blame.
- **Sam Ewing:** *Reader's Digest, December, 1992.*

1,437. Always listen to experts. They'll tell you what can't be done, and why. Then do it.
- **Robert A. Heinlein:** *Time Enough For Love, 1973.*

1,438. Expert: a man who makes three correct guesses consecutively.
- **Laurence J. Peter, *attributed.***

1.439. Even when experts all agree, they may well be mistaken.
- **Bertrand Russell:** *Skeptical Essays*, 1928.

1,440. If the world should blow itself up, the last audible voice would be that of an expert saying it can't be done.
- **Sir Peter Ustinov,** *attributed*.

FACTS

1,441. Facts are stubborn things; and whatever may be our wishes, our inclinations, or the dictates of our passion, they cannot alter the state of facts and evidence.
- **John Adams:** *in defence of British soldiers in the Boston Massacre Trials, December 4th, 1770.*

1,442. Facts mean nothing unless they are rightly understood, rightly related and rightly interpreted.
- ***anon:*** quoted in *Braude's Handbook of Stories for Toastmasters and Speakers* by Jacob M. Braude, 1957.

1,443. But facts are chiels that winna ding, an' downa be disputed.
- **Robert Burns:** *A Dream*, 1783. NB Scots: <u>chiels</u> = young lads: <u>winna</u> = will not: <u>ding</u> = be beaten: <u>downa</u> = cannot

1,444. *As a matter of fact* is an expression that precedes many an expression that isn't.
- **Evan Esar:** *20,000 Quips and Quotes*, 1968.

1,445. Get the facts, or the facts will get you. And when you get them, get them right, or they will get you wrong.
- **Thomas Fuller:** *Gnomologia: Adages and Proverbs*, 1732.

1,446. Facts are never neutral; they are impregnated with value judgements.
- **Peter Gay:** *Style in History*, 1988.

1,447. Facts do not cease to exist because they are ignored.
- **Aldous Huxley:** *Proper Studies*, 1927.

1,448. Obviously the facts are never just coming at you but are incorporated by an imagination that is formed by your previous experience. Memories of the past are not memories of facts but memories of your imaginings of the facts.
- **Philip Roth:** *The Facts: A Novelist's Autobiography*, 1988.

1,449. The Right Honourable gentleman is indebted to his memory for his jests, and to his imagination for his facts.
- **Richard Brinsley Sheridan:** *in a speech in reply to a Mr Dundas,* quoted in *Sheridaniana: Anecdotes of the Life of Richard Brinsley Sheridan,* 2007.

1,450. Facts may speak for themselves.
- **George Washington:** *in a letter, January, 1780*

FAILURE

1,451. Success comes in cans, failure in can'ts.
- *anon*.

1,452. Failure is the path of least persistence.
- *anon*.

1,453. Don't fear failure so much that you refuse to try new things. The saddest summary of a life contains three descriptions: could have, might have, and should have.
- **Louis E. Boone.**

1,454. A failure establishes only this, that our determination to succeed was not strong enough.
- **Christian Nestell Bovee:** *Intuitions and Summaries of Thought.* 1862.

1,455. The tragedy of life is not that man loses, but that he almost wins.
- **Heywood C. Broun:** *Pieces of Hate, and Other Enthusiasms,* 1922.

1,456. It's OK to fail, but it is not OK to give up.
- Kate, age 8: quoted in *Wit & Wisdom from the Peanut Gang: A Collection of Wise Words from Young Hearts* compiled by **H. Jackson Brown Jr**, 1994.

1,457. Failing once in a while builds character. I should know, I have more character than I know what to do with.
- **George Burns:** *Dr Burns' Prescription For Happiness,* 1986.

1,458. I honestly think it is better to be a failure at something you love than to be a success at something you hate.
- **George Burns:** *Readers' Digest, July, 1990.*

1,459. Never take "No" for an answer. Never submit to failure.
- **Sir Winston Churchill:** *The Wit & Wisdom of Winston Churchill* by James C. Humes, 1995.

1,460. If I had permitted my failures, or what seemed to me at the time a lack of success, to discourage me I cannot see any way in which I would ever have made progress.
- **Calvin Coolidge**, *The Autobiography of Calvin Coolidge*, 1929.

1,461. Be Persevering and Keep Digging. This is one of the most important rules. I've seen people within inches of success suddenly quit. By digging and digging, you can turn failure into success. Don't give up!
- **E. Joseph Cosman:** *How I Made $1,000,000 in Mail Order*, 1964.

1,462. Failure is success if we learn from it.
- **Malcolm Forbes:** *The Forbes Book of Business Quotations*.

1,463. You can do as much as you think you can,
But you'll never accomplish more;
If you're afraid of yourself, young man,
There's little for you in store.
For failure comes from the inside first,
It's there if we only knew it.
And you can win, though you face the worst,
If you feel that you're going to do it.
- **Edgar A. Guest:** *How Do You Tackle Your Work?* in *A Heap O' Livin'*, 1916.

1,464. He was a self-made man who owed his lack of success to nobody.
- **Joseph Heller:** *Catch-22*, 1961.

1,465. A little more persistence, a little more effort, and what seemed hopeless failure may turn to glorious success. There is no failure except in no longer trying. There is no defeat except from within, no really insurmountable barrier save our own inherent weakness of purpose.
- **Elbert Hubbard**.

1,466. Every great achievement has come after repeated failure. Virtually nothing came out right first time. Failures, repeated failures, are the posts on the road to achievement.
- **Charles F. Kettering:** *Toronto Globe and Mail, June, 2004*.

1,467. Remove failure as an option, and your chances for success become infinitely better.
- **Joan Lunden:** *Cable News Network Chat Show, 17/ 10/ 2000*

1,468. You can't let your failures define you – you have to let your failures teach you. You have to let them show you what to do differently the next time.
- **Barack Obama:** *in a speech to American school children, 8 / 9/ 09*

1,469. It is impossible to live without failing at something unless you live so cautiously that you might as well not have lived at all – in which case, you fail by default.
- **J. K. Rowling:** *2008 Harvard Commencement Speech.*

1,470. It is a mistake to suppose that men succeed through success, they much more oftener succeed through failures. Precept, study, advice, and example could never have taught them so well as failure has done.
- **Samuel Smiles:** *Self – Help*, 1859.

FAITH

1,471. Faith is the first factor in a life devoted to service. Without it, nothing is possible. With it, nothing is impossible.
- **Mary McLeod Bethune:** *Women of Faith and Spirit* by Dayna Beilenson and Mary Alice Warner, 1987.

1,472. There is nothing anti-intellectual in the leap of faith, for faith is not believing without proof but trusting without reservation.
- **William Sloane Coffin:** *Credo,* 2004.

1,473. Socrates had it wrong; it is not the unexamined but... the uncommitted life that is not worth living.
- *ibid.*

1,474. Faith moves mountains but you have to keep pushing while you are praying.
- **Mason Cooley:** *City Aphorisms, Fourth Selection,* 1987.

1,475. Faith is the belief that in God the impossible is possible, that in Him time and eternity are one, that both life and death are meaningful.
- **Peter Drucker:** *The Ecological Vision,* 1993.

1,476. Faith means belief in something concerning which doubt is theoretically possible.
- **William James:** *Princeton Review, 1882.*

1,477. It takes a lot of intellect to have faith, which is why so many people only have religiosity.
- **Madeleine L'Engle:** *Newsweek, May 7th, 2003.*

1,478. Faith doesn't mean that you don't have doubts.
- **Barack Obama:** *in a speech, June, 2006.*

1,479. It is the heart which experiences God and not the reason. That is what faith is: God felt by the heart, not by the reason.
- **Blaise Pascal:** *Pensees*, 1670.

1,480 . There lives more faith in honest doubt,
 Believe me, than in half the creeds.
- **Alfred Lord Tennyson:** *In Memoriam*, 1850.

1,481. 'Tis not the dying for a faith that's so hard - 'tis the living up to it that's difficult, as I know to my cost.
- **William Makepeace Thackeray:** *The History of Henry Esmond*, 1852.

THE FAMILY

1,482. Keeping peace in a large family requires patience, love, understanding and at least two television sets.
- ***anon***.

1,483. The family is the association established by nature for the supply of man's everyday need.
- **Aristotle:** *Politics*, 4th century BC.

1,484. The bond that links your true family is not one of blood, but of respect and joy in each other's life.
- **Richard Bach:** *Illusions*, 1977.

1,485. I know it is too late now, but I have long felt that I was foolish not to limit my family... to a parakeet with his tongue clipped.
- **Erma Bombeck:** *Wait Till You Have Children of Your Own!* 1971.

1,486. Good family life is never an accident but always an achievement by those who share it.
- **James H. S. Bossard:** *The Large Family System: An Original Study in the Sociology of Family Behaviour*, 1956.

1,487. The family defines our past and shapes our character. It is here that we learn the important lessons of self-discipline, the art of compromise, forgiveness, honesty, and fair play.
- **H. Jackson Brown, Jr:** Family Preface in *Wit and Wisdom from the Peanut Butter Gang: A Collection of Wise Words From Young Hearts*, 1994

1,488. It does not matter how much money a family has. If there is a lot of love in a home, that family is richer than any millionaire could ever be.
- Whitney, age 16, quoted in *Wit & Wisdom from the Peanut Butter Gang*, compiled and edited by **H. Jackson Brown, Jr**, 1994.

1,489. Where does the family start? It starts with a young man falling in love with a girl – no superior alternative has yet been found.
- **Sir Winston Churchill:** quoted in *A Churchill Reader* by Colin Coote, 1954.

1,490. Family life may survive as a form of evening and weekend entertainment.
- **Mason Cooley:** *City Aphorisms, Second Selection*, 1985.

1,491. You've simply got to get on with your family and friends and tell them how much you love them because you never know whether they'll be there tomorrow, do you? People seem afraid of sentimentality, more's the pity.
- **Jilly Cooper:** *Saga Magazine, 1998.*

1,492. At best the family teaches the finest things human beings can learn from one another - generosity and love. But it is also, all too often, where we learn nasty things like hate, rage and shame.
- **Barbara Ehrenreich:** *The Snarling Citizen*, 1995.

1,493. Family: A social unit where the father is concerned with parking space, the children with outer space, and the mother with closet space.
- **Evan Esar:** *Esar's Comic Dictionary*, 1943.

1,494. In some families, the problems are relative.
- **Sam Ewing:** *Mature Living, April, 1999.*

1,495. In truth a family is what you make it. It is made strong, not by the number of heads counted at the dinner table, but by the rituals you help family members create, by the memories you share, by the commitment of time, caring, and love you show to one another, and by the hopes for the future you have as individuals and as a unit.
- **Marge Kennedy:** *The Single Parent Family*, 1994.

1,496. The first and fundamental structure for human ecology is the family, in which man receives his first ideas about truth and goodness and learns what it means to love and be loved, and thus what it means to be a person.
- **Pope John Paul 2nd:** *Pastoral letter on the 100th anniversary of the papal encyclical on the conditions of the workers by Pope Leo 13th in 1891.*

1,497. Govern a family as you would cook a small fish- very gently.
- ***Chinese Proverb.***

1,498. A family in harmony will prosper in everything.
- *Chinese Proverb*.

1,499. Feelings of worth can flourish only in an atmosphere where individual differences are appreciated, mistakes are tolerated, communication is open, and rules are flexible- the kind of atmosphere that is found in a nurturing family.
- **Virginia Satir**: *The Winning Family* by Louise Hart,1988

1,500. Rearing a family is probably the most difficult job in the world.
- **Virginia Satir:** *The New Peoplemaking,* 1972.

- **1,501** Effective family life does not just happen; it's the result of deliberate intention, determination and practice.
- **Charles R. Swindoll***: The Strong Family*, 1993.

FARMERS AND FARMING

1,502 There are three easy ways of losing money- racing is the quickest, women the most pleasant, and farming the most certain.
- **Lord Amherst**.

1,503. If you complain about farmers, don't talk with your mouth full!
- *On a billboard in the American Midwest:* quoted in *The Speaker's Book of Quotations* compiled by **Henry O. Dorman**, 1987.

1,504. Agriculture represents the single most profound ecological change in the entire 3.5 billion-year history of life.
- **Niles Eldredge:** *The Sixth Extinction,* 2001.

1,505. If you work hard and long enough on a farm you can make a fortune – if you strike oil on it.
- **Evan Esar:** *20,000 Quips and Quotes,* 1968.

1,506. The farmer will never be happy again;
He carries his heart in his boots.
For either the rain is destroying his grain
Or the drought is destroying his roots.
- **A. P. Herbert:** *Tinker, Tailor: A Child's Guide to the Professions,* 1922.

1,507. Italians come to ruin most generally in three ways: women, gambling and farming. My family chose the slowest one
- **Pope John 23rd**.

1,508. Happy the man whose wish and care
A few paternal acres bound,
Content to breathe his native air,
In his own ground.
- **Alexander Pope:** *Ode on Solitude* **circa** 1700. In this poem, written when he was only 12 years old, Pope romanticizes the life of the farmer.

1,509. A farmer's daughter, newly returned from University with a degree in English, was finding some of her father's ways a trifle coarse. After her father announced that he was "awa' to scatter a wheen o' dung," she asked her mother, "Can we not persuade him to say manure instead of dung?"

"Wheesht, lassie," her mother replied, "It's taken me twenty years to get him to say dung."

- **Tom Sheilds:** *Tom Shield's Diary*, 1991. NB Scots: a wheen o' = a considerable amount. wheesht = be quiet!

1,510. He is now rising fast from affluence to poverty.
- **Mark Twain:** *Henry Ward Beecher's Farm*, 1885..

FASHION

1,511. People are more violently opposed to fur than leather because it's safer to harass rich women than motorcycle gangs.
- *anon.*

1,512. Stretch pants- the garment that made skiing a spectator sport.
- *anon.*

1,513. If the hindsight of some women was as good as their foresight, they wouldn't wear slacks.
- *anon.*

1,514. Said an envious, erudite ermine, / "There's one thing I cannot determine; / When a girl wears my coat, / She's a person of note, / When I wear it, I'm called only vermin."
- *anon.*

1.515. There was a young lady (a doll!) / Who wore a newspaper dress to a ball. / The dress caught fire / And burned her entire / Front page, sports section and all.
- *anon.*

1,516. I bought myself a Wonderbra / For fourteen ninety nine, / It looked so good on the model girl's chest, / And I hoped it would on mine, /I took it from the packaging / And when I tried it on, / The Wonderbra restored to me all I believed had gone.
- **Pam Ayres:** *The Wonderbra Song* in *With These Hands, A Collection of Work,* 1997.

1,517. She was a large woman who seemed not so much dressed as upholstered.
- **Sir J. M. Barrie:** quoted in *The Treasury of Humorous Quotations* edited by Evan Esar, 1955.

1,518. The leading cause of death among fashion models is falling through street grates.
- **Dave Barry:** *New York News, November, 1986.*

1,519. You always hear about fashion's success stories, How a starlet lost an earing one night and by the next morning the entire country was wearing one earing.
- **Erma Bombeck:** *If Life is a Bowl of Cherries, What am I Doing in the Pits?* 1978.

1,520. There comes a point in a man's life when he is no longer able to wear a T-shirt... As soon as the merest hint of a belly begins to emerge, nothing looks quite so idiotic as a T-shirt. And if, like me, you have what amounts to an overinflated space hopper down there, you know that in a T-shirt you couldn't look more ridiculous even if you were going round in a scuba suite.
- **Jeremy Clarkson:** *The Sunday Times, 12th July, 2009.*

1,521. A woman wears a sweater to accentuate the positive, and a girdle to eliminate the negative.
- **Evan Esar:** *20,000 Quips and Quotes*, 1968.

1,522. Some women dress to please their husbands, while others never bother about the expense.
- *ibid.*

1,523. Fashions come and fashions go, but pockets are usually the same. There's little change in them.
- **Sam Ewing:** *The Reader's Digest, June, 1998.*

1,524. Short skirts make women look shorter – and men look longer.
- **Sam Ewing:** *The Sun, September 21st, 1999.*

1,525. A girdle is a device that holds a girl in when she's going out.
- **Leopold Fechtner:** *5,000 One-and-Two-Line Jokes*, 1973.

1,526. She ordered a bra by mail. Now she waits for her shape to come in.
- *ibid.*

1,527. The only thing that separates us from the animals is our ability to accessorize.
- Olympia Dukakis in her role as Claire Belcher in the **1989 Film** *Steel Magnolias*.

1,528. There's so much plastic in this culture that vinyl leopard skin is becoming an endangered synthetic.
- Lily Tomlin in her role as the housewife Judith Beasley in the **1981 Film**: *The Incredible Shrinking Woman.*

1,529. In 1949 bikinis were introduced. Never had so little done as much for so many.
- **Bob Hope:** *Don't Shoot, It's Me* with Melville Shavelson, 1990.

1,530. A woman's dress should be like a barbed-wire fence – serving it's purpose without obstructing the view.
- **Sophia Loren:** *Good Morning America, August 10ᵗʰ, 1979.*

1,531. Most husbands want their wives to wear their dresses longer – about two years longer.
- **Bob Monkhouse:** *Just Say A Few Words,* 1988.

1,532. Sure, deck your lower limbs in pants; / Yours are the limbs, my sweeting. / You look divine as you advance - / Have you seen yourself retreating?
- **Ogden Nash:** *What's The Use?* in *Free Wheeling,* 1931.

1,533. I base most of my fashion taste on what doesn't itch
- **Gilda Radner:** *It's Always Something,* 1981. CP Ogden Nash's sentiments expressed in *Taboo to Boot:* One bliss for which / There is no match / Is when you itch / To up and scratch.

1,534. A bikini is not a bikini unless it can be pulled through a wedding ring.
- **Louis Reard:** *The Oxford Dictionary of Modern Quotations, 3ʳᵈ Edition* edited by Elizabeth Knowles, 2007.

1,535. I never expected to see the day when girls would get sunburned in the places they now do.
- **Will Rogers.**

1,536. She fitted into my biggest armchair as if it had been built round her by someone who knew they were wearing armchairs tight about the hips that season.
- **P. G. Wodehouse:** *Jeeves and the Unbidden Guest,* the second story in *My Man Jeeves,* 1919.

1,537. I wouldn't say her bathing suit was skimpy, but I saw more cotton on top of an aspirin bottle.

- **Henny Youngman:** *How Do You Like Me So Far?* 1963.

1,538. We find ourselves in complete accord with the etiquette expert who says that only well reared girls should wear slacks.

- **Henny Youngman:** *400 Travelling Salesmen's Jokes*, 1967.

FATHERS

1,539. My father never raised his hand to any one of his children except in self-defence.
- **Fred Allan:** *Much Ado About Me*, 1956.

1,540. A father is someone who carries photos where his money used to be.
- *anon.*

1,541. Anyone can be a father – but it takes someone special to be a dad.
- *anon.*

1,542. Whenever Junior misbehaves, / My wife, a thrifty woman, saves / The punishment till I return / from work, whereon, with grave concern, / She tells me whatsoever bad / Was done by Junior, naughty lad, / And says, "Now speak to him." And so, / When we're alone, I say... . "Hello."
- **Richard Armour:***Discipline and Dad* in *An Armoury of Light Verse*, 1942.

1,543. Fathers' Day - an observance that, while largely fuelled by greeting card companies, nevertheless provides us with an excellent opportunity to recognise the importance of a father in the lives of his children.
- **James C. Dobson:** *Dr Dobson's Newsletter, June, 2002.*

1,544. The best way for a father to bring up his children is to love their mother.
- **Evan Esar:** *20,000 Quips and Quotes*, 1968.

1,545. I cannot think of any need in childhood as strong as the need of a father's protection.
- **Sigmund Freud:** *Civilization and Its Discontents*, 1941.

1,546. One father is more than a hundred schoolmasters.
- **George Herbert:** *Outlandish Proverbs*, 1651.

1,547. My father only hit me once- but he used a Volvo.
- **Bob Monkhouse:** quoted in *Just Like Dad Says* by Geoff Tibballs, 2009.

1,548. Being a father/ Is quite a bother/ You improve them mentally/ And straighten them dentally/ They're no longer corralable / Once they find that you're fallible.
- **Ogden Nash:** *Soliloquy in Circles* in *Verses*, 1949.

1,549. It is much easier to become a father than to be one.
- **Kent Nerburn:** *Letters to My Son: a Father's Wisdom on Manhood, Life and Love*, 1994.

1,550. Fathers are no longer, if they ever were, merely a biological necessity - a social accident.They are an important influence on their child's development. and fathers need their children too.
- **Ross D. Parke:** *Fathering*, quoted in *Psychologically Speaking: A Book of Quotations* by Kevin Connolly and Margaret Martlew, 1999.

1, 551. No matter what, Dad was always there with solid words of advice... . "Go and ask your mother."
- **Alan Ray:** *Dick Enberg's Humorous Quotes for All Occasions*.

1,552. A man's desire for a son is usually nothing but the wish to duplicate himself in order that such a remarkable pattern may not be lost to the world.
- **Helen Rowland:** *Reflections of a Bachelor Girl*, 1903.

FAULT FINDING

1,553. Ignorance of your faults is a greater evil than the fault itself.
- **Muhammad ibn Zafar al-Siqilli:** quoted in *Geary's Guide to the World's Great Aphorists* by James Geary, 2007.

1,554. How easy it is to see your brothers' faults. How hard it is to face your own.
- **Buddha:** *The Dhammapada, The Wisdom of the Buddha,* **circa** 483 BC.

1,555. The greatest of faults, I should say, is to be conscious of none.
- **Thomas Carlyle:** *On Heroes, Hero-Worship, and the Heroic in History.*

1,556. It is the peculiar quality of a fool to see the faults in others, and be blind to his own.
- **Marcus Tullius Cicero.**

1,557. It's easy to see the faults in people, I know; and it's harder to see the good. Especially when the good isn't there.
- **Will Cuppy:** *The Decline and Fall of Practically Everybody* compiled posthumously by Fred Feldkamp, 1950.

1,558. Nothing will make us so charitable and tender to the faults of others as by self-examination thoroughly to know our own.
- **Francois Fenelon.**

1,559. Whose house is of glass, must not throw stones at another.
- **George Herbert:** *Jacula Prudentum ("Outlandish Aphorisms")* 1651.

1,560. We are keenly aware of the faults of our friends, but if they like us enough it doesn't matter.
- **Mignon McLaughlin:** *The Neurotic's Notebook,* 1980.

1,561. We should look long and carefully at ourselves before we pass judgement on our fellows.
- **Moliere:** *Le Misanthrope,* 1660.

1,562. When a man points a finger at someone else, he should remember that four of his fingers are pointing at himself.
 - **Louis Nizer:** *My Life in Court*, 1963.

1,563. A man can become so accustomed to the thought of his own faults that he will begin to cherish them as charming little personal characteristics.
 - **Helen Rowland:** *A Guide To Men*, 1922.

FEAR

1,564. You don't face your fears, you stand up to them.
- ***anon.***

1,565. God is our refuge and strength, an ever-present help in trouble. Therefore we will not fear.
- **The Bible:** *Psalm 46: 1 – 2a, NIV.*

1,566. God did not give us a spirit of timidity but a spirit of power, of love and of self-discipline.
- **The Bible:** *2ⁿᵈ Timothy 1: 7, NIV.*

1,567. Nothing is terrible except fear itself.
- **Francis Bacon:** *Advancement of Learning,*1623.

1,568. We fear things in proportion to our ignorance of them.
- **Christian Nestell Bovee:** *Intuitions and Summeries of Thought,* 1862

1,569. Half our fears are baseless, the other half discreditable.
- ***ibid.***

1,570. I don't have a fear of heights. I do, however, have a fear of falling from heights.
- **George Carlin:** *Napalm and Silly Putty,* 2001.

1,571. All we need to do is expose our fears to the sunlight and they shrink. They're persistent but not brave; or expose them to ridicule, and they flee. Laughing juries do not convict.
- **Dale Dauten:** *Arizona Republic, March 27ᵗʰ, 2000.*

1,572. They can conquer who believe they can.... He has not learned the lesson of life who does not every day surmount a fear.
- **Ralph Waldo Emerson:** *Courage* in *Society and Solitude,* 1870.

1,573. Do the thing you fear, and death of fear is certain.
- **Ralph Waldo Emerson:** *Letters and Social Aims*, 1875.

1,574. If there is one thing I would banish from the earth it is fear.
- **Henry Ford:** *The Theosophat Magazine, February, 1930.*

1,575. If we want to master fear and worry we must not only be willing to accept help from others, but also learn to accept ourselves and our abilities as well as our limitations.
- **Joshua Loth Liebman:** *Peace of Mind, 1948.*

1,576. Unlike any viral or bacterial illness, fear can be caught over the telephone, from reading newspapers, or from watching television.
- **Peter McWilliams:** *You Can't Afford the Luxury of a Negative Thought.*

1,577. I learned that courage was not the absence of fear, but the triumph over it. The brave man is not he who does not feel afraid, but he who conquers that fear.
- **Nelson Mandela:** *A Long Walk to Freedom.* 1995.

1,578. Things that go "bump" in the night / Should not really give one a fright / It's the hole in each ear / That lets in the fear, / That, and the absence of light!
- **Spike Milligan:** *Bump* in *The Little Pot Boiler,* 1963

1,579. You gain strength, courage and confidence by every experience in which you really stop to look fear in the face. You are able to say to yourself, "I have lived through this horror, I can take the next thing that comes along." You must do the thing you think you cannot do.
- **Eleanor Roosevelt:** *You Learn by Living: Eleven Keys for a More Fulfilling Life,* 1960.

1,580. Let me assert my firm belief that the only thing we have to fear is fear itself.
- **Franklin D. Roosevelt:** *Inaugeral Address, March 4th, 1933,* CP: Michel de Montaigne's comment: "The thing I fear most is fear."

1,581 Fear fades when facts are faced.
- **Frank Tyger**.

1,582. Courage is resistance to fear, mastery of fear — not absence of fear.
- **Mark Twain:** *Pudd'nhead Wilson,* 1894.

1,583. I think night-time is dark so you can imagine your fears with less distraction.
- **Bill Watterson:** *The Indispensable Calvin and Hobbs,* 1992.

1,584. Whatever you fear most has no power – it is your fear that has the power.
 - **Oprah Winfrey:** *O Magazine.*

FEMINISM

1,585. Yes, it's a man's world, but we are all right because they're making a total mess of it. We're chipping away at their control, taking the parts we want. Some women think it's difficult, but it's not.
- **Cher**.

1,586. Women must try to do things that men have tried. When they fail then failure must be but a challenge to others'.
 - **Amelia Earhart:** quoted in *The Sound of Wings* by Mary S. Lovell, 1989.

1,587. Miss Jenkyns had the appearance of a strong-minded woman; although she would have despised the modern idea of women being equal to men. Equal indeed! She knew they were superior.
- **Elizabeth Gaskell:** *Cranford*, 1853.

1,588. A man's got to do what a man's got to do. A woman must do what he can't.
- **Rhonda Hansome**.

1,589. Women who seek to be equal with men lack ambition.
- **Timothy Leary**.

1,590. The seahorse might well be a symbol for the more extreme branches of woman's lib, because the female seahorse lays her eggs in the male pouch and then he has to carry eggs to term, go through labour pains and bear the babies.
- **Madeleine L'Engle:** *The Irrational Season*, 1977.

1,591. But the fundamental thing is that women are more like men than anything else in the world. They are human beings. This is the equality claimed and the fact is that it is persistently evaded and denied.
- **Dorothy L. Sayers:** *Unpopular Opinions: Twenty-One Essays*, 1946.

1,592. We hold these truths to be self-evident: that all men and women are created equal.
- **Elizabeth Cady Stanton**.

1,593. Remember, Ginger Rogers did everything Fred Astaire did, but she did it backwards and in high heels.
- **Bob Thaves**.

1,594. I myself have never been able to find out precisely what feminism is: I only know that people call me a feminist whenever I express sentiments that differentiate me from a door mat or a prostitute.
- **Rebecca West:** *The Clarion, November, 1913.*

1,595. Whatever women do they must do twice as well as men to be thought half as good. Luckily, this is not difficult.
- **Charlotte Whitton:** *Canada Month, June, 1963.*

FIELD SPORTS

1,596. Nothing makes a fish bigger than almost being caught.
- *anon*

1,597. Help me, O Lord, to catch a fish
So large that even I,
In boasting of it afterwards,
Shall have no need to lie.
— *anon: The Angler's Prayer,* quoted in *Prayers and Graces:A Little Book of Extraordinary Piety* collected by Allan M. Laing, 1944.

1,598 I don't want to participate in any sport that has an ambulance at the bottom of the hill!
- **Erma Bombeck:** *Aunt Erma's Cope Book,* 1985.

1,599. The biggest fish he ever caught were those that got away.
- **Eugene Field:** *Our Biggest Fish* in *Poems of Childhood,* 1904.

1,600. Killing among animals is limited to the need for food, and "dog eat dog" is a human perversion, for individuals of the same animal species almost never kill, much less consume, their own kind.
- **Sydney J. Harris**.

1,601. Some people are under the impression that all that is required to make a good fisherman is the ability to tell lies easily and without blushing; but this is a mistake.
- **Jerome K. Jerome:** *Three Men in a Boat,* 1889.

1,602. Fly fishing may be a very pleasant amusement; but angling or float fishing I can only compare to a stick and a string with a worm at one end and a fool at the other.
- Attributed to **Samuel Johnson** by Peter Hawker in his *Instructions to Young Sportsmen,* 1824.

1,603. It takes a good deal of physical courage to ride a horse. This, however, I have. I get it at about forty cents a flask, and take it as required.
- **Stephen Leacock:** *Literary Lapses,* 1910.

1,604. I always will remember, / 'Twas a year ago November, / I went out to hunt some deer, / On a morning bright and clear / I went and shot the maximum the game laws would allow; / Two game wardens, seven hunters and a cow.
- **Tom Lehrer:** *The Hunting Song.*

1,605. The hunter crouches in his blind, / 'Neath camouflage of every kind, / And conjures up a quacking noise / To lend allure to his decoys. / This grown-up man, with pluck and luck / Is hoping to outwit a duck.
- **Ogden Nash:** *The Best of Ogden Nash* selected by Linell Smith. 2007.

1,606. The fascination of shooting as a sport depends almost wholly on whether you are at the right or wrong end of the gun.
- **P. G. Wodehouse.**

FILMS

1,607. What I want in the cinema is something that can't possibly happen to me.
- **James Agate:** *Halliwell's Who's Who in the Movies, 3rd Edition,* 1970.

1,608. The British film industry is alive and well and living in Los Angeles.
- **Michael Caine:** *The Observer, March 20th, 1994.*

1,609. Real Life is scarier than any movie these days.
- **John Carpenter:** *Halliwell's Who's Who in the Movies, 3rd Edition,* 1970.

1,610. Because the eye is the most sensitive and dependable of our sense organs, the motion picture offers the widest, direct avenue to our emotions.
- **Walt Disney:** *Quotable Walt Disney* by Dave Smith, 2001.

1,611. Do you realize that they show movies these days that couldn't even get developed a few years ago?
- **Sam Ewing:** *The Wall Street Journal, 22/4/99.*

1,612. A good opening and a good ending make a good film provided they come close together.
- **Federico Fellini:** *Fellini Lexicon* by Sam Rohdie, 1992.

1,613. Movies are one of the bad habits that corrupted our century... They have slapped into the American mind more human misinformation in one evening than the Dark Ages could muster in a decade.
- **Ben Hecht:** quoted in his autobiography, *A Child of the Century,* 1954.

1,614. The length of the film should be directly related to the endurance of the human bladder.
- **Sir Alfred Hitchcock:** *Halliwell's Who's Who in the Movies,* 1970.

1,615. A good film is when the price of the admission, the dinner and the baby-sitter was well worth it.

- *ibid.*

1,616. The cinema, like the detective story, makes it possible to experience without danger all the excitement, passion and desirousness which must be suppressed in a humanitarian ordering of society.

- **C. G. Jung:** quoted in *Halliwell's Filmgoer's Book of Quotes,* 1978.

1,617. The British film industry is not dead – it's alive and well and it's called television.

- **Lord Angus J. MacDonald:** *Edinburgh Television Festival Guide, 1977.*

FOOD AND DRINK

1,618. An epicure dining at Crewe / Found a rather large mouse in his stew, / Said the waiter, "Don't shout and wave it about, / Or the rest will be wanting one too."
- *anon.*

1,619. I eat my peas with honey / And have done so all my life. / It makes the peas taste funny, / But it keeps them on the knife.
- *anon.*

1,620. Mexican restaurants slip high-octane beans into virtually everything they serve, including breath mints. It is not by mere chance that most of Mexico is located outside.
- **Dave Barry:** *Dave Barry is Not Making This Up*, 1995.

1,621. Without question, the greatest invention in the history of mankind is beer. Oh, I grant you that the wheel was a fine invention, but the wheel does not go nearly as well with pizza.
- **Dave Barry:** *Dave Barry in Cyberspace*, 1996.

1,622. A lot of people say, "I'm no good in the morning until I've had my coffee!" I'm no good in the morning even after I've had my coffee.
- **Robert Benchley:** *My Ten Years in a Quandary*, 1939.

1,623. Better a meal of vegetables where there is love than a fattened calf with hatred.
- **The Bible:** *Proverbs 15: 17 NIV*.

1,624. I wasna fou, but just had plenty.
- **Robert Burns:** *Death and Dr Hornbook*. NB Scots: <u>wasna</u> = was not: <u>fou</u> = full, tipsy.

1,625. The world's costliest coffee, at $130 a pound, is called kopi luwak. Essentially, it is the droppings of a marsupial that eats only the very best coffee beans. Plantation workers track them down and scoop their

precious poop.
- **Irena Chalmers:** *The Great Food Almanac: A Feast of Facts from A to Z.*

1,626. French wine growers fear that this year's vintage may be entirely spoiled due to the grape treaders' sit in.
- **Ronnie Corbett:** *The Two Ronnies.*(English Television Series)

1,627. Good food is always a trouble and it's preparation should be recognised as a labour of love.
- **Elizabeth David:** *The Oxford Dictionary of Quotations,* 2004.

1,628. You've had too much to drink when you feel sophisticated but can't pronounce it.
- **Sam Ewing:** *The Sun, July 27th, 1999.*

1,629. Don't drink that one for the road, unless you want a police car as a chaser.
- **Sam Ewing:** *The Sun, 7th September, 1999.*

1,630. Food is an important part of a balanced diet.
- **Fran Lebowitz:** *Metropolitan Life,* 1978.

1,631. Everything you see I owe to spaghetti.
- **Sophia Loren:** *An Uncommon Scold* by Abby Adams, 1989.

1,632. One day some years ago, I awoke to find myself washed up on a beach in Hawaii. I made a mental note never again to partake of happy hour at a waterfront bar in Seattle.
- **Patrick F. McManus:** *Rubber Legs,*1987.

1,633. One must eat to live, and not live to eat.
- **Moliere:** *The Miser,* 1668.

1,634. One of the very nicest things about life is the way we must regularly stop whatever it is we are doing and devote our attention to eating.
- **Luciano Pavarotti:** *Pavarotti, My Own Story,* 1982.

1,635. Strange to see how a good dinner and feasting reconciles everybody.
Samuel Pepys: *Diary,* 9th November, 1665.

1,636. Eat at pleasure, drink by measure.
- ***English Proverb.***

1,637. A meal without wine is like a day without sunshine.
- *Italian Proverb*.

1,638. A nickel will get you on the subway, but garlic will get you a seat.
- *Old New York Proverb*.

1,639. Vegetables are interesting but lack a sense of purpose when unaccompanied by a good cut of meat.
- **Susan L. Rattiner:** *Food and Drink,* 2003.

1,640. Eating is not merely a material pleasure. Eating well gives a spectacular joy to life and contributes immensely to goodwill and happy companionship. It is of great importance to morale.
- **Elsa Schiaparelli:** *Shocking Life,* 1954.

1,641. Even those for whom cooking is an oppressive chore or a source of self-doubting anxiety, acknowledge that a meal shared by friends and family is one of the bonding rituals without which the family, society even, can fall apart.
- **Antonia Till:** *Loaves and Fishes: Writers Writing on Food,* 1992.

FORGIVENESS

1,642. To err is human; to forgive, infrequent.
- **Franklin P. Adams**.

 1,643. I can forgive, but I cannot forget, is only another way of saying I will not forgive. Forgiveness ought to be like a cancelled note - torn in two, and burned up, so that it never can be shown against one.
 - **Henry Ward Beecher**.

1,644. Forgiveness is almost a selfish act because of its immense benefits to the one who forgives.
- **Lawana Blackwell:** *The Dowry of Miss Lydia Clark*, 1999.

1,645. Nothing brings families together faster than forgiveness... but most of us find forgiving hard. We associate it with weakness and losing, when, actually, the reverse is true.
- **Joyce Brothers:** *Parade Magazine, 2001*.

1,646. To be wronged is nothing unless you continue to remember it.
- **Confucius:** *Analects*, 5th century BC.

1,647. Once a woman has forgiven her man, she must not reheat his sins for breakfast.
- **Marlene Dietrich:** *Marlene Dietrich's ABC*, 1962.

1,648. The weak can never forgive. Forgiveness is the attribute of the strong.
- **Mahatma Gandhi:** *Laura Moncur's Motivational Quotations*.

1,649. "To forgive oneself" - ? No, that doesn't work: we have to *be forgiven*. But we can only believe this is possible if we ourselves can forgive.
- **Dag Hammarskjold:** *Markings*, 1964.

1,650. He who forgiveth, and is reconciled unto his enemy, shall receive his reward from God, for He loveth not the unjust doers.
 - **The Koran:** *Sura 42* in George Sale's translation, *1887.*

1,651. To fail to forgive is to destroy the bridge over which one day you may want to travel.
- **Ann Landers**.

1,652. Holding on to anger, resentment and hurt only gives you tense muscles, a headache and a sore jaw from clenching your teeth. Forgiveness gives you back the laughter and the lightness in your life.
- **Ann Landers:** *in answer to a viewer's question on a TV chat show held on October 27th , 2000.*

1.653. To be in a state of unforgiveness is to know hell, at least in a small way.
- **Madeleine L'Engle:** *A Stone for a Pillow*, 1986.

 1,654. We achieve inner health only through forgiveness – the forgiveness not only of others, but also of ourselves.
- **Joshua Loth Liebman:** *Peace of Mind,* 1946.

1,655. Forgiveness is not a gift for the other person; it is a purely selfish act that allows you to put the past behind you.
- **Stephanie Marston:** *The Divorced Parent,* 1994.

1,656. When you forgive, you in no way change the past - but you sure do change the future.
- **Bernard Meltzer.**

 1,657. Sincere forgiveness isn't coloured with expectations that the other person apologize or change. Don't worry whether or not they finally understand you. Love them and release them. Love feeds back truth to people in its own way and time.
- **Sara Paddison:** *The Hidden Power of the Heart,* 1994.

1,658. As long as we love, we can forgive.
- **Francois, Duc de La Rochefoucauld:** *Maxims,* 1665.

1,659. I strongly suggest to everyone... that you give up a lot of the hostility you carry around from petty disagreements with friends and colleagues... it really will make a difference in how you'll feel about yourself.
 - **Lewis B. Smedes:** *The Art of Forgiving,* 1997.

1,660. When we forgive we set a prisoner free and discover that the prisoner we set free is us.
- *ibid.*

1,661. How unhappy is he who cannot forgive himself.
- **Publilius Syrus:** *Moral Maxims,* 1st century BC.

FRIENDS AND FRIENDSHIP

1,662. In time, little friends may prove to be great friends.
- The moral of **Aesop's Fable:** *The Lion and the Mouse.*

1,663. True friendship exists when friends can sit, in silence, completely at ease and comfortable in one another's company.
- *anon.*

1,664. You are known by the friends you keep.
- *anon.*

1,665. Old friends and old wine are best.
- *anon.*

1666. Friendship isn't a big thing – it's countless little things.
- *anon.*

1,667. A faithful friend is a secure shelter; whoever finds one has found a treasure. A faithful friend is beyond price; his worth is more than money can buy.
- **The Apocrypha:** *Ecclesiasticus 6: 14 & 15 NIV.*

1,668. A faithful friend is an elixir of life. (An older translation has: "A faithful friend is the medicine of life.")
 - **The Apocrypha:** *Ecclesiasticu*s *6: 16a.*

1,669. Do not desert an old friend; a new one is not worth as much. A new friend is like new wine; you do not enjoy drinking it until it has matured.
- **The Apocrypha:** *Ecclesiasticus 9: 10 NEB.*

1,670. I keep my friends as misers do their treasure, because, of all the things granted us by wisdom, none is greater or better than friendship.
- **Pietro Aretino**.

1,671. Without friends no one would choose to live, though he had all other goods.
- **Aristotle:** *Nicomachean Ethics*, 4th century BC.

1,672. The worst solitude is to be destitute of sincere friendship.
- **Francis Bacon:** *Essays*, 1625.

1,673. From quiet homes and first beginnings, / Out to the undiscovered ends, / There's nothing worth the wear of winning, / But laughter and the love of friends.
- **Hilaire Belloc:** *Dedicatory Ode*, 1910.

1,674. False friends are like our shadow, keeping close to us while we walk in the sunshine, but leaving us the instant we cross into the shade.
- **Christian Nestell Bovee:** *Intuitions and Summaries of Thought*, 1862

1,675. When you are sick, friends can sometimes be a better medicine than the kind the doctor gives you.
- Julie Anne, age 12 in *Wit & Wisdom from the Peanut Butter Gang* by **H. Jackson Brown**, 1994.

1,676. If you have true friends, you can get through anything.
- Jessica, age 15 *ibid.*

1,677. Do not keep the alabaster box of your friendship sealed up until your friends are dead. Fill their lives with sweetness. Speak approving, cheering words while their ears can hear them, and while their hearts can be thrilled and made happier. The kind of things you mean to say when they are gone, say before they go.
- **George W. Childs.**

1,678. Treat your friends as you do your pictures and place them in their best light.
- **Lady Randolph Churchill:** *Small Talks on Big Subjects*, 1916.

1,679. True friendship is like sound health, the value of it is seldom known until it be lost.
- **Charles Caleb Colton:** *Lacon Or Many Things in Few Words Addressed To Those who Think*, 1826, edited by George J. Barbour, 2001.

1,680. A friend is someone with whom you dare to be yourself.
- **Frank Crane:** *Four Minute Essays.*

1,681. Chance makes our relatives, we choose our friends.
- **Jacques Delille:** *Pitie*, 1802.

1,682. It's the friends you can call up at four a.m. that matter.
- **Marlene Dietrich**.

1,683. The only way to have a friend is to be one.
- **Ralph Waldo Emerson:** *Essays, First Series*, 1841.

1,684. A friend is a person with whom I may be sincere. Before whom I can think aloud.
- *ibid.*

1.685. The glory of friendship is not the outstretched hand, nor the kindly smile, nor the joy of companionship. It is the spiritual inspiration that comes to one when you discover that someone else believes in you and is willing to trust you with a friendship.
- **Ralph Waldo Emerson:** *Letters and Social Aims*.

1,686. Of all the means which wisdom acquires to ensure happiness throughout the whole life, by far the most important is friendship.
- **Epicurus:** *Principle Doctrines of Epicurus* translated by Robert D. Hicks.

1,687. Your best friends are those who speak well of you behind your back.
- **Sam Ewing:** *National Enquirer, July 16th, 1996*.

1,688. There are three faithful friends - an old wife, an old dog, and ready money.
- **Benjamin Franklin:** *Poor Richard's Almanack*, 1738.

1,689. An open foe may prove a curse / But a pretended friend is worse.
- **John Gay:** *Fables*, 1738.

1,690. Time is the only yardstick by which I can judge who are - and who aren't - really friends.
- **J. Paul Getty:** quoted by the American journalist Alden Whitman in Getty's obituary notice in *The New York Times, 6th June, 1976*.

1,691. In the sweetness of friendship let there be laughter and sharing of pleasures.
- **Khalil Gibran:** *The Prophet, chapter 19, On Friendship*, 1923.

1,692. True friendship multiplies the good life and divides its evils. Strive to have friends, for life without friends is like life on a desert island... to find one real friend in a lifetime is good fortune, to keep him is a blessing.
- **Baltasar Gracian:** *The Art of Worldly Wisdom*, 1647.

1,693. Every deed and every relationship is surrounded by an atmosphere of silence. Friendship needs no words – it is solitude delivered from the anguish of loneliness.
- **Dag Hammarskjold:** *Markings*, 1964.

1,694. Don't flatter yourself that friendship authorizes you to say disagreeable things to your intimates. The nearer you come into relation with a person, the more necessary do tact and courtesy become.
- **Oliver Wendell Holmes:** *The Autocrat at the Breakfast Table*, 1858.

1,695. A friend is one who knows you and loves you just the same.
- **Elbert Hubbard:** quoted in *Geary's Guide to the World's Great Aphorists* by James Geary, 2007.

1,696. Wherever you are it is your friends who make your world.
- **William James**.

1,697. If a man does not make new acquaintances as he advanced through life, he will soon find himself alone. A man, Sir, should keep his friendship in constant repair.
- **Samuel Johnson:** *Boswell's Life of Johnson*, 1755.

1,698. A true friend is one who overlooks your failures and tolerates your success.
- **Doug Larson**.

1,699. A cheerful friend is like a sunny day which sheds its brightness on all around.
- **John Lubbock**.

1,700. It is important to our friends to believe that we are unreservedly frank with them, and important to friendship that we are not.
- **Mignon McLaughlin:** *The Neurotic's Notebook*, 1960.

1,701. The best way to keep your friends is not to give them away.
- **Wilson Mizner:** quoted in *The Treasury of Humorous Quotations* edited by Evan Esar, 1955.

1,702. Care is the ingredient that keeps true friendships alive despite separation, distance, or time. Care gives latitude to another person and gets you past the dislikes and annoyances. Quite simply, caring sustains love.
- **Sara Paddison:** *The Hidden Power of the Heart*, 1994.

1,703. Few friendships would remain if each knew what his friend said of him when he wasn't there.
- **Blaise Pascal:** *Pensees*, 1670.

1,704. We need old friends to help us to grow old and new friends to help us stay young.
- **Letty Cottin Pogrebin:** *Among Friends*, 1986.

1,705. A broken friendship may be solder'd, but will never be sound.
- ***English Proverb.***

1,706. A friend is best found in adversity.
- ***English Proverb.***

1,707. To have a friend who knows you by name gives you a sense that you are not alone in the world.
- **Eleanor Roosevelt:** *Eleanor: The Years Alone* by J. P. Lassch, 1972.

1,708. A friend should bear his friend's infirmities.
- **William Shakespeare:** *Julius Caesar*, 1599.

1,709. The friends thou hast, and their adoption tried, Grapple them to thy soul with hoops of steel.
- **William Shakespeare:** *Hamlet*, 1601.

1,710. So long as we are loved by others I should say that we are almost indispensable, and no man is useless while he has a friend.
- **Robert Louis Stevenson:** *Lay Morals and Other Papers*, 1892.

1,711. Admonish your friends in secret, praise them openly.
- **Publilius Syrus:** *Moral Maxims*, 1st century BC.

1,712. Friends broaden our horizons. They serve as new models with whom we can identify. They allow us to be ourselves and accept us that way... we matter to them, and because they matter to us... they enrich the quality of our emotional life.
- **Judith Viorst:** *Necessary Losses: The Loves, Illusions, Dependencies and Impossible Expectations That All of Us Have to Give Up in Order to Grow*, 1987.

1,713. Close friends contribute to our personal growth. They also contribute to our personal pleasure, making the music sound sweeter, the wine taste richer, the laughter ring louder because they are there.
- *ibid.*

1,714. Things are never quite so scary when you've got a best friend.
- Calvin in *The Indispensable Calvin and Hobbs* by **Bill Watterson**, 1992.

1,715. Every one of us gets through the tough times because somebody is there, standing in the gap to close it for us.
- **Oprah Winfrey:** *O Magazine.*

FUNERALS

1,716. Funerals are very expensive, that's why people rarely have them until the last minute.
- *anon.*

1,717. The last wishes of a hen-pecked husband of a house-proud Edinburgh lady was that he be cremated and his ashes scattered over her living room carpet.
- *anon.*

1,718. If it looks like a lot of people aren't going to show up for my funeral, hold it in a phone booth so it'll look crowded.
- **Erma Bombeck:** *A Marriage Made in Heaven*, 1994.

1,719. In life one has to go to the funerals of the people we like and the birthdays of those we don't.
- **Wieslaw Brudzinski:** quoted in *Geary's Guide to the World's Great Aphorists* by James Geary, 2007.

1,720. At my age flowers scare me.
- **George Burns**.

1,721. No man should be afraid to die who hath understood what is is to live.
- **Thomas Fuller:** *Gnomologia*, 1732.

1,722. Anything awful makes me laugh. I misbehaved once at a funeral.
- **Charles Lamb:** *Letter to Robert Southey*, 1815.

1,723. We usually meet all our relatives only at funerals where someone always observes: "Too bad we can't get together more often."
- **Sam Levinson**.

1,724. The grave is but a covered bridge
Leading from light to light, through a brief darkness.
- **Henry Wadsworth Longfellow:** *The Golden Legend*, 1851.

1,725. No matter how rich you become, how famous or powerful, when you die the size of your funeral will still pretty much depend on the weather.
- **Michael Pritchard**.

1,726. An old man who was dying asked his wife if she would be willing to sit beside his sister at his funeral. His wife, who could not stand her sister-in-law, grudgingly agreed.

"But I hope you realize," she added, "that it will completely spoil my day."
- **James A Simpson:** *The Laugh Shall be First,* 1998.

1,727. Why is it that we rejoice at a birth and grieve at a funeral? Is it because we are not the person concerned?
 - **Mark Twain:** *Pudd'nhead Wilson,* 1894.

GAMBLING

1,728. I used to be a heavy gambler. But now I just make mental bets. That's how I lost my mind.
- **Steve Allen**.

1,729. The urge to gamble is so universal and its practice so pleasurable that I assume it must be evil.
- **Heywood Hale Broun:** quoted in *2,715 One-Line Quotations for Speakers, Writers and Raconteurs* by Edward F. Murphy, 1981.

1,730. I joined Gamblers Anonymous. They gave me two to one I don't make it.
- **Rodney Dangerfield**.

1,731. Money can be lost in more ways than won.
- **Sam Ewing:** *Mature Living, March, 1997*.

1,732. Gambling away the rent money is a moving experience.
- **Leopold Fechtner:** *5,000 One-And-Two-Line Jokes*, 1973.

1,733. Horse sense is the thing a horse has which keeps it from betting on people.
- **W. C. Fields**, *attributed*.

1,734. The only man who makes money following the horses is the one who does it with a broom and shovel.
- **Elbert Hubbard**.

1,735. The safest way to double your money is to fold it over and put it in your pocket.
- **Kin Hubbard**.

1,736. Man is a gambling animal. He must be always trying to get the better in something or other.
- **Charles Lamb:** *Essays of Elia*, 1878.

1,737. I backed this horse at twenty to one – and it came in at twenty-five past four.
- **Fred Metcalf:** *The Penguin Dictionary of Jokes*, 1993.

1,738. *Gambling:* The only certain way of getting nothing for something.
- **Wilson Mizner:** quoted in *Leo Rosten's Book of Laughter*, 1986.

1,739. The best throw of the dice is to throw them away.
- ***English Proverb.***

1,740. A wager is a fool's argument.
- ***English Proverb.***

1,741. Show me a gambler and I'll show you a loser.
- **Mario Puzo:** *Fools Die*, 1975.

1,742. No horse can go as fast as the money you put out on her.
- **Earl Wilson.**

1,743. Strip Poker is the only game in which the more you lose, the more you have to show for it.
- **Henny Youngman:** *The Best Little Book of One-Liners*, 1992.

GARDENS AND GARDENING

1,744. Gardeners all share a love of natural beauty and a passion to create order, however briefly, from chaos.
- **Diane Ackerman:** *Cultivating Delight: a Natural History of my Garden.*

1,745. For the worldwide regiment of gardeners, reveille sounds in Spring, and from then on its full parade march, pomp and circumstance, and ritualized tending until Winter.
- *ibid*, 2001.

1,746. A garden is a friend you can visit any time.
- *anon.*

1,747. God made rainy days so gardeners could get the housework done.
- *anon.*

1,748. A garden is a thing of beauty and a job forever.
- *anon.*

1,749. I've had enough of gardening – I'm just about ready to throw in the trowel.
- *anon.*

1,750. The earth and the sky / Conspire to grow it / And you and I / Perspire to mow it.
- **Richard Armour:** *Grass* in *An Armoury of Light Verse*, 1964.

1,751. God Almighty first planted a garden, and, indeed, it is the purest of human pleasures.
- **Francis Bacon:** *Essays*, 1625.

1,752. Build houses and settle down; plant gardens and eat what they produce.
- **The Bible:** *Jeremiah 29: 5 NIV.*

1,753. To cultivate a garden is to walk with God. To go hand in hand with nature in some of her most beautiful processes. -
- **Christian Nestell Bovee:** *Intuitions and Summaries of Thought*, 1862.

1,754. The best way to enjoy a beautiful, productive garden is to live next door to one, and cultivate your neighbour.
- **Jacob M. Braude:** *Braude's Treasury of Wit & Humour for all Occasions.*

1,755. The easiest way to tell the difference between young plants and weeds is to pull up everything. If they come up again, they are weeds.
- *ibid*, 1991.

1,756. Earth's crammed with heaven, / And every common bush afire with God; / But only he who sees, takes off his shoes; / The rest sit round and pluck blackberries.
- **Elizabeth Barrett Browning:** *Aurora Leigh*, 1857.

1,757. If you have a garden and a library, you have everything you need.
- **Cicero.**

1,758. The process of weeding can be as beneficial to the gardener as to the garden. It gives scope to the aggressive instinct – what satisfaction to pull up an enemy by the roots and throw him into a heap; and yet, paradoxically, weeding is the most peaceful of any outside task.
- **Bertha Damon:** *A Sense of Humus*, 1943.

1,759. Till to my garden back I come, / Where bumble-bees for hours and hours / Sit on their soft, fat, velvet bums, / To wriggle out of hollow flowers.
- **W. H. Davies:** *All in June*, in *Collected Poems of William H. Davies*, 1921.

1,760. Gardens are a form of autobiography.
- **Sydney Eddison:** *Horticulture Magazine, August/September, 1993.*

1,761. A perfect June day is when the sun is shining, a soft breeze is blowing, birds are singing, and the lawn mower is broken.
- **Sam Ewing:** *Mature Living.*

1,762. They now have a book on gardening called *Weeder's Digest.*
- **Leopold Fechtner:** *Encyclopedia of Ad-Libs, Crazy Jokes, etc*, 1977.

1,763. Gardening is civilizing. Finding ways to enhance and control nature, creating works of art, imagination and colour – it's not surprising that women make great gardeners.
- **Anna Ford:** *Life's Lessons* in *Saga Magazine, May, 2008.*

1,764. You can't make an instant garden, any more than an instant child. You have to watch and nurture plants, move them into the right position and soil, sun and shade. It's a long-term attachment.
- *ibid.*

1,765. Her crop was a miscellany / When all was said and done, / A little bit of everything, / And a great deal of none.
- **Robert Frost:** *A Girl's Garden*, in *Mountain Interval*, 1916.

1,766. He that plants trees, loves others besides himself.
- **Thomas Fuller:** *Gnomologia: Adages and Proverbs*, 1732.

1,767. The kiss of the sun for pardon, / The song of the birds for mirth, / One is nearer God's heart in a garden / Than anywhere else on earth.
- **Dorothy Frances Gurney:** *God's Garden* in *Family Book of Best Loved Poems*, edited by David L.George, 1952.

1,768. Experience teaches that love of flowers and vegetables is not enough to make a man a good gardener. He must also hate weeds.
- **Burton Hillis:** *The Toastmaster's Treasure Chest* by Herbert V. Prochnow and Herbert V. Prochnow Jr: 1979.

1,769. All gardeners live in beautiful places because they make them so.
- **Joseph Joubert**.

1,770. Our England is a garden, and such gardens are not made By singing: "Oh, how beautiful!" and sitting in the shade.....

And when your back stops aching and your hands begin to harden,
You will find yourself a partner in the Glory of the Garden.
- **Rudyard Kipling:** *The Glory of the Garden* in *A School History of England* by C.R.L. Fletcher and Rudyard Kipling, 1911. NB The full text of this poem is available on the internet at:
www.kipling.org.uk/poems_garden.

1,771. My neighbour asked if he could use my lawnmower and I told him of course he could, so long as he didn't take it out of my garden.
- **Eric Morecombe**.

1,772. People from a planet without flowers would think we must be mad with joy the whole time to have such things about us.
- **Iris Murdoch:** *A Fairly Honourable Defeat,* 1970.

1,773. Anyone who thinks that gardening begins in the Spring and ends in the Fall is missing the best part of the whole year. For gardening begins in January, beginning with the dream.
- **Josephine Nuese:** *The Country Garden,* 1970.

1,774. Pleasure for one hour, a bottle of wine. Pleasure for one year, a marriage. Pleasure for a lifetime, a garden.
- ***Chinese Proverb.***

1,775. More grows in the garden than the gardener sows.
- ***Old Spanish Proverb.***

1,776. A garden is always a series of losses set against a few triumphs, like life itself.
- **May Sarton.**

1,777. To own a bit of ground, to scratch it with a hoe, to plant seeds and watch their renewal of life, this is the commonest delight of the race, the most satisfying thing a man can do.
- **Charles Dudley Warner:** *My Summer in a Garden,* 1870.

GENEROSITY

1,778. You will make all kinds of mistakes, but as long as you are generous and true..... you cannot hurt the world or even seriously distress her.
- **Sir Winston Churchill:** *My Early Life. A Roving Commission* 1930.

1,779. Be kind whenever possible. It is always possible.
- Tenzin Gyatso, the 14ᵗʰ **Dalai Lama**.

1,780. I'm sorry, my good fellow, but all my money is tied up in currency.
- **W.C. Fields:** quoted in *The Funniest Thing You Never Said* by Rosemary Jarski, 2004.

1,781. As you grow older, you will discover that you have two hands, one is for helping yourself, the other is for helping others.
- **Audrey Hepburn**.

1,782. Remember that there is no happiness in having or in getting, but only in giving. Reach out. Share. Smile. Hug. Happiness is a perfume you cannot pour on others without getting a few drops on yourself.
- **Og Mandino**.

1,783. Give yourself entirely to those around you. Be generous with your blessings. A kind gesture can reach a wound that only compassion can heal.
- **Steve Maraboli:** quoted in *Life, the Truth, and Being Free*, 2009.

1,784. A small gift is better than a great promise.
- ***German Proverb***.

1,785. Think of giving not as a duty but as a privilege .
- **John D. Rockefeller Jr**.

1,786. Since you get more joy out of giving joy to others, you should put a good deal of thought into the happiness that you are able to give.
- **Eleanor Roosevelt**.

1,787. The purpose of human life is to serve and to show compassion and the will to help others.
- **Albert Schweitzer:** quoted in *The Scheitzer Album. A Portrait in Words and Pictures* by Erica Anderson, 1965.

1,788. We should give as we would receive, cheerfully, quickly, and without hesitation, for there is no grace in a benefit that sticks to the fingers.
- **Seneca**.

1,789. Do all the good you can,/ By all the means you can./ In all the ways you can/In all the places you can,/ At all the times you can./ To all the people you can/As long as ever you can/
- **John Wesley:** This statement, known as *John Wesley's Rule,* has long been attributed to Wesley, however, there is no evidence that he wrote it.

GIFTS AND GIVING

1,790. The best gifts are invariably tied with heartstrings.
- ***anon***.

1,791. The best thing to give your enemy is forgiveness; to an opponent tolerance; to a friend your heart; to your child a good example; to a father deference; to your mother, conduct that will make her proud of you; to yourself respect; and to all men charity.
- **Lady Frances Balfour**.

1,792. Blessed are those who give without remembering and take without forgetting.
- **Elizabeth Bibesco:** *Haven,* a collection of stories, poems and aphorisms published in 1951, six years after her death.

1,793. When it comes to giving, some people stop at nothing
- **Jacob M. Braude:** *Braude's Treasury of Wit and Humour for all Occasions,* 1991.

1,794. The trouble with some folks who give until it hurts is that they are so sensitive to pain.
- ***ibid***.

1,795. Generosity lies less in giving much than in giving at the right moment.
- **Jean de La Bruyere:** *Les Caracteres,* 1688.

1,796. When you have told anyone you have left him a legacy the only decent thing to do is to die at once.
- **Samuel Butler:** *Samuel Butler: A Memoir* by Henry Festing Jones, 1919.

1,797. He that gives quickly, gives twice.
- **Miguel de Cervantes:** *Don Quixote,* 1619

1,798. To have and not to give is often worse than stealing.
- **Marie von Ebner-Eschenbach:** *Aphorisms*, 1893.

1,799. What do you give a man who has everything ? - A burglar alarm.
- **Leopold Fechtner:** *5,000 One-And-Two-Line Jokes*, 1973.

1,800. You give but little when you give of your possessions. It is when you give of yourself that you truly give.
- **Kahlil Gibran:** *The Prophet*, 1923.

1.801. I have come to believe that giving and receiving are really the same. Giving and receiving - not giving and taking.
- **Joyce Grenfell:** *Joyce Grenfell Requests the Pleasure*, 1976.

1,802. People who think they're generous to a fault usually think that's their only fault.
- **Sydney J. Harris:** *On the Contrary*, 1964.

1,803. Presents, I often say, endear absents.
- **Charles Lamb:** *Essays of Elia*, 1818.

1,804. Not what we give, but what we share. / For the gift without the giver is bare.
- **James Russell Lowell:** *The Vision of Sir Launfal*, 1848.

1,805. Nobody is ever impoverished through the giving to charity.
- **Maimonides**.

1,806. When you give of yourself, something new comes into being. Two people, who, moments before, were trapped in separate worlds of private cares, suddenly meet each other over a simple act of sharing; warmth, even joy, is created. The world expands, a bit of goodness is brought forth and a small miracle occurs.
You must never underestimate this miracle. Too many good people think they have to become Mother Teresa or Albert Schweitzer, or even Santa Claus, and perform great acts if they are to be givers. They don't see the simple openings of the heart that can be practised anywhere with almost anyone.
- **Kent Nerburn:** *Letters to My Son: A Father's Wisdom on Manhood, Life and Love*, 1994.

1,807. If you have much, give of your wealth; if you have little, give of your heart.
- *Arabic Proverb.*

1,808. He gives twice that gives in a trice.
- *English Proverb.*

1,809. I believe the greatest gift I can conceive of having from anyone is to be seen by them, heard by them, to be understood and touched by them. The greatest gift I can give is to see, hear, understand and touch another person. When this is done I feel contact has been made.
- **Virginia Satir:** *Making Contact,*1976

1,810. He doubly benefits the needy who gives quickly.
- **Publilius Syrus:** *Moral Maxims,* 1st century, BC.

1,811. The excellence of a gift lies in its appropriateness rather than its value.
- **Charles Dudley Warner:** *Backlog Studies*, 1873.

1,812. He asked for an oriental rug for his birthday, and his wife got him a toupee that was made in Hong Kong.
- **Pat Williams:** *Winning With One-Liners*, 2002.

GOALS

1,813. If you aim at nothing, you'll hit it every time.
- ***anon***.

1,814. We must have a theme, a goal, a purpose to our lives, if you don't know where you're aiming, you don't have a goal. My goal is to live my life in such a way that when I die, someone can say, she cared.
- **Mary Kay Ash**.

1,815. Give yourself something to work towards – constantly.
- **Mary Kay Ash**.

1,816. A good goal is like strenuous exercise – it makes you stretch.
- **Mary Kay Ash**.

1,817. The achievement of one goal should be the starting point for another.
- **Alexander Graham Bell**.

1,818. Forgetting what is behind and straining towards what is ahead, I press on towards the goal to win the prize for which God has called me heavenwards in Christ Jesus.
- **The Bible:** *Philippians 3: 13b – 14 NIV*.

1,819. Ah, but a man's reach should exceed his grasp,/Or what's a heaven for?
- **Robert Browning:** *Andrea del Sarto* in *Men and Women*, 1855.

1,820. Beware what you set your heart upon. For it shall surely be yours.
- **Ralph Waldo Emerson:** quoted in *Inspiration and Motivation* by Alfred Armand Montapert, 1982.

1,821. The important thing in life is to have a great aim and to possess the aptitude and perseverance to attain it.
- **Johann Wolfgang von Goethe:** quoted in *The Speaker's Treasury of Stories for all Occasions* by Herbert V. Procknow, 1953.

1,822. Never look down to test the ground before taking your next step: only he who keeps his eyes fixed on the far horizon will find his right road.
- **Dag Hammarskjold:** *Markings* 1964.

1,823. A goal is a dream with a deadline.
- **Napoleon Hill**.

1,824. Establishing goals is all right if you don't let them deprive you of interesting detours.
- **Doug Larson**.

1,825. All who have accomplished great things have had a great aim, have fixed their gaze on a goal which was high, and one which sometimes seemed impossible.
- **Orison Swett Marden**.

1,826. It must be borne in mind that the tragedy of life does not lie in not reaching your goal. The tragedy of life lies in having no goal to reach.
- **Benjamin E. Mays**.

1,827. In life, the FIRST thing you must do is decide what you really want. Weigh the costs and the results. Are the results worthy of the costs? Then make up your mind completely. Then go after your goals with all your might. You are living only when you are useful and accomplishing things.
- **Alfred Armand Montapert:** *Inspiration and Motivation,* 1982.

1,828. A goal without a plan is just a wish.
- **Antoine de Saint Exupery**.

1,829. If we do not know what port we're steering for, no wind is favourable.
- **Seneca:** quoted in *The Life You Were Born to Live: Finding Your Life Purposes* by Dan Millman, 1995.

1,830. The value of the goal lies in the goal itself, and therefore the goal cannot be attained unless it is pursued for its own sake.
- **Arnold Toynbee:** *A Study of History.* NB: This is the title of Toynbee's 12 volume magnum opus, finished in 1961.

1,831. The big secret in life is that there is no big secret. Whatever your goal, you can get there if you are willing to work.
- **Oprah Winfrey:** *O Magazine.*

GOD

1,832. If only God would give me some clear sign! Like making a large deposit in my name at a Swiss bank.
- **Woody Allen:** *Without Feathers,* 1972.

1,833. Some people treat God like a lawyer - they go to Him only when they are in trouble.
- ***anon***.

1,834. When we lose God, it is not God who is lost.
- ***anon***.

1,835. God does not ask your ability or your inability. He asks only your availability.
- **Mary Kay Ash.**

1,836. You have made us for yourself, O Lord, and our hearts are restless until they rest in you.
- **St. Augustine of Hippo:** *Confessions,* ***circa*** 397 AD.

1,837. Nobody talks so consistently about God as those who insist that there is no God.
- **Heywood C. Broun:** *Collected Edition of Heywood Broun* compiled by Heywood Broun, 1941.

1,838. Everyday people are straying away from church and going back to God.
- **Lenny Bruce:** *The Essential Lenny Bruce* edited by John Cohen, 1967.

1,839. If God does not exist, then everything is permitted.
- **Fyodor Dostoevsky:** *The Demons,* 1871.

1,840. One who truly has God will have him in all places, in the streets, and in the world, no less than in the church.
- **Meister Eckhart:** *Meister Eckhart, from Whom God Hid Nothing, Sermons, Writings and Sayings* edited by David O'Neal, 1996.

1,841. As wider skies broke on his view, / God greatened in his growing mind; / Each year he dreamed his God anew, / And left his older God behind.
- **Sam Walter Foss:** *A Greater God* in *Songs of the Average Man,* 1907.

1,842. God does not die on the day when we cease to believe in a personal deity, but we die on the day when our lives cease to be illumined by the steady radiance, renewed daily, of a wonder, the source of which is beyond all reason.
- **Dag Hammarskjold:** *Markings,* 1964.

1,843. I have never understood why it should be considered derogatory to the Creator to suppose that he has a sense of humour.
 - **Dean Inge:** *A Rustic Moralist,* 1937.

GOLF

1,844. Golf is a lot of walking, broken up by disappointment and bad arithmetic.
- *anon.*

1,845. If it goes to the right, it's a slice. If it goes to the left, it's a hook. If it goes straight up the fairway, it's a miracle.
- *anon.*

1,846. The Scots invented golf, it's said, / And also good malt whisky; / If wearied when the first is played, / The other keeps them frisky.
- *anon:* quoted in *A Little Book of Scottish Quotations* by J. D. Sutherland.

1,847. N is for *nineteenth*, the hole that's best,
And the reason some golfers play all the rest.
- **Richard Armour:** *Golf is a Four Letter Word*, 1962.

1,848. Although golf was originally restricted to wealthy, overweight Protestants, today it's open to anybody who owns hideous clothing.
- **Dave Barry:** *Stay Fit and Healthy Until You're Dead*, 1985.

1,849. The thought came to me that perhaps I could take up the violin and take a few lessons – purely as a personal hobby, you know. After all, man does not live by golf alone.
- **Jack Benny:** *Sunday Nights at Seven :The Jack Benny Story* with his daughter Joan, 1990.

1,850. Give me golf clubs, fresh air and a beautiful partner, and you can keep the clubs and the fresh air.
- *ibid.*

1,851. The prospective bride rushed up to the prospective groom on the first tee. The groom looked at her in all her bridal finery and said, "I told you- only if it rained!"
- **Milton Berle:** *Milton Berle's Private Joke File*, 1989.

1,852. Bob Hope is convinced Gerry Ford was the first person to make golf a contact sport. "When he yelled, 'Fore!' " said Hope, "you never knew if he was telling people to get out of the way or predicting how many spectators he was going to hit."
- **Jacob M. Braude:** *Braude's Treasury of Wit & Wisdom for all Occasions.*

1,853. Golf is not, on the whole, a game for realists. By its exactitudes of measurement it invites the attention of perfectionists.
- **Heywood Hale Broun:** *Tumultuous Merriment,* 1979.

1,854. A noted psychiatrist's wife asked him why he never let her play golf with him. "My dear," he admonished her, "there are three things a man must do alone: testify, die, and putt."
- **Bennett Cerf:** *The Laugh's on Me,* 1963.

1,855. Golf is an ineffectual attempt to direct an uncontollable sphere into an inaccessible hole with instruments ill-adapted to the purpose.
- **Lord Randolph Henry Spencer Churchill:** quoted in *The Golf Quotations Book* by Michael Hobbs, 1992.

1,856. The real reason the golf pro tells you to keep your head down is so you can't see him laughing at you.
- **Phyllis Diller**.

1,857. My golf is improving. Yesterday I hit a ball in one!
- **Leopold Fechtner:** *5,000 One-And-Two-Line Jokes,* 1973.

1,858. I know I am getting better at golf because I'm hitting fewer spectators.
- **Gerald Ford:** quoted in *The Penguin Dictionary of Modern Humorous Quotations* edited by Fred Metcalf, 1986.

1,859. Golf is like a love affair: if you don't take it seriously it's boring, and if you do, it breaks your heart.
- **Rod Funseth**.

1,860. You know why they call it golf, don't you ? Because all the good four-letter words were already taken.
- **Lewis Grizzard:** quoted in *The Penguin Dictionary of Modern Quotations* edited by Fred Metcalf, 1986.

1,861. Golf does strange things to other people... It makes liars out of honest men, cheats out of altruists, cowards out of brave men and fools out of everybody.
- **Milton Gross:** quoted in *Eighteen Holes in My Head* by Milton Gross and John Pierotti, 1959.

1,862. Golf is a game in which you yell, "Fore", shoot six, and write down five.
- **Paul Harvey:** quoted in *Quotable Business* by Louis E. Boone, 1999.

1,863. If you watch a game it's fun. If you play a game it's recreation. If you work at it, it's golf.
- **Bob Hope:** quoted in *The Readers Digest, October, 1958.*

1,864. If profanity had an influence on the flight of the ball, the game would be played far better than it is now.
- **Horace G. Hutchinson:** *Hints on the Game of Golf,* 1895.

1,865. Golf is assuredly a mysterious game. It would seem that if a person has hit a golf ball correctly a thousand times, he should be able to duplicate the performance at will. But this is certainly not the case.
- **Bobby Jones:** *The Golfer's Book of Wisdom, Common Sense and. Uncommon Genius from 101 Golfing Greats* by Grisswell Freeman, 1995.

1,866. On a recent survey, 80% of golfers admitted cheating. The other 20% lied.
- **Bruce Lansky**: *Golf is Just a Game! The Best Jokes and Cartoons About Golf* selected by Bruce Lansky, 1996.

1,867. My pro said, "Practice makes perfect." He lied.
- *ibid.*

1,868. Talking to a golf ball won't do you any good unless you do it while your opponent is teeing off.
- *ibid.*

1,869. The hardest shot is a mashie at ninety yards from the green, where the ball has to be played against an oak tree, bounces back into a sand trap, hits a stone, bounces on the green, and then rolls into the cup. That shot is so difficult I have only made it once.
- **Zeppo Marx:** *The Book of Golf Quotations* by Pat Sullivan, 1985.

1,870. Every day I try to tell myself this is going to be fun today. I try to put myself in a great frame of mind before I go out- then I screw it up with the first shot.
- **Johnny Miller:** quoted in *Golf Magazine, 1984.*

1,871. Golf combines two favourite American pastimes: taking long walks and hitting things with a stick.
- **P. J. O'Rourke**: *Modern Manners: An Etiquette Book for Rude People,* 1984.

1,872. I have a tip that can take five strokes off anyone's golf game. It's called an eraser
- **Arnold Palmer:** *Golf is Just a Game!* by Bruce Lansky, 1996.

1,873. Golf is a game where you sock the ball hard and (then) walk four feet.
- **Herbert Procknow:** quoted in *Golfing Wit: Quips and Quotes for the Golf Obsessed* by Aubrey Malone, 2007.

1,874. Golf is a fascinating game. It has taken me nearly forty years to discover that I can't play it.
- **Ted Ray:** *Golf: My Slice of Life,* 1972.

1,875. Golf is like bicycle shorts. It reveals a lot about people.
Rick Reilly: quoted in *Sports Illustrated, 1995.*

1.876. I guess there is nothing that will get your mind off everything like golf will. I have never been depressed enough to take up the game, but they say you can get so sore at yourself that you forget to hate your enemies.
- **Will Rogers:** *The Best of Will Rogers* by Bryan Sterling, 1979.

1.877. A willing but wanting lady golfer on a Kilmarnock municipal course was experiencing great difficulty making contact with the ball. After her third fresh air shot, she turned to the party of schoolboys who were waiting their turn and apologised for the delay. "That's all right missus," one boy replied, "we started our school holidays today."
- **Tom Shields:** *More Tom Shields' Diary Too,* 1993.

1.878. Golf is a good walk spoiled.
- **Mark Twain:** quoted in *Quotations for our Time* by Laurence J. Peter.

1,879. As one of his retirement gifts, we wanted to give him something that he could use playing golf. But we found out he already had a calculator
- **Pat Williams:** *Winning With One-Liners,* 2002.

1,880. He asked the caddy, "What do you think of my game?" He said, "It's okay, but I like golf better."
- *ibid.*

1,881. He cut ten strokes off his golf score. He didn't play the last hole.
- *ibid.*

1.882. Golf.... is the infallible test. The man who can go into a patch of rough alone, with the knowledge that only God is watching him, and play his ball where it lies, is the man who will serve you faithfully and well.
- **P. G. Wodehouse:** *Golf Without Tears*, 1922.

1,883. The least little thing upset him on the links. He missed short putts because of the uproar of butterflies in the adjoining meadows.
- *ibid.*

1,884. While they were content to peck cautiously at the ball, he never spared himself in his efforts to do it a violent injury.
- **P.G. Wodehouse:** *The Heart of a Goof,* 1926.

1.885. The best year of my life was when I was eleven. I got straight A's, had two recesses a day, and the cutist girl friend and won 32 tournaments that year. Everything's been downhill since.
- **Tiger Woods:** *Las Vegas Review-Journal, 2000.*

GOOD AND EVIL

1,886. No man or woman can really be strong, gentle and good, without the world being better for it, without somebody being helped and comforted by the very existence of that goodness.
- **Alan Alda**.

1,887. Live so that when people speak ill of you no one will believe it.
- *anon.*

1,888. Every man is a walking civil war; there is a constant battle between the higher and lower side of man; man is always torn between the desire for good and the desire for evil
- **William Barclay:** *The Letters to the Galations and Ephesians.*

1,889. Goodness is achieved not in a vacuum, but in the company of other men, attended by love.
- **Saul Bellow:** *Dangling Man,* 1944.

1,890. Turn from evil and do good; seek peace and pursue it.
- **The Bible:** *Psalm 34: 14, NIV.*

1.891. I have the desire to do what is good, but I cannot carry it out. For what I do is not the good I want to do; no, the evil that I do not want to do - this I keep on doing.
- **The Bible:** *Romans 7: 18b – 19, NIV.* CP: Matthew Arnold: "We do not what we ought, / What we ought not, we do" from *Empedocles on Etna and Other Poems,* 1852.

1,892. The love of money is a root of all kinds of evil.
- **The Bible:** *1st Timothy 6: 10, NIV.*

1,893. Man's inhumanity to man / Makes countless thousands mourn.
- **Robert Burns:** *Man Was Made to Mourn,* 1786.

1,894. The evil that is in the world almost always comes of ignorance, and good intentions may do as much harm as malevolence if they lack understanding.
 - **Albert Camus:** *The Plague,* 1947.

1,895. If you see what is right and fail to act on it, you lack courage.
- **Confucius:** *The Analects.* 5th century, BC.

1,896. What after all is a halo? It's only one more thing to keep clean.
 - **Christopher Fry:** *The Lady's Not For Burning, Act 1,* 1949.

1,897. Necessary evils are never necessary and always evil.
- **Taro Gold:** *Open Your Mind, Open Your Life,* A Book of Eastern Wisdom.

1,898. Evil is a fact not to be explained away, but to be accepted; and accepted not to be endured, but to be conquered. It is a challenge neither to our reason nor to our patience, but to our courage.
- **John Andrew Holmes Jr:** *Wisdom in Small Doses,* 1927.

1,899. Into the hands of every individual is given a marvellous power for good or evil – the silent, unconscious, unseen influence of his life. This is simply the constant radiation of what man really is, not what he pretends to be.
- **William George Jordan:** *Majesty of Calmness,* 1900.

THE GOOD LIFE

1,900. I commend the enjoyment of life, because nothing is better for a man... than to eat and drink and be glad. Then joy will accompany him in his work all the days of the life God has given him.
- **The Bible:** *Ecclesiastes 8; 15,NIV*

1,901. Can we ever have too much of a good thing?
- **Miguel de Cervantes:** *Don Quixote*, 1615.

1,902. The Good Life.
- **Charles Colson:** *Book Title*, 2005. NB What the good life involves is given in the sub-title: *Seeking Purpose, Meaning, and Truth in Your Life.*

1,903. The hardest arithmetic to master is that which enables us to count our blessings.
- **Eric Heffer:** *Reflections on the Human Condition*, 1973.

1,904. Thank you, dear God, for this good life and forgive us if we do not love it enough.
- **Garrison Keillor:** *State Fair*, a short story in *Leaving Home*,1987

1,905. There are three ingredients in the good life; learning, earning and yearning.
- **Christopher Morley:** recalled after his death, 28th March, 1957.

1,906. The good life is one inspired by love and guided by knowledge.
- **Bertrand Russell:** *What I Believe*, 1925.

1,907. The good life is using your signature strengths every day to produce authentic happiness and abundant gratification.
- **Martin E. P. Seligman:** *Authentic Happiness: Using the New Positive Psychology to Realize Your Potential for Lasting Fulfilment*, 2002.

1,908. Good health and good sense are two of life's greatest blessings.
- **Publilius Syrus:** *Moral Maxims*, 1st century BC.

GOSSIP

1,909. You can tell more about a person by what he says about others than you can by what others say about him.
- **Leo Aikman**.

1,910. A gossip is a person with a keen sense of rumour.
- *anon*.

1,911. Gossip needn't be false to be evil - there's a lot of truth that shouldn't be passed around.
- *anon*.

1,912. Conversation is an exercise of the mind; gossip is merely an exercise of the tongue.
- *anon*.

1,913. The best way to spread the most news in the least time is to disguise it as a secret.
- *anon*.

1,914. One sort of knowledge / Good to lack / Is what is said / Behind your back.
- **Richard Armour:** *Blessed Ignorance* in *An Armoury of Light Verse*, 1964

1,915. A gossip separates close friends.
- **The Bible:** *Psalm 16: 28b, NIV*.

1,916. *Gossip:* One who usually gets caught in their own mouth trap.
- **Jacob M. Braude:** *Braude's Treasury of Wit & Wisdom*, 1991.

1,917. Whispering tongues can poison truth.
- **Samuel Taylor Coleridge:** *Christabel, part 2* in *The Cambridge History of English and American Literature*, edited by A.W. Ward and A.R. Waller.

1,918. None are as fond of secrets as those who do not mean to keep them; such persons covet secrets, as a spend-thrift covets money, for the purpose of circulation.
- **Charles Caleb Colton:** *Lacon, or Many Things in Few Words*, 1826, edited by George J. Barbour, 2001.

1,919. I know that's a secret, for its whispered everywhere.
- **William Congreve:** *Love for Love, Act 3, Sc 3*, 1695.

1,920. A gossip is anybody who is not too busy to be a busybody.
- **Evan Esar:** *20,000 Quips and Quotes*, 1968.

1,921. We have all seen the whispering process, which sometimes seems to be the fastest and most effective means of communication known to man.
- **Richard L. Evans:** *Music and the Spoken Word*, a talk from *The Mormon Tabernacle Choir Broadcasts*.

1,922. A gossip is a person who can give you all the details without knowing any of the facts.
- **Leopold Fechtner:** *5,000 One-And-Two-Line Jokes*, 1979.

1,923. Three may keep a secret, if two of them are dead.
- **Benjamin Franklin:** *Poor Richard's Almanack*, 1735.

1,924. Gossip is mischievous, light and easy to raise, but grievous to bear and hard to get rid of.
- **Hesiod:** Greek poet, 8th century BC.

1,925. There is so much good in the worst of us, / And so much bad in the best of us, / That it hardly behoves any of us / To talk about the rest of us.
- **Edward Wallis Hoch:** *Marion (Kansas) Record*. NB This quotation has also been attributed to the American writer James Truslow Adams.

1,926. To repeat an unkind truth is just as bad as to invent a lie.
- **Elbert Hubbard:** *A Thousand and One Epigrams*, 2005.

1,927. Of course we women gossip on occasion. But our appetite for it is not as avid as a man's. It is in the boys' gyms... the club locker rooms, the panelled offices of business that gossip reaches its luxuriant flower.
- **Phyllis McGinley:** quoted in *Province of the Heart*, 1959.

1,928. Before you speak ask yourself if what you are going to say is true, is kind, is necessary, is helpful. If the answer is no, maybe what you are about to say should be left unsaid.
- **Bernard Meltzer:** *What's Your Problem?* (US Radio Advice Program).

1,929. There are two kinds of people who blow through life like a breeze,
And one kind is gossipers, and the other kind is gossipees.
- **Ogden Nash:** *I Have It On Good Authority* in *I'm a Stranger Here Myself.*

1,930. Another good thing about gossip is that it is within everybody's reach,
And it is much more interesting than any other form of speech.
- **Ogden Nash,** ***ibid***, 1938.

1,931. A cruel story runs on wheels, and every hand oils the wheels as they run.
- **Ouida:** the pen name of a prolific 19th century English romantic novelist.

1,932. The flying Rumours gather'd as they roll'd,
Scarce any Tale was sooner heard than told;
And all who told it, added something new,
And all who heard it, made enlargement too,
In ev'ry Ear it spread, on ev'ry Tongue it grew.
- **Alexander Pope:** *The Temple of Fame: a Vision in Verse*, 1715.

1,933. At ev'ry word a reputation dies.
- **Alexander Pope:** *The Rape of the Lock and Other Poems* edited by Martin Price, 2003.

1,934. Where there is whispering, there is lying.
- ***English Proverb***.

1,935. What you don't see with your eyes, don't witness with your mouth.
- ***Jewish Proverb***.

1,936. Whoever gossips to you will gossip about you.
- ***Spanish Proverb***.

1,937. No one gossips about other people's secret virtues.
- **Bertrand Russell:** *On Education,* 1926.

1,938. Who steals my purse, steals trash.....
But he that filches from me my good name,
Robs me of that which not enriches him,
And makes me poor indeed.
- **William Shakespeare:** *Othello, Act 3, Sc. 3.*

1,939. Conversation is three woman standing on the corner talking. Gossip is when one of them leaves.
- **Herb Shriner**.

1,940. Who only sees ill is worse than blind.
- **Sir Philip Sidney:** quoted in *Geary's Guide to the World's Great Aphorists* by James Geary, 2007.

1,941. I heard the story, bit by bit, from various people, and, as generally happens in such cases, each time it was a different story.
 - **Edith Wharton:** *Ethan Frome,* 1911.

1,942. My wife never repeats gossip. You've got to listen the first time she tells you.
- **Pat Williams:** *Winning with One-Liners,* 2002.

GOVERNMENT

1,943. There is no worse heresy than that the office sanctifies the holder.
- **Lord Acton**.

1,944. The basic natural right that a just society or government should try to secure - and aid and abet – for every individual is not, and cannot be, the right to happiness, but is rather the right to its pursuit.
 - **Mortimer J. Adler:** *The Time of our Lives: the Ethics of Common Sense,* 1970.

1,945. What we lack in government is entrepreneurial ability.
 - **Tony Benn:** *speech, London, 6th June, 1974.*

1,946. It is frightening but indisputable that the longer a government is in office, the more afraid of ideas it becomes- this is true of governments of all persuasions.
- **David Blunkett:** *Quotes of the Day,The Press and Journal, 17/ 10 / 2000.*

1,947. The very essence of a free government consists in considering offices as public trusts, bestowed for the good of the country, and not for the benefit of an individual or a party.
- **John C. Calhoun:** *speech, 13th February, 1835.*

1,948. All government is an ugly necessity.
- **G. K. Chesterton**: *A Short History of England,* 1917.

1,949. Governing a large country is like frying a small fish. Too much poking spoils the meat
 - **Tao Te Ching:** from a translation by J. H. McDonald, 1996.

1,950. Government is a trust, and the officers of the government are trustees; and both the trust and the trustees are created for the benefit of the people.
- **Henry Clay:** *speech, March, 1829.*

1,951. The administration of government lies in getting proper men.
- **Confucius:** *The Analects*, 5th century, BC.

1,952. If you would govern a state... be true to your word, be economical in expenditure and love the people.
- *ibid.*

1,953. No government can be long secure without a formidable opposition.
- **Benjamin Disraeli:** *Coningsby*, 1844.

1.954. In government, a "highly placed source" is the person who started the rumour.
- **Sam Ewing:** *The Wall Street Journal, 3rd March. 1993.*

1,955. Only government can take perfectly good paper, cover it with perfectly good ink and make the combination worthless.
- **Milton Friedman.**

1,956. It doesn't matter who you vote for, the government always gets in.
- **Graffiti**, London, 1970's.

1,957. Well, fancy giving money to the Government!
Might as well have put it down the drain.
Fancy giving money to the Government!
Nobody will see the stuff again.
- **Sir A. P. Herbert.**

1,958. The essence of government is power, and power, lodged as it must be in human hands, will ever be liable to abuse.
- **James Madison:** *speech at the Virginia State Convention of 1829.*

1,959. Remember the good old days, when the government lived within its income and without most of yours?
- **Mad Magazine:** *Mad:The Half-Wit and Wisdom of Alfred Neuman*, 1997.

1,960. Standing up to your government can mean standing up for your country.
- **Bill Moyers.**

1,961. Giving money and power to government is like giving whisky and car keys to teenage boys.
- **P. J. O'Rourke:** *Parliament of Whores*, 1991.

1,962. It is a popular delusion that the government wastes vast amounts of money through inefficiency and sloth. Enormous effort and elaborate planning are required to waste this much money.
- *ibid.*

1,963. The motive power for government machinery is supplied by the tax payer harnessed to a treadmill.
- **Herbert V. Prochnow and Herbert V. Prochnow Jr:** *The Public Speaker's Source Book*, 1977.

1,964. Government is like a baby - an alimentary canal with a big appetite at one end and no sense of responsibility at the other.
- **Ronald Reagan:** *The Reagan Wit* edited by Bill Adler *et al*, 1981.

GRATITUDE

1,965. Give thanks to the Lord, for he is good; his love endures forever.
- **The Bible:** *Psalm 118: 1, NIV.*

1,966. Some hae meat and canna eat, / And some wad eat that want it; / But we hae meat, and we can eat, / And sae the Lord be thankit.
- **Robert Burns:** the so-called *Selkirk Grace*, **circa** 1790. NB Scots: <u>hae</u> = have: <u>canna</u> = cannot: <u>sae</u> = so: <u>thankit</u> = thanked.

1,967. O Thou who kindly dost provide / For every creature's want! / We bless Thee, God of Nature wide, / For all Thy goodness lent: / And, if it please Thee, heavenly Guide, / May never worse be sent; / But, whether granted or denied, / Lord, bless us with content. Amen.
- **Robert Burns:** *A Grace Before Dinner, Extempore.*

1,968. Never in the field of human conflict was so much owed by so many to so few.
- **Sir Winston Churchill:** *speech, 20th August, 1940.*

1,969. There is no quality I would rather have, and be thought to have, than gratitude. For it is not only the greatest virtue, but is the mother of all the others.
- **Cicero:** *On Duties,* **circa** 44 BC.

1,970. If the only prayer you ever say in your entire life is, "Thank you," it will be enough.
- **Meister Eckhart.**

1,971. If we stopped to think more, we would stop to thank more.
- **Evan Esar:** *20,000 Quips and Quotes,* 1968.

1,972. If your wife doesn't treat you as she should, be thankful.
- *ibid.*

1,973. "Do you say your prayers before meals?" a minister asked a small boy. "No sir, I don't need to," replied the lad, "my mother is a good cook."
- **Sam Ewing:** *National Enquirer, 20th August, 1996.*

1,974. Catherine, I'm afraid you'll have to ask the blessing. The Lord knows I'm not grateful for turkey hash and I can't fool him.
- Rev. Dr Peter Marshal (played by Richard Todd) to his wife (played by Jean Peters) in the **1955 Film**: *A Man Called Peter.*

1,975. Ingratitude is always a sign of weakness. I have never observed that accomplished people were ungrateful.
- **Johann Wolfgang von Goethe:** *Art and Antiquity,* 1823.

1.976. Gratitude is a fruit of great cultivation; you do not find it among gross people.
- **Samuel Johnson:** *Journal of a Tour to the Hebrides,* 1773.

1,977. Gratitude preserves old friendship, and procures new.
- *English Proverb.*

1,978. Gratitude is the least of virtues, but ingratitude is the worst of vices.
- *English Proverb.*

1,979. He who receives a benefit with gratitude repays the first instalment on his debt.
- **Seneca:** *On Benefits,* 1st century BC.

1,980. God bless the cakes and bless the jam,
Bless the cheese and the cold boiled ham.
Bless the scones aunt Jenny makes,
And save us all from bellyaches.
- **Robert W. Service**. NB: At his sixth birthday party Robert Service asked if he might say grace. His childish effort on that occasion gave promise of greater things to come.

1,981. Down with your head / Up with your paws / Thank the good Lord / For the use of your jaws.
- **James A. Simpson:** *Holy Wit,* 1986.

1,982. Gratitude takes three forms: a feeling in the heart, an expression in words, and a giving in return.
- **John Wanamaker**.

1,983. Feeling gratitude and not expressing it is like wrapping a present and not giving it.
- **William Arthur Ward**.

1,984. God gave you a gift of 86,400 seconds today. Have you used one to say "thank you"?
- **William Arthur Ward**.

1,985. Keep a grateful journal. Every night, list five things that happened this day that you are grateful for. What it will begin to do is change your perspective on your day and your life. If you can learn to focus on what you have, you will always see that the universe is abundant and you will have more. If you concentrate on what you don't have, you will never have enough.
- **Oprah Winfrey:** *O Magazine*.

GRIEF AND BEREAVEMENT

1,986. There is no pain so great as the memory of joy in present grief.
- **Joseph Addison:** *Cato, a Tragedy, Act 4, Sc 1*, 1713.

1.987. The Lord is close to the broken-hearted.
- **The Bible:** *Psalm 34: 18a, NIV.*

1,988. Tearless grief bleeds inwardly.
- **Christian Nestell Bovee:** *Intuitions and Summaries of Thought.* 1862.

1,989. Tears are nature's lotion for the eyes. The eyes see better for being washed by them.
- *ibid.*

1,990. I have lost the one I love, I must now live in this terrible solitude where memory is torture.
- **Albert Camus:** *The Misunderstanding, Act 2, Sc 2*, 1944 .

1,991. There is no grief which time does not lessen and soften.
- **Cicero:** *Epistles.* 1st century BC.

1,992. The path of sorrow, and that path alone,
Leads to the land where sorrow is unknown.
- **William Cowper:** *To an Afflicted Protestant Lady* in *The Poetical Works of William Cowper, Vol 1*, 1859.

1,993. Grief is itself a med'cine.
- **William Cowper:** *Charity, ibid.*

1,994. Grief is the agony of an instant. The indulgence of grief is the blunder of a life.
- **Benjamin Disraeli:** quoted in *Geary's Guide to the World's Great Aphorists* by James Geary, 2007.

1,995. Natural affections must have their course. The best remedy of grief is time.
- **Benjamin Franklin:** *The Wit and Wisdom of Benjamin Franklin* edited by James C. Humes, 1995.

1,996. Death leaves a heartache no one can heal, love leaves a memory no one can steal.
 - **From a headstone in an Irish cemetery**.

1,997. For all pairs of lovers without exception, bereavement is a universal and integral part of our experience of love.
- **C. S. Lewis:** *A Grief Observed*, 1961.

1,998. The pain now is part of the happiness then. That's the deal.
- **C. S. Lewis**: *Shadowlands*, the 1985 television film written by William Nicolson, with Joss Ackland playing the part of Jack Lewis.

1,999. In this sad world of ours, sorrow comes to all; and to the young, it comes with bitterest agony. The older have learned to ever expect it.
- **Abraham Lincoln:** *in a letter dated 23rd December, 1832.* Quoted in *Collected Works of Abraham Lincoln* by Roy P. Basler, 1953.

2,000. There is no grief like the grief which does not speak!
- **Henry Wadsworth Longfellow:** *Hyperion, a Romance*, 1839.

2,001. When we lose one we love, our bitterest tears are called forth by the memory of hours when we loved not enough.
 - **Maurice Maeterlinck:** *Wisdom and Destiny* translated by A Sutro, 1899.

2,002. Shared joy is double joy. Shared sorrow is half sorrow.
- *Swedish Proverb*.

2,003. He that conceals his grief finds no remedy for it.
- *Turkish Proverb*.

2,004. Give sorrow words; the grief that does not speak whispers the o'er-fraught heart and bids it break.
 - **William Shakespeare:** *Macbeth, Act 4, Sc. 3*

2,005. The bitterest tears shed over graves are for words left unsaid and deeds left undone.
- **Harriet Beecher Stowe:** *Little Foxes*, 1866.

2,006. Grief is a whole cluster of adjustments, apprehensions, and uncertainties that strike life in its forward progress and make it difficult to redirect the energies of life.
- **Charles Swindoll:** *Growing Strong in the Seasons of Life,* 1988.

2,007. Not until we express our grief fully do we fully recover.
- **Charles Swindoll:** *The Strong Family,* 1991.

2,008. I hold it true, whate'er befall;
I feel it when I sorrow most.
'Tis better to have loved and lost,
Than never to have loved at all.
- **Alfred Lord Tennyson:** *In Memoriam,* 1850.

2,009. Tears are the silent language of grief
- **Voltaire:** *A Philosophical Dictionary.*

HABIT

2,010. The best way to break a bad habit is to drop it.
- **Leo Aikman**.

2,011. Bad habits are like a comfortable bed, easy to get into, but hard to get out of.
- *anon*.

2,012. Know the difference between instinct and habit. Trust your instincts- question your habits.
- *anon*: *quoted* in *Open Your Mind, Open Your Life. A Book of Eastern Wisdom* by Taro Gold, 2002.

2,013. Our character is basically a composite of our habits. Because they are consistent, often unconscious patterns, they constantly, daily, express our character.
- **Stephen Covey:** *The 7 Habits of Highly Effective People*, 1990.

2,014. Habits are safer than rules; you don't have to watch them. And you don't have to keep them either. They keep you.
- **Frank Crane:** *Four Minute Essays*.

2,015. Early to bed and early to rise, makes a man healthy, wealthy and wise.
- **Benjamin Franklin:** *Poor Richard's Almanack,* 1735. **CP**: James Thurber's parody in his *Fables for Our Time,* published in 1940: "Early to rise and early to bed makes a male healthy, wealthy and dead."

2,016. Cultivate only the habits that you are willing should master you.
- **Elbert Hubbard**.

2,017. Habit is... the enormous flywheel of society, its most precious conservative agent.
- **William James:** *The Principles of Psychology*, 1890.

2,018. The chains of habit are too weak to be felt until they are too strong to be broken.
 - **Samuel Johnson**.

2,019. Habit, with its iron sinews, clasps us and leads us day by day.
- **Alphonse de Lamartine**.

2,020. We are quite ignorant of the real power of our habits until we try to give them up.
 - **C. S. Lewis**: *in a letter to a friend dated 26th May, 1942*.

2,021. Habit is a cable; we weave a thread of it each day, and at last we cannot break it.
- **Horace Mann**.

2,022. It's just like magic. When you live by yourself, all your annoying habits are gone.
- **Merrill Markoe:** quoted in *Loose Cannons* by Autumn Stephens.

2,023. There was a young belle of old Natchez
Whose garments were always in patchez.
When comment arose
On the state of her clothes,
She drawled, When Ah itchez, Ah scratchez!
 - **Ogden Nash:** *Requiem* in *I'm a Stranger Here Myself,* 1939.

HAPPINESS

2,024. True happiness in life is found always within.
- ***anon***: *quoted* in *Open Your Mind, Open Your Life. A Book of Eastern Wisdom* by Taro Gold, 2002.

2,025. Remember this - very little is needed to make a happy life.
- **Marcus Aurelius:** *The Meditations*, 3rd century BC.

2,026. A large income is the best recipe for happiness I ever heard of.
- **Jane Austin:** *Mansfield Park*, 1814.

2,027. Happiness is the real sense of fulfilment that comes from hard work.
- **Joseph Barbara:** *Success Secrets of Super Achievers* by Jim Stovall, 1999.

2,028. Money can't buy happiness. It just helps you look for it in more places.
- **Milton Berle:** *Milton Berle's Private Joke File*, 1989.

2,029. A man doesn't know what true happiness is until he gets married. Then it's too late.
- ***ibid.***

2,030. All who joy would win / Must share it - happiness was born a twin.
- **Lord Byron:** *Don Juan*, 1824.

2,031. Happiness is not easily won; it is hard to find it in ourselves, and impossible to find it elsewhere.
- **Nicolas Chamfort:** *Maxims and Considerations* translated by E. Powys Mathers, 1926.

2,032. Happiness is a mystery, like religion, and should never be rationalized.
- **G. K. Chesterton:** *Heretics*, 1905.

2,033. The happiness of life is made up of minute fractions – the little, soon forgotten charities of a kiss, a smile, a kind look, a heartfelt compliment, and the countless infinitesimals of pleasurable and genial feeling.
- **Samuel Taylor Coleridge**.

2,034. Happiness, that grand mistress of the ceremonies in the dance of life, impels us through all its mazes and meanderings, but leads none of us by the same routes.
- **Charles Caleb Colton:** *Lacon, or Many Things in Few Words Addressed to Those Who Think,* 1826, edited by George J. Barbour, 2001.

2,035. My mother, who was a lovely person, had a saying that, "If you are unhappy, surround yourself with people who love you." Like most mothers, she was right.
- **Jilly Cooper:** *OK Magazine, 1995*.

2,036. Happiness seems made to be shared.
- **Pierre Corneille**.

2,037. Happiness depends, as Nature shows,
Less on exterior things than most suppose.
- **William Cowper:** *Table Talk and Other Poems,* 1782.

2,038. Happiness is always a by-product... it is not something that can be demanded from life.
 - **Robertson Davies:** *The Enthusiasms of Robertson Davies,* 1979.

2,039. If you will make a man happy, add not to his riches, but take away from his
desires.
- **Epicurus:** *The Meditations,* 3rd century BC.

2,040. If you do not have the capacity for happiness with a little money, great wealth will not bring it to you.
- **William Feather:** *The Business of Life,* 1949.

2,041. Plenty of people miss their share of happiness, not because they never found it, but because they didn't stop to enjoy it.
 - *ibid.*

2,042. My wife is so happy that I'm not perfect. She loves to nag.
- **Leopold Fechtner:** *5,000 One-And-Two-Line Jokes,* 1973.

2,043. Some people cause happiness wherever they go. Others whenever they go.
- *ibid.*

2,044. Is there a pleasure upon Earth to be compared with that which arises from the sense of making others happy ?
- **Benjamin Franklin:** *The Wit and Wisdom of Benjamin Franklin* edited by James C. Humes, 1995.

2,045. Happiness in this world depends on internals, not externals.
- *ibid.*

2,046. Story book happiness involved every form of pleasant thumb-twiddling; true happiness involved the full use of one's powers and talents.
- **John W. Gardner:** *Self - Renewal: the Individual and the Innovative Society*, 1963.

2,047. Looking for lasting happiness outside yourself is meaningless. It is like expecting to become fit by watching other people exercise.
- **Taro Gold:** *Open Your Mind, Open Your Life: A Little Book of Eastern Wisdom*, 2001.

2,048. Most people today fail to recognize that happiness is a fairly recent aspiration of the human race. For most of history, survival was the goal – coping, making do, struggling against the caprices of natural disasters and the blows of social and economic justice.
- **Sydney J. Harris:** *Clearing the Ground.* 1986.

2,049. What we need for our happiness is often close at hand, if we knew but how to seek for it.
- **Nathaniel Hawthorne:** *American Note Books*, 1837.

2,050. Happiness is watching the TV at your girl friend's house during a power failure.
- **Bob Hope:** quoted in *Women on Men / Men on Women: Love and Life with the Opposite Sex* edited by Barb Karg, 2007.

2,051. Get happiness out of your work or you may never know what happiness is.
- **Elbert Hubbard**.

2,052. The supreme happiness in life is the conviction that we are loved – loved for ourselves, or rather, loved in spite of ourselves.
- **Victor Hugo:** *Les Miserables,* 1862.

2,053. Happiness is not achieved by the conscious pursuit of happiness; it is generally the by-product of other activities.
- **Aldous Huxley:** *Vedanta for the Western World* by Christopher Isherwood, 1945.

2,054. Happiness is like a kiss. You must share it to enjoy it.
- **Bernard Meltzer**.

2,055. Happiness is having a scratch for every itch.
- **Ogden Nash:** *Jokes, Quotes and One-Liners,Vol 2* by Herbert V. Prochnow and Herbert V. Prochnow Jr, 1983.

2,056. The thirst after happiness is never extinguished in the heart of man.
- **The Confessions of Jean-Jacques Rousseau**; 1782.

2,057. To be happy with a man you must understand him a lot and love him a little. To be happy with a woman you must love her a lot and not try to understand her at all.
- **Helen Rowland:** *A Guide to Men,* 1922.

2,058. Of all forms of caution, caution in love is perhaps the most fatal to true happiness.
- **Bertrand Russell:** *Conquest of Happiness,* 1930.

2,059. Happiness is not having what you want, but wanting what you have.
- **Rabbi Hyman Judah Schachtel:** *The Real Enjoyment of Living,* 1954.

2,060. We have no more right to consume happiness without producing it than to consume wealth without producing it.
- **George Bernard Shaw:** *Candida,* 1898.

2,061. No man is happy who does not think himself so.
- **Publilius Syrus:** *Moral Maxims,* 1st century BC.

2,062. Seize the moments of happiness, love and be loved! That is the only reality in the world, all else is folly.
- **Leo Tolstoy:** *War and Peace,* 1865 – 1869

2,063. Happiness is an inside job.
- **William Arthur Ward**.

2,064. Happiness is being famous for your financial ability to indulge in every kind of excess.
- Calvin's sentiments in *The Authoritative Calvin and Hobbs*, by **Bill Waterson**, 1990.

2, 065. What good is happiness ? It can't buy you money.
 - **Henny Youngman:** *How Do You Like Me So Far?* 1963.

HATE

2,066. Lord, make me an instrument of your peace.
Where there is hatred let me sow love;
Where there is injury, pardon;
Where there is doubt, faith;
Where there is despair, hope;
Where there is darkness, light;
Where there is sadness, joy.
- **anon**, **circa**, 1912. NB The story behind this prayer – long attributed to St. Francis – is available on the Internet at:
 www.franciscan-archive.org/patriarcha/peace.html

2,067. Better a meal of vegetables where there is love than a fattened calf with hatred.
- **The Bible:** *Proverbs 15: 17, NIV.*

2,068. Hatred stirs up dissension, but love covers all wrongs.
- **The Bible:** *Proverbs 10: 12, NIV.*

2,069. The hatred you're carrying is a live coal in your heart – far more damaging to yourself than to them.
- **Lawana Blackwell:** *The Dowry of Miss Lydia Clark*, 1999.

2,070. Life appears to me too short to be spent in nursing animosity or registering wrongs.
- **Charlotte Bronte:** *Jane Eyre*, 1847.

2,071. In this world
Hate never yet dispelled hate,
Only love dispels hate.
- **Gautama Buddha:** *The Dhammapada*, 6th century, BC.

2,072. Heav'n has no rage like love to hatred turn'd,
Nor hell a fury like a woman scorned.
- **William Congreve:** *The Mourning Bride, Act 3, Sc 8*, 1697.

2,073. 'Tis strange how men find time to hate
When life is all too short for love.
- **W. H. Davies:** *Come, Let Us Find* in *Forty New Poems*, 1918.

2,074. There are glances of hatred that stab, and raise no cry of murder.
- **George Eliot:** *Felix Holt, the Radical,* 1866.

2,075. I never hated a man enough to give him diamonds back.
- **Zsa Zsa Gabor:** *The Observer, August 25, 1957.*

2,076. Hatred can be overcome only by love.
- **Mahatma Gandi,** *attributed*

2,077. Hate is like acid. It can damage the vessel in which it is stored as well as destroy the object on which it is poured.
- **Ann Landers:** *Bits and Pieces, September, 1992.*

2,078. No one is born hating another person because of the colour of his skin, or his background, or his religion. People must learn to hate, and if they can learn to hate, they can be taught to love, for love comes more naturally to the human heart than its opposite.
- **Nelson Mandela:** *A Long Walk to Freedom: the Autobiography of Nelson Mandela,* 1994.

2,079. Hate is not the opposite of love; apathy is.
- **Rollo May:** *Love and Will,* 1969.

2,080. Hate can only flourish where love is absent.
- **William C. Menninger.**

2,081. When our hatred is too fierce, it places us beneath those we hate.
- **Francois, Duc de la Rochefoucauld:** *Maxims,* 1665.

2,082. Throughout life people will make you mad
Disrespect you and treat you bad
Let God deal with the things they do
Cause hate in your heart will consume you too.
- **Will Smith:** *Just the Two Of Us,* 2001.

2,083. I learned the lesson that great men cultivate love, and that only little men cherish a spirit of hatred.
- **Booker T. Washington**: *Up From Slavery – The Autobiography of Booker T. Washington,* 1901.

2,084. I would permit no man, no matter what his colour might be, to narrow and degrade my soul by making me hate him.
- *ibid.*

2,085. I think that hate is a thing, a feeling, that can only exist where there is no understanding.
- **Tennessee Williams:** *Sweet Bird of Youth,* 1959.

HEALTH AND FITNESS

2,086. Cheerfulness is the best promoter of health and is as friendly to the mind as to the body.
- **Joseph Addison:** *The Spectator.*

2,087. Health and cheerfulness mutually beget each other.
- *ibid.*

2,088. Happiness gives us the energy which is the basis of health.
- **Henri-Frederic Amiel:** *Journal Intime,* 1882.

2,089. Fitness is a philosophy of life, a revolutionary new concept in personhood, and, ultimately, a way for people like me to become wealthy via the sales of fitness-related items such as this book.
- **Dave Barry:** *Dave Barry's Stay Fit and Healthy Until You're Dead,* 1989.

2,090. A cheerful heart is good medicine.
- **The Bible:** *Proverbs 17: 22a, NIV.*

2,091. There's a lot of people in this world who spend so much time watching their health that they haven't the time to enjoy it.
- **Josh Billings**.

2,092. The secret of health for both mind and body is not to mourn for the past, nor to worry about the future, but to live the present moment wisely and earnestly.
- **Gautama Buddha** (The authenticity of this quotation is in doubt)

2,093. The first wealth is health.
- **Ralph Waldo Emerson:** *The Conduct of Life,* 1860.

2,094. Health is not valued till sickness comes.
- **Thomas Fuller:** *Gnomologia; Adages and Proverbs,* 1732.

2,095. Everyone has a doctor in him or her; we just have to help it in its work. The natural healing force within each one of us is the greatest force in getting well.
- **Hippocrates.**

2,096. Walking is man's best medicine.
- **Hippocrates.**

2,097. Our food should be our medicine, our medicine should be our food.
- **Hippocrates.**

2,098. The wise man should consider that health is the greatest of human blessings.
- **Hippocrates.**

2,099. Of all the home remedies, a good wife is best.
- **Kin Hubbard.**

2,100. You can tell how healthy a man is by what he takes two of at a time – stairs or pills.
- **Kin Hubbard:** *The Laughs on Me* by Bennett Cerf, 1959.

2,101. Laughter is the most healthful exertion.
- **Christoph Wilhelm Hufeland.**

2,102. Life's not just being alive, but being well.
- **Martial.**

2,103. The picture of health requires a happy frame of mind.
- **Laurence J. Peter:** *The Laughter Prescription*, 1982.

2,104. What some call health, if purchased by perpetual anxiety about diet, isn't much better than tedious disease.
- **George D. Prentice.**

2,105. To get his wealth he spent his health
And then with might and main
He turned around and spent his wealth
To get his health again.
- **Herbert V. Prochnow and Herbert V. Prochnow Jr:** *Jokes, Quotes and One-Liners, Vol 2. 1983.*

2,106. He who has health has hope; and he who has hope has everything.
- *Arabian Proverb*.

2,107. A good laugh and a long sleep are the best cures in the doctor's book.
- *Irish Proverb*.

2,108. An imaginary ailment is worse than a disease.
- *Yiddish Proverb*.

2,109. Looking after my health gives me a better hope for tomorrow.
- **Ann Wilson Schaef**.

2,110. I am always busy, which is perhaps the chief reason why I am always well.
- **Elizabeth Cady Stanton**.

2,111. Look to your health; and if you have it, praise God, and value it next to a good conscience; for health is the second blessing that we mortals are capable of; a blessing that money cannot buy.
- **Izaak Walton:** *The Compleat Angler,* 1653.

2,112. Health is a state of complete physical, mental and social well-being, and not merely the absence of disease or infirmity.
- The first principle of the **Constitution of the World Health Organization**

HISTORY

2,113. History repeats itself because no one listens the first time.
- ***anon***.

2,114. After the war, Prohibition was passed, and with liquor no longer legally available, the nation plunged headlong into the Great Depression.
- **Dave Barry:** *Dave Barry Hits Below the Belt,* 2001.

2,115. History. n. An account mostly false, of events mostly unimportant, which are brought about by rulers mostly knaves, and soldiers mostly fools.
- **Ambrose Bierce:** *The Devil's Dictionary,* 1911.

2,116. History is the essence of innumerable biographies.
- **Thomas Carlyle:** *Critical and Miscellaneous Essays,* 1837.

2,117. Psychology keeps trying to vindicate human nature. History keeps undermining the effort.
- **Mason Cooley**.

2,118. One of the lessons of history is that nothing is often a good thing to do and always a clever thing to say.
- **Will Durant:** *Reader's Digest, 1972.*

2,119. History teaches us that men and nations behave wisely once they have exhausted all other alternatives.
- **Abba Eban:** *in a speech delivered in London, December 16th, 1970.*

2,120. History... is, indeed, little more than the register of the crimes, follies, and misfortunes of mankind.
- **Edward Gibbon:** *The History of the Decline and Fall of the Roman Empire (* Six Volumes published between 1776 and 1788)

2,121. History repeats itself. Historians repeat each other.
- **Philip Guedalla:** *Supers and Supermen: Studies in Politics, History and Letters,* 1922.

2,122. What experience and history teach us is this - that people and governments never have learned anything from history.
- **G. W. F. Hegel**.

2,123. A generation which ignores history has no past – and no future.
- **Robert Heinlein:** *Time Enough for Love*, 1973.

2,124. That we do not learn much from the lessons of history is the most important of all the lessons of history.
- **Aldous Huxley:** *Collected Essays*, 1958.

2,125. Thanks to television, for the first time the young are seeing history made before it is censored by their elders.
- **Margaret Mead:** recalled on her death, 15th November, 1978. Quoted in *Simpson's Contemporary Quotations* compiled by James B. Simpson, 1988.

2,126. There is no reason to repeat bad history.
- **Eleanor Holmes Norton:** *Sisterhood is Powerful* edited by Robin Morgan, 1970.

HOME

2,127. A House is not a Home.
 - The title of the autobiography of **Polly Adler**, the Russian-born American madam who ran New York's most notorious brothel in the 1920'a and 1930s.

2,128. It takes hands to build a house, but only hearts can build a home.
- *anon*.

2,129. All that keeps some families from having a home of their own is a popular teenage daughter.
- **anon:** 20,000 *Quipes and Quotes* by Evan Esar, 1969.

 2,130. Our house is a three-ring circus,
As all who have seen it have known.
And these are the rings I refer to:
The front door, the back door, the phone.
- **Richard Armour:** *Three-Ring Circus* in *An Armoury of Light Verse*, 1942.

2,131. Our home's a railway carriage
And it cannot be denied
That you might describe our dwelling
As a little bit on the side.
Yet it has the odd advantages
Where other housing fails,
And we're on the straight and narrow
So we can't go off the rails!
- **Pam Ayres:** *The Railway Carriage Couple* in *Thoughts of a Late Night Knitter*, 1979.

2,132. All mortgages work basically the same way. You sign a bunch of papers, then you make large monthly payments until the Second Coming.
- **Dave Barry:** *Dave Barry's Homes and Other Black Holes*, 1988.

2,133. Do you know what it means to come home at night to a woman who'll give you a little love, a little affection, a little tenderness ? It means you are in the wrong house.
- **George Burns**. (Also attributed to Henny Youngman.)

2,134. Home is Where the Heart Is.
- **David Cassidy**. Title of his 2nd Album issued in 1976. NB This saying is attributed to Pliny the Younger, 2nd century AD.

2,135. Home is where one starts from.
- **T. S. Eliot:** *East Coker*, 1940.

2,136. Home is the place where you're treated best and complain most.
- **Sam Ewing:** *National Enquirer, 7th March, 1995*

2,137. Close your eyes and tap your heels together three times and think to yourself,
"There's no place like home."
- Billie Burke in the role of Glinda the Good Witch of the North in the **1939 Film**: *The Wizard of Oz*.

2,138. Home is the place where, when you have to go there, they have to take you in.
- **Robert Frost:** *The Death of the Hired Man*, 1914.

2,139. I wanted a house that would have four bedrooms for the boys, all of them located some distance from the living room – say in the next country somewhere.
- **Jean Kerr:** *Please Don't Eat the Daisies*, 1960.

2,140. There is no fireside like your own fireside.
- *Irish Proverb*.

2,141. Home is any four walls that enclose the right person.
- **Helen Rowland:** *Reflections of a Bachelor Girl*, 1903.

2,142. I have a great house. It's just twenty minutes from the city – by phone.
- **Henny Youngman:** *How Do You Like Me So Far?* 1963..

HONEYMOON

2,143. A honeymoon is the short period between the bridal toast and the burnt toast.
- *anon*.

2,144. Honeymoon: a short period of doting between dating and debting.
- *anon*.

2,145. The taxi arrived at the hotel. Getting out, the new bride asked her husband, "What can we do to hide the fact that we've just been married?" The groom said, "You carry the luggage!"
- **Milton Berle:** *Milton Berle's Private Joke File*, 1989.

2,146. Next to hot chicken soup, a tattoo of an anchor on your chest, and penicillin, I consider a honeymoon one of the most overrated events in the world.
- **Erma Bombeck:** *If Life is a Bowl of Cherries, What Am I Doing in the Pits?* 1971.

2,147. The honeymoon is over...
A. When he stops helping her with the dishes, and starts doing them himself.
B. When she stops dropping her eyes and starts raising her voice.
C. When she starts wondering what happened to the man she married, and he starts wondering what happened to the girl he didn't.
D. When the bride who took her husband for better or for worse, starts taking him for granted.
E. When he finds out he married a big spender, and she finds out she didn't.
- **Evan Esar:** *The Comic Encyclopedia,* 1978.

2,148. I went alone on my honeymoon. My wife had already seen Niagra Falls.
- **Leopold Fechtner:** *5,000 One-And-Two-Line Jokes,* 1973.

2,149. I would have liked to take my wife along on our honeymoon, but she had to go to work next day.
- *ibid*.

2,150. Conversation like television set on honeymoon... unnecessary.
- Peter Sellers in the role of Mr Wang in the **1976 Film**: *Murder By Death*.

2,151. Camped on a tropical riverside, / One day he missed his lovely bride. / She had, the guide informed him later, / Been eaten by an alligator. / Professor Twist could not but smile, / "You mean," he said, "a crocodile."
- **Ogden Nash:** *The Purist* in *The Oxford Book of Children's Verse in America* edited by Donald Hall, 1985.

HUMOUR

2,152. Humour is a social lubricant that helps us get over some of the bad spots.
- **Steve Allen:** *The Center Magazine, 1991*.

2,153. Mark my words, when a society has to resort to the lavatory for it's humour, the writing is on the wall.
- **Alan Bennett:** *Plays End*, 1996.

2,154. Total absence of humour renders life impossible.
- **Colette:** *Acquaintances*.

2,155. Healthy humour is a symptom of physical, emotional and psychological well being. Laughing eases fear, reduces stress and brings greater self awareness. It brings people together and enriches all aspects of life.
- **Cathy Fenwick:** author of *Healing with Humour*, 1995.

2,156. Humour gives us the ability to detach from the situation and has a cathartic effect. Our ability to recognize some humorist aspect of a situation can give us a relief from the negative impact of emotions such as fear, anger, depression, disappointment, embarrassment, and chagrin. Humour helps to release the hold these emotions have on an individual.
- **William Fry Jr**.

2,157. Humour is the affirmation of dignity, a declaration of man's superiority to all that befalls him.
- **Romain Gary:** *Promise at Dawn*, 1962.

2,158. A keen sense of humour helps us overcome the unbecoming, understand the unconventional, tolerate the unpleasant, overcome the unexpected, and outlast the unbearable.
- **Billy Graham:** *Readers' Digest, March, 1993*.

2.159. Humour is a rubber sword – it allows you to make a point without drawing blood.
- **Mary Hirsch**.

2,160. There is always something to chuckle about. Sometimes we see it. Sometimes... we don't. Still, the world is filled with humour. It is there when we are happy and it is there to cheer us up when we are not.
- **Allen Klein:** *The Lift-Your-Spirits Quote Book*, 2001.

2,161. Good humour is a tonic for mind and body. It is the best antidote for anxiety and depression. It is a business asset. It attracts and keeps friends. It lightens human burdens. It is the direct route to serenity and contentment.
- **Grenville Kleiser:** *The Forbes Book of Business Quotations*.

2,162. Humour, it cannot be too often said, must be kind.
- **Stephen Leacock:** *How To Write*, 1943.

2,163. There is no evidence that humour is capable of reversing any disease, but it does help assure that your body's natural health and healing systems are fully engaged in the battle.
- **Paul E. McGee**.

2,164. To succeed in life, you need three things: a wishbone, a backbone and a funny-bone.
-**Reba McIntyre:** *Comfort From a Country Quilt*, 1991.

2,165. After God created the world, he made man and woman. Then, to keep the whole thing from collapsing, he invented humour.
- **Guillermo Mordillo**.

2,166. Show me a patient who is able to laugh and play, who enjoys living and I'll show you someone who is going to live longer. Laughter makes the unbearable bearable, and a patient with a well developed sense of humour has a better chance of recovery than a stolid individual who seldom laughs.
- **Bernie S. Siegel**.

2,167. Humour can be dangerous to your illness.
- **Steve Sultanoff**.

2,168. I have always felt that humour was a wonderful vehicle to let us become connected with each other and ourselves.
- **Lily Tomlin:** *Variety Magazine*.

HUSBANDS

2,169. My husband will never chase another woman. He's too fine, too decent, too old.
- **Gracie Allen:** *Halliwell's Who's Who in the Movies*, 2003.

2,170. Hold on to your husband, in time he may come back into fashion.
- *anon*.

2,171. Some mornings I wake up grumpy, on other days I let him sleep in.
- *anon*.

2,172. Many poor husbands were once rich bachelors.
- *anon*.

2,173. A smart husband is one who thinks twice before saying nothing.
- *anon*.

2,174. I told my wife that a husband is like a fine wine, he gets better with age. Next day she locked me in the cellar!
- *anon*

2,175. Being a husband is a full-time job. That is why so many husbands fail. They cannot give their entire attention to it.
- **Arnold Bennett:** *The Title, Act 1,1918*

2,176. He stopped calling her "the little woman," when she started calling him "the big mistake."
- **Milton Berle:** *Milton Berle's Private Joke File*, 1989.

2,177. Husbands, love your wives and do not be harsh with them.
- **The Bible:** *Colossians 3: 19, NIV*.

2,178. Your husband drinks too much if he says he never drinks alone, but considers the goldfish somebody.
- **Phyllis Diller:** *Phyllis Diller's Marriage Manual* 1967.

2,179. Personally, I can't see why it would be any less romantic to find a husband in a nice four-colour catalogue than in the average down town bar at happy hour.
- **Barbara Ehrenreich:** *The Oxford Dictionary of Thematic Quotations* by Susan Ratcliffe, 2000.

2,180. Being a husband is like any other job – it helps if you like the boss!
- **Evan Esar:** *20,000 Quips and Quotes*, 1968.

2,181. He knows little who will tell his wife all he knows.
- **Thomas Fuller:** *The Holy State and the Profane State*, 1642.

2,182. All women should know how to take care of children. Most of them will have a husband some day.
- **Franklin P. Jones**.

2,183. A husband who says that he is the boss of the house will probably lie about other things too
- **Pat Williams:** *Winning with One-Liners*. 2002.

IDEAS

2,184. Not to engage in the pursuit of ideas is to live like ants instead of like men.
- **Mortimer Adler:** *The Saturday Review, 22nd November, 1958.*

2,185. Eureka! (I have got it!)
- **Archimedes**.

2,186. A mediocre idea that generates enthusiasm will go further than a great idea that inspires no one.
- **Mary Kay Ash:** *Mary Kay on People Management*, 1985.

2,187. Any powerful idea is absolutely fascinating and absolutely useless unless we choose to use it.
- **Richard Bach:** *One*, 1988.

2,188. One of the greatest pains to human nature is the pain of a new idea.
- **Walter Bagehot:** *Physics and Politics*, 1869.

2,189. An idea can turn to dust or magic, depending on the talent that rubs against it.
- **William Bernbach:** *New York Times, 6th October, 1982.*

2,190. An idea that is developed and put into action is more important than an idea that exists only as an idea.
- **Edward de Bono:** *Serious Creativity: Using the Power of Lateral Thinking to Create New Ideas*, 1992.

2,191. One can live in the shadow of an idea without grasping it.
- **Elizabeth Bowen:** *The Heat of the Day*, 1949.

2,192. Every new idea has something of the pain and peril of childbirth about it.
- **Samuel Butler:** *Notebooks*, 1912.

2,193. The ideas I stand for are not mine. I borrowed them from Socrates, I swiped them from Chesterfield, I stole them from Jesus, and I put them in a book. If you don't like their rules, whose would you use?
- **Dale Carnegie:** *How to Win Friends and Influence People*, 1936.

2,194. A man is not necessarily intelligent because he has plenty of ideas, any more than he is a good general because he has plenty of soldiers.
- **Nicolas Chamfort:** *Maxims and Considerations* translated by E. Powys Mathers, 1926.

2,195. Ideas are somewhat like babies - they are born small, immature, and shapeless. They are promise rather than fulfilment. In the innovative company executives do not say, "This is a damn-fool idea," instead they ask, "What would be needed to make this embryonic, half-baked, foolish idea into something that makes sense, that is an opportunity for us?"
- **Peter Drucker:** *The Frontiers of Management*, 1986.

2,196. The value of an idea lies in the using of it
- **Thomas Edison, *attributed*.**

2,197. Man's fear of ideas is probably the greatest dyke holding back human knowledge and happiness.
- **Morris L. Ernst**.

2,198. No matter what people tell you, words and ideas can change the world.
- Robin Williams in the role of the charismatic teacher, Mr Keating, in the **1989 Film**: *Dead Poets Society*.

2,199. Ideas are the raw material of progress. Everything first takes shape in the form of an idea, but an idea by itself is worth nothing. An idea, like a machine, must have power applied to it before it can accomplish anything.
- **B. C. Forbes:** *Reader's Digest, February, 1993*.

2,200. It's not an idea unless you're willing to take action on it.
- **Doug Hall:** *Jump Start Your Brain*, 1995.

2,201. Every now and then a man's mind is stretched by a new idea or sensation, and never shrinks back to its former dimensions.
- **Oliver Wendell Holmes Sr:** *The Autocrat of the Breakfast Table*, 1858.

IGNORANCE

2,202. To be ignorant of one's ignorance is the malady of the ignorant.
- **Amos Bronson Alcott:** *Table Talk*, 1977.

2,203. If ignorance is bliss, why aren't more people jumping up and down?
- *anon*.

2,204. I have tried to know absolutely nothing about a great many things, and I have succeeded fairly well.
- **Robert Benchley**.

2,205. Ignorance more frequently begets confidence than does knowledge; it is those who know little, and not those who know much, who so positively assert that this or that problem will never be solved by science.
- **Charles Darwin:** *The Descent of Man*, 1871.

2,206. To be conscious that you are ignorant is a great step to knowledge.
- **Benjamin Disraeli:** *Sybil* or *The Two Nations*, 1845.

2,207. His ignorance is encyclopaedic.
- **Abba Eban**.

2,208. Fear always springs from ignorance.
- **Ralph Waldo Emerson:** *Essays and Lectures* edited by Joel Porte, 1983.

2,209. It is harder to conceal ignorance than to acquire knowledge.
- **Arnold H. Glasgow**.

2,210. Nothing is more terrible than ignorance in action.
- **Johann Wolfgang von Goethe:** *Maxims and Reflections* translated by Elizabeth Stopp, 1998.

2,211. Children begin by honestly saying, "I don't know," until they are taught (mistakenly) to be ashamed of ignorance; and this is why so many adults remain ashamed of saying, "I don't know," when they should say it. Ignorance is shameful only when we have had the opportunity to learn something and rejected it.
- **Sydney J. Harris:** *Pieces of Eight,* 1975.

2,212. The recipe for perpetual ignorance is: be satisfied with your opinions and content with your knowledge.
- **Elbert Hubbard**.

2,213. As hunger is cured by food, so ignorance is cured by study
- *Chinese Proverb*

2,214. The more one learns, the more one sees one's ignorance
- *Chinese Proverb*.

2,215. It is not a shame not to know, it is a shame not to ask.
- *Turkish Proverb*.

2,216. The only good is knowledge and the only evil is ignorance.
- **Socrates:** *Lives of Eminent Philosophers* by Diogenes Laertius.

2,217. The doorstep to the temple of wisdom is the knowledge of our own ignorance
- **Charles H. Spurgeon:** quoted in *Selling With Emotional Intelligence* by Mitch Anthony, 2003.

IMAGINATION

2,218. A lady's imagination is very rapid; it jumps from admiration to love, from love to matrimony in a moment.
- **Jane Austen:** *Pride and Prejudice*, 1813.

2,219. Imagination is the highest kite we can fly.
- **Lauren Bacall:** *Lauren Bacall by Myself*, 1978.

2,220. Every great advance in science has issued from a new audacity of imagination.
- **John Dewey:** *The Quest for Certainty, a Study of the Relation of Knowledge and Action*, 1929.

2,221. Imagination is more important that knowledge. Knowledge is limited. Imagination encircles the world.... When I examine myself and my methods of thought, I come close to the conclusion that the gift of imagination has meant more to me than my talent for absorbing absolute Knowledge.
- **Albert Einstein:** *The New Quotable Einstein* collected and edited by Alice Calaprice, 2005.

2,222. Solitude is as needful to the imagination as society is wholesome for the character.
- **James Russell Lowell:** *Among My Books*, 1870.

2,223. Imagination is the outreaching of the mind... It is the capacity to "dream dreams and see visions."
- **Rollo May:** *The Courage to Create*, 1975.

2,224. We do not need magic to change the world. We carry all the power we need inside ourselves already; we have the power to imagine better.
- **J. K. Rowling:** *The Fringe Benefits of Failure, and the Importance of Imagination.* Speech at the annual meeting of the Harvard Alumni Association, 5th June, 2008.

2,225. The Right Honourable gentleman is indebted to his memory for his jests, and to his imagination for his facts.

Richard Brinsley Sheridan: in a speech in reply to a certain Mr Dundas, quoted in *Sheridaniana*, 1826.

2,226. Every child is born blessed with a vivid imagination. But just as a muscle grows flabby with disuse, so the bright imagination of a child pales in later years if he ceases to use it.

- **Dave Smith**: *The Quotable Walt Disney*, 2002.

INDIFFERENCE

2,227. ...he passed by on the other side.
- **The Bible:** *Luke 10: 31b, NIV*.

 2,228. The opposite of love is not hate, as many believe, but rather indifference. Nothing communicates disinterest more clearly than distancing. A child cannot feel valued by parents who are forever absorbed in their own affairs.
- **Dorothy C. Briggs:** *Your Child's Self-Esteem, the Key to His Life,* 1970.

2,229. Science may have found a cure for most evils; but it has found no remedy for the worst of them all - the apathy of human beings.
- **Helen Keller:** *My Religion,* 1927.

2,230. The greatest sin of our time is not the few who have destroyed but the vast majority who sat idly by.
 - **Martin Luther King Jr:** *in a speech.*

2,231. Tolerance is only another name for indifference.
- **W. Somerset Maugham:** *A Writer's Notebook,* 1949.

2,232. There is nothing harder than the softness of indifference.
- **Juan Montalvo**.

2,233. Throughout history, it has been the inaction of those who could have acted, the indifference of those who should have known better, the silence of the voice of justice when it mattered most, that has made it possible for evil to triumph.
- **Haile Selassie:** in a speech in Addis Ababa. Quoted in *Simpson's Contemporary Quotations,* 1988.

2,234. The worst sin towards our fellow creatures is not to hate them, but to be indifferent to them; that's the essence of inhumanity.
- **George Bernard Shaw:** *The Devil's Disciple* (1897) in *Three Plays for Puritans,* 1901.

2,235. I regard you with an indifference closely bordering on aversion.
- **Robert Louis Stevenson:** *The New Arabian Nights* (1882). Quoted in *Encarta Book of Quotations* edited by Bill Swainson, 2000.

2,236. The opposite of love is not hate, it's indifference.
- **Elie Wiesel:** *US News and World Report, 27th October, 1986.*

2,237. Indifference, to me, is the epitome of evil.
- *ibid.*

INDOLENCE

2,238. The man who has nothing to do always gives it his personal attention.
- **anon:** *2,000 Quips and Quotes* by Evan Esar, 1968.

2,239. Doing nothing is the most tiresome job in the world because you can't stop and rest.
- **anon**, **ibid**.

2,240. The worst thing about time-wasters is that so much of the time they waste doesn't belong to them
- **anon**, **ibid**.

2,241. I never worry about action, but only about inaction.
- **Sir Winston Churchill:** *The Wit and Wisdom of Winston Churchill* by James C. Humes, 1994.

2,242. Defer not till tomorrow to be wise,
 Tomorrow's sun to thee may never rise
 - **William Congreve:** *in a letter to the Right Honourable the Lord Viscount Cobham* (in verse), 1729

2,243. Inactivity is one of the great indignities of life. The need to work is always there, bugging me.
- **Joan Crawford** as Sadie Thompson in the **1932 Film**: *Rain*.

 2,244. You could see it in the way she carried herself; she was the kind of employee always looking for nothing to do.
- **Dale Dauten**.

2,245. He that is busy is tempted by but one devil; he that is idle, by a legion.
- **Thomas Fuller:** *Gnomologia: Adages and Proverbs*, 1732.

2,246. Some people have a perfect genius for doing nothing, and doing it assiduously.
- **Thomas Chandler Haliburton**.

2,247. Idling always has been my strong point. I take no credit to myself in the matter – it is a gift. Few possess it.
- **Jerome K. Jerome**: *Idle Thoughts of an Idle Fellow*, 1886.

2,248. Idleness, like kisses, to be sweet must be stolen.
- *ibid.*

2,249. Iron rusts from disuse; stagnant water loses it's purity and in cold weather becomes frozen; even so does inaction sap the vigour of the mind.
- **Leonardo da Vinci**: *The Notebooks of Leonardo Da Vinci* translated by Jean Paul Richter, 1888.

2,250. Your hair may be brushed, but your mind's untidy.
You've had about seven hours of sleep since Friday,
No wonder you feel that lost sensation,
You're sunk from a riot of relaxation.
- **Ogden Nash**: *We'll All Feel Better by Wednesday*, in *Verses*, 1949.

2,251. Of all our faults, the one that we excuse most easily is idleness.
- **Francois, Duc de la Rochefoucauld**: *Maxims*, 1665.

2,252. I am happiest when I am idle. I could live for months without performing any kind of labour, and at the expiration of that time I should feel fresh and vigorous enough to go right on in the same way for numerous more months.
- **Artemus Ward**: *Artemus Ward in London: and Other Papers*, 1867.

THE INTERNET

2,253. Give a person a fish and you feed him for a day, teach that person to use the Internet and he won't bother you ever again.
- *anon*.

2,254. A journey of a thousand sites begins with a single click.
- *anon*.

2,255. The Internet is the single most important development in the history of communications since the invention of "call waiting."
- **Dave Barry:** *Dave Barry in Cyberspace*, 1996.

2,256. When I first began tinkering with a software program that eventually gave rise to the idea of the World Wide Web, I named it Enquire, short for *Enquire for Everything*, a musty old book of Victorian advice I noticed as a child in my parent's house outside London. With its title suggestive of magic, the book served as a portal to a world of information, everything from how to remove clothing stains to tips on investing money. Not a perfect analogy for the Web, but a primitive starting point.
- **Tim Berners-Lee**: *Weaving the* Web. *The Original Design and Ultimate Destiny of the World Wide Web*, 1999.

2,257. The Internet is like alcohol in some sense. It accentuates what you would do anyway. If you want to be a loner, you can be more alone. If you want to connect, it makes it easier to connect. In my own experience it has drawn my family closer, as we post pictures on Flickr.
- **Esther Dyson**.

2,258. Few influential people involved with the Internet claim that it is good in and of itself. It is a powerful tool for solving social problems, just as it is a tool for making money, finding lost relatives, receiving medical advice, or, come to that, trading instructions for making bombs.
- **Esther Dyson:** *Time Magazine, 16th October, 2005*.

2,259. The Internet is becoming the town square for the global village of tomorrow.
- **Bill Gates:** *Business @ the Speed of Thought.* 1999.

2,260. We never thought to ask how will our lives, our way of thinking, be changed by this Internet, which has seduced a whole generation with its inanities so that even quite reasonable people will confess that once they are hooked, it is hard to cut free.
- **Doris Lessing**: *Nobel Prize Acceptance Speech,* 2002.

2,261. Human beings are human beings. They say what they want, don't they? They used to say it across the fence while they were hanging wash. Now they just say it on the Internet.
- **Dennis Miller.**

2,262. The Internet is a telephone system that's got uppity.
- **Clifford Stoll:** *Silicon Snake Oil,* 1995.

2,263. Electronic communication is an instantaneous and illusory contact that creates a sense of intimacy without the emotional investment that leads to close friendships.
- *ibid.*

2,264. Anyone can post messages on the Net. Practically everyone does. The resulting cacophony drowns out serious discussion.
- *ibid.*

2,265. Yes, there is a ton of information on the Web, but much of it is egregiously inaccurate, unedited, unattributed and juvenile.
- **John Updike:** *speech at Book Expo, 2006.* NB Egregiously, *adv,* derived from egregious *adj.* outstandingly bad.

IRELAND AND THE IRISH

2,266. May you always have work for your hands to do, / May your pockets hold always a coin or two. / May the sun shine bright on your window pane, / May the rainbow be certain to follow each rain. / May the hand of a friend always be near you, /And may God fill your heart with gladness to cheer you.
- **anon:** *An Irish Blessing.*

2,267. May you live as long as you want, and never want as long as you live.
- **anon:** *An Irish Toast,*

2,268. An Irishman is never at peace except when he's fighting.
- **anon**.

2,269. Other people have a nationality. The Irish and the Jews have a psychosis.
- **Brendan Behan:** *Richard's Cork Leg,* 1972.

2,270. IRISH: An English-piquing people.
- **Jacob M**. **Braude:** *Braude's Treasury of Wit and Humour for all Occasions,* 1991.

2,271. Have you heard about the Irishman who reversed into a car boot sale and sold the engine.
- **Frank Carson**.

2,272. An Irishman had a ship, a cargo ship, full of yo-yos and he hit this rock and it sank 44 times.
- **Tommy Cooper:** *The Very Best of Tommy Cooper,* 1999.

2,273. The Irish gave the bagpipes to the Scots as a joke, but the Scots haven't seen the joke yet.
- **Oliver Herford**.

2,274. In some parts of Ireland the sleep which knows no waking is always followed by a wake which knows no sleeping.
- **Mary Wilson Little:** *An Uncommon Scold* by Abby Adams,1989.

2,275. The Irish are often nervous about having the appropriate face for the occasion. They have to be happy at weddings, which is a strain so they get depressed: they have to be sad at funerals, which is easy, so they get happy.
 - **Peggy Noonan:** *What I Saw at the Revolution: a Political Life in the Reagan Era*, 1990.

2,276. It's not a sin not to be Irish, but it is a great shame.
 - **Sean O'Huiginn:** *Reader's Digest,March,1987*

2,277. An Englishman thinks, seated; a Frenchman, standing; an American, pacing; an Irishman, afterwards.
- **Austin O'Malley**.

JEALOUSY

2,278. It is the character of very few men to honour without envy a friend who has prospered.
- **Aeschylus:** *Agamemnon*, 6ᵗʰ century BC.

2,279. As iron is eaten by rust, so are the envious consumed by envy.
- **Antisthenes**.

2,280. Of all the passions, jealousy is that which exacts the hardest service, and pays the bitterest wages. Its service is to watch the *success* of our enemy; its wages - to be *sure* of it.
- **Charles Caleb Colton:** *Lacon, or Many Things in Few Words*, 1826, edited by George J. Barbour, 2101.

2,281. My wife's jealousy is getting ridiculous. The other day she looked at my calendar and wanted to know who May was.
- **Rodney Dangerfield**.

2,282. It is not love that is blind, but jealousy.
- **Lawrence Durrell:** *Justine*, 1957.

2,283. One of the tortures of jealousy is that it can never turn its eyes from the thing that pains it.
- **George Eliot:** *Scenes from Clerical Life*, 1858.

2,284. Anger and jealousy can no more bear to lose sight of their objects than love.
- **George Eliot:** *The Mill on the Floss*, 1860.

2,285. Jealousy is a mental cancer.
- **B. C. Forbes**.

2,286. The jealous are troublesome to others, but a torment to themselves.
- **William Penn:** *Some Fruits of Solitude*, 1693.

2,287. Jealousy is the greatest of all evils, and the one which arouses the least pity in the person who causes it.
- **Francois, Duc de la Rochefoucauld:** *Maxims,* 1665.

2,288. O, beware, my Lord, of jealousy; / It is the green-ey'd monster which doth mock / The meat it feeds on.
- **William Shakespeare:** Othello, Act 3, Sc 3.

2,289. Trifles light as air / Are to the jealous confirmations strong / As proofs of holy writ.
- *ibid.*

JOY AND SORROW

2,290. Do not give yourself over to sorrow or distress yourself deliberately. A merry heart keeps a man alive, and joy lengthens his span of days.
- **The Apocrypha:** *Ecclesiasticus 3: 21 – 22, NEB.*

2,291. It is good to grow wise by sorrow.
- **Aeschylus:** *Eumenides*, 6th century BC.

2,292. Those who bring sunshine into the lives of others, cannot keep it from themselves.
- **Sir James M. Barrie**.

2,293. Man was made for joy and woe; / And when this we rightly know / Through the world we safely go. / Joy and woes are woven fine, / A clothing for the soul divine.
- **William Blake:** *Auguries of Innocence*, 1803.

2,294. Not only is there a right to be happy, there is a duty to be happy. So much sadness exists in the world that we are all under obligation to contribute as much joy as lies within our powers.
- **John Sutherland Bonnell**.

2,295. Tearless grief bleeds inwardly.
- **Christian Nestell Bovee:** *Intuitions and summaries of Thought*, 1862.

2,296. The path of sorrow, and that path alone,
Leads to the land where sorrow is unknown.
- **William Cowper:** *To an Afflicted Protestant Lady in France.*

2,297. ... There is no greater sorrow,
Than to be mindful of the happy time
 In misery.
 - **Dante Alighieri:** *The Divine Comedy, Inferno V. 121*, 1321.

2,298. The selfsame well from which your laughter rises was often-time filled with your tears.
- **Kahlil Gibran:** *The Prophet,* 1923.

2,299. I walked a mile with Pleasure, / She chattered all the way; / But left me none the wiser, / For all she had to say./ I walked a mile with Sorrow / And ne'er a word said she; / But, Oh, the things I learned from her / When Sorrow walked with me.
- **Robert Browning Hamilton:** *Along the Road* in *Best Loved Poems of the American People* by Hazel Felleman, 1936.

2,300. One can endure sorrow alone, but it takes two to be glad. Only by giving out our joy do we make it our own – by sharing, we double it.
- **Elbert Hubbard:** *A Thousand and One Epigrams,* 1911.

2,301. Into each life some rain must fall, /Some days must be dark and dreary.
- **Henry Wadsworth Longfellow:** *The Rainy Day* in *Voices of the Night,* 1839.

2,302. I believe humans were born to have joy and to have it more abundantly, that the birthright of everyone is loving, caring, sharing and abundance.
- **Peter McWilliams:** *You Can't Afford the Luxury of a Negative Thought.* 1991.

2,303. He truly sorrows who sorrows unseen.
- **Martial:** *Epigrams,* **circa** 86 AD.

2,304. Joy increases as you give it, and diminishes as you try to keep it for yourself. In giving it, you will accumulate a deposit of joy greater than you ever believed possible.
- **Norman Vincent Peale:** *Positive Thinking Every Day,* 1993.

2,305. You cannot prevent the birds of sorrow from flying over your head, but you can prevent them from building nests in your hair.
- *Chinese Proverb.*

2,306. Happiness is beneficial for the body but it is grief that develops the powers of the mind.
- **Marcel Proust:***The Past Recaptured,* 1927.

2,307. A joy that's shared is a joy made double.
- **John Ray:** *A Complete Collection of English Proverb*s, 1670.

2,308. To live through a period of stress and sorrow with another human being creates a bond which nothing seems able to break.. People can be happy together and look back on their contacts very pleasantly, but such contacts will not make the same kind of bond that sorrow lived through together will create.
- **Eleanor Roosevelt:** *The Public Speaker's Source Book* by Herbert V. Prochnow and Herbert V. Prochnow Jr, 1977.

2,309. There may be sorrow and suffering around the corner for anyone at any time. Nevertheless, life is worth living and it is worthwhile to love, even though that very love may bring you suffering.
- **Eleanor Roosevelt:** *My Day: 2nd October, 1946.*

2,310. Give sorrow words; the grief that does not speak
 Whispers the o'er-fraught heart and bids it break.
- **William Shakespeare:** *Macbeth, Act 4, Sc 3*, 1611.

2,311. I hold it true, what 'er befall, / I feel it when I sorrow most, / 'Tis better to have loved and lost / Than never to have loved at all.
- **Alfred**, **Lord Tennyson:** *In Memoriam*, 1850.

2,312. Pleasure is always derived from something outside you, whereas joy arises from within.
- **Eckhart Tolle:** *The Power of Now*, 1997.

2,313. Grief can take care of itself; but to get the full value of a joy you must have someone to divide it with.
- **Mark Twain:** *The Tragedy of Pudd'nhead Wilson*, 1894.

2,314. Joy is not in things, it is in us.
- **Richard Wagner**.

2,315. Joy is what happens to us when we allow ourselves to recognize how good things really are.
- **Marianne Williamson**.

KINDNESS

2,316. No act of kindness, no matter how small, is ever wasted.
- The moral of **Aesop's Fable:** *The Lion and the Mouse.*

2,317. A small good deed is better that a great intention.
- *anon.*

2,318. Cato said the best way to keep good acts in memory was to refresh them with new.
- **Francis Bacon:** *Apophthegms, New and Old,* 1625. NB This is Bacon's collection of wise sayings of personalities of the past.

2,319. Shall we make a new rule of life from tonight: always try to be a little kinder.
- **Sir J. M. Barrie:** *The Little White Bird,* 1902.

2,320. But deep this truth impress'd my mind - / Thro' all His works abroad, / The heart benevolent and kind / The most resembles God.
- **Robert Burns:** *A Winter Night,* 1787, quoted in *The Complete Illustrated Poems, Songs and Ballads of Robert Burns,* 1990.

2,321. Too often we underestimate the power of a touch, a smile, a kind word, a listening ear, an honest compliment, or the smallest act of caring, all of which have the potential to turn a life around.
- **Leo F. Buscaglia:** *Love,* 1985.

2,322. The best way to keep good acts in memory is to refresh them with new.
- **Cato the Elder:** *Apothegms No 247.*

2,323. You can never do a kindness too soon, for you never know how soon it will be too late.
- **Ralph Waldo Emerson:** *The Conduct of Life,* 1860..

,324. Life is mostly froth and bubble, / Two things stand like stone - / Kindness in another's trouble, / Courage in your own.
- **Adam Lindsay Gordon:** *Finis Exoptatus (A Metaphysical Song)*, quoted in *The Oxford Book of Australian Verse* edited by Walter Murdoch, 1918.

2,325. I expect to pass through this world but once. Any good therefore that I do, or any kindness that I can show to any fellow creature, let me do it now. Let me not defer or neglect it, for I shall not pass this way again.
- **Stephen Grellet:** early 19th century Frenchman who spent the greater part of his life as a Quaker missionary in America. NB This statement is also attributed to William Penn and Mahatma Gandhi.

2.326. If you haven't any charity in your heart, you have the worst kind of heart trouble.
- **Bob Hope**.

2,327. Verily God commands justice and kindness.
- **The Koran**.

2,328. A word of kindness is seldom spoken in vain, while witty sayings are as easily lost as the pearls slipping from a broken string.
- **George D. Prentice**.

2,329. How far that little candle throws his beams! / So shines a good deed in a naughty world.
- **William Shakespeare:** *The Merchant of Venice, Act 5. Sc 1*.

2,330. That best portion of a good man's life, / His little, nameless, unremembered acts / Of kindness and of love. - **William Wordsworth:** *Lines Composed a Few Miles Above Tintern Abbey* in *Lyrical Ballads*, 1798.

KISSING

2,331. Seventy per cent of the body's sense perceptors cluster in the eyes, and it is mainly through seeing the world that we appraise and understand it. Lovers close their eyes when they kiss because, if they didn't, there would be too many visual distractions to notice and analyse.
- **Diane Ackerman:** *A Natural History of the Senses,* 1990.

2,332. A kiss is a pleasant reminder that two heads are better than one.
- *anon.*

2,333. There was a young lady of Florence / Who for kissing professed great abhorrence. / But when she'd been kissed / And found what she had missed,/ She cried till her tears came in torrents.
- *anon.*

2,334. A kiss is something you cannot give without taking, and cannot take without giving.
- *anon.*

2,335. Stolen kisses require an accomplice.
- **"Texas" Bix Bender:** *Just One Thing After Another,* 1994.

2,336. A kiss is a lovely trick designed by nature to stop speech when words become superfluous.
- **Ingrid Bergman**.

2,337. Kiss: n. A word invented by the poets as a rhyme for "bliss" It is supposed to signify, in a general way, some kind of rite or ceremony appertaining to a good understanding, but the manner of its performance is unknown to this lexicographer.
- **Ambrose Bierce:** *The Devil's Dictionary,* 1911.

2,338. Not everyone is comfortable with the kissing ritual. My husband is one of them. He refuses to press lips with anyone except his wife, mother, and dog. If someone wanted to give him mouth-to-mouth

resuscitation, he would refuse until he had been formally introduced.
- **Erma Bombeck:** *All I Know About Animal Behaviour I Learned in Loehmann's Dressing Room*, 1995.

2,339. It is the passion that is in a kiss that gives it its sweetness; it is the affection in a kiss that sanctifies it.
- **Christian Nestell Bovee:** *Intuitions and Summaries of Thought*. 1862.

2,340. Take good aim... the lips meet... the eyes close... the heart forgets all bitterness, and the incomparable art of kissing is learned.
- *The Art of Kissing:* from an 1896 edition of **The Farmers' Almanac**. NB *The Farmers' Almanac* is one of the oldest magazines in America, it has been in continuous print since 1818.

2,341. I do not know how to kiss, or I would kiss you. Where do the noses go?
- Ingrid Bergman in the role of Maria in the **1943 Film:** *For Whom the Bell Tolls.*

2,342. You need to be kissed, and often, and by someone who knows how!
- Clark Gable in the role of Rhett Butler, to Scarlett O'Hara, played by Vivien Leigh, in the **1939 Film:** *Gone With the Wind.*

2.343. Oh, innocent victims of Cupid, / Remember this terse little verse; / To let a fool kiss you is stupid, / To let a kiss fool you is worse.
- **E. Y. Harburg:** *Inscriptions on a Lipstick* in *Lighten Up! Bk 1,* edited by Bruce Lansky, 1998.

2,344. You may conquer with the sword, but you are conquered by a kiss.
- **Daniel Heinsius**.

2,345. People who throw kisses are hopelessly lazy.
- **Bob Hope**.

2,346. Stealing a kiss sometimes leads to marriage, a perfect example of crime and punishment.
- **Bob Monkhouse:** *Just Say a Few Words,* 1988.

2,347. Any man who can drive safely while kissing a pretty girl is simply not giving the kiss the attention it deserves.
- **Helen Rowland:** *A Guide to Men,* 1922.

2,348. Why does a man take it for granted that a girl who flirts with him wants him to kiss her - when, nine times out of ten, she only wants him to want to kiss her?
- *ibid.*

2,349. Lord, I wonder what fool it was that first invented kissing!
- **Jonathan Swift:** *Polite Conversation, Dialogue 2,* 1738.

2,350. Strephon kissed me in the Spring, / Robin in the Fall, / But Colin only looked at me / And never kissed at all./ Strephon's kiss was lost in jest, / Robin's lost in play, / But the kiss in Colin's
eyes / Haunts me night and day.
- **Sara Teasdale:** *The Look* in *Love Songs,* 1917.

2,351. I smoked my first cigarette and kissed my first woman on the same day. I have never had time for tobacco since.
- **Arturo Toscanini:** *The Oxford Dictionary of Thematic Quotations* edited by Susan Ratcliffe, 2000.

KNOWLEDGE

2,352. The utmost extent of man's knowledge, is to know that he knows nothing.
- **Joseph Addison:** *Essay on Pride*, 1794.

2,353. Knowledge doesn't pay – it's what you do with your knowledge that pays.
- **anon:** *20,000 Quips and Quotes* by Evan Esar, 1968.

2,354. Knowledge is power.
- **Francis Bacon:** *Sacred Meditations*, 1597.

2,355. Experience is the only thing that brings knowledge, and the longer you are on earth the more experience you are sure to get.
- **L. Frank Baum:** *The Wonderful Wizard of Oz*, 1900.

2,356. Many will go here and there to increase knowledge.
The Bible: *Daniel 12: 4b, NIV*.

2,357. Practically all knowledge resolves itself into four forms: the knowledge of what to do, how to do it, and when to do it, and of what to do.
- **Christian Nestell Bovee:** *Intuitions and Summaries of Thought*, 1862.

2,358. The knowledge of the world is only to be acquired in the world, and not in a closet.
- **Lord Chesterfield:** *Letters to His Son*, 4th October, 1774.

2,359. Real knowledge is to know the extent of one's ignorance.
- **Confucius:** *Analects*, 5th century BC.

2,360. Knowledge is the antidote to fear.
- **Ralph Waldo Emerson:** *Courage*. CP:"Fear always springs from ignorance", stated by Emerson in a lecture he gave at Harvard in 1837.

2,361. A little learning is a dangerous thing – almost as dangerous as a lot of ignorance.
- **Evan Esar:** *20,000 Quips and Quotes*, 1968.

2,362. Whoso neglects learning in his youth, loses the past and is dead to the future.
- **Euripides:** *Fragment*, 5th century BC.

2,363. I would never buy an encyclopaedia. My wife knows everything.
- **Leopold Fechtner:** *5,000 One-And-Two-Line Jokes*, 1979.

2,364. Knowledge is of two kinds: we know a subject ourselves, or we know where we can find information upon it.
- **Samuel Johnson:** *The Life of Samuel Johnson* by James Boswell, 1791.

2,365. All wish to possess knowledge, but few are prepared to pay the price.
- **Juvenal:** *Satires*, 1st - 2nd centuries, AD.

2,366. There is a great difference between knowing a thing and understanding it.
- **Charles F. Kettering:** *Prophet of Progress*, 1961.

2,367. Reading furnishes the mind only with materials of knowledge; it is thinking that makes what we read ours.
- **John Locke:** *in an essay on reading.*

2,368. A good education is no longer a pathway to opportunity - it is a pre-requisite.
- **Barack Obama:** *in a speech to Congress, 24th February, 2009.*

2,369. Knowledge in youth is wisdom in age.
 - ***English Proverb.***

2,370. Knowledge is a treasure but practice is the key to it.
- ***English Proverb.***

2,371. Not to know is bad, not to wish to know is worse.
- ***Nigerian Proverb.***

2,372. The desire of knowledge, like the thirst of riches, increases ever with the acquisition of it.
- **Laurence Sterne:** *Tristram Shandy, Bk 2*, 1760.

2,373. The most difficult thing in life is knowledge of yourself,
- **Thales**: *Reader's Digest Pocket Treasury of Great Quotations*, 1978.

2,374. The more I read, the more I meditate; and the more I acquire, the more certain I am that I know nothing.
 - **Voltaire:** *Philosophical Dictionary*,1764

LANGUAGE

2,375. We have too many high sounding words, and too few actions that corresponds with them.
- **Abigail Adams:** *in a letter to John Adams, 1774.*

2,376. Be careful of the words you say, / Keep them short and sweet, / You never know, from day to day, / Which ones you'll have to eat.
- ***anon.***

2,377. Drawing on my fine command of language, I said nothing.
- **Robert Benchley:** *The Treasury of Humorous Quotations* edited by Evan Esar, 1955.

2,378. The good man brings good things out of the good stored up in his heart, and the evil man brings evil things out of the evil stored up in his heart. For out of the overflow of his heart his mouth speaks.
- **The Bible:** *Luke, chapter 6, verse 45, NIV.*

2,379. Language was given to us that we might say pleasant things to each other.
- **Christian Nestell Bovee:** *Intuitions and Summaries of Thought,* 1862.

2,380. However many holy words you read, / However many you speak, / What good will they do you / If you do not act upon them?
- **Buddha.**

2,381. Language is called the garment of thought.
- **Thomas Carlyle:** *Sartor Resartus, Bk 1,* 1833 – 1834.

2,382. There is all the difference in the world between having something to say, and saying something.
- **John Dewey:** *Book of Quotations* edited by Judy Hamilton, 2004.

2,383. No one has a better command of the language than the man who knows just when to talk and when to shut up.
- **Evan Esar:** *20,000 Quips and Quotes.*

2,384. They call our language the mother tongue because father seldom gets a chance to use it.
- **Leopold Fechtner:** *5,000 One-And-Two-Line Jokes,* 1986.

2,385. Words - so innocent and powerless as they are, as standing in a dictionary, how potent for good and evil they become in the hands of one who knows how to combine them.
- **Nathaniel Hawthorne:** *The American Notebooks,* 1848.

2,386. Good words are worth much, and cost little.
 - **George Herbert:** *Jacula Prudentum,*(pithy proverbs), 1651.

2,387. Language is the most imperfect and expensive means yet discovered for communicating thought.
- **William James:** *The Thought and Character of William James,* Volume 2, by Ralph Barton Perry. 1935.

 2,388. Words are, of course, the most powerful drug used by mankind.
- **Rudyard Kipling**, *in a speech delivered on February 14th, 1923.*

2,389. The language is alive and constantly moving.
- **W**. **Somerset Maugham:** *The Summing Up,* 1938.

2.390. Words are like leaves, and where they most abound,
Much fruit of sense beneath is rarely found.
- **Alexander Pope:** *An Essay on Criticism,* 1711.

2,391. I am under the spell of language, which has ruled me since I was ten.
 - **V. S. Pritchett:** *New York Times, 4th December, 1980.* NB Pritchett made this statement shortly before his 80th birthday.

2,392. Words are loaded pistols.
- **Jean-Paul Sarte:** *What is Literature and Other Essays,* 1949.

2,393. Language has created the word loneliness to express the pain of being alone, and the word solitude to express the glory of being alone.
- **Paul Tillich:** *The Eternal Now* (1963)

2,394. I think we developed language because of our deep down need to complain.

- **Lily Tomlin:** as Trudy in the one woman stage show, *The Search for Signs of Intelligent Life in the Universe,* written by Jane Wagner, 1985. NB "Man invented language to satisfy his deep inner need to complain" is an unsourced variant.

LAUGHTER

2,395. The amount of energy spent laughing at a joke should be directly proportional to the hierarchical status of the joke teller.
- **Scott Adams:** *Build a Better Life by Stealing Office Supplies: Dogbert's Big Book of Business,* 1994.

2,396. Man is distinguished from all other creatures by the faculty of laughter.
- **Joseph Addison:** *The Spectator, 26th September, 1712.*

2,397. When I think about all the good that laughter does for people, I get the feeling that making people laugh can be noble work.
- **Allan Alda:** from the *Commencement Speech* he made when his daughter, Eve, graduated from Connecticut College in 1980.

2,398. We would all agree that even if laughter were nothing more than sheer silliness and fun, it would still be a precious boon. But we now know that it is far more than that, that it is, in fact, an essential element in emotional health.
- **Steve Allan:** *The Laughter Prescription* by Laurence J. Peter, 1982.

2,399. If you are too busy to laugh, you are altogether too busy.
- *anon.*

2,400. A laugh a day keeps the psychiatrist away.
- *anon.*

2,401. Laughter, n. An interior convulsion, producing a distortion of the features and accompanied by inarticulate noises. It is infectious and, though intermittent, incurable.
- **Ambrose Bierce:** *The Devil's Dictionary*, 1911.

2,402. Laughter sets the spirit free to move through even the most tragic of circumstances. It helps us shake our heads clear, get our feet back under us, restoring our sense of balance and purpose. Humour is integral

to our peace of mind and to our ability to go beyond survival.
- **Captain Gerald Coffee:** *Beyond Survival,* 1991. NB *Beyond Survival* is Captain Coffee's account of his seven year incarceration as a Viet Nam prisoner of war.

2,403. The newspaper accounts had made it appear that I had laughed my way out of a serious illness. Careful readers of my book, however, knew that laughter was just a metaphor for the entire range of positive emotions. Hope, faith, love, the will to live, cheerfulness, humour, creativity, playfulness, confidence, great expectations – all these, I believe, had therapeutic value. Since the negative emotions could set the stage for illnesses, it seemed to me reasonable to believe that the positive emotions might help set the stage for recovery. I never regarded the positive emotions, however, as a substitute for scientific treatment. I saw them as providing an auspicious environment for medical care, a method of optimising prospects of recovery.
- **Norman Cousins:** *Anatomy of an Illness as Perceived by the Patient,* 1979.

2,404. In my mind, there is nothing so illiberal and so ill bred, as audible laughter.
- **Lord Chesterfield:** *Modern Manners: An Etiquette Book for Rude People* by P. J. O'Rourke. 1983.

2,405. The only medicine that needs no prescription, has no unpleasant taste, and costs no money is laughter.
- **Evan Esar:** *20,000 Quips and Quotes,* 1968.

2,406. Laughter is great medicine for what ails you, and there are only good side effects.
- **Sam Ewing:** *Mature Living Magazine, July, 1998.*

2,407. A laugh at your own expense costs nothing.
- **Sam Ewing:** *National Enquirer.*

2,408. There is nothing in which people more betray their character than in what they laugh at.
- **Johann Wolfgang von Goethe:** *Elective Affinities,* 1808.

2,409. Healthy, non-ridiculing and connecting laughter provides physiological, psychological and spiritual benefits you probably never realized or imagined. We are born with the gift of laughter - it's being serious that we learn.
- **Annette Goodheart.**

2,410. God cannot be solemn, or he would not have blessed man with the incalculable gift of laughter.
- **Sydney J. Harris:** *Quotations for Our Time* compiled by Laurence J, Peter, 1977.

2,411. I have been driven by the sound of laughter. All that good energy in the air. Someone once pointed out that the human being is the only being on the planet that has the ability to laugh. I guess that's why I always found my best audience to be humans.
- **Bob Hope:** *My Life in Jokes*, 2003.

2,412. Laughter is sunshine; it chases Winter from the human face.
- **Victor Hugo:** *Les Miserables, Vol 2*, 1862.

2,413. Laughing is my favourite acrobic exercise (right after breathing and eating), and *shared* laughter is my favourite form of fun.
 - **Barbara Johnson:** *Humour Me, I'm Your Mother*, 2003,

2.414. You can't deny laughter; when it comes, it plops down in your favourite chair and stays as long as it wants.
- **Stephen King:** *Stephen King Goes to the Movies (Hearts in Atlantis)*, 2009.

2,415. The sound of laughter is like the vaulted dome of a temple of happiness.
- **Milan Kundera:** *The Book of Laughter and Forgetting*, 1980.

2,416. You can't stay mad at someone who makes you laugh.
- **Jay Leno:** *O Magazine, February, 2003.*

2,417. Laughter is by definition healthy.
- **Doris Lessing:** *Summer Before the Dark*

2,418. I have always done that (laugh at my own jokes), not because I think they are funny but because Papa had told me, "Never depend on strangers".
- **Sam Levenson:** *In One Era and Out the Other*, 1973.

2,419. Gentlemen... with the fearful strain that is upon me night and day, if I did not laugh I should die, and you need this medicine as much as I do.
- **Abraham Lincoln:** speaking to his cabinet after Edwin M. Stanton, the Secretary of War, objected to the President opening the meeting by reading an amusing sketch by Artemus Ward.

2,420. It may be possible to incorporate laughter into daily activities, just as is done with other heart-healthy activities, such as taking the stairs instead of the elevator. The recommendation for a healthy heart may one day be exercise, eat right and laugh a few times a day.
- **Michael Miller**.

2,421. Laughter is... the hilarious declaration made by man that life is worth living.
- **Sean O'Casey:** *Simpson's Contemporary Quotations* compiled by James B. Simpson, 1988.

2,422. For a long time, medical doctors have known that happy patients generally respond more favourably to treatment and recover faster than do cheerless and complaining ones.
- **Laurence J. Peter:** *The Laughter Prescription*, 1982.

2,423. Examination of available findings... indicates that the physical benefits of humour have a firm scientific basis.
- *ibid.*

2,424. He who laughs, lasts!
- **Mary Pettibone Poole:** quoted in her book of epigrams: *A Glass Eye at a Keyhole*, 1938.

2,425. Laughter is the most beautiful and beneficial therapy God ever granted humanity.
- **Charles Swindoll:** *Laugh Again*, 1992.

2,426. A good laugh is sunshine in the house.
- **William Makepeace Thackeray**.

2,427. Against the assault of laughter nothing can stand.
- **Mark Twain:** *The Mysterious Stranger*, published postumously, 1916.

2,428. I was irrevocably betrothed to laughter, the sound of which has always seemed to me the most civilized music in the world.
- **Sir Peter Ustinov:** quoted in his autobiography, *Dear Me*, 1977.

2,429. Laughter is a smile that engages the entire body.
- **Patty Wooten**.

THE LAW AND LAWYERS

2,430. Education is worth a whole lot. Just think – with enough education and brains the average man would make a good lawyer – and so would the average lawyer.
- **Gracie Allen:** *Gracie: A Love Story* by George Burns,1989.

2,431. Lawyers are the only persons in whom ignorance of the law is not punished.
- **Jeremy Bentham:** *The Canadian Bar Journal, 1966.*

2,432. Most attorneys practice because it gives them a grand and glorious feeling. Hand them a grand and they feel glorious!
- **Milton Berle:** *Milton Berle's Private Joke File*, 1989.

2,433. This lawyer helped a woman lose a hundred and eighty pounds of fat. He got her a divorce.
- *ibid.*

2,434. If there were no bad people, there would be no good lawyers.
- **Charles Dickens:** *The Old Curiosity Shop*, 1841.

2,435. A lawyer with his brief case can steal more than a hundred men with guns.
- Marlin Brando as Don Corleone in the **1960 Film:** *The Godfather.*

2,436. Don't mess with me, man, I'm a lawyer!
- **Robin Williams** in his role as Peter Pan in the **1991 Film:** *Hook*, based on the play by Sir J. M. Barrie.

2,437. I am delighted to see so many lawyers here. I hope you are not all charging for your time or we'll be bankrupt.
- **Christine Hamilton:** at the launch of her autobiography, *For Better For Worse. Quotes of the Day* in the *Press & Journal, 24th March, 2005.*

2,438. You can hire logic, in the shape of a lawyer, to prove anything that you want to prove.
- **Oliver Wendell Holmes:** *Autocrat at the Breakfast Table*, 1858.

2,439. I do not care to speak ill of any man behind his back, but I believe the gentleman is an attorney.
- **Samuel Johnson.**

2,440. Anyone who thinks talk is cheap should get some legal advice.
- **Franklin P. Jones.**

2,441. If you must take the law into your own hands, strangle a solicitor.
- **Bob Monkhouse:** *Just Say a Few Words*, 1988.

2,442. The minute that you read something that you can't understand, you can almost be sure it was drawn up by a lawyer.
- **Will Rogers:** *Illiterate Digest*.

2,443. We live in a ridiculously litigatious society. Opportunists know that a wet floor or a hot cup of coffee can put them in easy street.
- **Morgan Spurlock:** *Don't Eat This Book. Fast Food and the Supersizing of America, 2005*.

2,444. I always figured that being a good robber was like being a good lawyer.
- **Willie Sutton:** *Where the Money Was: The Memoir of a Bank Robber*, 1976.

2,445. Laws are like cobwebs, which may catch small flies, but let wasps and hornets break through.
- **Jonathan Swift:** *A Critical Essay Upon the Faculties of the Mind*, 1707.

2,446. My lawyer has never given me bad advice. He sells it to me.
- **Pat Williams:** *Winning With One-Liners, 2002*.

2,447. He's such a dedicated lawyer that he even named his daughter Sue.
- *ibid.*

LEARNING

2,448. Learning is not attained by chance, it must be sought for with ardour and attended to with diligence.
- **Abigail Adams:** *Letter to her son, John, 1780.*

2,449. The purpose of learning is growth, and our minds, unlike our bodies, can continue growing as long as we live.
- **Mortimer J. Adler**.

2,450. All genuine learning is active, not passive. It involves the use of the mind, not just the memory. It is the process of discovery in which the student is the main agent, not the teacher.
- **Mortimer J. Adler**.

2,451. If you study to remember, you will forget, but if you study to understand, you will remember.
- ***anon***.

2,452. Anything that we have to learn we learn by the actual doing of it. We become just by performing just acts, temperate by performing temperate ones, brave by performing brave ones.
- **Aristotle:** *Nicomachean Ethics,* 4th century BC.

2,453. Learning should be a joy and full of excitement. It is life's greatest adventure, it is an illustrated excursion into the minds of the noble and the learned.
- **Taylor Caldwell:** *The Sound of the Thunder,* 1957.

2,454. I am always ready to learn although I do not always like to be taught.
- **Sir Winston Churchill:** *The Observer, 9th November, 1952.*

2,455. Learning is a kind of natural food for the mind.
- **Marcus Tullius Cicero**.

2,456. Develop a passion for learning. If you do so, you will never cease to grow.
- **Anthony J. D'Angelo:** *The College Blue Book*, 1995.

2,457. Learning is not compulsory, neither is survival.
- **W. Edwards Deming**.

2,458. Universities won't survive. The future is outside the traditional campus, outside the traditional classroom. Distance learning is coming on fast.
- **Peter Drucker**.

2,459. It is impossible for a man to begin to learn what he thinks he knows.
- **Epictetus:** *Discourses*, 1st - 2nd century BC.

2,460. Whoso neglects learning in his youth loses the past and is dead for the future.
- **Euripides**.

2,461. To teach one's self is to be forced to learn twice.
- **Ellen Glasgow:** *The Woman Within* NB Ellen Glasgow's autobiography, *The Woman Within*, was published posthumously in 1954.

2,462. All wish to be learned, but no one is willing to pay the price.
- **Juvenal:** *Satires*, 1st - 2nd century AD

2,463. Erudition can produce foliage without bearing fruit.
- **Georg Christoph Lichtenberg:** *Notebook C*, 1772 – 1773.

2,464. Those who have not distinguished themselves at school need not on that account be discouraged. The greatest minds do not necessarily ripen the quickest.
- **Sir John Lubbock**. NB A list of well known people who made major achievements in old age is available on the Internet at:
www.medrounds.org/achievements-at-advanced-age-action.html

2,465. If we succeed in giving the love of learning, the learning itself is sure to follow.
- **Sir John Lubbock**.

2,466. When I learn something new – and it happens every day – I feel a little more at home in this universe, a little more comfortable in the nest.
- **Bill Moyers**.

2,467. A little learning is a dangerous thing.
- **Alexander Pope:** *An Essay on Criticism*, 1711.

2,468. Gold has a price, but learning is priceless.
- *Chinese Proverb*.

2,469. Learning is like rowing upstream; not to advance is to stop.
- *ibid*.

2,470. I hear; I forget, / I see; I remember, / I do; I understand
- *Chinese Proverb:* quoted in *Creative Thinking. How to Generate Ideas and Turn Them Into Reality* by Michael Le Boeuf, 1994.

2,471. Whilst doing one learns.
- *Dutch Proverb*.

2,472. A maiden in college, Miss Breeze,
Weighed down with BA's and PhD's,
Collapsed from the strain,
Said her doctor, "It's plain
You are killing yourself – by degrees."
- **Leo Rosten:** *Leo Rosten's Book of Laughter*, 1985.

2,473. When you stop learning, stop listening, stop looking and asking questions, always new questions, then it is time to die.
- **Lillian Smith**.

2,474. The illiterate of the 21st century will not be those who cannot read and write, but those who cannot learn, unlearn and relearn.
- **Alvin Toffler:** *Future Shock*, 1970.

2,475. Why waste time learning, when ignorance is instantaneous?
- **Bill Watterson:** *Attack of the Deranged Mutant Killer Monster Snow Goons*, 1992.

2,476. The joy of learning is as indispensable in study as breathing is in running. Where it is lacking there are no real students.
- **Simone Weil:** *Waiting for God*, 1951.

LEISURE AND RECREATION

2,477. Periods of wholesome laziness, after days of energetic effort, will wonderfully tone up the mind and body.
- **Grenville Kleiser.**

2,478. Every now and then go away, have a little relaxation, for when you come back to your work your judgement will be surer since to remain constantly at work will cause you to lose power of judgement.
- **Leonardo Da Vinci:** *The Notebooks of Leonardo Da Vinci.*

2,479. Rest is not idleness, and to lie sometimes on the grass under trees on a Summer's day, listening to the murmur of water, or watching the clouds float across the blue sky, is by no means a waste of time.
- **Sir John Lubbock:** *The Use of Life,* 1894.

2,480. The time to relax is when we don't have time for it.
- **Joan Lunden.**

2,481. For Fast Acting Relief, Try Slowing Down!
- **Joan Lunden,** chapter title in *Wake-Up Calls,* 2001.

2.482. Our minds need relaxation and give way Unless we mix with work a little play.
 - **Moliere:** *School for Husbands,* 1661.

2,483. In our leisure we reveal what kind of people we are.
- **Ovid.**

2,484. The best intelligence test is what we do with our leisure.
- **Laurence J. Peter:** *Quotations For Our Time,* 1977.

2,485. That indolent but agreeable condition of doing nothing.
- **Pliny the Younger:** 1st and 2nd century BC.

2,486. If a man is to be liberated to enjoy more leisure, he must also be prepared to enjoy this leisure fully and creatively
Eleanor Roosevelt: *My Day. The Best of Eleanor Roosevelt's Acclaimed Newspaper Column, 1936 – 1962.*

2,487. There's never enough time to do all the nothing you want.
- **Bill Watterson:** *The Authoritative Calvin and Hobbes,* 1991.

2,488 It is not when he is working in his office but when he is lying idly on the sand that his soul utters, "Life is beautiful."
- **Lin Yutang:** *The Importance of Living,* 1937.

LENDING AND BORROWING

2,489. If you borrow a hundred pounds from the bank and you cannot repay it, you have a problem. If you borrow a million pounds from the bank and you cannot repay it, the bank has a problem.
- ***anon***.

2,490. How times have changed: in the old days it was much harder getting a loan than paying it back.
- **Evan Esar:** *20,000 Quips and Quotes*, 1968.

2,491. Never lend books, for no one ever returns them; the only books I have in my library are books that other folks have lent to me.
- **Anatole France:** *On Life and Letters*, 1924.

2,492. He that goes a-borrowing goes a-sorrowing.
- **George Herbert:** *Outlandish Proverbs*, 1630.

2,493. The human species, according to the best theory I can form of it, is composed of two distinct races: the men who borrow and the men who lend.
- **Charles Lamb:** *The Two Races of Men* in *London Magazine, Dec., 1820*.

2,494. Your borrowers of books – those mutilators of collections, spoilers of the symmetry of shelves, and creators of odd volumes.
- ***ibid***.

2,495. Always borrow from a pessimist – he never expects it back anyhow.
- **Herbert V. Prochnow and Herbert V. Prochnow Jr:** *Jokes, Quotes and One-Liners, Vol 2*, 1983.

2,496. To know the price of money one must be compelled to borrow some.
- ***French Proverb***.

2,497. Neither a borrower, nor a lender be;
For loan oft loses both itself and friend.
- **William Shakespeare:** *Hamlet, Act 1, Sc 3,* 1601.

2,498. The holy passion of friendship is of so sweet and steady and loyal and enduring nature that it will last through a whole lifetime, if not asked to lend money.
 - **Mark Twain:** *The Tragedy of Pudd'nhead Wilson,* 1894.

2,499. Let us all be happy and live within our means, even if we have to borrer the money to do it with.
- **Artemus Ward:** *Punch, 1866.*

LETTERS

2,500. Letters are expectation packaged in an envelope.
- **Shana Alexander:** *Life Magazine, 30th June, 1967.*

2.501. Never answer an anonymous letter.
- **Yogi Berra:** *The Yogi Book: I Really Didn't Say Everything I Said,* 1998.

2,502. I found a letter to my sister the other day that I had forgotten to mail. It just needed a little updating to send. After "The baby is..." I crossed out, "toilet trained" and wrote in, "graduating from high school this month."
 - **Erma Bombeck:** *If Life is a Bowl of Cherries – What Am I Doing in the Pits?* 1981.

2,503. It's against the law to send threatening letters through the post, except when the Inland Revenue does it.
- **Evan Esar:** *20,000 Quips and Quotes,* 1968.

2,504. Letters are among the most significant memorial a person can leave behind them.
- **Johann Wolfgang von Goethe.**

2,505. When a man sends you an impudent letter, sit right down and give it back to him with interest ten times compounded, and then throw both letters in the wastebasket.
- **Elbert Hubbard**. NB: The Chinese proverb "Never write a letter while you are angry":

2,506. Read my heart for "the quill cannot express good will"
- **Michelangelo:** *in a letter to Tommaso dei Cavalieri, 1st January, 1533.*

2,507. The present letter is a very long one, simply because I have had no leisure to make it shorter.
- **Blaise Pascal:** *The Provincial Letters. Letter XVI (to the Reverend Fathers, the Jesuits), 4th December, 1656.*

2,508. And oft, the pangs of absence to remove
By letters, soft interpreters of love.
- **Matthew Prior:** *Henry and Emma*,1793

2,509. Correspondences are like small clothes before the invention of suspenders, it is impossible to keep them up.
- **Sydney Smith:** *in a letter to Catherine Crowe, 31ˢᵗ January, 1841.*

2,510. Unlike a telephone call, letters take commitment and concentration. They're like paper kisses, some short and sweet, others long and deep.
- **Susan Besze Wallace:** *Love and War: 250 Years of Wartime Love Letters,* 1997.

LIES AND LIARS

2,511. There is no believing a liar, even when he speaks the truth.
- The moral of **Aesop's Fable**: *The Shepherd Boy and the Wolf.*

2,512. Any fool can tell the truth, but it requires a man of some sense to know how to lie well.
- **Samuel Butler**, *Notebooks*, 1912.

2,513. I do not mind lying, but I hate inaccuracy.
- *ibid.*

2,514. I know nothing more criminal, more mean, and more ridiculous than lying... for lies are always detected sooner or later.
- **Lord Chesterfield**, *Letters to His Son*, 21st September, 1747.

2,515. Thou liar of the first magnitude.
- **William Congreve**, *Time for Love*, Act 2, Sc 2, 1695.

2,516. Keep your lies short and simple.
- **Masson Cooley**, *City Aphorisms, Eighth Selection*, 1991.

2,517. It takes good memory to keep up a lie.
- **Pierre Corneille**, *The Liar*, Act 4, Sc 5, 1642.

2,518. Permit your child to tell white lies, and he will grow up colour-blind.
- **Evan Esar**, *20,000 Quips and Quotes*, 1968.

2,519. Don't tell a lie! Some men I've known / Commit the most appalling acts, / Because they happen to be prone / To an economy of facts / And if to *lie* is bad, no doubt, / 'Tis even worse to get *found out.*
- **Harry Graham**, *Ruthless Rhymes for Heartless Homes*, 1899.

2,520. That's not a lie, it's a terminological inexactitude (and) also a tactical misrepresentation.
- **Alexander Haig**.

2,521. The slickest way to tell a lie is to tell the right amount of truth – then shut up.
 - **Robert A. Heinlein**, *Strangers in a Strange Land*, 1961.

2,522. The great masses of the people... will more easily fall victims to a big lie than to a small one.
 - **Adolph Hitler**, *Mein Kampf*, 1927.

2,523. By means of shrewd lies, unremittingly repeated, it is possible to make people believe that heaven is hell, and hell is heaven. The greater the lie, the more readily it will be believed.
 - *ibid.*

2,524. We lie loudest when we lie to ourselves.
 - **Eric Hoffer:** *The Passionate State of Mind*, 1955.

2,525. Sin has many tools, but a lie is the handle which fits them all.
- **Oliver Wendell Holmes:** *The Autocrat at the Breakfast Table*, 1858.

2,526. The most dangerous of all falsehoods is a slightly distorted truth.
 - **Georg Christoph Lichtenberg:** *Notebook H*, 1784 – 1788.

2,527. No man has a good enough memory to make a successful liar.
- **Abraham Lincoln:** *The Wit and Wisdom of Abraham Lincoln* edited by Alex Ayres, 1992.

2,528. They say George Washington could never tell a lie. My wife can. As soon as she hears it.
- **Bob Monkhouse:** *Just Say a Few Words*, 1988.

2,529. Unless a man feels he has a good enough memory, he should never venture to lie.
- **Michel de Montaigne**.

2,530. It is twice as hard to crush a half truth as a whole lie.
- **Austin O'Malley:** *Keystones of Thought*. 1914.

2,531. Those that think it permissible to tell white lies soon grow colour blind.
 - *ibid.*

2,532. Telling lies is a fault in a boy, an art in a lover, an accomplishment in a bachelor, and second nature in a married man.
- **Helen Rowland:** *A Guide to Men*, 1922.

2,533. A little inaccuracy sometimes saves tons of explanation.
- **Saki:** *The Square Egg and Other Stories*, 1924.

2,534. We should keep so close to facts that we never have to remember the second time what we said the first time.
- **Francis Marion Smith**.

2,535. A lie never lives to be old.
- **Sophocles:** *Fragment*, 5th century BC.

2,536. The cruellest lies are often told in silence.
- **Robert Louis Stevenson:** *Virginibus Puerisque*, 1881.

2,537. Minor white lies permeate our daily lives, especially when we feel the need to protect someone else's feelings.
- **Mitch Thrower:** *The Attention Deficit Workplace*, 2005.

2,538. There was things which he stretched, but mainly he told the truth.
- **Mark Twain:** *The Adventures of Huckleberry Finn*, 1884.

2,539. There are three kinds of lies: lies, damned lies, and statistics.
- **Mark Twain:** *Autobiography*. 1924.
NB Mark Twain may not be the originator of this saying. It has been suggested that he may have been quoting Benjamin Disraeli.

LIFE AND LIVINGS

2,540. When we are motivated by goals that have deep meaning, by dreams that need completion, by pure love that needs expressing, then we truly live life.
- **Greg Anderson:** *The 22 Non-Negotiable Laws of Wellness*, 1996.

2,541. Having nothing to carry is life's heaviest burden, having nothing to do is life's hardest work, and having nothing to look forward to is life's darkest picture.
- *anon.*

2,542. Live to make the child you were proud of the person you are.
- *anon:* quoted in *Open Your Mind, Open Your Life* by Taro Gold, 2002.

2,543. Life is not measured by the number of breaths we take, but by the moments that take our breath away.
- *anon.*

2,544. Life is a journey and love is what makes the journey worthwhile
- *anon: Voyages: A Travel Journal* by Evelyn Loeb, 2002.

2,545. Life is a game, play it. Life is a challenge, meet it. Life is an opportunity, seize it.
- *anon.*

2,546. Life requires us to live with the consequences of our choices.
- **Richard Bach:** *Running From Safety*, 1994.

2,547. The life of every man is a diary in which he means to write one story, and writes another; and his humblest hour is when he compares the volume as it is with what he vowed to make it.
- **Sir James M. Barrie:** *The Little Minister*, 1891.

2,548. From the hour you're born you begin to die, but between birth and death there's life.
- **Simone de Beauvoire:** *All Men Are Mortal*, 1946.

2,549. Life is rather like a tin of sardines – we're all of us looking for the key.
 - **Alan Bennett:** *Beyond the Fringe*, 1960.

2,550. Life consists not in holding good cards but in playing well those you hold.
- **Josh Billings**.

2,551. If I had my life to live over again I would have talked less and listened more. But mostly, given another shot at life, I would seize every moment of it, look at it and really see it. try it on, live it, exhaust it, and never give that moment back until there was nothing left of it.
- **Erma Bombeck:** *Aunt Erma's Cope Book*, 1985.

2,552. It's a great life if you don't weaken.
- **John Buchan:** *Mr Standfast*, 1919.

2,553. Here's to life. Let's live it.
- **Anthony Burgess:** *Enderby's Dark Lady*, 1984.

2,554. Life is a struggle, but not a warfare.
- **John Burroughs:** *The Summit of the Years*, 1913.

 2,555. It's not enough to have lived. We should be determined to live for something. May I suggest that it be creating joy for others, sharing what we have, bringing hope to the lost and love to the lonely.
- **Leo Buscaglia:** *Love,*1982

2,556. He has spent his life best who has enjoyed it most.
- **Samuel Butler:** *The Way of all Flesh*, 1903.

 2,557. We must understand that life is a more profound experience than we are told it is. After all, the likelihood of life beginning by chance is about as great as a hurricane blowing through a scrap yard and assembling a Rolls Royce.
- **Charles, Prince of Wales:** *Thought for the Day, BBC Radio 4, 1/ 1 / 01*

2,558. What is the use of living, if it be not to strive for noble causes and to make this muddled world a better place to live in after we are gone?
- **Sir Winston Churchill:** *The Wit and Wisdom of Winston Churchill* by. James C. Humes, 61994.

2,559. We make a living by what we get, but we make a life by what we give.
- *ibid.*

2,560. Our span of life is brief, but it is long enough for us to live well and honestly.
- **Marcus Tullius Cicero.**

2,561. Life is too short to waste.
- **Ralph Waldo Emerson:** *Essays, 2nd Series,* 1844.

2,562. Only a life lived for others is a life worthwhile.
- **Albert Einstein:** *New York Times, 20th June, 1932.*

2,563. Life can be grim when you pass 80, especially if there is a police car behind you.
- **Sam Ewing:** *The Sun, 11th May, 1999.*

2,564. Life is like a box of chocolates. You never know what you're gonna get.
- Sally Field in her role as Mrs Gump, to her son, played by Tom Hanks, in the **1994 Film:** *Forrest Gump.*

2,565. Carpe Diem, seize the day boys, make your lives extraordinary.
- Robin Williams in his role as the unorthodox English teacher in the **1989 Film:** *Dead Poets Society.*

2,566. Those who have a "why" to live, can bear with almost any "how."
- **Victor Frankl:** *Man's Search for Meaning,* 1946.

2,567. In three words I can sum up everything I've learned about life – it goes on.
- **Robert Frost.**

2,568. Life is the childhood of our immortality.
- **Johann Wolfgang von Goethe.**

2,569. If I were asked what I thought life is for I'd say it was for making discoveries, and I think the greatest gift anyone can have is an unending sense of discovery, and with it an increasing awareness of delight and wonder.
- **Joyce Grenfell:** *Thought For the Day, BBC Radio 4.*

2,570. Life only demands from you the strength you possess. Only one feat is possible - not to have run away.
- **Dag Hammarskjold:** *Markings.* 1964.

2,571. Life grants nothing to us mortals without hard work.
- **Horace:** *Satires*, 1st century BC.

2,572. It is only life and love that give love and life.
- **Elbert Hubbard:** *The Notebook of Elbert Hubbard*, 1927.

2,573. Believe that life is worth living and your belief will create the fact.
- **William James:** *The Verities of Religious Experience*, 1902.

2,574. The best use of life is to spend it for something that outlasts life.
- *ibid.*

2,575. Life is a gift. Unwrap your present !
- **Barbara Johnson:** *Splashes of Joy, 365 Gems to Sparkle Your Day*, 2000.

2,576. The love of life is necessary to the vigorous prosecution of any undertaking.
- **Samuel Johnson:** *The Rambler*, 1751 – 1752.

2,577. Thank you God for this good life and forgive us if we do not love it enough.
- **Garrison Keiller:** *Leaving Home*, 1987.

2,578. Redeem thy mis-spent time that's past; Live this day as if twere thy last.
- **Bishop Thomas Ken:** *A Morning Hymn* in the Church of Scotland's *Church Hymnary, Fourth Edition*, 2005.

2,579. When we were children, we used to think that when we were grown up we would no longer be vulnerable. But to grow up is to accept vulnerability... to be alive is to be vulnerable.
- **Madeleine L'Engle:** *Walking on Water. Reflections on Faith & Art*, 1980.

2,580. I like living. I have sometimes been wildly, despairingly, acutely miserable, racked with sorrow, but through it all I still know quite certainly that just to be alive is a grand thing.
- **Evelyn Loeb:** *Count Your Blessings*, 2003.

2,581. We cannot choose how many years we will live. But we can choose how much life those years will have.
- **John C. Maxwell:** *Developing the Leader Within You*, 2001.

2,582. Life is an endlessly creative experience, and we are shaping ourselves at every moment by every decision we make.
- **Kent Nerburn:** *Simple Truths: Clear and Gentle Guidance on the Big Issues of Life*, 1996.

2,583. We are all functioning at a small fraction of our capacity to live fully in it's total meaning of loving, caring, creating and adventuring. Consequently, the actualizing of our potential can become the most exciting adventure of our life-time.
- **Herbert Otto:** *Love: What Life is All About* , 1972.

2,584. The whole life of man is but a point of time; let us enjoy it, therefore, while it lasts, and not spend it to no purpose.
- **Plutarch:** *Moralia* , ***circa*** 100 AD

2,585. While we have the gift of life, it seems to me the only tragedy is to allow part of us to die – whether it is our spirit, our creativity, or our glorious uniqueness.
- **Gilda Radner:** *It's Always Something*, 1989.
NB In this book Gilda Radner tells of her battle with ovarian cancer. This was published in the year of her death at the age of 42.

2,586. The purpose of life is to live it - to taste the experience to the utmost, to reach out eagerly and without fear for newer and richer experiences.
- **Eleanor Roosevelt:** *Older and Wiser* by J. Cranfield **et al**, 2008.

2,587. Life was meant to be lived, and curiosity must be kept alive.One must never, for whatever reason, turn one's back on life.
- **Eleanor Roosevelt:** *The Autobiography of Eleanor Roosevelt*, 1961

2.588. Life's but a walking shadow, a poor player
That struts and frets his hour upon the stage
And then is heard no more; it is a tale
Told by an idiot, full of sound and fury,
Signifying nothing.
- **William Shakespeare:** *Macbeth Act V*.

2,589. To be what we are, and to become what we are capable of becoming, is the only end of life.
- **R. L. Stevenson:** *Familiar Studies of Men and Books.*

2,590. Life is not simply about diligence and duty, vigilance and crusading. It is also about play and relaxation, fun and laughter, about glad to be alive.
- **James A. Simpson:** *The Laugh Shall be First.* 1998.

2,591. There are two things to aim at in life; first to get what you want, and, after that, enjoy it. Only the wisest of mankind achieve the second.
- **Logan Pearsall Smith:** *Aftrethoughts,* 1931.

2,592. Life's meaning has always eluded me, but I guess it always will. But I love it.
- **E. B. White:** *in a letter to Mary Virginia Parrish, 29ᵗʰ August, 1969.*

LISTENING

2,593. Children have never been very good at listening to their elders, but they have never failed to imitate them.
- **James Baldwin:** *Nobody Knows My Name.*

2,594. The way of a fool seems right to him, but a wise man listens to advice.
- **The Bible:** Proverbs 12: 15, NIV.

2,595. Nature gives us one tongue and two ears so we could hear twice as much as we speak.
- **Epictetus:** *Discoveries, 2nd century, AD.*

2,596. Some men are naturally good listeners; others get married and have to be.
- **Evan Esar:** *20,00 Quips and Quotes,* 1968.

2,597. A good listener is sometimes a man with nothing to say, and sometimes a woman with a sore throat.
- ***ibid.***

2,598. One often reads about the art of conversation - how it's dying, or what's needed to make it flourish, or how rare good ones are. But wouldn't you agree that the infinitly more valuable rara avis is a good listener?
- **Malcolm Forbes:** *The Forbes Book of Business Quotations,* 1997.
NB rara avis *n.* a person rarely encountered.

2,599. The opposite of talking isn't listening. The opposite of talking is waiting.
- **Fran Lebowitz:** *Social Studies,* 1981.

2,600. No one really listens to anyone else, and if you try it for a while you'll see why.
- **Mignon McLaughlin:** *The Neurotic's Notebook,* 1960.

2,601. A good listener is not only popular everywhere, but after a while he gets to know something.
- **Wilson Mizner:** *Dreamers, Schemers & Scalawags*, 1994.

2,602. Know how to listen, and you will profit even from those who talk badly.
- **Plutarch:** *Morals*, 1st and 2nd century AD

2,603. From listening comes wisdom.
- *Italian Proverb.*

2,604. The first duty of love is to listen.
- **Paul Tillich:** recalled on his death on 22nd October, 1965. Quoted in *Simpson's Contemporary Quotations* compiled by James Simpson, 1988.

2,605. Hearing is one of the body's five senses; but listening is an art.
- **Frank Tyger:** an oft-quoted aphorist about whom little is known.

2,606. Learn to listen. Opportunity could be knocking at your door very softly.
- **Frank Tyger.**

2,607. Be a good listener. Your ears will never get you into trouble.
- **Frank Tyger.**

LOVE

2,608. The greatest thing you'll ever learn
Is just to love and be loved in return.
- From *Nature Boy:* the 1848 song with lyrics and music by **Eden Ahbez**.

2,609. Love is a great beautifier.
- **Louisa May Alcott:** *Little Women.* 1868.

2,610. True love is that which ennobles the personality, fortifies the heart and sanctifies the existence.
- **Henri Frederic Amiel:** *Journey in Time,* 1882.

2,611. We are weaned from our timidity,
In the flush of love's light we dare to be brave,
And suddenly we see that love costs all
that we are and will ever be.
Yet it is only love which sets us free.
- **Maya Angelou:** the final stanza of her poem *Touched By An Angel.*

2,612.
A. Falling in love is awfully simple, but falling out of love is simply awful.
B. A philosopher defined the difference between life and love as follows: "Life is just one fool thing after another, love is just two things after each other."
C. Like the measles, love is most dangerous when it comes late in life.
D. To love you must show your love.
- *anon.*

2,613. Love is, above all else, the gift of oneself.
- **Jean Anouilh:** *The Cry of the Peacock,* 1948.

2,614. Sand is also a good place on which to write, "I love you," as it would be difficult to get into court after several years had passed.
- **Robert Benchley:** *No Poems, or Around the World Backwards and Sideways,* 1932.

2,615. Love is patient, love is kind... it is not easily angered, it keeps no record of wrongs... It always protects, always trusts, always hopes, always perseveres.
- **The Bible:** *1ˢᵗ Corinthians 13: 4 – 7, NIV.*

2,616. There is no fear in love. . . perfect love drives out fear.
- **The Bible:** *1ˢᵗ John 4: 18, NIV.*

2,617. Love: n. A temporary insanity curable either by marriage or by the removal of the influence under which he incurred the disorder..
- **Ambrose Bierce:** *The Devil's Dictionary,* 1911.

2,618. Love to faults is always blind.
- **William Blake:** *Poems from William Blake's Notebook,* 1792.

2,619. Love comes when manipulation stops; when you think more about the other person than about his or her reactions to you. When you dare to reveal yourself fully. When you dare to be vulnerable.
- **Joyce Brothers:** *Courage: The Choice That Makes the Difference* by Dwight Goldwinde, 2004.

2,620. How do I love thee? Let me count the ways.
- **Elizabeth Barrett Browning:** *Sonnets From the Portuguese,* 1850.

2,621. Love is a lot like backache, it doesn't show up on X-rays, but we know that it's there.
- **George Burns:** *Gracie: A Love Story,* 1987.

2,622. We need others to love and we need to be loved by them. There is no doubt that without it, we too, like the infant left alone, would cease to grow.
- **Leo Buscaglia:** *Love,* 1962.

2,623. One does not fall "in" or "out" of love. One grows in love.
- ***ibid.***
CP Sam Keen's assertion noted in 2,640.

2,624. What the world needs now is love, sweet love
It's the only thing that there's just too little of,
What the world needs now is love, sweet love.
No, not just for some but for everyone.
- *What the World Needs Now is Love:* 1965 song, lyrics by **Hal David,** music by Burt Bacharach.

2,625. The pleasures of love are for those who are hopelessly addicted to another human person. The reasons for such addiction are so many that I suspect they are never the same in any two cases.
- **Robertson Davies:** *The Pleasures of Love*, 1961.

2,626. True love always makes a man better, no matter what woman inspires it.
- **Alexander Dumas:** *Camille*, 1852.

2,627. I was born when she kissed me. I died when she left me. I lived a few weeks while she loved me.
- Humphrey Bogart in his role as Dixon Steele in the **1950 Film:** *In a Lonely Place*.

2,628. Love is a Many-Splendoured Thing.
- The Academy Award-winning song from the **1955 Film:** *Love is a Many Splendoured Thing*, starring William Holden and Jennifer Jones. Lyrics by Paul Francis Webster, music by Sammy Fain.

2,629. I never knew it could be like this.
- Deborah Kerr as Karen Homes speaking to Sergeant Milton Warden, played by Burt Lancaster, in the **1955 Film:** *From Here to Eternity*.

2,630. When you fall in love, it is a temporary madness. It erupts like an earthquake and then subsides. And when it subsides you have to make a decision. You have to work out whether your roots have become so entwined together that it is inconceivable that you should ever part. Because that is what love is.
- **John Hurt** in his role as Dr Iannis in the **2001 Film:** *Captain Corelli's Mandolin*.

2,631. If two people who have been strangers let the wall between them break down, and feel close, feel one, this moment of oneness is one of the most exhilerating, most exciting experiences in life.
- **Eric Fromm:** *The Art of Loving*, 1957.

2,632. Love is an irresistible desire to be irresistibly desired.
- **Robert Frost**.

2,633. Love that is not expressed in loving actions does not really exist, just as talent that does not express itself in creative works does not exist; neither of these is a state of mind or a feeling, but an *activity*, or it is a myth.
- **Sydney J. Harris:** *Pieces of Eight*, 1975.

2,634. The story of love is not important – what is important is that one is capable of love. It is perhaps the only glimpse we are permitted of eternity.
- **Helen Hayes:** *Guideposts Magazine, January, 1960.*

2,635. Love is that condition in which the happiness of another person is essential to your own.
- **Robert A. Heinlein:** *Stranger in a Strange Land,* 1961.

2,636. If I know what love is, it is because of you.
- **Hermann Hesse:** *Narcissus and Goldmund,* 1930.

2,637. When you're away, I'm restless, lonely,
Wretched, bored, dejected; only
Here's the rub, my darling dear,
I feel the same when you are here.
- **Samuel Hoffenstein:** *Poems of Passion Carefully Restrained So as to Offend Nobody* in *The Complete Poetry of Samuel Hoffenstein.* 1954.

2,638. Love grows by giving. The love we give away is the only love we keep. The only way to retain love is to give it away.
- **Elbert Hubbard:** *Love, Life and Work,* 1906.

2,639. Do you want me to tell you something subversive ? Love is everything it's cracked up to be. That's why people are so cynical about it. It really is worth fighting for, being brave for, risking everything for, and the trouble is, if you don't risk everything, you risk even more.
- **Erica Jong:** *How to Save Your Own Life,* 1977.

2,640. Love is not something we "fall" into, but a complex art combining many skills and talents that take a lifetinme to learn.
- **Sam Keen:** *To Love and be Loved,* 1997.

2,641. When one has once fully entered the realm of love, the world - no matter how imperfect - becomes rich and beautiful, it consists solely of opportunities for love.
- **Soren Kierkegaard:** *Works of Love,* 1847.

2,642. To be with those we love is happiness; even if both are silent, the mere fact of being together is sufficient.
- **Jean de La Bruyere:** *The Morals and Manners of the Seventeenth Century; Being the Characters of La Bruyere* translated by Helen Stott, 1890.

2,643. Life is a journey, and love is what makes the journey worthwhile.
- **Evelyn Loeb:** *Voyages Journal,* 2002.

2,644. Love is a living thing. Anything living must be nurtured. It takes time, effort, attention, and sometimes work, but the return is way over tenfold.
- **Reba McEntire:** *Reba: My Story,* 1994.

2,645. In the arithmetic of love, one plus one equals everything, and two minus one equals nothing.
- **Mignon McLaughlin:** *The Second Neurotic's Notebook,* 1966.

2,646. It seems like the whole world is obsessed with love, although no one can really agree what it actually *is*... For a thing we really can't identify, we are all certainly very preoccupied with finding it, keeping it, maintaining it, reviving it, getting rid of it, and then starting all over again anew.
- **Merrill Markoe:** *Merrill Markoe's Guide to Love,* 1997.

2,647. To love means to open ourselves to the negatives as well as the positives – to grief, sorrow and disappointment, as well as to joy, fulfilment, and an intensity of consciousness we did not know was possible before.
- **Rollo May:** *Love and Will,* 1969.

2,648. If you want to be loved, be lovable.
- **Ovid:** *The Art of Love,* **circa** 16 BC.

2,649. Love ever gives, forgives, outlives, and ever stands with open hands.and while it lives it gives. For this is love's prerogative, to give and give and give.
- **John Oxenham**.

2,650. Oh, life is a glorious cycle of song,
A medley of extemporanea;
And love is a thing than can never go wrong;
And I am Marie of Roumania.
- **Dorothy Parker:** *Comment* in *Enough Rope,* 1926.
2,651. But though first love's impassion'd blindness
Has pass'd away in colder light,
I still have thought of you with kindness,
And shall do, till our last good-night.
- **Thomas Love Peacock:** *Love and Age* in *The Oxford Book of English Verse (1250 – 1900)* edited by Arthur Quiller-Couch, 1919.

2,652. When we love something it is of value to us, and when something is of value to us we spend time with it, time enjoying it and time taking care of it.
- **M. Scott Peck:** *The Road Less Travelled: A New Psychology of Love, Traditional Values and Spiritual Growth*, 1979.

2,653. Ultimately love is everything.
- *ibid.*

2,654. I've learned that when you're in love, it shows.
- **Andy Rooney:** *CBS Television Show: 60 Minutes.*

2,655. I've learned… that love, not time, heals all wounds.
- *ibid.*

2,656. It takes courage to love, but pain through love is the putrefying fire which those who love generously know.
- **Eleanor Roosevelt:** *My Day*, April, 1939.

2,657. Falling in love consists in uncorking the imagination and bottling the common sense.
- **Helen Rowland:** *A Guide to Men: Being the Reflections of a Bachelor Girl*, 1922.

2,658. To fear love is to fear life. And those who fear life are already three parts dead.
- **Bertrand Russell:** *Marriage and Morals*, 1929.

2,659. Life has taught us that love does not consist in gazing at each other but in looking outward together in the same direction.
- **Antoine de Saint-Exupery:** *Wind, Sand and Stars*, 1939.

2,660. Please note that the greatest gift you can both give and receive costs no money, it is not a material thing. It is the essence of love that you are giving and receiving and its only costs are time and acceptance.
- **Virginia Satir:** *Making Contact*, 1976.

2,661. All you really need is love, but a little chocolate now and then doesn't hurt.
- Lucy van Pelt in the Peanuts cartoon strip by **Charles M. Schulz.**

2,662. I love humanity – it's people I can't stand.
- Linus van Pelt in the Peanuts cartoon strip by **Charles M. Schulz.**

2,663. Nothing takes the taste out of peanut butter quite like unrequited love.
- Charlie Brown in the Peanuts cartoon strip by **Charles M. Schulz**.

2,664. Love is not love
Which alters when it alteration finds,
Or bends with the remover to remove:
Oh no! It is an ever-fixed mark,
That looks on tempests and is never shaken.
- **William Shakespeare** *Sonnet 116*.

2,665. The course of true love never did run smooth.
- **William Shakespeare:** *A Midsummer Night's Dream, Act 1, Sc 1*, 1596.

2,666. Love sought is good, but given unsought is better.
- **William Shakespeare:** *Twelfth Night, Act 3, Sc 1*, 1601.

2,667. Doubt thou the stars are fire,
Doubt that the sun doth move;
Doubt truth to be a liar,
But never doubt I love.
- **William Shakespeare:** *Hamlet, Act 2, Sc 2*, 1601.
NB This quotation comes from Hamlet's love poem to Ophelia, read by Polonius to Claudius and Gertrude.

2,668. First love is only a little foolishness and a lot of curiosity.
- **George Bernard Shaw:** *John Bull's Other Island*, 1907.

2,669. To love and be loved is the greatest happiness of existence.
- **Sydney Smith:** *Lady Holland's Memoir*, 1855.

2,670. One word frees us of all the weight and pain of life; that word is love.
- **Sophocles:** *Oedipus at Colonus*, 5th century BC.

2,671. I hold it true, whate'er befall;
I feel it when I sorrow most:
'Tis better to have loved and lost
Than never to have loved at all.
- **Alfred, Lord Tennyson:** *In Memoriam, Canto 27*, 1849.

2,672. It is best to love wisely, no doubt, but to love foolishly is better than not to be able to love at all.
- **William Makepeace Thackery:** *Pendennis*, 1848 – 1850.

2,673. Seize the moment of happiness, love and be loved! That is the only reality in the world, all else is folly.
- **Leo Tolstoy:** *War and Peace,* 1863 – 1869.

2,674. The language of love is spoken with a look, a touch, a sigh, a kiss and sometimes with a word.
- **Frank Tyger:** quoted in *The Forbes Book of Business Quotations* edited by Ted Goodmen, 1997.

2,675. Love is an act of endless forgiveness, a tender look which becomes a habit.
- **Sir Peter Ustinov:** *The Christian Science Monitor, 9th December, 1958.*

2,676. Love is much nicer to be in than an automobile accident, a tight girdle, a higher tax bracket or a holding pattern over Philadelphia.
- **Judith Viorst:** *The Redbook Magazine, 1975.*

2,677. Love is nature's way of giving a reason to be living.
- *Love is a Many-Splendored Thing* by **Paul Francis Webster**, 1955.

2,678. All love that has not friendship for its base, is like a mansion build upon sand.
- **Ella Wilcox:** *Upon the Sand* in *Poems of Passion,* 1883.

2,679. Love is the essential reality and our purpose on earth. To be consciously aware of it, to experience love in ourselves & others, is the meaning of life.
- **Marianne Williamson:** *A Return to Love,* 1992.

MARRIAGE

2,680. In every marriage more than a week old, there are grounds for divorce. The trick is to find, and continue to find, grounds for marriage.
- **Robert W. Anderson:** *Solitaire and Double Solitaire.* 1972.

2,681. Marriage is a three ring circus. There is the engagement ring, the wedding ring and the suffering.
- *anon.*

2,682. If you are determined to have a long-lasting and happy marriage you must each cultivate a sense of humour and a short memory.
- *anon.*

2,683. Love is one glorious dream, and marriage is the alarm clock.
- *anon.*

2,684. If marriages did not exist men and women would have to quarrel with total strangers.
- *anon.*

2,685. Marriage is the mourning after the knot before.
- *anon.*

2,686. Some hoist the windows, gasp for air, / While others find it chilly.
Some turn up thermostats a hair, / While others think them silly. /
Some like it cold, some like it hot, / Some freeze while others smother,
/ And by some fiendish, fatal plot, / They marry one another.
- **Richard Armour:** *Light Armour: Playful Poems on Practically Everything,*
1954.

2,687. The bride, white of hair, is stooped over her cane
Her faltering footsteps need guiding.
While down the church aisle, with wan toothless smile,
The groom in a wheelchair comes riding.
And who is this elderly couple you ask?

You'll find, when you've closely explored it,
That here is that rare, most conservative pair,
Who waited 'till they could afford it.
- **Richard Armour:** *To Have and Too Old,* quoted in *Lighten Up: 100 Funny Little Poems* selected by Bruce Lansky, 1998.

2,688. Anything is to be preferred or endured rather than marriage without affection.
- **Jane Austin:** *in a letter to her niece,* quoted in *Jane Austin's Letters to her Sister Cassandra and Others,* 1952.

2,689. A lady's imagination is very rapid; it jumps from admiration to love, from love to matrimony, in a moment.
- **Jane Austin:** *Pride and Prejudice,* 1813.

2,690. Happiness in marriage is entirely a matter of chance.
- **Jane Austin, *ibid.***

2,691. Yes, I'll marry you, my dear, / And here's the reason why; /
So I can push you out of bed / When the baby starts to cry, /
And if we hear a knocking / And it's creepy and it's late, /
I hand you the torch you see, / And you investigate.
- **Pam Ayres:** *Pam Ayres - In Her Own Words, DVD,* 2006.

2,692. Marriage is one of the few institutions that allow a man to do as his wife pleases.
- **Milton Berle:** *Milton Berle's Private Joke File,* 1989.

2.693. Marriage is not just spiritual communion and passionate embraces; marriage is also three meals a day, sharing the workload and remembering to carry out the trash.
- **Joyce Brothers:** *When Your Husband's Affection Cools* in *Good Housekeeping, May 1972.*

2,694. At Blenheim I took two very important decisions: to be born and marry. I am content with the decision I took on both occasions. I have never had cause to regret either.
- **Sir Winston Churchill:** *The Wit and Wisdom of Winston Churchill* by James C. Humes, 1995.

2,695. An honest man may really love a pretty girl, but only an idiot marries her merely because she is pretty.
- **Lord Chesterfield:** *Letters to His Son,* 3rd December, 1734.

2,696. A man has been lucky in marrying the woman he loves. But he is luckier in loving the woman he marries.
- **G. K. Chesterton:** *Brave New Family: G. K. Chesterton on Men and Women, Children, Sex, Divorce, Marriage and the Family* edited by Alvaro Da Silva, 1992.

2,697. I am not against hasty marriages where a mutual flame is fanned by an adequate income.
- **Wilkie Collins:** *No Name,* 1862.

2,698. Thus grief still treads upon the heels of pleasure; Married in haste, we may repent at leisure.
- **William Congreve:** *The Old Bachelor, Act 5, Sc 1,* 1693.

2,699. Marriage is a wonderful invention; then again, so is a bicycle repair kit.
- **Billy Connolly:** *Gullible's Travels* by Duncan Campbell, 1982.

2,700. My wife and I were married in a toilet: it was a marriage of convenience.
- **Tommy Cooper**.

2,701. Let us now set forth one of the fundamental truths about marriage: the wife is in charge.
- **Bill Cosby:** *Love and Marriage,* 1989.

2,702. For two people in a marriage to live together day after day is unquestionably the one miracle the Vatican has overlooked.
- ***ibid***.

2,703. She was the most intelligent woman of her day and she refused to get married in nine languages.
- **Will Cuppy:** *The Decline and Fall of Practically Everybody* compiled after his death by Fred Feldkam, 1950.
NB The statement above was Cuppy's comment on Queen Elizabeth 1st.

2,704. He let me know that he had been led into his marriage by love, and love alone, though he did not say so it was clear he owed Cupid a grudge.
- **Robertson Davies:** *Fifth Business,* 1970.

2,705. I am constantly astonished by the people, otherwise intelligent, who think that anything so complex and delicate as a marriage can be left to take care of itself. One sees them fussing about all sorts of lesser concerns, apparently unaware that side by side with them - often in the same bed - a human creature is perishing from lack of affection, of emotional malnutrition.

- **Robertson Davies:** *The Pleasures of Love* (1961), reprinted in *The Enthusiasms of Robertson Davies*, 1990.

2,706. Matrimony and Other Painful Pleasures.
- **Max Eastman:** Chapter title in his book - *Enjoyment of Laughter*, 1939.

2,707. A sound marriage is not based on complete frankness, it is based on sensible reticence.
- **Morris L. Ernst**.

2,708. I was married for five years and never told anybody. I like to keep my troubles to myself.
- **Leopold Fechtner:** *5,000 One-And-Two-Line Jokes*, 1973.

2.709. If you have half a mind to get married, do it. That is all it takes.
- *ibid*.

2,710. We're equal partners in our marriage. I'm the silent one.
- *ibid*.

2,711. Marriage isn't a word - it's a sentence.
- From the **1928 Film:** *The Crowd*, directed and written by King Vidor et al.

2,712. Keep your eyes wide open before marriage, half shut afterwards.
- **Benjamin Franklin:** *Poor Richard's Almanack*, 1738.

2,713. Love one another but make not a bond of love.
- **Kahlil Gibran:** *The Prophet, Chapter 3, Marriage*, 1926.

2,714. Let there be spaces in your togetherness.
- *ibid*.

2,715. To wed, or not to wed; that is the question;
Whether 'tis nobler in the mind to suffer
The bills and house rent of a wedded fortune,
Or to say "nit" when she proposes,
And by declining cut her. To wed; to smoke
No more; and have a wife at home to mend

The holes in socks and shirts
And underwear and so forth. 'Tis a consummation
Devoutly to be wished. To wed for life;
To wed; perchance to fight; ay, there's the rub.
- **Edgar Albert Guest:** *Home Rhymes from Breakfast Table Chat*, 1909.

2,716. The most important element in marriage, bar none, is learning what to overlook.
- **Sydney J. Harris:** *Pieces of Eight*, 1975.

2,717. The conception of two people living together for 25 years without having a cross word suggests a lack of spirit only to be admired in sheep.
- **Sir A. P. Herbert**.

2,718. The critical period in matrimony is breakfast time.
- **Sir A. P. Herbert:** *Uncommon Law*, 1935.

2,719. Marriage has many pains, but celibacy has no pleasures.
- **Samuel Johnson:** *The History of Rasselas*, 1759.
NB *The History of Rasselas* is a novel about happiness.

2,720. All married couples should learn the art of battle as they should learn the art of love. Good battle is objective and honest – never vicious, or cruel. Good battle is healthy and constructive, and brings to a marriage the principle of equal partnership.
- **Ann Landers:** *Ann Landers Says, "Truth is Stranger"*

2,721. There is no more lovely, friendly and charming relationship, communion or company than a good marriage.
- **Martin Luther:** *Table Talk*, 1569.

2,722. Marriage is like a bath; once you're into it and you're used to it, it's not so hot.
- **Mad Magazine:** *Mad, The Half-Wit and Wisdom of Alfred E. Neuman*.

2,723. A successful marriage is an edifice that must be rebuilt every day.
- **Andre Maurois:** *The Art of Living*, 1941.

2,724. A great marriage is not when the "perfect couple" come together. It is when an imperfect couple learns to enjoy their differences.
- **Dave Meurer:** *Daze of our Wives: A Semi-Helpful Guide to Marital Bliss*, 2000.

2,725. After seven years of marriage I'm sure of two things - first, never wallpaper together and second, you'll need two bathrooms, both for her. The rest is a mystery I love to be involved in.
- **Dennis Miller**.

2,726. Marriage is an investment which pays dividends if you pay interest.
- **Bob Monkhouse**: *The Times Online Obituary, 29th December, 2003.*

2,727. There once was an old man of Lyme, / Who married three wives at a time. / When asked, "Why the third?" / He replied, "One's absurd, / And bigamy, sir, is a crime."
- **William Cosmo Monkhouse:** *Limerick.*

2,728. The beauty of a long-term marriage is the unfolding discovery that young love can grow into mature love.
- **Tom Mullen:** *A Very Good Marriage*, 2001.

2,729. With children no longer the universally accepted reason for marriage, marriages are going to have to exist on their own merits.
- **Eleanor Holmes Norton:** quoted in *Sisterhood is Powerful* edited by Robin Morgan, 1970.

2,730. Marriage is wonderful when it lasts forever, and I envy the old couple in *When Harry Met Sally* who reminisce tearfully about the day they met fifty years before.
- **Peggy O'Mara:** *Mothering Magazine, Autumn, 1989.*

2,731. In California, marriages break up so fast wedding photographers are using Polaroid cameras.
- **Robert Orben:** *2,000 Sure-Fire Jokes For Speakers.*

2,732. "Till death us do part" was not a sweet nothing to be muttered when love was young, but a real commitment and an unbreakable promise.
- **Tony Parsons:** commenting on the attitude to marriage of the generation born before the Second World War, exemplified by his parents and the Queen and Prince Philip, in *Mirror. co. uk. 19th November, 2007.*

2,733. They call it the sea of matrimony because husbands have such a hard job keeping their heads above water.
- **Herbert V. Prochnow and Herbert V. Prochnow Jr:** *The Public Speaker's Source Book*, 1977.

2,734. Marriage halves our griefs, doubles our joys and quadruples our expenses.
- *ibid.*

2,735. Married couples tell each other a thousand things without talking.
- *Chinese Proverb.*

2,736. Never advise anyone to go to war or to marry.
- *Spanish Proverb.*

2,737. The clearest explanation for the failure of any marriage is that the two people are incompatible - that is, that one is male and the other female.
- **Anna Quindlen**, *Living Out Loud*, 1988.

2,738. Marriage is like twirling a baton, turning hand springs or eating with chopsticks. It looks easy until you try it.
- **Helen Rowland**.

2.739. It has been said that the supreme test of marriage is when husbands and wives put up wallpaper together.
- *ibid*

2,740. Men who have pierced ears are better prepared for marriage. They've experienced pain and bought jewellery.
- **Rita Rudner**.

2,741. I love being married. It's so great to find that one special person you want to annoy for the rest of your life.
- *ibid.*

2,742. There is no subject on which more dangerous nonsense is talked and thought than marriage.
- **George Bernard Shaw:** in the Preface to the play, *Getting Married*, 1908.

2,743. When two people are under the influence of the most violent, most insane, most delusive, and most transient of passions, they are required to swear that they will remain in that excited, abnormal, and exhausting condition continuously until death do them part.
- *ibid.*

2,744. Marriage is popular because it combines the maximum of temptation with the maximum of opportunity.
- **George Bernard Shaw:** *Man and Superman, Act 4*, 1903.

2,745. Marriage is one long conversation, chequered by disputes.
- **Robert Louis Stevenson:** *Talk and Talkers, paper 2: Memories and Portraits*, 1887.

2,746. Love seems the swiftest, but it is the slowest of all growths. No man or woman really knows what perfect love is until they have been married a quarter of a century.
- **Mark Twain:** *Notebook*, 1894.

2,747. One advantage of marriage is that, when you fall out of love with him or he falls out of love with you, it keeps you together until you fall in again.
- **Judith Viorst:** *Redbook Magazine, February, 1975*.

2,748. He is the most married man I ever saw in my life.
- **Artemus Ward:** *Moses, the Sassy* – a short story.

2,749. The first part of our marriage was very happy, But then on the way back from the ceremony.
- **Henny Youngman:** *How Do You Like Me So Far?* 1963.

2,750. Some people ask the secret of our long marriage. We take time to go to a restaurant twice a week – a little candlelight, dinner, soft music, and dancing. She goes Tuesdays, I go Fridays.
- **Henny Youngman:** *The Best Little Book of One-Liners*, 1992.

2,751. I've been married for fifty years and I'm still in love with the same woman. If my wife ever finds out, she'll kill me.

MARITAL DISPUTES

2,752. The only person who listens to both sides of an argument is the woman next door.
- **Joey Adams:** *Joey Adams' Encyclopedia of Humour*, 1968.

2,753. Arguments out of a pretty mouth are unanswerable.
- **Joseph Addison:** *The Free Holder: or Political Essays*, 1739.

2,754. Arguments with furniture are rarely productive.
- **Kehlog Albran:** the pseudonym of the authors of *The Profit*, 1973.
NB: *The Profit* is a parody of Kahlil Gibran's *The Prophet*, 1923.

2,755. It takes two flints to make a fire.
- **Louisa May Alcott:** *Little Women*, 1868.

2,756. "You say you have never quarrelled with your wife?"
"Never. She goes her way and I go hers."
- ***anon***.

2,757. Arguing with my wife can be quickly described: "I came! I saw! I concurred!"
- ***anon***.

2,758. My wife and I have arguments, / But they don't last very long. / In fact, they're over just as soon / As I admit I'm wrong.
- **Richard Armour:** *The Peacemaker*.

2,759. Most young couples begin married life knowing very little about how to argue, and are forced to learn through trial and error.
- **Dave Barry:** *Dave Barry's Guide to Marriage and / or Sex*, 1987.

2,760. Creative arguing is the key to a long-lasting marriage.
- ***ibid***.

2,761. A good argument, when conducted properly, takes the time and full attention of two people.
- **Erma Bombeck:** *When You Look Like Your Passport Photo, It's Time to go Home*, 1992.

2,762. The story of some marriages should be told in a scrapbook.
- **Jacob M. Braude:** *Braude's Treasury of Wit and Humour for all Occasions* 1991.

2,763. It is not he who gains the exact point in dispute who scores most in controversy - but he who has shown the better temper.
- **Samuel Butler:** *Notebooks*, 1912.

2,764. I don't complain of Betsy or any of her acts, Exceptin' when we've quarrelled and told each other facts.
- **Will Carleton:** *Betsy and I Are Out*, 1871.

2,765. When married, one has to get into an argument once in a while since in this way one learns about the other.
- **G. K. Chesterton:** *Elective Affinities*, 1809.

2,766. Tears are great peace-makers.
- **Mason Cooley:** *Aphorisms, 5th Selection*, 1988.

2,767. My wife had a go at me last night. She said, "You'll drive me to my grave." - I had the car out in thirty seconds.
- **Tommy Cooper.**

2,768. Feminine logic is fallacious, shallow, inconsistent, irrelevant, capricious, transparent - and irrefutable.
- **Harold Coffin.**

2.769. You have such strong words at command, that they make the smallest argument seem formidable.
- **George Eliot:** *Felix Holt, the Radical*, 1866.
NB The statement above was made by a woman to a male protagonist.

2,770. In case of dissension, never dare to judge till you've heard the other side.
- **Euripides:** *Heraclidae*, **circa**. 428 BC.

2,771. A good time to keep your mouth shut is when you're in deep water.
- **Sam Ewing:** *Reader's Digest, August, 1995*.

2,772. Much may be said on both sides.
- **Henry Fielding:** *The Covent Garden Tragedy, Act 5, Sc 1*, 1732.

2,773. The concept of two people living together for 25 years without having a cross word suggests a lack of spirit only to be admired in sheep.
- **Sir A. P. Herbert**.

2,774. My wife and I have resolved not to go to bed angry. As of now we have been awake for three weeks.
- **Bob Monkhouse:** *Just Say a Few Words*, 1988.

2,775. He who establishes his argument by noise and command shows that his reason is weak.
 Michel de Montaigne: *Instant Quotations Dictionary* by Donald Bolander **et al**, 1979.

2,776. To keep your marriage brimming,
With love in the loving cup.
Whenever you're wrong, admit it;
Whenever you're right, shut up.
- **Ogden Nash:** *A Word to Husbands* in *Everyone But Thee and Me*, 1962.

2,777. I find my wife hath something in her gizzard that only wants an opportunity of being provoked to bring up; but I will not, for my content-sake, give it.
 - **Samuel Pepys:** *Diary*, June, 1668.

2,778. My dead love came to me, and said: / "God gives me one hour's rest, / To spend with thee on earth again; / How shall we spend it best?"
"Why, as of old," I said; and so / We quarrelled as of old. / But, when I turned to make my peace, / That one short hour was told.
- **Stephen Philips:** *A Dream* in *Modern British Poetry* edited by Louis Untermeyer, 1920.

2,779. When two quarrel, both are to blame.
- *Dutch Proverb*.

2,780. A woman's strength is in her tongue.
- *English Proverb*.

2,781. Argument seldom convinces any one against his inclination.
- *English Proverb*.

2,782. It takes two to quarrel, but only one to end it.
- ***Spanish Proverb***.

2,783. Problems in marriage often arise because a man too often shows his worst side to his better half.
- **Herbert V. Prochnow and Herbert V. Prochnow Jr:** *The Public Speaker's Source Book*, 1977.

2,784. The weaker the argument, the stronger the words.
- ***ibid.*** 1977.

2,785. Quarrels would not last so long if the fault were only on one side.
- **Francois, Duc de La Rochefoucauld:** *Maxims*, 1665.

2,786 The test of a man or woman's breeding is how they behave in a quarrel.
- **George Bernard Shaw:** *The Philanderer, Act 4*, 1893.

MEMORY

2,787. Smells detonate softly in our memory like poignant land mines hidden under the weedy mass of the years. Hit a tripwire of smell and memories explode all at once.
- **Diane Ackerman:** *A Natural History of the Senses*, 1990.

2,788. Inscribe it in the remembering tablets of your mind.
- **Aeschylus:** *Prometheus Bound.* **circa**, 410 BC.

2,789. Memory is the mother of all wisdom.
- *ibid.*

2,790. To improve your memory lend people money.
- *anon.*

2,791. A man with a terrible memory forgets everything, a woman with a terrible memory remembers everything.
- *anon: 20,000 Quips and Quotes* by Evan Esar, 1968.

2,792. Life brings us tears, smiles and memories. The tears dry, the smile fades, but the memories will last forever.
- *anon.*

2,793. Someone said that God gave us memory so that we might have roses in December.
- **Sir J. M. Barrie:** *Rectorial Speech, St. Andrew's University, 3rd May, 1922.*

2.794. Everybody needs his memories. They keep the wolf of insignificance from the door.
- **Saul Bellow:** *Mr Sammler's Planet*, 1970.

2,795. Just because you're old doesn't mean you're more forgetful. The same people whose names I can't remember now I couldn't remember fifty years ago.
- **George Burns:** *The Third Time Around: Autobiography*, 1980.

2,796. To live in hearts we leave behind / Is not to die.
- **Thomas Campbell:** *Hallowed Ground, 1825*, reproduced in *Complete Poetical Works* edited by J. L. Robertson, 1907.

2,797. Memory is the treasury and guardian of all things.
- **Marcus Tullius Cicero:** *On the Orator.* 1st century BC.

2,798. In plucking the fruit of memory one runs the risk of spoiling the bloom.
- **Joseph Conrad:** *The Arrow of Gold*, 1919.

2,799. The heart of marriage is memories, and if the two of you happen to have the same ones and can savour your reruns, then your marriage is a gift from the gods.
- **Bill Cosby:** *Love and Marriage*, 1990.

2,800. There's no disappointment in memory, and one's exaggerations are always on the good side.
- **George Eliot:** *Daniel Deronda*, 1876.

2,801. Oh may I join the choir invisible / Of those immortal dead who live again / In minds made better by their presence.
- **George Eliot:** *Oh May I Join the Choir Invisible and Other Favourite Poems*, 1867.

2,802. My wife has a terrible memory. She doesn't forget anything.
- **Leopold Fechtner:** *5,000 One-And-Two-Line Jokes*, 1973.

2,803. A retentive memory may be a good thing, but the ability to forget is the true token of greatness.
- **Elbert Hubbard:** *The Notebook of Elbert Hubbard.*

2,804. Memory is not just the imprint of the past time upon us; it is the keeper of what is meaningful for our deepest hopes and fears.
- **Rollo May:** *Man's Search for Himself*, 1953.

2,805. Oft in the stilly night, / Ere slumber's chain has bound me, / Fond memory brings the light / Of other days around me.
- **Thomas Moore:** *Oft in the Stilly Night* in *Melodies, Songs and Sacred Songs,* 1822.

2,806. How vast a memory has Love!
- **Alexander Pope:** *Sappho to Phaon,* 1712.

2,807. When they begin the beguine, / It brings back the sound of music so tender, / It brings back the night of tropical splendour, / It brings back a memory evergreen.
- Words and music by **Cole Porter:** for a 1935 stage musical.
NB: The beguine was a dance similar to a slow rumba, popular in the 1930's

2,808. Memories, pressed between the pages of my mind,
Memories, sweetened through the ages just like wine.
- An **Elvis Presley** song; words and music by Bill Strange and Scott Davis.

2,809. Write the bad things that are done to you in the sand, but write the good things that happen to you on a piece of marble.
- *Arabian Proverb.*

2,810. Memory is the treasurer of the mind.
- *English Proverb.*

2,811. Cherish all your happy moments; they make a fine cushion for your old age.
- **Booth Tarkington.**

2,812. I have no riches but my thoughts, / Yet these are wealth enough for me; / My thoughts of you are golden coins / Stamped in the mint of memory.
- **Sara Teasdale:** *Riches* in *Love Songs,* 1907.

MEN

2,813. Far out in the unchartered backwaters of the unfashionable end of the western spiral arm of the galaxy lies a small, unregarded yellow sun, orbiting this at a distance of roughly ninety-eight million miles is an utterly insignificant little blue-green planet whose ape-descended life forms are so amazingly primitive that they still think digital watches are a pretty neat idea.
- **Douglas Adams:** *The Hitchhiker's Guide to the Galaxy*, 1979.

2,814. A man is known by the company he keeps.
- The moral of **Aesop's Fable:** *The Ass and His Purchaser.*

2,815. Man - because of a tragic genetic flaw - cannot see dirt until there is enough of it to support agriculture.
- **Dave Barry:** *The Miami Herald, 23rd November, 2003.*

2,816. Man is his own worst enemy.
- **Marcus Tullius Cicero.**

2,817. No man is an Island, entire of itself; every man is a piece of the continent, a part of the main... any man's death diminishes me, because I am involved in mankind.
- **John Donne:** *Devotions Upon Emergent Occasions*, 1624.

2,818. Men are but children of a larger growth.
- **John Dryden:** *All For Love, Act 4*, 1678.

2,819. Men are what their mothers made them.
- **Ralph Waldo Emerson:** *Essays: First Series, Compensation*, 1841.

2,820. I believe that man will not merely endure; he will prevail. He is immortal, not because he alone among creatures has an inexhaustible voice, but because he has a soul, a spirit capable of compassion and sacrifice and endurance.
- **William Faulkner:** *in a speech at the Nobel Prize Banquet, after he received the Nobel Prize for Literature, 10th December, 1950.*

2,821. Every man has a wild beast within him.
- **Frederick 2nd of Prussia:** *in a letter to Voltaire, 1759.*

2,822. A bird is known by its note, and a man by his talk.
- **Thomas Fuller:** *Gnomologia: Adages and Proverbs,* 1732.

2,823. The proof that man is the noblest of all creatures is that no other creature has ever contested this claim.
- **George Christoph Lichtenberg:** *Notebook D,* 1773 – 1775.

2,824. The four stages of man are infancy, childhood, adolescence and obsolescence.
- **Art Linkletter:** *A Child's Garden of Misinformation,* 1965.

2,825. Brad Pitt's hair, Tom Cruise's smile, George Clooney's body and Bill Gate's wallet.
Miss Piggy: the star of the Muppet Show, gave this as her perfect, composite man in *The Marie Claire Magazine.*

2,826. Telling lies is a fault in a boy, an art in a lover, an accomplishment in a bachelor, and second-nature to a married man.
- **Helen Rowland:** *A Guide to Men,* 1922.

2,827. Numberless are the world's wonders but none more wonderful than man.
- **Sophocles:** *Antigone.* 5th century BC.

2,828. No man has ever lived that had enough of children's gratitude or woman's love.
- **W. B. Yeats:** *Vacillation,* 1932.

MEN AND WOMEN

2,829. God certainly created man before woman, and rightly so for it is always best to make a rough draft before the final masterpiece.
- *anon.*

2,830. Most women, given the choice, would much prefer to have beauty rather than brains, because most men can see much better than they can think.
- *anon.*

2,831. Women have their faults, men have only two, everything they say, and everything they do.
- *anon.*

2,832. Very few women tell their age, and fewer men act theirs.
- *anon.*

2,833. Man forgives woman anything save the wit to outwit him.
- **Minna Antrim:** *Naked Truths and Veiled Allusions*, 1901.

2,834. Until Eve arrived, this was a man's world.
- **Richard Armour:** quoted in *Sisterhood is Powerful: An Anthology of Writings from the Women's Liberation Movement* by Robin Morgan, 1970.

2,835. If a woman is partial to a man, and does not endeavour to conceal it, he must find out.
- **Jane Austin:** *Pride and Prejudice*, 1813.

2,836. Life is not bearable with the opposite sex until it is unbearable without 'em.
- **Texas Bix Bender:** *Just One Fool Thing After Another: a Cowfolks' Guide to Romance* with Gladioli Montana, 1994.

2,837. About the only time a woman really succeeds in changing a male is when he's a baby.
- **Jacob M. Braude:** *Braude's Treasury of Wit and Humour*, 1991.

2,838. A pompous gentleman once asked the sharp-tongued actress, Mrs Patrick Campbell, "Why do you suppose it is that women so utterly lack a sense of humour?"
"God did it on purpose," Mrs Campbell answered without batting an eyelash, "so that we may love you men instead of laughing at you."
- *ibid.*

2,839. Both men and women are fallible. The difference is, women know it.
- **Eleanor Bron:** *The Times, 28th July, 1992.*

2,840. Man's love is man's life a thing apart, 'Tis woman's whole existence.
- **Lord Byron:** *Don Juan*, 1824.

2,841. The only solid and lasting peace between a man and his wife is, doubtless, separation.
- **Lord Chesterfield:** *Letters to his Son,* 1st September, 1763.

2,842. Women encourage men to be childish, then scold them.
- **Mason Cooley:** *City Aphorisms, Eighth Selection*, 1991.

2,843. Men and women belong to different species and communications between them is still in its infancy.
- **Bill Cosby**.

2,844. When a man courts a woman, he talks and she listens. After the wedding, she talks and he listens, and usually, after ten years of married life, they both talk and the neighbours listen.
- **Les Dawson:** *Listen to Les: BBC Radio Collection.*

2,845. Most women set out to change a man, and when they have changed him they do not like him.
- **Marlene Dietrich:** *The Last Word: A Treasury of Women's Quotes* by Carolyn Warner, 1992.

2,846. A different taste in jokes is a great strain on the affections.
- **George Eliot:** *Daniel Deronda*, 1876.

2,847. Adam and Eve were the first book-keepers; they invented the loose-leaf system.
- **Evan Esar:** *Esar's Comic Dictionary*, 1943.

2,848. The battle between the sexes will go on forever, there's just too much fraternizing with the enemy.
- **Sam Ewing:** *Wall Street Journal, 17th January, 1992.*

2,849. Women lie about their age - men lie about their income.
- **William Feather:** *Talk About Women,* 1960.

2,850. A man well on in years was taken to task for still paying attention to a young woman. "It's the only way," he replied, "to rejuvinate oneself, and surely that's what everybody wants."
- **Johann Wolfgang von Goethe:** *Maxims and Reflections* translated by Elizabeth Stopp edited by Peter Hutchison, 1998.

2,851. Men are motivated when they feel needed, while women are motivated when they feel cherished.
- **John Gray:** *Men Are From Mars, Women Are From Venus,* 1992.

2,852. Men primarily need a kind of love that is trusting, accepting and appreciative. Women primarily need a kind of love that is caring, understandable and respectful.
- *ibid.*

2,853. Man has his will - but woman has her way!
- **Oliver Wendell Holmes:** *The Autocrat of the Breakfast Table,* 1858.

2,854. The female of her species is more deadly than the male.
- **Rudyard Kipling:** *The Female of the Species* in *The Collected Poems of Rudyard Kipling,* 1994.

2,855. Women are different from us men, most are, in fact superior./ Though both may look the same inside, a woman has a more rounded exterior.
- **Walter McCorrisken:** *Women* in *A Wee Dribble of Dross,* 1993.

MEN ACCORDING TO WOMEN

2,856. For all their strength, men were sometimes like little children.
- **Lawana Blackwell:** *The Dowry of Miss Lydia Clark,* 1999.

2,857. Men should be like kleenex, soft, strong and disposable.
- **Cher**.

2,858. Men are luxuries, not necessities.
- **Cher:** quoted in *Halliwell's Who's Who in the Movies, 3rd Edition,* 1970.

2,859. I don't think I've learned too many lessons about men, other than you have to kiss a lot of frogs before you meet your prince.
- **Joan Collins:** *Press and Journals "Quote of the Day" 30th August, 2011.*

2,860. Men know best about everything except what women know better.
- **George Eliot:** *Middlemarch,* 1871 – 1872.

2,861. There wouldn't be half as much fun in the world if it weren't for children and men, and there aint a mite of difference between them under the skins.
- **Ellen Glasgow:** *Letters of Ellen Glasgow,* 1958.

2,862. A man's got to do what a man's got to do. A woman must do what he can't.
- **Rhonda Hansome**.

2,863. Women speak because they wish to speak, whereas a man speaks only when driven to speech by something outside himself - like, for instance, he can't find clean socks.
- **Jean Kerr:** *The Snake Has All The Lines,* 1958.

2,864. A man wants his virility regarded, a woman wants her femininity appreciated.
- **Ursula K. Le Guin:** *The Left Hand of Darkness,* 1969.

2,865. I don't deny that an odd man here and there, if he's caught young and trained up proper, and if his mother has spanked him well before hand, may turn out a decent being.
- **Lucy Maude Montgomerie:** *Anne's House of Dreams.*

2,866. There's so much saint in the worst of them, / And so much devil in the best of them, / That a woman who's married to one of them, / Has nothing to learn of the rest of them.
- **Helen Rowland:** *A Guide to Men,* 1922.

2,867. Men would like monogamy better if it sounded less like monotony.
- **Rita Rudner:** *Rita Rudner's Guide to Men,* 1998.

MIDDLE AGE

2,868. Years ago we discovered the exact point, the dead centre of middle age. It occurs when you are too young to take up golf and too old to rush up to the net.
- **Franklin P. Adams:** *Nods and Becks,* 1944.

2,869. Middle age is that time of life when a woman won't tell her age, and a man won't act his.
- *anon.*

2,870. Middle age is the time of your life when everything wears out, falls out, or spreads out.
- *anon.*

2,871. Every young man starts out in life expecting to find a pot of gold at the end of the rainbow. By the time they reach middle age, most of them have at least found the pot.
- *anon.*

2,872. Middle age is when a man starts turning off the lights for economic rather than romantic reasons.
- *anon.*

2,873. You know you've reached middle age when a doctor, not a policeman, tells you to slow down.
- *anon.*

2,874. Middle age is having a choice of two temptations and choosing the one that will get you home earlier.
- **Dan Bennett:** quoted in *Age Happens: The Best Quotes and Cartoons About Growing Old* selected by Bruce Lansky, 1996.

2,875. It's a frightening feeling to wake up one morning and discover that while you were asleep you went out of style.
- **Erma Bombeck:** *If Life is a Bowl of Cherries What Am I Doing in the Pits?* 1979.

2,876. MIDDLE AGE: That time of your life when the broad mind and narrow waist change places.
- **Jacob M. Braude:** *Braude's Treasury of Wit and Wisdom*, 1991.

2,877. A. Middle age is when you begin to exchange your emotions for symptoms.
B. Middle age is the period when too much food and too little sleep make a person thick and tired.
C Middle age is when you don't care where you go just so long as you're home by ten.
D. Another sign of middle age is when you want to see how long your car will last instead of how fast it will go.
- **Irvin S. Cobb:** *20,000 Quips and Quotes*, 1968.

2,878. The really frightening thing about middle age is the knowledge that you'll grow out of it.
- **Doris Day:** *Doris Day, Her Own Story* by A.E. Hotchner, 1976.

2,879. The years between 50 and 70 are the hardest. You are always being asked to do things, and yet you are not decrepit enough to turn them down.
- **T. S. Eliot:** *Time Magazine, 23rd October, 1950.*

2,880. Middle age is when you are old enough to know better, but still young enough to keep on doing it.
- **Sam Ewing:** *The Saturday Evening Post, December, 1991.*

2,881. Setting a good example for children takes all the fun out of middle age.
- **William Feather**.

2,882. Whoever, in middle age, attempts to realize the wishes and hopes of his early youth, invariably deceives himself.
- **Johann Wolfgang von Goethe:** from his novel, *Elective Affinities*, 1809.

2,883. Middle age is when your age starts to show around the middle.
- **Bob Hope:** *New York Times, 15th February, 1954.*

2,884. You've reached middle age when all you exercise is caution.

- **Franklin P. Jones:** quoted in *Braude's Handbook of Stories for Toastmasters and Speakers*, 1979.

2,885. Perhaps middle-age is, or should be, a period of shedding shells; the shell of ambition, the shell of material accumulations and possessions, the shell of the ego.

- **Anne Morrow Lindbergh:** quoted in *The Last Word: A Treasury of Women's Quotes* by Carolyn Warner, 1992.

2,886. Middle age is the time when a man is always thinking that in a week or two he will feel as good as ever.

- **Don Marquis:** *O Rare Don Marquis* a biography by E. Anthony, 1962.

2,887. Middle age is when, whenever you go on holiday, you pack a sweater.

- **Denis Norden:** *The BBC Radio Panel Game: My Word.*

2,888. No matter how old a mother is she watches her middle-aged children for signs of improvement.

- **Florida Scott-Maxwell:** *Measure of My Days,* 1968

THE MIND

2,889. Old minds are like old horses; you must exercise them if you wish to keep them in working order.
- **John Adams:** *Looking Toward Sunset* by Lydia Maria Child, 1865.

2,890. By the time most people are thirty years old, their bodies are as good as they will ever be, in fact, many persons' bodies have begun to deteriorate by that time. But there is no limit to the amount of growth and development that the mind can sustain. The mind does not stop growing at any particular age.
- **Mortimer Adler:** *How to Read a Book: The Classic Guide to Intellectual Reading*, 1972.

2,891. A man's mind may be likened to a garden, which may be intelligently cultivated or allowed to run wild; but whether cultivated or neglected, it must, and will, bring forth. If no useful seeds are put into it, then an abundance of useless weed seeds will fall therein, and will continue to produce their kind.
- **James Allen:** *As A Man Thinketh*, 1902.

2,892. A mind unemployed is a mind un-enjoyed.
- **Christian Nestell Bovee**.

2,893. Mind is the forerunner of all actions.
- **Buddha:** *Dhammapada*, **circa** 483 BC.

2,894. The human mind ever longs for occupation.
- **Marcus Tullius Cicero**.

2,895. It is not enough to have a good mind. The main thing is to use it well.
- **Rene Descartes:** *Discourse on Method*, 1638.

2,896. Minds are like parachutes – they only function when open.
- **Sir Thomas Dewar:** *Wit and Wisdom of Tommy Dewar* by Ian Robert Buxton, 2001.

2,897. The human mind is like a TV schedule - subject to change without notice.
- **Sam Ewing:** *The Sun Newspaper, 14th September, 1999.*

2,898. To see a thing clearly in the mind makes it begin to take form.
- **Henry Ford:** *Theophist Magazine. February, 1930.*

2,899. To be capable of steady friendship or lasting love are the two greatest proofs, not only of goodness of heart, but of strength of mind.
- **William Hazlit:** *Selected Essays of William Hazlitt* edited by Geoffrey Keynes, 1930.

2,900. A woman's mind is cleaner than a man's – she changes it oftener.
- **Oliver Herford:** *Braude's Handbook of Stories for Toastmasters and Speakers,* by Jacob M. Braude, 1971.

2,901. A man must use his mind; he must feel that he is doing something that will develop his highest powers and contribute to the development of his fellow men, or he will cease to be a man.
- **Robert Maynard Hutchins:** *Great Books of the Western World,* 1952.

2,902. Of all the things I've lost it's my mind I miss the most.
- **Barbara Johnson:** *I'm So Glad You Told Me What I Didn't Wanna Hear.* 1996.

2,903. I have a bone to pick with Fate,
Come here and tell me, girlie,
Do you think my mind is maturing late,
Or simply rotted early?
- **Ogden Nash:** *Lines on Facing Forty* in *Good Intentions,* 1942.

2,904. Carl Jung used the term *SHADOW* to designate that part of our mind containing those things that we would rather not own up to: traits that we are not only trying to hide from others but also from ourselves, that we are continually trying to sweep under the rug of consciousness.
- **M**. **Scott Peck:** *A World Waiting to be Born,* 1993.

2,905. The mind is not a vessel to be filled but a fire to be kindled.
- **Plutarch**.

2,906. As it is the characteristic of great minds to say much in a few words, so is it of small minds to talk much and say nothing.
- **Francois Duc de La Rochefoucauld:** *Maxims,* 1665.

2,907. Reason is God's crowning gift to man.
- **Sophocles:** *Antigone,* 5th century BC.

2,908. I have a prodigious quantity of mind, it takes me as much as a week sometimes to make it up.
- **Mark Twain:** *The Innocents Abroad,* 1869.

2,909. Once we are destined to live out our lives in the prison of our mind, our one duty is to furnish it well.
- **Sir Peter Ustinov:** *Dear Me,* 1977. NB *Dear Me* is Sir Peter Unstinov's autobiography.

MISFORTUNES

2,910. Learn from the misfortunes of others.
- The moral of **Aesop's Fable:** *The Ass, the Fox, and the Lion.*

2,911. I am not afraid of storms, for I am learning how to sail my ship.
- **Louisa May Alcott:** *Little Women,* 1868.

2,912. Misfortune shows those who are not really friends.
- **Aristotle:** *Eudemian Ethics.* 4th century BC.

2,913. Anything can happen, but it usually doesn't.
- **Robert Benchley:** *My Ten Years in a Quandary and How They Grew.* 1951.

2,914. Man is born to trouble as surely as sparks fly upward.
- **The Bible:** *Job 5: 7 , NIV.*

2,915. Weeping may remain for a night, but rejoicing comes in the morning.
- **The Bible:** *Psalms 30: 5b. NIV.*

2,916. Misfortunes seldom come singly.
- **Miguel de Cervantes:** *Don Quixote.*

2,917. Most of our misfortunes are more supportable than the comments of our friends upon them.
- **C. C. Colton**: *Lacon,* or *Many Things in Few Words,* 1922, edited by George J. Barbour. 2001.

2,918. Reflect upon your present blessings – of which every man has many – not on your past misfortunes, of which all men have some.
- **Charles Dickens:** *Sketches by Boz,* 1836 – 1837.

2,919. Some of your hurts you have cured,
And the sharpest you still have survived,
But what torments of grief you endured

From evils which never arrived!
- **Ralph Waldo Emerson:** *May-Day and Other* Pieces. 1867.

2,920. Man does not understand woman - that is his misfortune; woman understands man - that is also his misfortune.
- **Evan Esar:** *20,000 Quips and Quotes* by Evan Esar, 1968.

2,921. There is no defence against adverse fortune which is so effectual as an habitual sense of humour.
- **Thomas W. Higginson.**

2,922. Acceptance of what has happened is the first step to overcoming the consequences of any misfortune.
- **William James.**

2,923. He knows not his own strength that hath not met adversity.
- **Ben Jonson:** *Timber: or Discoveries,* 1640.

2,924. Although the world is full of suffering, it is also full of the overcoming of it.
- **Helen Keller:** *Optimism,* 1903.

2,925. Be still, sad heart and cease repining;
Behind the clouds is the sun still shining;
Thy fate is the common fate of all,
Into each life some rain must fall.
- **Henry Wadsworth Longfellow:** *Rainy Day* in *Voices of the Night,* 1839.

2,926. The misfortunes hardest to bear are those which never come.
- **James Russell Lowell:** *Democracy, and Other Addresses,* 1886.

2,927. Fortune knocks but once, but misfortune has much more patience.
- **Laurence J. Peter:** *Quotations for Our Time,* 1977.

2,928. Socrates thought that if all our misfortunes were laid in one common heap, whence everyone must take an equal portion, most persons would be contented to take their own and depart.
- **Plutarch:** *Consolation to Apollonius,* 1st - 2nd AD

2,929. Misfortunes seldom come alone.
- ***English Proverb.***

2,930. All of us have sufficient fortitude to bear the misfortunes of others.
- **Francois, Duc de La Rochefoucauld:** *Maxims*, 1665.

2,931. Fire is the test of gold; adversity of strong men.
- **Lucius Annaeus Seneca (Seneca the Younger):** *Moral Essays*.

2,932. I consider you unfortunate because you have never been unfortunate.
- *ibid*

2,933. Never find your delight in another's misfortune.
- **Publilius Syrus:** *Maxims*, 1st century BC.

2,934. The longer we dwell on our misfortunes, the greater is their power to harm us.
- **Voltaire**.

MISTAKES

2,935. It's no crime to make a mistake,it's a crime if you don't learn from it.
- ***anon.***

2,936. Learn from your mistakes and build on your successes.
- **John C. Calhoun.**

2,937. To make a mistake and not correct it - that, indeed, is a mistake.
- **Confucius:** *The Analects of Confucius,* 5th century BC.

2,938. When you make a mistake, admit it, correct it, and learn from it immediately.
- **Stephen Covey:** *The 7 Habits of Highly Effective People,* 1990.

2,939. Teach yourself by your own mistakes; people learn only by error.
- **William Faulkner:** Advice to young writers in an *Interview in The Paris Review, 1956.*

2,940. The greatest mistake you can make in life is to be continually fearing you will make one.
- **Elbert Hubbard:** *The Note Book of Elbert Hubbard,* 1927.

2,941. People think I'm this whiter-than-white girl who's never made any mistakes. But I've made loads of mistakes. . . I'm very conscious of the fact that people put me on this pedestal, but I'm as human and flawed as anyone else. What is true is that every time I make a mistake, I try to learn from it.
- **Katherine Jenkins**: *magazine interview, 17th November, 2009.*

2,942. One day my skydiving uncle Newt forgot to pack his parachute. "That's one mistake," said auntie Jen, "that he will never make again."
- **Bruce Lansky:** *A Lesson Learned* in *Lighten Up, Bk 1* by B.Lansky, 1998.

2,943. It seems that the necessary thing to do is not to fear mistakes, to plunge in, to do the best that one can, hoping to learn enough from blunders to correct them eventually.
- **Abraham Maslow:** *Motivation and Personality,* 1954.

2,944. A man must be big enough to admit his mistakes, smart enough to profit from them, and strong enough to correct them.
- **John C. Maxwell.**

2,945. We often discover what *will* do, by finding out what will not do; and probably he who never made a mistake never made a discovery.
- **Samuel Smiles:** *Self Help,* 1859.

2,946. Mistakes are the usual bridge between inexperience and wisdom.
- **Phyllis Theroux:** *Night Lights: Bedtime Stories for Parents,* 1988.

MONEY

2,947. The true value of money is not in its possession, but in its use.
- The moral of **Aesop's Fable:** *The Miser and His Gold.*

2,948. Money is a needful and precious thing, and when well used, a noble thing, but I never want you to think it is the first or only prize to strive for.
- **Louisa May Alcott:** The sentiments of Marmee, the girls' mother, in *Little Women*, 1868.

2,949. Money is like muck, of very little use except it be spread.
- **Francis Bacon:** *Essays*, 1626.

2,950. I'm tired of love; I'm tired of Rhyme
But Money gives me pleasure all the time.
- **Hilaire Belloc:** *Fatigued* in *The Oxford Book of Twentieth Century English Verse* edited by Philip Larkin, 1973.

2,951. People who want to get rich fall into temptation and a trap and into many foolish and harmful desires that plunge men into ruin and destruction. For the love of money is a root of all kinds of evil.
- **The Bible:** *1ˢᵗ Timothy 6: 9 - 10a, NIV*

2,952. Money is like promises - easier made than kept.
- **Josh Billings:** *Josh Billings, His Book*, 1865.

2,953. We all need money, but there are degrees of desperation.
- **Anthony Burgess:** *The Face Magazine, December, 1984.*

2,954. It has been said that the love of money is the root of all evil. The want of money is so quite as truly.
- **Samuel Butler:** *Erewhon*, 1872.

2,955. Ready money is Aladdin's lamp.
- **Lord Byron:** *Don Juan*, 1819 – 1824.

2,956. Money doesn't talk these days. It just goes without saying.
- **Bennett Cerf:** *The Laugh's On Me*, 1963.

2,957. Preoccupation with money is the great test of small natures, but only a small test of great ones.
- **Nicolas Chamfort:** *Maxims and Considerations of Chamfort* translated by Edward Powys Mathers, 1926.

2,958. I knew once a very covetous, sordid fellow who used to say, "Take care of the pence, for the pounds will take care of themselves."
- **Lord Chesterfield:** *Letters to His Son*, 6th November, 1747.

2,959. I and my companions suffer from a disease of the heart that can be cured only with gold.
- **Hernan Cortes:** Message sent to Montezuma, quoted in *The Hutchinson Dictionary of Biography*, 1993.

2,960. I am living so far beyond my income that we may almost be said to be living apart.
- **E. E. Cumming:** *Quotable Business* by Louis E. Boone, 1999.

2,961. Annual income twenty pounds, annual expenditure nineteen pounds nineteen and six, result happiness. Annual income twenty pounds, annual expenditure twenty pounds ought and six, result misery.
- **Charles Dickens:** Micawber's sentiments in *David Copperfield*, 1850.

2,962. My kids never had the advantage I had, I was born poor.
- **Kirk Douglas:** *Halliwell's Who's Who in the Movies, 3rd Edition* edited by John Walker, 1997.

2,963. The mint makes it first, and it's up to you to make it last.
- **Evan Esar:** *20,000 Quips and Quotes*, 1968.

2,964. Money isn't everything - for one thing, it isn't plentiful.
- *ibid*.

2,965. Money is far more persuasive than logical argument.
- **Euripides**.

2,966. Money is really only important if you don't have any.
- **Harrison Ford:** *Reader's Digest, May, 2008*

2,967. The desire seems to be to find a short cut to money and to pass over the obvious short cut - which is work.
- **Henry Ford:** *My Life and Work – an Autobiography of Henry Ford* in collaboration with Samuel Crowther. 1922.

2,968. Money is worth what it will help you to produce or buy and no more.
- **Henry Ford:** *Theosophist Magazine, February, 1930.*

2,969. One of the evils of money is that it tempts us to look at it rather than at the things that it buys.
- **E. M. Forster:** *Two Cheers for Democracy- Essays and Broadcasts,* 1951.

2,970. A. He that is of the opinion money will do everything may well be suspected of doing everything for money.
B. Wealth is not his that has it, but his that enjoys it.
C. There are three faithful friends - an old wife, an old dog, & ready money.
D. A penny saved is a penny earned.
E. The use of money is all the advantage there is in having money.
- **Benjamin Franklin:** *Poor Richard's Almanack.*

2,971. If you can actually count your money, then you are not really a rich man.
- **J. Paul Getty:** *The Observer, 3rd November, 1957.*

2,972. I only ask that Fortune send
A little more than I shall spend.
- **Oliver Wendell Holmes:** *The Autocratic at the Breakfast Table,* 1858.

2,973. Money never made a fool o' anybuddy; it only shows 'em up.
- **Kin Hubbard:** *Abe Martin Hoss Sense and Nonsense,* 1926.

2,974. The love of money grows as the money itself grows.
- **Juvenal:** *Satires,* 1st & 2nd centuries AD

2,975. It's good to have money and the things money can buy, but it's good, too, to check up once in a while and make sure that you haven't lost the things that money can't buy.
- **George Horace Lorimer:** Editor-in-Chief of *The Saturday Evening Post* from 1899 till 1936.

2,976. Too much money is as demoralizing as too little, and there's no such thing as exactly enough.
- **Mignon McLaughlin:** *The Second Neurotic's Notebook*, 1966.

2,977. Money is just the poor man's credit card.
- **Marshall McLuhan:** *Understanding Media: The Extensions of Man*, 1964.

2,978. Today, money still talks. Trouble is, you have to increase the volume a lot!
Mad Magazine: *MAD. The Half-Wit and Wisdom of Alfred E. Neuman* 1997.

2,979. I have enough money to last me the rest of my life, unless I buy something.
- **Jackie Mason:** *Jackie Mason's America*, 1983.

2,980. The further through life I drift the more obvious it becomes that I am lacking in thrift.
- **Ogden Nash:** *A Penny Saved* in *Good Intentions*, 1942.

2,981. Money on its most basic level is a hard fact - you either have it or you don't. But on its emotional level it is purely a fiction. It becomes what you let it become.
- **Kent Nerburn:** *Letters to My Son: A Father's Wisdom on Manhood, Life. And Love*, 1994.

2,982. Money may not bring happiness, but it is nice to find out for yourself.
- **Herbert V. Prochnow and Herbert V. Prochnow Jr:** *The Public Speaker's Source Book.* 1977.

2,983. If you want to know what God thinks of money, look at the people he gives it to.
- ***New England Proverb***.

2,984. Having money is rather like being a blonde. It is more fun but not vital.
- **Mary Quant:** *The Observer, 2nd November, 1986.*

2,985. Money is only a tool. It will take you wherever you wish, but it will not replace you as the driver.
- **Ayn Rand:** *Atlas Shrugged*, 1957.

2,986. The use of money is all the advantage there is in having money.

- **John Ray:** *A Complete Collection of English Proverbs*, 1670.

2,987. Money has never made anyone rich.

- **Seneca:** quoted in *The Tao of Dad. The Wisdom of Fathers Near and Far* by Taro Gold, 2006.

2,988. Lack of money is the root of all evil.

- **George Bernard Shaw:** *Man and Superman*, 1903.

2,989. Let us all be happy and live within our means, even if it means we have to borrow money to do it.

- **Artemus Ward:** *Artemus Ward in London and Other Papers*, 1867.

2,990. The only way not to think about money is to have a great deal of it.

- **Edith Wharton:** *The House of Mirth*. 1905.

2,991. Always remember, money isn't everything - but also remember to make a lot of it before talking such fool nonsense.

- **Earl Wilson**

MOTHERS

2,992. A Freudian slip is when you say one thing but mean your mother.
- *anon*.

2,993. If at first you don't succeed, do it like your mother told you.
- *anon*.

2,994. If being a mum was easy, a man could do it.
- *anon*.

2,995. A man's work is from sun to sun, but a mother's work is never done.
- *anon*.

2,996. Every mother hopes her daughter will get a better husband than she did, but she knows her son will never get as good a wife as his father did.
- *anon*: *20,000 Quips and Quotes* by Evan Esar, 1968.

2,997. The art of motherhood involves much silent, unobtrusive self-denial, an hourly devotion which finds no detail too minute.
- **Honore de Balzac:** *Letters of Two Brides*, 1842.

2,998. When somebody writes a script about life, usually the leading role will be the man, because mostly what women do is at home taking care of the children. That's the most important job there is on earth. And why shouldn't women have it since they are the better of the two sexes.
- **Anne Bancroft:** *Associated Press Interview*, 1992.

2,999. A child needs a mother more than all the things money can buy. Spending time with your children is the greatest gift of all.
- **Ezra Taft Benson**.

3,000. Honour your father and your mother.
- **The Bible:** *Exodus 20: 12a, NIV*

3,001. I love my mother for all the times she said absolutely nothing. I thank her for her virtues, but mostly for never once having said, "I told you so."
- **Erma Bombeck:** *Motherhood, the Second Oldest Profession,* 1983.

3,002. I was one of the luckier women who came to motherhood with some experience. I owned a Yorkshire Terrier for three years.
- *ibid.*

3,003. Motherhood is the biggest on-the-job-training program in existence.
- *ibid*

3,004. Some are kissing mothers and some are scolding mothers, but it is love just the same, and most mothers kiss and scold.
- **Pearl S. Buck:** *To My Daughters, With Love,* 1967.

3,005. Pride is one of the seven deadly sins; but it cannot be the pride of a mother in her children, for that is a compound of two cardinal virtues - faith and hope.
- **Charles Dickens:** *The Life and Adventures of Nicholas Nickleby,* 1839.

3,006. Tired mothers find that spanking takes less time than reasoning and penetrates sooner to the seat of the memory.
- **Will Durant.**

3,007. Take Motherhood: nobody ever thought of putting it on a moral pedestal until some brash feminist pointed out, about a century ago, that the pay is lousy and the career ladder non-existent.
- **Barbara Ehrenreich:** *The Worst Years of Our Lives,* 1990.

3,008. Men are what their mothers made them.
- **Ralph Waldo Emerson:** *The Conduct of Life,* 1860.

3,009. A mother takes twenty years to make a man of her boy, and another woman makes a fool of him in twenty minutes.
- **Robert Frost:** quoted in *The Dictionary of Humorous Quotations* edited by Evan Esar, 1955.

3,010. Motherhood isn't For Wimps.
- **Barbara Johnson:** chapter title in *Splashes of Joy,* 2003.

3,011. If I were drowned in the deepest sea
Mother o' mine, O mother o' mine
I know whose tears would come down to me
Mother o' mine, O mother o' mine.
- **Rudyard Kipling:** *Collected Poems of Rudyard Kipling*, 1994.

3,012. Mothers are Like Miracles: They Make Everything Possible.
- **Janet Lanese:** book title, 1998.

3,013. It isn't easy being a mother.. If it were, fathers would do it.
- **Fred Metcalf:** *The Penguin Dictionary of Jokes*, 1993.

3,014. Her mother was a cultivated woman - she was born in a greenhouse.
- **Spike Milligan**: *Lady Chatterley's Lover According to Spike Milligan*.

3,015 More than any other human relationship, overwhelmingly more, motherhood means being instantly interruptible, responsive, responsible.
- **Tillie Olson:** *Silences*, 1995.

3.016. A man loves his sweetheart the most, his wife the best but his mother the longest.
- *Irish Proverb*.

3,017. An ounce of mother is worth a pound of clergy.
- *Spanish Proverb*.

3,018. God could not be everywhere so he created mothers.
- *Yiddish Proverb*.

3,019. The world is full of women blinded by the increasing demands of motherhood, still flabbergasted by how a job can be terrific and torturous, involving and utterly tedious, all at the same time. The world is full of women made to feel strange because what everyone assumes comes naturally is so difficult to do – never mind to do well.
- **Anne Quinlen:** *Thinking Out Loud*, 1993.

3,020. The role of a mother is probably the most important career a woman can have.
- **Janet Mary Riley:** *Times, November 2nd 1986*. Quoted in *Encarta Book of Quotations* edited by Bill Swainson, 2,000.

3,021. Into a woman's keeping is committed the destiny of the generations to come.
- **Theodore Roosevelt:** quoted in *Mother: A Book of Quotations* edited by Herb Galewitz, 2002.

3,022. My doctors told me I would never walk again. My mother told me I would, I believed my mother... My mother taught me very early to believe I could achieve any accomplishment I wanted to. The first was to walk without braces.
- **Wilma Rudolph:** American Olympic Gold medalist, quoted in her autobiography, *Wilma: The Story of Wilma Rudolph*, 1977.

3,023. You may have tangible wealth untold;
Caskets of jewels and coffers of gold.
Richer than I you can never be...
I had a Mother who read to me.
- **Gillian Strickland:** *The Reading Mother* in *Best Loved Poems of the American People*, 1936.

3,024. Who ran to help me when I fell,
And would some pretty story tell,
Or kiss the place to make it well?
My mother.
- **Ann Taylor:** *My Mother* in *Original Poems for Infant Minds*, 1804.

MOTHER'S DAY

3,025. Unpleasant questions are being raised about Mother's Day. Is this day necessary? No politician with half his senses, which a majority of politicians have, is likely to vote for its abolition, however, as a class, mothers are tender and loving, but as a voting bloc they would not hesitate for an instant to pull the seat out from behind any member of parliament who suggests that Mother is not entitled to a box of chocolates each year on Mother's Day.
- **Russell Baker:** *The Mother Book* edited by Liz Smith. 1978.

3,026. A lot of things have been done in bed in the name of love, but nothing comes close to the traditional Mother's Day breakfast in bed.
- **Erma Bombeck:** *Motherhood: The Second Oldest Profession*, 1983.

3,027. Mothers, in fact, organize the day as precisely as Patton planned an attack. They make a list of things they want, summon their children, and say, "Go see your father, get some money from him, and surprise me with some of these."
- **Bill Cosby:** *Fatherhood*, 1986.

3,028. Don't forget Mother's Day, or as they call it in Beverley Hills, "Dad's Third Wife Day."
- **Jay Leno**.

3,029. The only mothers it is safe to forget on Mother's Day are the good ones.
- **Mignon McLaughlin:** *The Neurotic's Notebook*, 1960.

MOTHERS-IN-LAW

3,030. There are only three basic jokes, but since the mother-in-law joke is not a joke, but a very serious question, there are only two.
- **George Ade:** *The Treasury of Humorous Quotations* edited by Evan Esar. English edition edited by Nicolas Bentley, 1955.

3,031. English law prohibits a man from marrying his mother-in-law. This is our idea of useless legislation.
- *anon.*

3,032. Every mother-in-law forgets she was once a daughter-in-law.
- *anon.*

3,033. Behind every successful man is a surprised woman, his mother-in-law.
- *anon: 20,000 Quips and Quotes* edited by Evan Esar, 1968.

3,034. An ill humoured mother-in-law is no laughing matter.
- *anon, ibid.*

3,035. If you tell your motherr-in-law that the house is too small for all three of you to live in, she'll raise the roof.
- *anon, ibid.*

3,036. Adam was not only the first man, he was also the first man to have no mother-in-law. That is how we know he lived in paradise.
- *anon: The Comic Encyclopedia* written by Evan Esar, 1978.

3,037. Can the police come round and take my mother-in-law away? She has been here for 18 days.
- *anon: The Press and Journal Quotes for the Day, 1st Feb. 2008.*
NB This plea was made by a caller to South Wales Police 999 Service during the 2007 Christmas holidays.

3,038. The home for the aged came for a contribution. He gave them his mother-in-law.
- **Milton Berle:** *Milton Berle's Private Joke File*, 1989.

3.039. Happiness is your mother-in-law developing an untreatable allergy to something in your house.
- **George Burns:** *Dr Burns' Prescription for Happiness,* 1986.

3,040. My mother-in-law has come round to our house at Christmas seven years running. This year we're having a change. We're going to let her in.
- **Les Dawson**.

3,041. The wife's mother said, "When you're dead, I'll dance on your grave." I said, "Good, I'm being buried at sea."
- **Les Dawson**.

3.042. I took my mother-in-law to Madame Tussaud's Chamber of Horrors, and one of the attendants said, "Keep her moving, Sir, we're stock taking."
- **Les Dawson**.

3,043. The wife's mother said, "How would you like to have a chat with me?" I said, "Through a medium."
- **Les Dawson**.

3,044. My car has had stereo for a long time. My wife in the front and my mother-in-law in the back.
- **Leopard Fechtner:** *5,000 One-And-Two-Line Jokes*, 1979.

3,045. Everything has its drawbacks, as the man said when his mother-in-law died and they came down on him for the funeral expenses.
- **Jerome K. Jerome:** *Three Men in a Boat,* 1889.

3,046. Give up all hope of peace so long as your mother-in-law is alive.
- **Juvenal:** *Satires,* **circa** 120 AD

3,047. I just came back from a pleasure trip. I took my mother-in-law to the bus station.
- **Pat Williams:** *Winning With One-Liners*, 2002.

MOURNING

3,048. When someone you love becomes a memory, the memory becomes a treasure.
- ***anon.***

3,049. Nothing happens to anybody which he is not fitted by nature to bear.
- **Marcus Aurelius:** *Meditations,* 2nd century AD.

3,050. Blessed are those who mourn, for they will be comforted.
- **The Bible:** *Matthew 5: 4, NIV*

3,051. I cannot force you to believe in God. Believing in God amounts to coming to terms with death. When you have accepted death, the problem of God will be solved – and not the reverse.
- **Albert Camus**.

3,052. There is no grief which time does not lessen and soften.
- **Marcus Tullius Cicero:** *Epistles,* 1st century, BC.

3,053. Let mourning stop when one's grief is fully expressed.
- **Confucius:** *Analects,* 6th centurey, BC.

3,054. Grief is itself a medicine.
- **William Cowper:** *Charity,* 1782.

3,055. There is no greater grief than to remember days of joy when misery is at hand.
- **Dante:** *Inferno, Canto v,* 14th century AD.

3,056. Grief is the agony of an instant, the indulgence of grief the blunder of a life.
- **Benjamin Disraeli:** *Vivian Grey,* 1826.

3,057. Time is a physician that heals every grief.
- **Diphilus:** Greek physician, 3rd century BC.

3,058. When you are sorrowful look again in your heart, and you shall see that in truth you are weeping for that which has been your delight.
- **Kahlil Gibran:** *The Prophet*, 1923.

3,059. To spare oneself from grief at all cost can be achieved only at the price of total detachment, which excludes the ability to experience happiness.
- **Erich Fromm:** *The Art of Loving*, 1957.

3,060. I have lived with you and loved you, / And now you are gone away,/ Gone where I cannot follow, / Until I have finished all my days.
- **Victoria Hanley:** *The Seer and the Sword*, 1999.

3,061. People in mourning have to come to grips with death before they can live again.
- **Elizabeth Kubler-Ross:** quoted in *And I Quote* by William R. Evams. *et al*, 2003.

3,062. Grief knits two hearts in closer bonds than happiness ever can, and common sufferings are far stronger links than common joys.
- **Alphonse de Lamartine**.

3,063. Expect trouble as an inevitable part of life and repeat to yourself, the most comforting words of all: This, too, shall pass.
- **Ann Landers:** *Chicago Sun-Times Advice Column*.

3,064. The turning point in the process of growing up is when you discover the core of strength within you that can survive all hurt.
- **Max Lerner:** *The Unfinished Country*, 1959.

3,065. There is no grief like the grief which does not speak.
- **Henry Wadsworth Longfellow:** *Hyperion*, 1839.

3,066. If we have been pleased with life, we should not be displeased with death, since it comes from the hand of the same master.
- **Michelangelo:** *circa* 1564 AD

3,067. For death begins with life's first breath, and life begins at the touch of death.
- **John Oxenham**.

3,068. Happiness is beneficial for the body but it is grief that develops the powers of the mind.
- **Marcel Proust:** *In Search of Lost Time,* 1927.

3,069. A: He who has hope has everything.
- ***Arabian Proverb.***
B: You cannot stop the birds of sorrow from flying over your head, but you can prevent them from building a nest in your hair.
- ***Chinese Proverb***
C: Friendship doubles joy and halves grief.
- ***Egyptian Proverb.***
D: Say not in grief; "He is no more", but live in thankfulness that he was.
- ***Hebrew Proverb.***
E: He that conceals his grief finds no remedy for it.
- ***Turkish Proverb.***

3.070. Here is one of the worst things about having someone you love die: It happens every single morning.
- **Anna Quinlen:** *Every Last One,* 2010.

3,071. Give sorrow words;
the grief that does not speak
whispers the o'er fraught heart
and bids it break.
- **William Shakespeare:** *Macbeth, Act IV, Scene III.*

3,072. The bitterest tears shed over graves are for words left unsaid and deeds left undone.
- **Harriet Beecher Stowe:** *Little Foxes: The Insignificant Little Habits Which Mar Domestic Happiness,* 1866.

3,073. The risk of love is loss, and the price of loss is grief. But the pain of grief is only a shadow when compared with the pain of never risking love.
- **Leonard M. Zunin and Hilary Stanton Zunin:** *The Art of Condolence.*

MUSIC

3,074. There are seventy stanzas in the Uruguay national anthem, which fact may account for the Uruguay standing army.
- **Franklin Pierce Adams:** quoted in *The Treasury of Humorous Quotations* edited by Evan Esar, English edition edited by Nicolas Bentley, 1955.

3,075. I play a musical instrument some, but only for my own amazement.
- **Fred Allen:** *The Treasury of Humorous Quotations* by Evan Esar.

3,076. He often broke into song because he couldn't find the key.
- *anon.*

3,077. Many a husband, knowing nothing about music, learns he can produce real harmony in the home by playing second fiddle.
- *anon.*

3,078. Music therapy is the treatment of physical and mental ills by means of music... One of the special advantages of music as a therapeutic device is that it takes up where medicine leaves off. The latter prescribes for the physical man; the former seeks to restore balance to the person as a whole. Music bolsters the morale and spirits of the sick one and tones up the body as well.
- **Doron K. Antrim:** *The Musical Quarterly, 1944.*

3,079. I close my eyes at concerts which / Are rather long and boring, / And people think, "Ah, he's enthralled / A music lover I am called, / Until they hear me snoring.
- **Richard Armour:** *Expert Listener* in *An Armoury of Light Verse.* 1942.

3,080. Music is the fourth great material want of our natures. First food, then raiment, then shelter, then music.
- **Christian Nestell Bovee**.

3,081. Music hath charms to soothe the savage breast.
- **William Congreve:** *The Mourning Bride, Act 1, Sc 1*, 1697.

3,082. Music produces a kind of pleasure which human nature cannot do without.
- **Confucius:** *Analects,* 5th century BC.

3,083. At night, as I tried to go to sleep, I listened to Mr Fox play the piano, and I learned from those evening recitals that music could ache and hurt, that beautiful music was a place a suffering man could hide.
- **Pat Conway:** *Beach House,* 1995

3,084. There is no feeling, except the extreme of fear and grief, that does not find relief in music.
- **George Eliot:** *The Mill on the Floss,* 1860.

3,085. Life seems to go on without effort when I am filled with music.
- ***ibid.***

3,086. He did not see any reason why the devil should have all the good tunes.
- Said of **Rowland Hill** in *The Rev. Rowland Hill* by E. W. Broome, 1881.

3,087. Music is the universal language of mankind.
- **Henry Wadsworth Longfellow:** *Outre-Mer,* a prose travelogue, 1835.

3,088. And the night shall be filled with music, / And the cares that infest the day, / Shall fold their tents, like the Arabs, / And silently steal away.
- **Henry Wadsworth Longfellow:** the last stanza of *The Day is Done* in *The Yale Book of American Verse* edited by Thomas R. Lounsbury, 2008.

3,089. There are many theories about the bagpipes, otherwise known as the missing link between music and noise. Some say they were invented by a Scotsman who trod on his cat and liked the noise. Others claim that they are based on the noise made by a dying octopus.
- **Des MacHale:** *The World's Best Scottish Jokes,* 1993.

3,090. My singing got mixed reception the other night. I liked it, but my audience didn't.
- **Pat Williams:** *Winning With One-Liners,* 2002.

NAMES

3,091. At the school I attended there was a boy who was forever being teased because his name was Norman Conquest. When he came of age he changed his surname by deed poll, taking his mother's maiden name. He is now known as Norman Castle.
- *anon.*

3,092. Some parents have difficulty deciding on a name for the new baby, while others have rich relatives.
- *anon: 20,000 Quips and Quotes* by Evan Esar, 1968.

3,093. A reckless driver is called a lot of names before he is finally called, "the deceased".
- *anon, ibid.*

3,094. A good name is more desirable than great riches; to be esteemed is better than silver or gold.
- **The Bible:** *Proverbs 22: 1, NIV.*

3,095. Always end the name of your child with a vowel, so that when you yell the name will carry.
- **Bill Cosby:** *Fatherhood*, 1986.

3,096. Nicknames stick to people, and the most ridiculous are the most adhesive.
- **Thomas Chandler Haliburton**.

3,097. A nickname is the hardest stone that the devil can throw at a man.
- **William Hazlitt:** *Sketches and Essays*, 1839.

3,098. I keep six honest serving men / (They taught me all I knew); / Their names are What and Why and When / And How and Where and Who.
- **Rudyard Kipling:** *Just So Stories*, 1902.

3,099. This is unfortunately a world in which things find it difficult, frequently impossible, to live up to their names.
- **J. B. Priestley:** *All About Ourselves and Other Essays,* 1956.

3,100. What's in a name ? that which we call a rose
By any other name would smell as sweet.
- **William Skakespeare:** *Romeo and Juliet, Act 2, Sc 2,* 1595.

3,101. Who steals my purse, steals trash... But he that filches from me my good name, / Robs me of that which not enriches him, / And makes me poor indeed.
- **William Shakespeare:** *Othello, Act 3, Sc 3,* 1603.

3.102. Never described as a sylph, Wright had no objection to the memorable name of her show (Two Fat Ladies). When asked if she found the name vulgar, she replied, "We don't mind 'two', and there's nothing wrong with 'fat', but we don't like 'ladies', it makes us sound like a public convenience."
- Quoted in an American University Student Newspaper review of *Clarissa and the Countryman* by **Clarissa Wright** and John Scott, 200.

NEIGHBOURS

3,103. People who live in glass houses nake the most interesting neighbours.
- **anon:** *20,000 Quips and Quotes* by Evan Esar, 1968.

3,104. My life was perfect until a new neighbour with a greeen thumb moved in.
- **Milton Berle:** *Milton Berle's Private Joke File*, 1989.

3,105. The Bible tells us to love our neighbours, and also to love our enemies, probably because they are generally the same people.
- **G. K. Chesterton:** *Illustrated London News, 7th October, 1916.*

3.106. The neighbour's grass may be greener, but their water bills are higher.
- **Sam Ewing:** *The Wall Street Journal, 17th April, 1996.*

3,107. My neighbours are keeping me broke. They are always buying things I cannot afford.
- **Leopold Fechtner:** *5,000 One-And-Two-Line Jokes*, 1973.

3.108. Good fences make good neighbours.
- **Robert Frost:** *Mending Wall* in *North of Boston*, 1915.

3,109. A bad neighbour is a great misfortune, as much as a good one is a great blessing.
- **Hesiod:** *Works and Days*, 8th century BC.

3,110. It is easier to love humanity as a whole than to love one's neighbour.
- **Eric Hoffer:** *New York Times Magazine.*

3,111. The best part of a real estate bargain is the neighbour.
- **Austin O'Malley**.

NEWSPAPERS

3,112. A newspaper is lumber made malleable. It is ink made into words and pictures. It is conceived, born, grows up and dies of old age in a day.
- **Jim Bishop**.

3,113. A newspaper reports all sorts of events, including misfortunes like deaths and marriages.
- **Evan Esar:** *20,000 Quips and Quotes*, 1968.

3,114. A newspaper is a circulating library with high blood pressure.
- *ibid*.

3,115. A good way to get youjr name in a newspaper is to walk across the street reading one.
- **Leopold Fechtner:** *5,000 One-and-Two Line Jokes*, 1973.

3,116. People who read the tabloids deserve to be lied to.
- **Jerry Seinfeld**.

3,117. An editor is someone who separates the wheat from the chaff and prints the chaff.
- **Adlai Stevenson:** *The Stevenson Wit* by Bill Adler.

NEW YEAR

3,118. The New Year is not the time to make a new start on old habits.
- ***anon***.

3,119. For auld lang syne, my dear,
For auld lang syne,
We'll take a cup o' kindness yet
For auld lang syne!
- **Robert Burns:** *Auld Lang Syne* (Chorus), 1788.
NB *For auld lang syne* might loosely be translated: *For the sake of old times*.

3,120. This is the day when people reciprocally offer, and receive, the kindest and warmest wishes, though, in general, without meaning them on one side, or believing them on the other.
- **Lord Chesterfield:** *Letters to His Son*, 1st January, 1753.

3,121. A New Year resolution is something that goes in one year and out the other.
- **Leopold Fechtner:** *5,000 One-And-Two-Line Jokes*, 1973.

3,122. Be always at war with your vices, at peace with your neighbours, and let each new year find you a better man.
- **Benjamin Franklin**.

3,123. I said to the man who stood at the gate of the year,
"Give me a light that I may tread safely into the unknown."
And he replied, "Go into the darkness and put your hand
Into the hand of God, that shall be to you better than light
And safer than a known way!"
So I went forth and finding the hand of God trod gladly.
Into the night.
- **Minnie Louise Haskins:** *God Knows*, 1908.
NB King George VI incorporated these lines into his 1939 Christmas message to the nation.

3,124. May all your troubles last as long as your New Year resolutions.
- **Barbara Johnson:** *Daily Splashes of Joy*, 2000.

3,125. A guid new year to ane an' a' / An' mony may ye see,
An' during a' the years to come / O happy may ye be.
- **Peter Livingstone:** *A Guid New Year – Poets' Box*, 1865.

3,126. Let us celebrate the occasion with wine and sweet words.
- **Plautus**.

3,127. Cheers to a new year and another chance for us to get it right.
Oprah Winfrey: *O Magazine*.

NUDITY

3,128. Living in a nudist camp must take all the fun out of Hallowe'en.
- *anon*.

3,129. All nudists are optimists who grin and bare it.
- *anon*.

3,130. Let's not criticize the nudists – remember, they were born that way.
- *anon: 20,000 Quips and Quotes* by Evan Esar, 1968.

3,131. I have always felt that if the good Lord had meant for people to go nude he would never have invented the wicker chair.
- **Emma Bombeck:** *The Grass is Always Greener Over the Septic Tank*, 1976.

3,132. When a nudist couple gets a divorce, it's usually because they have been seeing too much of each other.
- **Leopold Fechtner:** *5,000 One-And-Two-Line Jokes*, 1973.

3,133. It's not true that I had nothing on. I had the radio on.
- **Marilyn Monroe:** *Time Magazine, 1952,* commenting on a photograph of her naked on a calandar.

3,134. Nudist camps are places where, if you see a sign saying: "PUT YOUR BUTS HERE" it isn't an ash tray, it's a bench!
- **Robert Orben:** *2,000 New Laughs for Speakers, the Ad Libbers's . Handbook,* 1978.

OBESITY

3,139. Push-ups, sit-ups, run in place.
Each night I keep a gruelling pace.
With bleak results, I must divulge -
I've lost the battle of the bulge.
- **Charles Ghigna:** *Age Happens: The Best Quotes and Cartoons About Growing Older* selected by Bruce Lansky, 1996.

3,140. I see no objection to stoutness, in moderation.
- **Sir W. S. Gilbert:** *Iolanthe, Act 1*, 1882.

3,141. Yesterday my gun exploded
When I thought it wasn't loaded;
Near my wife I pulled the trigger,
Chipped a fragment off her figure;
'Course I'm sorry, and all that,
But she shouldn't be so fat.
- **Harry Graham:** *The Perils of Obesity* quoted in *The Fireside Book of Humorous Poetry* edited by William Cole, 1959.

3,142. Fatness is not a state of mind and mustn't be allowed to become so.
- **Miriam Margolyes**.

3,143. Life, if you're fat, is a minefield – you have to pick your way, otherwise you blow up.
- **Miriam Margolyes:** *London Observer.*

3,144. "The global epidemic of obesity is completely out of control", the BBC noted, reporting from the first international obesity conference in 2004. "Obesity rates are escalating everywhere. Doctors at the meeting are warning that unless something is done, health care services in both the developed and developing world will not be able to cope with treating people with diseases linked with obesity."
- **Morgan Spurlock:** *Don't Eat This Book: Fast Food and the Supersizing of America*, 2005.

3,145. She fitted into my biggest armchair as if it had been built round her by someone who knew they were wearing armchairs tight about the hips that season.

- **P. G. Wodehouse:** *Very Good Jeeves*, 1930.

OBITUARIES

3,146. Dead men tell no tales, but their obituaries often do.
- *anon.*

3,147. A good way to get your name in the newspapers is to walk across the street reading one.
- *anon: 20,000 Quips and Quotes* by Evan Esar, 1968.

3,148. He was my North, my South, my East and West
My working week and my Sunday rest,
My noon, my midnight, my talk, my song;
I thought that love would last forever, I was wrong
- **W. H. Auden:** *Funeral Blues,* stanza 3, 1936.
NB All four stanzas of this poem were read at the funeral of Gareth – played by Simon Gallow – in the 1994 film: *Four Weddings and a Funeral.*

3,149. There's no such thing as bad publicity, except your own obituary.
- **Brendan Behan:** *My Brother Brendan* by Dominic Behan, 1965.

3,150. When I wrote obituaries, my mother said the only thing I ever got them to do was die in alphabetical order.
- **Erma Bombeck:** *Times Magazine, 2nd July, 1984.*

3,151. Like everyone else who makes the mistake of getting older, I begin each day with coffee and obituaries.
- **Bill Cosby:** *Time Flies,* 1987.

3,152. I never wanted to see anybody die, but there are a few obituary notices I have read with pleasure.
- **Clarence Darrow:** *The Story of My Life,* 1932.

3,153. I always wait for *The Times* each morning. I look at the obituary column, and if I'm not in it, I go to work.
- **A.E. Matthews:** *The Filmgoer's Book of Quotes.*

3,154. Live so that when the final summons comes you will leave something more behind you than an epitaph on a tombstone or an obituary in a newspaper.

- **Billy Sunday**.

3,155. Called upon for a few words of condolence at the death of one he cordially detested, Voltaire at first refused. He was finally persuaded and penned this brief but reluctant statement: "I have just been informed that Monsieur is dead. He was a sturdy patriot, a gifted writer, a loyal friend and an affectionate husband and father - provided he really is dead."

- **Voltaire**.

OBSTACLES

3,156. The obstacles of life are intended to make us better, not bitter.
- **anon:** *20,000 Quips and Quotes* by Evan Esar, 1968.

3,157. Obstacles are things a person sees when he takes his eyes off his goal.
- **E. Joseph Cossman.**

3,158. The longer you gaze on an obstacle the bigger it becomes.
- **B. C. Forbes:** *20,000 Quips and Quotes* by Evan Esar, 1968.

3,159. The best way out of a difficulty is through it.
- **B. C. Forbes:** *Forbes Epigrams*, 1922.

3,160. It still holds true that man is most uniquely human when he turns obstacles into opportunities.
- **Eric Hoffer:** *Reflections on the Human Condition*, 1973.

3,161. The boulder which was an obstacle in the path of the weak becomes a stepping stone in the pathway of the resolute.
- **Orison Swett Marden:** *Pushing to the Front or Success Under Difficulties*, 1911.

3,162. The only value the story of my life may have is to show that one can, even without any particular gifts, overcome obstacles that seem insurmountable if one is willing to face the fact that they must be overcome; that in spite of timidity and fear, in spite of a lack of special talents, one can find a way to live widely and fully.
- **Eleanor Roosevelt:** *The Autobiography of Eleanor Roosevelt*, 1961.

3,163. Imaginary obstacles are insurmountable. Real ones aren't.
- **Barbara Sher.**

OLD AGE

3,164. I am not interested in age. People who tell me their age are silly. You're as old as you feel.
- **Henri Frederic Amiel:** *Journal Intime*, 1882.

3,165. To know how to grow old is the master work of wisdom, and one of the most difficult chapters in the great art of living.
- *ibid.*

3,166. Growing old is mandatory, growing up is optional.
- *anon.*

3,167. Growing old is when you're told to slow down by the doctor instead of the police.
- *anon.*

3,168. I am old and I don't give a damn!
- **Lauren Bacall:** *Press and Journals 'Quotes of the Day', 10th August, 2007.*

3,169. Age appears to be best in four things – old wood best to burn, old wine to drink, old friends to trust, and old authors to read.
- **Francis Bacon:** *Apophthegms,* 1625.

3,170. I take it for granted that I am growing older, although, except for a slight arteriosclerosis and an inability to hear, I would never know it.
- **Robert Benchley:** *No Poems, or Around the World Backwards and Sideways,* 1932.

3,171. Age is no guarantee of maturity.
- **Lawana Blackwell:** *The Courtship of the Vicar's Daughter,* 1998.

3,172. To resist the frigidity of old age one must combine the body, the mind and the heart - and to keep them in parallel vigour one must exercise, study and love.
- **Karl von Bonstetten**.

3,173. Grow old along with me!
The best is yet to be.
- **Robert Browning:** *Rabbi Ben Ezra* in *Dramatis Personae,* 1864.

3,174. When I was young I was called a rugged individualist. When I was in my fifties I was considered eccentric. Here I am doing and saying the same things I did then and I'm labelled senile.
- **George Burn:** in his role as an elderly former vaudevillian in the 1979 film *Just You And Me Kid.*

3,175. Old age is really not so bad, may you come to know the condition.
- **Marcus Tullius Cicero:** *On Old Age,* 1st century BC.

3,176. Slowly and imperceptibly old age comes creeping on.
- *ibid.*

3,177. The folly of old age which is called dotage is peculiar to silly old men, not to age itself.
- *ibid.*

3,178. In middle age I practised feeling old, but the real thing has been a rude surprise.
- **Mason Cooley:** *City Aphorisms, Thirteenth Selection,* 1994.

3,179. "Don't worry about senility," my grandfather used to say, "when it hits you, you won't know it."
- **Bill Cosby:** *Time Flies,* 1987.

3,180. Old age isn't for sissies.
Bette Davis: *Old Age Comes at a Bad Time: Wit and Wisdom for the Young at Heart* selected by Eliakim Katz, 2002.

3,181. Indeed, he would sometimes remark, when a man fell into his anecdotage, it was a sign for him to retire from the world.
- **Benjamin Disraeli:** *Lothair,* 1870.

3,182. I was a young fellow once, and now I'm getting an old and wise one. Old at any rate; which is a gift that comes to everybody if they live long enough.
- **George Eliot:** *Daniel Deronda,* 1876.

3,183, As Groucho Marx once said, "Anyone can get old - all you have to do is to live long enough."
- **Queen Elizabeth 2nd**: *in a s peech at her official 80th birthday lunch.*

3,184. Another candle on your cake ? / Well, that's no cause to pout. / Be glad that you have strength enough / To blow the damn thing out.
- **William R. Evans III and Andrew Frothingham:** *Lighten Up! Book 2* edited by Bruce Lansky, 1999.

3,185. In today's world a person can live to a gripe old age.
- **Sam Ewing:** *The Sun, 6th July, 1999.*

3,186. Of all the self-fulfilling prophecies in our culture, the assumption that ageing means decline and poor health is probably the deadliest.
- **Marilyn Ferguson:** *The Aquarian Conspiracy,* 1980.

3,187. Old age, Mr Thomson, is the only disease you don't look forward to being cured of.
- Dialogue from the **1941 Film** *Citizen Kane,* partly written, directed and starring Orson Welles.

3,188. All my life I've been taught how to die, but no one ever taught me how to grow old.
- **Billy Graham:** *Newsweek, 14th August, 2006.*

3,189. To be seventy years young is sometimes far more cheerful and hopeful than to be forty years old.
- **Oliver Wendell Holmes, Sr:** *in a letter written to a lady of his acquantance on her 70th birthday.*

3,190. I'm so old they have cancelled my blood type.
- **Bob Hope**.

3,191. You're not old until your 80.... that is the new theory and with that comes the belief that old age has been postponed.... not indefinitely but certainly for longer than before.
- **Annie Hulley:** *How to Spend the Kids' Inheritance,* 2006.

3,192. I look forward to growing old and wise and audacious.
- **Glenda Jackson**.

3,193. Talking is the disease of age.
- **Ben Jonson:** *Timber or Discoveries Made Upon Men and Matter,* 1641.

3,194. Nothing makes one old so quickly as the ever present thought that one is growing older.
- **Georg Christoph Lichtenberg**: *Notebook K,* 1789 – 1793.

3,195. As life runs on, the road grows strange / with faces new - and, near the end / The milestones into headstones change, / 'Neath every one a friend.
- **James Russell Lowell**.

3,196. That's the purpose of old age. To give us a breathing space before we die, in which to see why we did what we did.
- **Colleen Mc Cullough**: *The Thornbirds,* 1977.

3,197. Old age has it's pleasures, which, though different, are not less than the pleasures of youth.
- **W. Somerset Maugham**: *The Summing Up,* 1938.

3,198. Old age is ready to undertake tasks that youth shirked because they would take too long.
- *ibid.*

3,199. I never lie about my age.. I just tell people I'm as old as my wife – and then I lie about *her* age!
- **Fred Metcalf**: *The Penguin Dictionary of Jokes.* 1993.

3,200. He is so old he can remember when Heinz had only one variety.
- *ibid.*

3,201. You know you're getting older when you decide to procrastinate but never seem to get round to it.
- **Bob Monkhouse**: *Just Say a Few Words,* 1988.

3,202. How confusing the beams from memory's lamp are; / One day a bachelor, the next a grampa, / What is the secret of the trick? / How did I get so old so quick?
- **Ogden Nash**: *Preface to the Past* in *You Can't Get There From Here,* 1957.

3,203. I used to think that getting old was about vanity – but actually it's about losing people you love.
- **Joyce Carol Oates**: *The Guardian,* 1987.

3,204. I'm not old but mellow like good wine.
- **Stephen Phillips**.

3,205. About the only thing that comes to us without effort is old age.
- **Gloria Pitzer:** *Reader's Digest, 1979.*

3,206. Old people love to give good advice to console themselves for no longer being able to set a bad example.
- **Francois, Duc de La Rochefoucauld:** *Maxims,* 1665.

3,207. As one grows older one becomes wiser and more foolish.
- *ibid.*

3,208. One of the blessings of age is to learn not to part in a note of sharpness, to treasure the moments spent with those we love, and to make them whenever possible good to remember, for time is short.
- **Eleanor Roosevelt:** *My Daily Column,* 5th February, 1943.

3,209. Getting old has its advantages. I can no longer read the bathroom scales.
- **Brad Schreiber:** *Laugh Twice & Call Me In The Morning: The Best Quotes And Cartoons To Cure What Ails You* by Bruce Lansky, 1999.

3,210. Old age is rather like another country. You will enjoy it more if you have prepared yourself to go.
- **B. F. Skinner & M. E. Vaughan:** *Enjoy Old Age: A Practical Guide.* 1997.

3,211. No man loves life like him that's growing old.
- **Sophocles:** *Fragment,* 5th century BC.

3,212. Getting older is like being a moneyed teenager. The same freedom, but more pennies. You have to grab the bonuses; you can spend the day in bed, reading a book.
- **Una Stubbs:** *Life's Lessons, The Saga Magazine, June, 2007.*

OPINIONS

3,213. You cannot prevent others from having a poor opinion of you, but you can keep them from being right in their opinion.
- *anon*.

3,214. I've never had a humble opinion in my life. If you are going to have one, why be humble about it.
- **Joan Baez:** *International Herald Tribune, 2/12/92.*

3,215. Patterning your life around other's opinions is nothing more than slavery.
- **Lawana Blackwell:** *The Dowry of Miss Lydia Clark*, 1999.

3,216. If in the last few years you haven't discarded a major opinion or acquired a new one, check your pulse, you may be dead.
- **Gelett Burgess**.

3,217. Fight for your opinions, but do not believe that they contain the whole truth or the only truth.
- **Charles Anderson Dana**.

3,218. One must judge men not by their opinions, but by what their opinions have made of them.
- **Georg Christoph Lichtenberg:** *Aphorisms and Letters* translated by F. Mautner and H. Hatfield, 1970.

3,219. New opinions are always suspected, and usually opposed, without any other reason but because they are not already common.
- **John Locke:** *An Essay Concerning Human Understanding* edited by Pauline Phemister, 2008.

3,220. The foolish and the dead alone never change their opinion.
- **James Russell Lowell**.

3,221. Any clod can have the facts, but having opinions is an art.
- **Charles McCabe**.

3,222. We credit scarcely any person with good sense except those who are of our opinion.
- **Francois, Duc de La Rochefoucauld:** *Maxims,* 1665.

3,223. The greatest deception men suffer is from their own opinions.
- **Leonardo da Vinci:** *The Notebooks of Leonardo da Vinci* translated by Jean Paul Richter, 1880.

OPPORTUNITY

3,224. Make time to listen because opportunity sometimes knocks very quietly.
- ***anon.***

3,225. Opportunities are never lost; someone will take the one you miss.
- ***anon.***

3,226. A wise man will make more opportunities than he finds.
- **Francis Bacon:** *Essays,* 1625.

3,227. There are no little events in life, those we think of no consequence may be full of fate, and it is at our own risk if we neglect the acquaintances and opportunities that seem to be casually offered, and of small importance.
- **Amelia Barr:** quoted in her autobiography *All The Days Of My Life,* 1913.

3,228. When one door closes another door opens; but we often look so long and so regretfully upon the closed door that we do not see the ones which open for us.
- **Alexander Graham Bell.**

3,229. Opportunitays, like eggs, don't kum but one at a time.
Josh Billings.

3,230. Small opportunities are often the beginnings of great enterprises.
- **Demosthenes.**

3,231. Nothing is so often irretrievably missed as a daily opportunity.
- **Marie von Ebner-Eschenback:** *Aphorisms,* 1905.

3,232. Opportunity is missed by most people because it is dressed in overalls and looks like work.
- **Thomas Edison:** *An Enemy Called Average* by John L. Mason.

3,233. Mediocre men wait for opportunities to come to them. Strong, able, alert men go after opportunity.
- **B. C. Forbes**.

3,234. The man who is intent on making the most of his opportunities is too busy to bother about luck.
- **B. C. Forbes**.

3,235. We are continually faced with a series of great opportunities brilliantly disguised as insoluble problems.
- **John W. Gardner**.

3,236. He who seizes the right moment, is the right man.
- **Johann Wolfgang von Goethe**: *Faust*, 1808.

3,237. You miss 100% of the shots you don't take.
- **Wayne Gretzky**.

3,238. The pessimist sees the difficulty in every opportunity; the optimist sees the opportunity in every difficulty.
- **L. P. Jacks**.

3,239. Sometimes opportunity knocks, but most of the time it sneaks up and then quietly steals away.
- **Doug Larson**.

3,240. Life pulsates with chances. They may not be dramatic or great, but they are important to him who would get on in the world.
- **Orison Swett Marden**: *Pushing to the Front, Vol 1*, 1911.

3,241. Open eyes will discover opportunities everywhere.
- *ibid*.

3,242. Four things come not back - the spoken word, the sped arrow, time past, and the neglected opportunity.
- ***Arabian Proverb***

3,243. Perhaps the most important thing that has come out of my life is the discovery that if you prepare yourself at every point as well as you can, with whatever means you have, however meagre they may seem, you will be able to grasp opportunity for broader experience when it appears. Without preparation you cannot do it.
- **Eleanor Roosevelt:** *The Autobiography of Eleanor Roosevelt*, 1961.

3,244. There is a tide in the affairs of men,
Which, taken at the flood, leads to fortune;
Omitted, all the voyage of their life
Is bound in shallows and in miseries.
- **William Shakespeare:** *Julius Caesar, Act 1V, Sc 111,* 1599.

3,245. Men who are resolved to find a way for themselves will always find opportunities enough; and if they do not find them, they will make them.
- **Samuel Smiles:** *Self-Help,* 1859.

3,246. Opportunities multiply as they are seized.
- **Sun Tzu:** *The Art of War.*

PAIN AND PLEASURE

3,247. In giving till it hurts, some people are extremely sensitive to pain.
- ***anon***.

3,248. The reason some people won't suffer in silence is because it would take all the pleasure out of it.
- ***anon***.

3,249. There was a faith-healer from Deal
Who said, "Although pain isn't real,
When I sit on a pin
And it punctures my skin
I dislike what I fancy I feel."
- ***anon***.

3,250. God Almighty first planted a garden; and indeed it is the purest of human pleasures.
- **Francis Bacon:** *Essays*, 1625.

3,251. The greatest pleasure in life is doing what people say you cannot do.
- **Walter Bagehot**.

3,252. I'm tired of Love; I'm still more tired of Rhyme
But Money gives me pleasure all the time.
- **Hilaire Belloc:** *Fatigued* in *Sonnets and Verse*, 1896.

3,253. But pleasures are like poppies spread,
You seize the flow'r, its bloom is shed;
Or like the snow falls in the river,
A moment white – then melts forever.
- **Robert Burns:** *Tam O' Shanter, a Tale*, 1791.

3.254. Enjoy pleasures, but let them be your own, and then you will taste them.
- **Lord Chesterfield:** *Letters to His Son*, 8th May, 1750.

3,255. Lying in bed would be an altogether perfect and supreme experience if only one had a coloured pencil long enough to draw on the ceiling.
- **G. K. Chesterton:** *Tremendous Trifles*, 1909.

3,256. In youth the absence of pleasure is pain, in old age the absence of pain is pleasure.
- **Evan Esar:** *20,000 Quips and Quotes*, 1968.

3,257. Short is the joy that guilty pleasure brings.
- **Euripides:** 4th century BC.

3,258. Enjoy what you can, and endure what you must.
- **Johann Wolfgang von Goethe.**

3,259. Do not bite at the bait of pleasure till you know that there is no hook beneath it.
- **Thomas Jefferson:** *in a private letter dated 12th October, 1786.*

3,260. Life affords no higher pleasure than that of surmounting difficulties, passing from one step of success to another, forming new wishes and seeing them gratified.
- **Samuel Johnson:** *Braude's Handbook of Stories for Toastmasters and Speakers* by Jacob M. Braude, 1957.

3,261. Although the world is full of suffering, it is also full of the overcoming of it.
- **Helen Keller:** *Optimism*, 1903.

3,262. The most delicate, the most sensible of all pleasures, consists in promoting the pleasures of others.
- **Jean de La Bruyere:** *Characters*, 1688.

3,263. The greatest pleasure I know, is to do a good action by stealth, and to have it found out by accident.
- **Charles Lamb:** *The Athenaeum, 4th January, 1834.*
NB *The Athenaeum* was a weekly periodical published in London between 1824 - 1923.

3,264. An hour of pain is as long as a day of pleasure.
- ***English Proverb.***
3,265. Anticipating pleasure is also a pleasure.
Johann Christoph Friedrich von Schiller.

3,266. For my pleasure I'll suffice with Woman, Wine and Song.
But though it be with jocund glee my tavern voice is ringing,
Had I to chuck one of the three, by gad ! I'd give up singing.
- **Robert Service**.

3,267. The sight of you is good for sore eyes.
- **Jonathan Swift:** *Polite Conversation*, 1738.

3,268. All the things I really like to do are either immoral, illegal or fattening.
- **Alexander Woollcott**

PARENTS AND PARENTING

3,269. Properly understood, child rearing... involves a continuous process of teaching, some of it formal, like that of the schools, but most of it informal, unconscious, and so minutely incidental that both pupil and teacher are largely unaware of what is going on.
- **James H. S. Bossard:** *The Large Family System: An Original Study of the Sociology of Family Behaviour*, 1956.

3,270. Being a parent is life's most important responsibility.
- ***ibid.***

3,271. I was a surprise to my parents, I was. They found me on the doorstep - they were expecting a pint of milk.
- **Tommy Cooper:** *The Very Best of Tommy Cooper, Vol 2*, 2005.

3,272. Raising children is an incredibly hard and risky business in which no cumulative wisdom is available. Each generation repeats the mistakes the previous one made.
- **Bill Cosby:** *Fatherhood*, 1986.

3,273. Parents are often so busy with the physical rearing of children that they miss the glory of parenthood, just as the grandeur of the trees is lost when raking leaves.
- **Marcelene Cox**.

3,274. Parenting Isn't For Cowards.
- **James C. Dobson:** *Book title*, 1987.

3,275. Raising children is like being taken hostage by midget terrorists.
- **Ben Elton:** *The Press and Journal's 'Quotes of the Year', April, 2007.*

3,276. Having a child does not make you a parent, just as having a kitchen does not make you a chef.
- **Taro Gold:** *Open Your Mind, Open Your Life: A Book of Eastern Wisdom* 2002.

3,277. We have become unsure of the rules and unsure of our roles. Parenting, like brain surgery, is now all-consuming, fraught with anxiety, worry and self-doubt. We have allowed what used to be simple and natural to become bewildering and intimidating.
- **Fred G. Gosman:** *How to be a Happy Parent in Spite of Your Children,* 1995.

3,278. Simply because our times are complex, does it follow that our parenting must also be? Must we reject the common sense that worked so well in the past just because our times are hightech? We live in such fear of being "old fashioned" that we are cutting ourselves off from that which is proven.
- *ibid.*

3,279. The more we shelter children from every disappointment, the more devastating future disappointments will be.
- *ibid.*

3.280. Nurses nurse
And teachers teach
And tailors mend
And preachers preach
And barbers trim
And chauffeurs haul
And parents get to do it all.
- **Babs Bell Hajdusiewicz** (pronounced Hi-doo-shev-its): *Familiarity Breeds Children* edited by Bruce Lansky, 1994.

3,281. A suspicious parent makes an artful child.
- **Thomas Chandler Haliburton**.

3,282. Youth is a time of rapid changes. Between the ages of twelve and seventeen a parent can age thirty years.
- **Sam Levenson**.

3,283. Any kid who has two parents who are interested in him and has a house full of books isn't poor.
- **Sam Levenson:** *Reader's Digest, January, 1972.*

3,284. The best academy, a mother's knee.
- **James Russell Lowell**.

3,285. Oh high is the price of parenthood,
And daughters may cost you double,
You dare not forget, as you thought you could,
That youth is a plague and a trouble.
- **Phyllis McGinley:** *Homework for Anabelle* in *Times Three*, 1960.

3,286. Children aren't happy with nothing to ignore,
And that's what parents were created for.
- **Ogden Nash:** *The Parent* in *Happy Days*. 1933.

3,287. Many terms are popular today – attachment, natural, empathetic –
to describe a way of parenting that is really not new at all. Being with
children in the way these terms describe is what parents all over the
world have done since the beginning of time.
- **Peggy O'Mara:** *The Natural Child: Parenting From the Heart* by Jan Hunt
2001.

3,288. Life was a lot simpler when what we honoured was father and
mother rather than all major credit cards.
- **Robert Orben:** *Wall Street Journal, March 17th, 1980.*

3,289. If a child sees his parents day in and day out behaving with self-
discipline, restraint, dignity and a capacity to order their own lives, then
the child will come to feel in the deepest fibres of his being that this is
the way to live. If a child sees his parents day in and day out living
without self-restraint or self-discipline, then he will come in the deepest
fibres of his being to believe that this is the way to live.
- **M. Scott Peck:** *The Road Less Travelled*, 1990.

3,290. This is what no one warns you about, when you decide to have
children. There is so much written about the cost and the changes in
your life, but no one ever tells you that what they are going to hand to
you in the hospital is power, whether you want it or not. . . I should have
known, but somehow over-looked for a time, that parents become,
effortlessly, just by showing up, the most influential totems in the lives
of their children.
- **Anna Quinlen:** *Living Out Loud*, 1988.

3,291. I got a fortune cookie that said, "To remember is to understand":
I have never forgotten it. A good judge remembers what it was like to be
a lawyer. A good editor remembers being a writer. A good parent
remembers what it was like to be a child.
- **Anna Quinlen:** *Thinking Out Loud*, 1994.

3,292. If you need to read a book about raising kids, you are in big trouble, and so are your kids.
- **Andy Rooney:** *CBS's TV Show: 60 Minutes.*

3,293. Parents' needs and children's needs are often opposed. When we need to hurry, they need to dawdle. When we crave ten minutes of solitude after a trying day, they issue eighteen demands for immediate attention. When we get a long distance phone call, they interrupt us with a crisis.
- **Nancy Samalin:** *Loving Your Child is Not Enough; Positive Discipline That Works*, 1987.

3,294. If you take every possible opportunity to point out what children do well, praise them descriptively for it and express appreciation, your child will become more co-operative, competent and confidence.
- *ibid.*

3,295. I regard parenting as the hardest, most complicated, anxiety-ridden, sweat-and-blood producing job in the world, succeeding requires the ultimate in patience, common sense, commitment, humour, tact, love, wisdom, awareness and knowledge.
- **Virginia Satir:** *The New People Making*, 1988.

3,296. (Parenting) holds the possibility for the most rewarding, joyous experience of a lifetime, namely, that of being successful guides to a new and unique human being.
- *ibid.*

3,297. Every word, facial expression, gesture or action on the part of a parent gives the child some message about self-worth. It is sad that so many parents don't realize what messages they are sending.
- **Virginia Satir:** *The Winning Family: Increasing Self-Esteem In Your Children and Yourself* by Dr Louise Hart, 1987.

3,298. One of the great privileges of being a parent is witnessing, close up, the flourishing of a young mind. But that's not the only benefit. In trying to make the world a more interesting and comprehensive place for their child, parents often find their own intellectual interests rekindled.
- **Michael Schulman:** *The Passionate Mind: Bringing Up a Creative and Intelligent Child*, 1991.

3,299. Parents learn a lot from their children about coping with life.
- **Dame Muriel Spark:** *The Comforters*, 1957.

3,300. What good mothers and fathers instinctively feel like doing for their babies is usually best after all.
- **Benjamin Spock:** *Baby and Child Care,* 1946.

3.301. Parenthood remains the greatest single preserve of the amateur.
- **Alvin Toffler:** *Future Shock,* 1973.

3.302. Before I got married I had six theories about bringing up children, and now I have six children and no theories.
- **John Wilmot, 2nd Earl of Rochester:** *The Treasury of Humorous Quotations* edited by Evan Esar, 1951.

PARTING

3,303. Ae fond kiss, and then we sever;
Ae fareweel, and then forever!
- **Robert Burns:** *Ae Fond Kiss, And Then We Sever.*
NB: Scots: ae = one

3,304. I can generally bear the separation, but I don't like the leave-taking.
- **Samuel Butler:** *Notebooks,* 1912.

3,305. Say what you will, 'tis better to be left than never to have been loved.
- **William Congreve:** *The Way Of The World, Act 11, Sc 1,* 1700.

3,306. The day he moved was terrible
That evening she went through hell.
His absence wasn't a problem
But the corkscrew had gone as well.
- **Wendy Cope:** *Loss* in *Kiss and Part Laughing at the End of Romance* edited by Gail White, 2005.

3,307. The pain of parting is nothing to the joy of meeting again.
- **Charles Dickens:** *Nicholas Nickleby,* 1839.

3,308. Pip, dear chap, life is made of ever so many partings welded together.
- **Charles Dickerns:** *Great Expectations,* 1860 – 1862.

3,309. You can leave in a taxi. If you can't leave in a taxi you can leave in a huff. If that's too soon, you can leave in a minute and a huff.
- Groucho Marx in his role as Rufus T. Firefly in the **1933 Paramount Film**: *Duck Soup.*

3,310. Love knows not it's own depth until the hour of separation.
- **Kahlil Gibran:** *The Prophet,* 1923.

3,311. Beloved, let our love be quite
Intense and splendid, but polite,
That in the hour of parting we
May end the matter pleasantly.
- **Samuel Hoffenstein**.

3,312. When love has brought no joy or gladness / Parting shall have little sadness.
- **Mikhail Lermontov:** *Geary's Guide to the World's Great Aphorists* by James Geary, 2007.

3,313. Ev'rytime we say goodbye I die a little.
- Lyrics and music by **Cole Porter:** featured in the 1944 musical review, *Seven Lively Arts*.

THE PAST

3,314. One day your life is going to flash before your eyes. Make sure it's worth watching.
- ***anon***.

3,315. In every age "the good old days" were a myth. No one ever thought they were good at the time. For every age has consisted of crises that seemed intolerable to the people who lived through them.
- **Brooks Atkinson:** *Once Around the Sun*, 1951.

3,316. Today expect something good to happen to you no matter what occurred yesterday. Realize the past no longer holds you captive. It can only continue to hurt you if you hold on to it. Let the past go. A simply abundant world awaits you.
- **Sarah Ban Breathnach:** *Simple Abundance: A Daybook of Comfort and Joy*, 1995.

3,317. Even though I know you can't live in the past, it's nice to have one.
- **George Burns:** *Third Time Around*, 1980.

3,318. I tend to live in the past because most of my life is there.
- **Herb Caen**.

3,319. The past is not what it was.
- **G. K. Chesterton:** *A Short History of England*.

3,320. I love my past, I love my present. I am not ashamed of what I have had, and I am not sad because I no longer have it
- **Colette:** *The Last of Cheri*, 1926.

3,321. Regretting the past does not prevent me from repeating it.
- **Mason Cooley:** *City Aphorisms*.

3,322. It is a mistake to think that the past is dead. Nothing that has ever happened is quite without influence at this moment.
- **Will Durant:** *The Story of Civilization, Vol VI, The Reformation*, 1957.

3,323. A man's past always colours his views.
- *ibid.*

3,324. There are two occasions when a man's past life is brought up before him; when he is drowning, and when he quarrels with his wife.
- **Evan Esar:** *20,000 Quips and Quotes*, 1968.

3,325. Half the pleasure of recalling the past lies in the editing.
- *ibid*

3,326. The Moving Finger writes, and having writ,
Moves on; nor all your Piety and Wit
Shall lure it back to cancel half a Line,
Nor all your Tears wash out a Word of it
- **Edward Fitzgerald:** *The Rubaiyat of Omar Khayyam*, LXX1, 1889.

3,327. Let today embrace the past with remembrance and the future with longing.
- **Kahlil Gibran:** *The Prophet*, 1923.

3,328. Yesterday is but today's memory, and tomorrow is today's dream.
- *ibid.*

3,329. You can clutch the past so tightly to your chest that it leaves your arms too full to embrace the present.
- **Jan Glidewell:** *The St. Petersburg Times.*

3,330. The illusion that times that were are better than those that are, has probably pervaded all ages.
- **Horace Greeley:** *The American Conflict*, 1865.

3,331. "Oh, give me back the good old days of fifty years ago," has been the cry ever since Adam's fifty-first birthday.
- **Jerome K. Jerome:** *Idle Thoughts of an Idle Fellow*, 1889.

3,332. The present is what slips by us while we're pondering the past and worrying about the future.
- **Barbara Johnson:** *Daily Splashes of Joy: 365 Gems to Sparkle Your Day*, 2000.

3,333. A nation that forgets its past can function no better than an individual with amnesia.
- **David C. McCullouch:** *LA Times, April 23rd, 1978,* quoted in *Simpson's Contemporary Quotations* compiled by James Simpson, 1988.

3,334. To be able to enjoy one's past life is to live twice.
- **Martial:** *Epigrams, **circa** 103 AD.*

3,335. Progress, far from existing in change, depends on retentiveness. Those who cannot remember the past are condemned to repeat it.
- **George Santayana:** *The Life of Reason, Vol 1, Introduction,* 1905.

3,336. What's past is prologue.
- **William Shakespeare:** *The Tempest,* Act 2, Scene 1

3,337. Well time slips away and leaves you with nothing mister but boring stories… of glory days.
- **Bruce Springsteen:** *Glory Days* from his 1984 Album *Born in the USA.*

3,338. Everything that is past is either a learning experience to grow on, a beautiful memory to reflect on, or a motivating factor to act upon.
- **Denis Waitley**

PATIENCE

3,339. How can a society that exists on frozen dinners and micro-wave ovens teach patience to the young!
- *anon.*

3,340. There wouldn't be nearly as many pedestrian patients if there were more patient pedestrians.
- *anon.*

3,341. Patience is the companion of wisdom.
- **St. Augustine of Hippo:** *Sermons, **circa** 430* AD.

3,342. There is no road too long for the man who advances deliberately and without undue haste; no honours too distant to the man who prepares himself for them with patience.
- **Jean de La Bruyere:** *Characters,* 1688.

3,343. Some people will hold anything except their tongues, keep anything except their word, and lose nothing but their patience.
- **Charles Caleb Colton:** *Lacon, or Many Things in Few Words,* 1826.

3,344. The time when patience is most needed is when it is exhausted.
- **Evan Esar:** *20,000 Quips and Quotes,* 1968.

3,345. To lose patience is to lose the battle.
- **Mohandas Karamchand Gandh:** *Geary's Guide to the World's Great Aphorists* by James Geary, 2007.

3,346. The key to everything is patience. You get the chicken by hatching the egg, not by smashing it open.
- **Arnold H. Glasgow.**

3,347. You can learn many things from children. How much patience you have for instance.
- **Franklin P. Jones:** quoted in *The Toastmaster's Treasure Chest* by Herbert

V. Prochnow and Herbert V. Prochnow Jr. 1979.

3,348. If you are patient in one moment of anger, you will escape a hundred days of sorrow.
- *Chinese Proverb*.

3,349. Patience is a flower that grows not in every garden.
- *English Proverb*.

3,350. Only those who have the patience to do simple things perfectly will acquire the skill to do difficult things easily.
- **Johann Friedrich von Schiller**.

3,351. I am extraordinarily patient, provided I get my own way in the end.
- **Margaret Thatcher:** *The Observer, 4th April, 1989.*

3,352. Everything comes in time to him who knows how to wait.
- **Leo Tolstoy:** *War and Peace,* 1865 – 1869.

PERSEVERANCE

3,353. Perseverance wins the race.
- The moral of **Aesop's Fable:** *The Hare and the Tortoise*.

3,354. The difference between perseverance and obstinacy is that one often comes from a strong will, and the other from a strong won't.
- **Henry Ward Beecher**.

3,355. Consider the postage stamp: its usefulness consists in the ability to stick to one thing till it gets there.
- **Josh Billings**.

3,356. With ordinary talent and extraordinary perseverance, all things are attainable.
- **Sir Thomas Fowell Buxton**.

3,357. Press on: nothing in the world can take the place of perseverance. Talent will not; nothing is more common than unsuccessful men with talent. Genius will not; unrewarded genius is almost a proverb. Education will not; the world is full of educated derelicts. Persistence and determination alone are omnipotent.
- **Calvin Coolidge:** *Wit and Wisdom of the American Presidents: A Book of Quotations* edited by Joslyn Pine, 2001.

3,358. How you start is important, but it is how you finish that counts. In the race for success, speed is less important than stamina. The sticker outlasts the sprinter.
- **B. C. Forbes:** *Reader's Digest, January, 1991*.

3,359. Perseverance is the most overrated of traits if it is unaccompanied by talent. Beating your head against a wall is more likely to produce a concussion in the head rather than a hole in the wall.
- **Sydney J. Harris**.

3,360. Great works are performed, not by strength but perseverance. He that shall walk with vigour three hours a day will pass in seven years a space equal to the circumference of the globe.
- **Samuel Johnson:** *The History of Rasselas.* (A novel), 1759.
NB The circumference of the earth at the equator is 24,902 miles or 40,076 kilometres. Over a period of seven years, to walk this distance, one would be obliged to travel 9.75 miles or 15,69 kilometres each day.

3,361. God is with those who persevere.
- **The Koran:** *Chapter 8.*

3,362. Perseverance is the ability to keep going in the face of continuous challenges. It is the ability to disregard distractions and to stay focused.
- **Catherine Pulsifer:** American author of inspiration words of wisdom.
NB Inspirational words of wisdom are available on the Internet at :www.wow4u.com

3,363. I think a hero is an ordinary individual who finds the strength to persevere and endure in spite of overwhelming obstacles.
- **Christopher Reeve:** in an interview following the publication of his autobiography, *Still Me.* Four years earlier he had sustained such severe injuries when thrown from a horse that he was a quadriplegic for the rest of his life. He died on October 10th, 2004.

PESSIMISTS AND OPTIMISTS

3,364. An optimist is someone who hasn't got around to reading the daily paper.
- **anon:** *Quotable Quotes for Quoters* by Aubrey Malone, 1990.

3,365. A real optimist is a man who pulls up at a hat shop to pick up his wife and keeps the engine running.
- **anon**.

3,366. One of the things I learned the hard way was that it doesn't pay to be discouraged. Keeping busy and making optimism a way of life can restore your faith in yourself.
- **Lucille Ball:** *The Last Word: A Treasury of Women's Quotes* byCarolyn Warner, 1992.

3,367. An optimist looks forward to marriage. A pessimist is a married optimist.
- **Milton Berle:** *Milton Berle's Private Joke File*, 1989.

3,368. On awakening, optimists opens the window and say with a smile, "Good morning, God!" Pessimists? They rub their eyes; clear their throats; look out of the window and say with a frown, "Good god, morning!"
- **Chuck Gallozzi:** *Pessimists and Optimists* – one of many splendid essays by Gallozzi to be found on the Internet at: **www.personal-development.com/chuck-gallozzi-articles.html.**

3,369. An optimist is a girl who mistakes a bulge for a curve.
- **Ring Lardner:** *The Dictionary of Humorous Quotations* edited by Evan Esar, 1949.

3,370. Optimists seek to increase good fortune, pessimists seek to avoid disaster.
- **Li Ao:** *Geary's Guide to the World's Great Aphorists* by James Geary, 2002.

3,371. A pessimist is a man who looks both ways before crossing a one way street.
- **Laurence J. Peter:** *Peter's Quotations: Ideas For Our Time*, 1977.

3,372. A stumbling block to the pessimist is a stepping stone to the optimist.
- **Eleanor Roosevelt:** *My Day*.(A syndicated newspaper column,1935 - 1962)

3,373. Both optimists and pessimists contribute to society. The optimist invents the aeroplane, the pessimist the parachute.
- **Gladys B. Stern**.

3,374. An optimist stays up until midnight to see the New Year in, a pessimist stays up to make sure the Old Year leaves.
- **Bill Vaughan:** *Kansas City Star*

PHOTOGRAPHY

3,375. Sometimes I do get to places just when God's ready to have someone click the shutter.
- **Ansel Adams**; *American Way,* 1974.

3,376. There are always two people in every picture: the photographer and the viewer.
- **Ansel Adams**; *magazine interview, 1983.*

3,377. A photograph can be as striking and as haunting as a great painting or a fine poem.
- *anon.*

3,378. The man who coined the phrase *as pretty as a picture* had evidently never seen a passport photograph.
- *anon.*

3,379. The virtue of the camera is not the power it has to transform the photographer into an artist, but the impulse it gives him to keep on looking.
- **Brooks Atkinson**; *Once Round the Sun,* 1951.

3,380. Most things in life are moments of pleasure and a lifetime of embarrassment; photography is a moment of embarrassment and a lifetime of pleasure.
- **Tony Benn**; *The Independent Newspaper, 21st October, 1989.*

3,381. Blessed be the inventor of photography!I set him above even the inventor of chloroform! It has given more positive pleasure to poor suffering humanity than anything else that has cast up in my time or is like to - this art by which even the poor can possess themselves of tolerable likenesses of their absent dear ones.
- **Jane Welsh Carlyle:** *The Collected Letters of Thomas and Jane Welsh Carlyle.*

3,382. If you really look like your passport photo, chances are you're not well enough to travel.

- **Leopold Fechtner:** *5,000 One-And-Two-Line Jokes*, 1986.

3,383. A photo of a girl in a bikini is not a snapshot - it's an exposure!

- *ibid.*

3,384. Passport Picture: A photo of a man that he can laugh at without realizing it looks exactly the way his friends see him.

- **Herbert V. Prochnow and Herbert V. Prochnow Jr:** *Jokes, Quotes and One-Liners for Public Speakers, Vol 2, 1983*

POLICE

3,385. On her way to work a nurse had driven through a set of lights and was now being questioned by a traffic policeman in a lay-by near the scene of the incident.

"Tell me, miss," the policeman asked, "does a red light mean *anything* to you?"

"Oh, yes it does officer,"said the nurse, "it means someone wants a bed pan."
- ***anon.***

3,386. The owner of a Florida massage parlour has been arrested by police. "There weren't any serious violations," said the officers, "she just rubbed us up the wrong way."
- **George Carlin:** *Napalm and Silly Putty*, 2001.

3,387. My ignorance of science is such that if anyone mentioned copper nitrate I should think he was talking about policemen's overtime.
- **Donald Coggan**.

3,388. Police arrested two kids yesterday, one was drinking battery acid, the other was eating fireworks. They charged one and let the other one off.
- **Tommy Cooper**.

3,389. When constabulary duty's to be done / A policeman's lot is not a happy one.
- **Sir W. S. Gilbert:** *Pirates of Penzance, Act 2*, 1879.

3,390. If you haven't seen your wife smile at a traffic cop, you haven't seen her smile her prettiest.
- **Kin Hubbard**.

3,391. A recent police study found that you're much more likely to get shot by a fat cop if you run.
- **Denis Miller**.

3,392. Policemen are numbered in case they get lost.
- **Spike Milligan:** *The Last Goon Show of All*, broadcast on 5th October,1972.
NB This was broadcast on 5th October, 1972.

3,393. An exhaustive study of police records shows that no woman has ever shot her husband while he was doing the dishes.
- **Earl Wilson:** *Field Newspaper Syndicate.*

POLITICIANS

3,394 The trouble with this country is that there are too many politicians who believe, with a conviction based on experience, that you can fool all of the people all of the time.
- **Franklin Pierce Adams:** *Nods and Becks,* 1944.

3,395. There's an old saying that if all the politicians in the world were laid end to end, they'd still be lying.
- **Fred Allen**.

3,396. The Prime Minister held a meeting with the cabinet today. He also spoke to the book case and argued with the chest of drawers.
- **Ronnie Barker:** *The Two Ronnies.*

3,397. People are fed up with soundbites, spin, sensation and scandal from politicians.
- **Tony Benn:** *The Press and Journal's Quotes for the Day, Wednesday, 9ᵗʰ May, 2012.*

3,398. Politicians often take umbrage but they prefer cash.
- **James Boren**.

3,399. When a politician is in opposition he is an expert on the means to some end; and when he is in office, he is an expert on the obstacles to it.
- **G. K. Chesterton:** *Illustrated London News, 4ᵗʰ June, 1918.*

3,400. The incompetence of our politicians is a never-ending subject of coversation. But why do those who are charged with running the country do it so badly ? The answer is that those who could really do it efficiently are too busy driving taxis or cutting other peoplel's hair.
- **Christopher Hamel Cooke:** *A Time To Laugh,* 1993.

3,401. A perfect politician is a person who can lie to the press, then believe what he reads.
- **Will Durst:** *The Reader's Digest Quotable Quotes,* 1988.

3,402. All of the great leaders have had one characteristic in common: it was the willingness to confront unequivocally the major anxiety of their people in their time. This, and not much else, is the essence of leadership.
- **John Kenneth Galbraith:** *The Age of Uncertainty*, 1977.

3,403. I don't think I'd like to go into politics, not at all. I'm too honest to be a politician.
- **Loan Gruffudd:** *The Press and Journal's QuotesFor The Day, 22nd March, 2007.*

3,404. There is one sure way of telling when politicians aren't telling the truth – their lips move.
- **Felicity Kendal**.

3,405. Ninety percent of the politicians give the other ten percent a bad reputation.
- **Henry Kissinger**.

3,406. A successful politician must be a master of ambiguity.
- **Abraham Lincoln:** *The Wit and Wisdom of Abraham Lincoln* by Alex Ayres, 1992.

3,407. These days, the only time politicians tell the truth is when they call each other a liar.
- **Mad Magazine:** *Mad:The Half-Wit and Wisdom of Alfred E. Neuman* 1997.

3,408. It's no wonder politicians don't listen to their conscience. They don't want to take advice from a total stranger.
- *ibid.*

3,409. A good politician is quite as unthinkable as an honest burglar.
- **H. L. Mencken:** *Newsweek, 1955.*

3,410. Friends, my grandfather was a politician, my father was a politician, I'm a politician - and my son's not going to work either!
- **Chic Murray:** *The Chic Murray Bumper Fun Book*, 1991.

3,411. Giving money and power to government is like giving whisky and car keys to teenage boys.
- **P. J. O'Rourke:** *Parliament of Whores*, 1991.

3,412. *English Proverbs* for politicians to ponder on :
A: It is easier to know how to speak, than how to be silent.
B: It is one thing to speak much, and another to speak pertinently.
C: Sometimes words hurt more than swords.
D: Time and words can never be recalled.
E: Speak little and to the purpose, and you will pass for somebody.

3,413. The only people who say worse things about politicians than reporters do are other politicians.
- **Andy Rooney:** *CBS TV 60 Minutes.*

3,414. Honesty is not so much a credit as an absolute prerequisite to efficient service to the public. Unless a man is honest, we have no right to keep him in public life; it matters not how brilliant his capacity.
- **Theodore Roosevelt:** *in a speech delivered while he was Governor of New York.*
NB Roosevelt served as New York's Governor from 1898 - 1900. His words are just as pertinent today as they were over a century ago.

3,415. Prime Ministers are wedded to the truth, but like other married couples they sometimes live apart.
- **Saki:** *The Unbearable Bassington,* 1912.

3,416. A politician is a person who approaches every subject with an open mouth.
- **Adlai Stevenson:** *in a speech delivered in Chicago, 3rd June, 1952.*

3,417. Politicians? They are slippery, evasive, irresponsible liars in the main.
- **Julie Walters:** *The Press and Journal's Quotes of the Day, Wednesday, 27th January, 2010.*

POLITICS

3,418. Practical politics consists in ignoring facts.
- **Henry Brooks Adams:** *The Education of Henry Adams*, 1906.

3,419. In politics, merit is rewarded by the possessor being raised, like a target, to a position to be fired at.
- **Christian Nestell Bovee**.

3,420. A passion for politics stems usually from an insatiable need, either for power, or friendship and adulation, or a combination of both.
- **Fawn M. Brodie:** *Thomas Jefferson: An Intimate History*, 1974.

3,421. Politics and the fate of mankind are formed by men without ideals and without greatness. Those who have greatness within them do not go into politics.
- **Albert Camus:** *Notebooks*, 1935 – 1942.

3,422. Politics is almost as exciting as war and quite as dangerous. In war you can only be killed once, but in politics many times.
- **Sir Winston Churchill:** *The Wit and Wisdom of Winston Churchill* by James C. Humes. 1994.

3,423. Nothing is so admirable in politics as a short memory.
- **John Kenneth Galbraith**.

3,424. In politics, you do not always have to keep your promises, but you have to know how to make them.
- **Roberto Gervaso:** quoted in *Geary's Guide to the.World's Great Aphorists* by James Geary, 2007.

3,425. The word 'politics' is derived from the word 'poly', meaning 'many', and the word 'ticks', meaning 'blood-sucking parasites'.
- **Larry Hardiman:** This quotation – the only one attributed to Hardiman - appears frequently on the Internet, however nothing is known about its author.

3,426. What hasn't been so nice is to discover just how dirty high politics can get.
- **Vaclav Havel:** former President of the Czech Republic, quoted in *The Press and Journal Quote of the Day, 5th November, 2009.*

3,427. A good speech isn't one where we can prove that we're telling the truth – it's one where nobody else can prove we're lying.
- **Anthony Jay and Jonathan Lynn:** *The Complete Yes Minister,* 1984.

3,428. A career in politics is no preparation for government.
- *ibid.*

3,429, "The public," said Sir Humphrey, "do not know anything about wasting public money. We are the experts."
- *ibid.*

3,430. There is more clap-trap, insincerity and humbug on the surface of politics than over any equal area on the face of any institution.
- **Stephen Leacock:** *The Hohenzollerns in America,* 1919.

3,431. Politics is the art of looking for trouble, finding it everywhere, diagnosing it incorrectly and applying the wrong remedies.
- **Groucho Marx:** quoted in *Power Quotes* by Daniel B. Baker, 1992.

3,432 Politics is the one way to achieve power without merit or risk.
- **P. J. O'Rourke:** *Give War a Chance,* 1992.

3,433. People who are wise, good, smart, skilful, or hard working, don't need politics, they have jobs.
- **P. J. O'Rourke:** *All the Trouble in the World,* 1994.

3,434. I used to think that politics was the second oldest profession. I have come to know that it bears a very close resemblance to the first.
- **Ronald Reagan:** *Wit and Wisdom of the American Presidents* edited by Joslyn Pine, 2001.

3,435. The more you read and observe about this politics thing, you got to admit that each party is worse than the other. The one that's out always looks the best.
- **Will Rogers:** *Illiterate Digest, 1924.*

3,436. Politics is perhaps the only profession for which no preparation is thought necessary.
- **Robert Louis Stevenson:** *Familiar Studies of Men and Books.* 1882.

3,437. Politics is a dirty business for a gentleman.
- **Booth Tarkington:** *The Magnificent Ambersons,* 1918.

3,438. An honest man in politics shines more than he would elsewhere.
- **Mark Twain:** *A Tramp Abroad,* 1880.

3,439. Politics is the art of preventing people from taking part in affairs which properly concern them.
- **Paul Valery:** *Tel Quel,* 1943.

3,440. Politics makes strange bedfellows.
- **Charles Dudley Warner:** *My Summer in a Garden,* 1870.

POTTY POETRY AND NONSENSE RHYMES

3,441. When I had my operation I displayed a lot of guts.
I could take it, and like it. But the bed-pans drove me nuts.
- **anon:** *Verse and Worse: A Private Collection* by Arnold Silcock.

3,442. One mirror does not constitute a vital threat to me,
But when I'm trying on a suit and see myself in three,
I get a sudden, full-length view of profile and of rear.
A sight I'm not accustomed to and which I always fear.
- **Richard Armour:** *Undone With Mirrors* in *An Armoury if Light Verse*.

3,443. Physicians of the utmost fame were called at once; but when they came.
They answered, as they took their fees, 'There is no cure for this disease.'
- **Hilaire Belloc:** *Henry King*, in *Cautionary Tales For Children*, 1908.

3,444. Here I sit, alone and sixty,
Bald and fat and full of sin.
Cold the seat and loud the cistern,
As I read the Harpic tin.
- **Alan Bennett:** *Place-Names of China*, quoted in *The New Oxford Book of English Light Verse* edited by Kingsley Amis, 1978.

3,445. The rain it raineth on the just and also on the unjust fella,
But chiefly on the just, because the unjust steals the just's umbrella.
- **Lord Bowen:** quoted in *The Fireside Book of Humorous Poetry* edited by William Cole, 1959. NB: Compare the seasonal variant written, with apologies to Lord Bowen, by Ross Miller of Stonington, Connecticut, USA: *The snow it snoweth on the just/ And also on the unjust's hovel / But chiefly on the just, because / The unjust steals the just's snow shovel.*

3,446. Aunt Jane observed, the second time she stumbled off the bus.
The step is short from the Sublime to the Ridiculous.
- **Harry Graham:** *More Ruthless Rhymes for Heartless Homes*, 1930.

3,447. The day my favourite goldfish died I'm not ashamed to say, I cried.

I prayed for its departed soul, then flushed it down the toilet bowl.
- **Bruce Lansky:** *Good-Bye, Goldfish,* in *Lighten up! 100 Funny Little Poems, Book Two*, 1999.

3,448. Imagine you've shopped in a posh little store.

You start to depart through a wide-open door.

When *crash* goes your forehead ! The glass door was closed.

It's not standing open, the way you supposed.

Your grin, you feel foolish. The door was too clean,

All glass should be dirty enough to be seen!
- **Irene Livingston:** *Is My Face Red!* in *Lighten Up! By Bruce Lansky*,1999.

3,449. A bridge I know where ladies go

Is watched by a thousand eyes below.

It came as no surprise,

That bridge is known

As the bridge of thighs.
- **Walter McCorrisken:** *Bridge of Thighs* in *Hairy Knees and Heather Hills*, 1995.

3,450. A three-legged dog rode westward one day

Down to the jail in Moose Jaw,

"Sheriff," he said on unsteady leg,

"Sheriff , ah've I've come for may paw!"
- **Walter McCorrisken,:** *A Three-Legged Dog* in *Hairy Knees and Heather Hills*, 1995.

3,451. The mosquito, with syringe built in, will plunge it underneath your skin,

And draw a droplet of your sap because he likes his drinks on tap.

And then, with overbearing gall, alight on newly-painted wall,

Full knowing that you dare not swot for fear he'll leave a crimson spot.
- **Bob McKenty:** *Light – A Quarterly of Light Verse, Summer, 1999.*

3,452. Now, having supped on woollen cloth,

The silly, suicidal moth,

Inexorably drawn to flame,

Takes fervent, final, fatal aim

At taper's top. He is tonight

Disposed to dyin' by candlelight.
- **Bob McKenty:** *Light – A Quarterly of Light Verse, Spring 2000.*

3,453. You baked me a cake in the shape of a heart,
I eagerly ate it, thus doing my part.
The way to my heart is my stomach, it's true -
And both are much bigger today, thanks to you.
 - **Bob McKenty:** quoted in *Lighten Up" Book 2* edited by Bruce Lansky.

3,454. The firefly's flame
Is something for which science has no name.
I can think of nothing eerier
Than flying around with an unidentified glow on a person's posterior.
 - **Ogden Nash:** *The Firefly,* in *Good Intentions,* 1942.

3,455. The python has, and I fib no fibs, 318 pairs of ribs. In stating this I place reliance on a séance with one who died for science; This figure is sworn to and attested; he counted them while being digested.
 - **Ogden Nash:** *The Python,* in *The Old Dog Barks Backwards,* 1972.

3,456. Doctor Bell fell down the well and broke his collar-bone,
Doctors should attend the sick and leave the well alone.
 - An 18th century nursery rhyme quoted in *Verse and Worse: A Private Collection* by **Arnold Silcock**, 1952.

POWER

3,457. Power tends to corrupt and absolute power corrupts absolutely.
- **John Acton**, **1ˢᵗ Baron Acton:** *in a letter to Bishop Mandell Creighton, dated 3ʳᵈ April, 1887.*

3,458. I was allowed to ring the bell for five minutes until everyone was in Assembly. It was the beginning of power.
- **Jeffrey Archer:** recalling his school days in *The Telegraph, March,1988.*

3,459. Knowledge itself is power.
- **Francis Bacon:** *Sacred Meditations,* 1597.

3.460. The greater the power the more dangerous the abuse.
- **Edmund Burke:** *in a speech in the House of Commons, 7ᵗʰ February, 1771.*

3.461. Too often we underestimate the power of a touch, a smile, a kind word, a listening ear, an honest compliment, or the smallest act of caring, all of which have the potential to turn a life around.
- **Leo F. Buscaglia:** *Love,* 1985.

3,462. Power will intoxicate the best hearts, as wine the strongest heads. No man is wise enough, nor good enough to be trusted with unlimited power.
- **Charles Caleb Colton:** *Lacon, or Many Things In Few Words,* 1822, edited by George J. Barbour, 2001.

3,463. The love of liberty is the love of others; the love of power is the love of ourselves.
- **William Hazlitt:** *Political Essays,* 1819.

3,464. Our scientific power has outrun our spiritual power. We have guided missiles and misguided men.
- **Martin Luther King:** *Strength to Love,* 1963.

3,465. Power is the ultimate aphrodisiac.
- **Henry Kissinger:** *New York Times, January, 1971.*

3.466. Nearly all men can stand adversity, but if you want to test a man's character, give him power.
- **Abraham Lincoln:** quoted in *The Most Brilliant Thoughts of all Time* by John M. Shanahan, 1999.

3,467. The most effective water power in the world – women's tears.
- **Wilson Mizner:** quoted in *The Treasury of Humorous Quotations* edited by Evan Esar, 1955.

3,468. Unlimited power is apt to corrupt the minds of those who possess it.
- **William Pitt, the Elder:** *in a speech delivered in the House of Lords on 9th January, 1770.*

3,469. In a democratic nation, power must be linked with responsibility, and obliged to defend and justify itself within the framework of the general good.
- **Franklin Delano Roosevel:** *in a speech to Congress, January, 1945.*

3,470. Knowing others is intelligence; / Knowing yourself is true wisdom. / Mastering others is strength; / Mastering yourself is true power.
- **Lao Tzu:** *Tao Te Ching: The Book of the Way* by Lao Tzu interpreted by Stephen Mitchell, 1992.

3,471. In every community, there is work to be done. In every nation, there are wounds to heal. In every heart, there is the power to do it.
- **Marianne Williamson:** *A Return to Love* quoted in *Reader's Digest Quotable Quotes*, 1989.

PRAISE AND ENCOURAGEMENT

3,472. Falsely praising a person is lying.
- **St Augustine of Hippo:** *Sermons*. 430AD.

3,473. Judicious praise is to children what the sun is to flowers.
- **Christian Nestell Bovee:** quoted in *The Lift-Your-Spirits Quote Book* compiled by Allen Klein, 2001.

3,474. Give people a feeling of importance; praise the good parts of them.
- **Dale Carnegie:** *How to Win Friends and Influence People*, 1936.

3,475. Praise makes good men better, and bad men worse.
- **Thomas Fuller:** *Gnomologia: Adages and Proverbs*, 1732.

3,476. Praising is pleasing to him who thinks he deserves it.
- ***ibid***.

3,477. Fools may our scorn, not envy raise, for envy is a kind of praise.
- **John Gay:** *Fables*, 1727.

3,478. He who praises everybody praises nobody.
- **Samuel Johnson:** *Johnson's Works, Vol XI*, 1787.

3,479. Reprove your friend in secret and praise him openly.
- **Leonardo da Vinci:** quoted in *Geary's Guide to the World's Great Aphorists* by James Geary, 2007.

3.480. Consider carefully before you say a hard word to a man, but never let a chance to say a good one go by. Praise judiciously bestowed is money invested.
- **George Horace Lorimer**.

3,481. Praise is warming and desirable, but it is an earned thing. It has to be deserved like a hug from a child.
- **Phyllis McGinley:** *The Saturday Evening Post*.

3,482. Praise is always pleasing.
- **Michel de Montaigne:** *Essays*, 1665.

3,483. Do not believe those who praise you.
- *Latin Proverb*.

3,484. Get someone else to blow your horn and the sound will carry twice as far.
- **Will Rogers:** quoted in *20,000 Quips and Quotes* by Evan Esar, 1968.

3,485. You can tell the character of every man when you see how he receives praise.
- **Seneca:** *Epistles*, 1st century BC.

3,486. Among the smaller duties of life I hardly know any one more important than that of not praising when praise is not due.
- **Sydney Smith:** *Sketches of Moral Philosophy*, 1856.

3,487. I don't really mind a little praise - as long as it's fulsome.
Adlai Stevenson.

3,488. The most powerful and predictable people-builders are praise and encouragement.
- **Brian Tracy:** quoted in *The Treasury of Quotes* by Jim Rohn, 1996.

3,489. The love of praise, howe'er concealed by art,
Reigns more or less, and glows in ev'ry heart.
- **Edward Young:** *Love of Fame*, 1725 – 1728.

PRAYER

3,490. It is foolish to expect our prayers to be heard, if we do not strive as well as pray.
- The moral of **Aesop's Fable:** *Hercules and the Waggoner.*

3,491. Some people are so busy asking God for favours, they have no time to thank him.
- *anon.*

3,492. God may not be too busy to listen to your prayers, but that's no reason why you shouldn't keep them short.
- *anon.*

3,493. Derek Nimmo in his book *O Come On All Ye Faithful* relates the story of the little girl who was asked if she said her prayers at night.
"Mummy says them for me," she replied.
"What does she say?"
"When she tucks me in she says, 'Thank God, you're in bed at last'"
- **Christopher Hamel Cooke:** quoted in *A Time To Laugh,* 1993.

3,494. Prayer is petition, intercession, adoration, and contemplation; great saints and mystics have agreed on this definition. To stop short at petition is to pray only in a crippled fashion. Further, such prayer encourages one of the faults which is most reprehended by spiritual instructors – turning to God without turning from self.
- **Robertson Davies:** *A Voice From the Attic,* 1960.

3,495. If the only prayer you said in your whole life was, "Thank You", that would suffice.
- **Meister Eckhart:**quoted in *A Bucket of Surprises,* by John and Mark Stibbe, 2002.

3,496. And that inverted Bowl they call the Sky,
Whereunder crawling coop'd we live and die,

Lift not your hands to it for help for it
As impotently moves as you or I.
- **Edward Fitzgerald:** *The Rubaiyat of Omar Khayyam*, 1857.

3,497. None can pray well but he that lives well.
- **Thomas Fuller:** *Gnomologia: Adages and Proverbs*, 1732.

3,498. You pray in your distress and in your need, would that you might also in the fullness of your joy and in your days of abundance.
- **Khalil Gibran:** *The Prophet*, 1923.

3,499. I have lived to thank God that all my prayers have not been answered.
- **Jean Ingelow**.

3,500. Prayer doesn't change God, but changes him who prays.
- **Soren Kierkegaard**.

3,501. I pray because I can't help myself. I pray because I am helpless. I pray because the need flows out of me all the time, waking and sleeping. It doesn't change God, it changes me.
- Anthony Hopkins, in his role as **C.S Lewis** in the 1993 Film *Shadowlands,* screenplay by William Nicholson, directed by Sir Richard Attenborough.

3,502. I have been driven many times to my knees by the overwhelming conviction that I had nowhere else to go. My own wisdom and that of all about me seemed insufficient for that day.
- **Abraham Lincoln:** *Lincoln Observed: The Civil War Dispatches of Noah Brooks* edited by Professor Michael Burlingame, 1998.

3,503. Think of prayer less as an activity for God and more as an awareness of God. Seek to live in uninterrupted awareness. Acknowledge his presence everywhere you go.
- **Max Lucano:** *Today's Christian, Nov /Dec, 2004*.

3,504. Prayer indeed is good but . . .a man should himself lend a hand.
- **Peter McWilliams:** *You Can't Afford the Luxury of a Negative Thought* 1995.

3,505. Who rises from prayer a better man, his prayer is answered.
- **George Meredith:** *The Ordeal of Richard Feverel,* 1859.

3,506. Prayer should be the key of the day, and the lock of the night.
- ***English Proverb***.

3,507. The trouble with our praying is we just do it as a means of last resort.
- **Will Rogers:** *The Best of Will Rogers* by Bryan Sterling, 1979.

3,508. My words fly up, my thoughts remain below;
Words without thoughts never to heaven go.
- **William Shakespeare:** *Hamlet, Act 3, Sc 3*, 1600.

3,509. If thou shouldst never see my face again,
Pray for my soul. More things are wrought by prayer,
Than this world dreams of.
- **Alfred**, **Lord Tennyson:** *The Passing of Arthur* in *Idylls of the King*, 1869.

PREJUDICE

3,510. Perhaps the briefest of all definitions of prejudice is: *thinking ill of others without sufficient warrant.*
- **Gordon W. Allport:** *The Nature of Prejudice.* 1954.

3,511. Many a man makes the mistake of developing his opinions in the dark room of prejudice.
- **anon:** *20,000 Quips and Quotes* by Evan Esar, 1968.

3,512. Prejudice, n. A vagrant opinion without visible means of support.
- **Ambrose Bierce:** *Devil's Dictionary,* 1911.

3,513. The difference between a conviction and a prejudice is that you can explain a conviction without getting angry.
- **Jacob M. Braude:** quoted in *Braude's Handbook of Stories for Toastmasters and Speakers,* 1957.

3,514. Prejudice can be defined as a judgement which does not change, and is impervious to facts and reason.
- **Stuart Chase:** American economist in his review of *The Nature of Prejudice* by Gordon W. Allport, 1954.

3,515. There are only two ways to be quite unprejudiced and impartial. One is to be completely ignorant. The other is to be completely indifferent.
- **Charles P. Curtis:** *A Commonplace Book,* 1957.

3,516. I am free of all prejudice.. I hate everyone equally.
- **W. C. Fields,** *attributed.*

3,517. Prejudice is the child of ignorance.
- **William Hazlit:** *On Prejudice* in *Sketches and Essays,* 1837.

3,518. Prejudice is always accompanied by a rigidity of attitude, an unwillingness to see all sides of a question or to face facts that are not to one's liking.
- **Elizabeth B. Hurlock**.

3,519. I have no race prejudices. All that I care to know is that man is a human being - that is enough for me; he can't be any worse.
- **Mark Twain:** *Harpers Magazine, December, 1899.*

3,520. Prejudice is a great time saver. You can form opinions without having to get the facts.
- **E. B. White**.

THE PRESENT

3,521. Every man's life lies within the present; for the past is spent and done with, and the future is uncertain.
- **Marcus Aurelius:** *Meditations. **circa** 180 AD.*

3,522. The present time has one advantage over every other - it is our own. Past opportunities are gone, future has not come.
- **Charles Caleb Colton:** *Lacon* or *Many Things in Few Words,* 1826 edited by George J. Barbour, 2001.

3,523. The past is a ghost, the future a dream, and all we ever have is now.
- **Bill Cosby.**

3,524. Enjoy now, another now is coming.
- **Sir Thomas Dewar:** author of witticisms now known as Dewarisms.

3,525. The present is the necessary product of all the past, the necessary cause of all the future.
- **Robert G. Ingersoll.**

3,526. The present is what slips by us while we're pondering the past and worrying about the future.
- **Barbara Johnson:** *Daily Splashes of Joy,* 2000.

3,527. There are many fine things which you mean to do some day, under what you think will be more favourable circumstances. But the only time that is yours is the present, hence this is the time to speak the word of appreciation and sympathy, and to do the generous deed, to forgive the fault of a thoughtless friend, to sacrifice self a little more for others.
- **Grenville Kleisler.**

3,528. Yesterday is a cancelled cheque; tomorrow is a promissary note; today is the only cash you have, so spend it wisely.
- **Kim Lyons.**

3,529. The time is now, the place is here. Stay in the present, you can do nothing to change the past, and the future will never come exactly as you plan or hope for.
- **Dan Millman**.

3,530. Yesterday is history, tomorrow is a mystery, and today ? Today is a gift, that's why we call it the present.
- **Babatunde Olatunji**.

3,531, Let others praise ancient times; I am glad I was born in these.
- **Ovid:** *The Art of Love* **circa** 2 AD

3,532. In regard to the present, let us remember Seneca's advice, and live each day as if it were our whole life... let us make it as agreeable as possible, it is the only real time we have.
- **Arthur Schopenhaur:** *Counsels and Maxims* translated by T. Bailey Saunders, 1890.

3,533. Another important element in the wise conduct of life is to preserve a proper proportion between our thought for the present and our thought for the future; in order not to spoil the one by paying over-great attention to the other.
- *ibid.*

3,534. We should never forget that the present is the only reality, the only certainty; that the future almost always turns out contrary to our expectations; that the past, too, was very different from what we supposed it to have been.
- *ibid.*

3,535. One day at a time - this is enough. Do not look back and grieve over the past, for it is gone; and do not be troubled about the future, for it has not yet come. Live in the present and make it so beautiful that it will be worth remembering.
- **Ida Scott Taylor**.

PROBLEMS AND SOLUTIONS

3,536. One of the nice things about problems is that a good many of them do not exist except in our imagination.
- **Steve Allen:** *The Reader's Digest, November, 1989.*

3.537. Why can't life's problems come to us at eighteen, when we know everything?
- *anon.*

3,538. Life's problems wouldn't be called 'hurdles' if there wasn't a way to get over them.
- *anon.*

3,539. It's much easier to suggest solutions when you don't know too much about the problem.
- **Malcolm Forbes:** *The Sayings of Chairman Malcolm, 1978.*

3,540. The answer to life's problems aren't at the bottom of a bottle, they're on TV!
- The sentiments of Homer Simpson, the head of the family in the animated cartoon series, *The Simpsons,* created and produced by **Matt Groening**.

3,541. Turn Your Problems Into Opportunities.
- Chapter title in *Attitude is Everything: Change Your Attitude and You Change Your Life* by **Jeff Keller**, 1999.

3,542. A problem well stated is a problem halve solved.
- **Charles F. Kettering**.

3,543. To every problem there is already a solution, whether you know it or not. To every sum there is already a correct answer, whether the mathematician has found it or not.
- **Grenville Kleiser:** quoted in *The Forbes Book of Business Quotations* by Ted Goodman and Steve Forbes, 1997.

3,544. The right angle to solve a difficult problem is the 'try-angle'.
- **Ellis I. Levitt.**

3,545. When Goliath came up against the Israelites, the soldiers all thought, "He's so big we can never kill him." David looked at the same giant and thought, "He's so big I cannot miss him."
- **John C. Maxwell:** *The Winning Attitude: Your Pathway to Personal Success,* 1993.

3,546. There is always an easy solution to every human problem – neat, plausible and wrong.
- **H. L. Mencken:** *The New York Evening Mail, 16ᵗʰ November, 1917.*

3,547. Problems are to the mind what exercise is to the muscles, they toughen and make strong.
- **Norman Vincent Peale:** *Positive Thinking Every Day: An Inspiration for Each Day of the Year,* 1993.

3,548. The 'how' thinker gets problems solved effectively because he wastes no time with futile 'ifs', but goes right to work on the creative 'how'.
- *ibid.*

3,549. Problems do not go away. They must be worked through or else they remain forever a barrier to the growth and development of the spirit.
- **M. Scott Peck:** *The Road Less Travelled,* 1978.

3,550. It is only because of problems that we grow mentally and spiritually.
- *ibid.*

3,551. Again and again, the impossible problem is solved when we see that the problem is only a tough decision waiting to be made.
- **Robert H. Schuller.**

3,552. Never underestimate your problem or your ability to deal with it.
- *ibid.*

3,553. There's no problem so big you can't run away from it.
- Linus van Pelt in **Charles Schultz's** cartoon *Peanuts.*

3.554. I've come to the realization that a lot of our problems are because of a dearth of spiritual values.
- **Benjamin Spock:** *Associated Press Interview, 1992.*

3,555. Prevent problems before they arise. Take action before things get out of hand.
- **Tao Te Ching:** translated by J. H. McDonald, 1996.

3,556. It's not a problem that we have a problem. It's a problem if we don't deal with the problem.
- **Mary Kay Utecht**.

PROCRASTINATION

3,557. Procrastination is the grave in which opportunity is buried.
- *anon.*

3,558. I always wanted to be a procrastinator, but I kept putting it off.
- *anon.*

3,559. Always put off till tomorrow what you shouldn't do at all.
- *anon.*

3,560. Procrastination: A hardening of the oughteries.
- *anon.*

3,561. Procrastination is the greatest labour-saving invention of all time.
- *anon.*

3,562. Whate'er there be of sorrow
I'll put off till tomorrow,
And when tomorrow comes, why then
'Twill be today and joy again.
- **John Kendrick Bangs**.

3,563. From here on in, my life is going to be orderly. I'm going to think before I talk; plan before I act; act before I procrastinate.
- **Erma Bombeck:** *Aunt Erma's Cope Book,* 1985.

3,564. Know the true value of Time; snatch, seize, and enjoy every minute of it. No idleness, no laziness, no procrastination; never put off till tomorrow what you can do today.
- **Lord Chesterfield:** *Letters to His Son.*

3,565. Defer not till tomorrow to be wise,
Tomorrow's sun to thee may never rise.
- **William Congreve**.

3,566. Procrastination makes easy things hard, and hard things harder.
- **Mason Cooley:** *City Aphorisms, Tenth Selection,* 1992.

3,567. Procrastination gives you something to look forward to.
- **Joan Konner.**

3,568. My evil genius Procrastination has whispered me to tarry 'til a more convenient season.
- **Mary Todd Lincoln:** *In a letter dated June, 1841* in *Mary Todd Lincoln: Her Life And Letters* by Justin G. Turner and Linda Levitt, 1987.

3,569. There is no pleasure in having nothing to do, the fun is in having lots to do and not doing it.
- **Mary Wilson Little:** *The Forbes Book of Business Quotations* edited by Ted Goodman, 1997.

3,570. Don't fool yourself that important things can be put off till tomorrow; they can be put off for ever, or not at all.
- **Mignon McLaughlin:** *The Neurotic's Notebook,* 1960.

3,571. Procrastination is the art of keeping up with yesterday.
- **Don Marquis:** *Archy and Mehitabel,* 1927.

3,572. I had a terrible fight with my wife on New Year's Eve. She called me a procrastinator. So I finished addressing the Christmas cards and left.
- **Robert Orben:** quoted in *Dick Enberg's Humorous Quotes For All Occasions,* 2000.

3,573. The celebrated Spanish composer Manuel de Falia was devastated when he received the news about the death of Ignacio Zuloaga, the Spanish painter. Deeply distressed over his friend's death, Falia lamented, "What a pity! He died before I answered his letter which he sent me five years ago."
Victor M. Parachin: in an article on *Procrastination* in the July / August 1997 issue of *Vibrant Life.*

3,574. Procrastination is my sin, / It brings me naught but sorrow./ I know that I should stop it, / In fact, I will – tomorrow!
- **Gloria Pitzer.**

3,575. Procrastination slams the breaks on the wheels of progress.
- **James R. Sherman:** *Stop Procrastination – Do It,* 1988.

3,576. Procrastination is the thief of time.
- **Edward Young:** *Night Thoughts*, 1742 - 1745.

PROGRESS

3,577. If we want progress we must take the forward look.
- *anon.*

3,578. Progress always means change,but change doesn't always mean progress.
- *anon.*

3,579. We have finally reached a state of affairs where a man can fly into space safely, but cannot cross the road without putting his life in danger.
- *anon.*

3.580. All progress is based upon a universal innate desire on the part of every organism to live beyond its income.
- **Samuel Butler:** *Notebooks,* 1912.

3,581. I have always considered that the substitution of the internal combustion engine for the horse marked a very gloomy milestone in the progress of mankind.
-   **Sir Winston Churchill:** *A Churchill Reader* edited by Colin Coote, 1954.

3,582. The perfecting of one's self is the fundamental base of all progress and all moral development.
- **Confucius:** 5th century BC.

3,583. Progress isn't made by early risers. It's made by lazy men trying to find easier ways to do something.
- **Robert Heinlein:** *Time Enough For Love,* 1973.

3,584. There can be no progress if people have no faith in tomorrow.
- **John F. Kennedy:** *in a speech delivered in Miami Beach, 18th November, 1963.*
NB Kennedy was assassinated four days later in Dallas, Texas.

3,585. The world hates change; yet it is the only thing that has brought progress.
- **Charles F. Kettering**.

3,586. The means by which we live have outdistanced the ends for which we live. Our scientific power has outrun our spiritual power. We have guided missiles and misguided men.
- **Martin Luther King:** *Strength To Love*, 1963.

3,587. The chief obstacle to the progress of the human race is the human race.
- **Don Marquis**.

3,588. Do not confuse motion and progress. A rocking-horse keeps moving, but does not make any progress.
- **Alfred A. Montapert**.

3,589. Not to go forward is to go back.
- *Chinese Proverb*

3,590. Progress, however, of the best kind, is comparatively slow. Great results cannot be achieved at once; and we must be satisfied to advance in life as we walk, step by step.
- **Samuel Smiles:** *Self-Help*, 1859.

3,591. Progress . . . is not an accident, but a necessity.
- **Herbert Spencer:** *Social Statics: The Conditions Essential to Human Happiness*, 1851.

3,592. All progress has resulted from people who took unpopular positions.
- **Adlai Stevenson**, *in a speech delivered on 22nd March, 1954.*

3,593. Progress depends upon the belief that things can always get better.
- **Frank Tyger**.

3,594. And step by step, since time began, I see the steady gain of man.
- **John Greenleaf Whittier:** *Poetical Works*, 1894.

PROMISES

3,595. When a man gives his word to another man, it's his bond; when he gives his word to a woman, it's his bondage.
- *anon.*

3,596. A politician is remembered by the promises he forgot to keep.
- *anon.*

3,597. I would never do anything to harm the country or anything improper. I think most people who have dealt with me think I'm a pretty straight sort of a guy.
- **Tony Blair:** *in an interview with John Humphrys on BBC TV's "On The Record," 16th November, 1997.*

3,598. My first rule – the golden rule – ensures that over the economic cycle the Government will borrow only to invest, and that current spending will be met from taxation. My second rule is that, as a proportion of national income, public debt will be held at a prudent and stable level over the economic cycle.
- **Gordon Brown:** *in a speech to Parliament, 2nd July, 1997.*

3,599. I have nothing to offer but blood, toil, tears and sweat.
- **Sir Winston Churchill:** *in a speech delivered on 13th May, 1940.*

3,600. Make small commitments and keep them.
- **Stephen R. Covey:** *Seven Habits of Highly Effective People,* 1989.

3,601. I promised I would take Rotherham out of the Second Division, I did – into the Third Division.
- **Tommy Docherty:** quoted in *Great British Wit,* by Rosemarie Jarski, 2005. NB Docherty was Manager of Rotherham United Football Club for 1 year.

3,602. Make a point of promising; for what harm can it do to promise? Anyone can be rich in promises.
- **Ovid:** *The Art of Love*, **circa** 2 AD.

3,603. Promises are like pie-crust, made to be broken.
- ***English Proverb***.

3,604. Promises may get friends, but 'tis performances that keep them.
- ***ibid***

3,605. Now a promise made is a debt unpaid.
- **Robert W. Service:** *Best Tales of the Yukon*, 1983.

3,606. He was ever precise in promise keeping.
- **William Shakespeare:** *Measure for Measure, Act 1, Sc 2*, 1604.

3,607. Never promise more than you can perform.
- **Publilius Syrus:** *Moral Sayings (Maxim 528)*. 1st century BC.

PUNCTUALITY

3,608. "Better late than never," is not half so good a maxim as "Better never late."
- *anon*.

3,609. It's easy to tell those who have never had much experience in committee work - they always get to the meeting on time.
- *anon*.

3,610. Punctuality is a virtue – if you don't mind being on your own for a time.
- *anon*.

3,611. The trouble with being punctual is that nobody's there to appreciate it.
- **Franklin P. Jones**.

3,612. I have noticed that the people who are late are often so much jollier than the people who have to wait for them.
- **Edward Verrall Lucas**.

3,613. Unfaithfulness in the keeping of an appointment is an act of clear dishonesty. You may as well borrow a person's money as his time.
- **Horace Mann**.

3,614. Punctuality is one of the cardinal business virtues: always insist on it in your subordinates.
- **Don Marquis**.

3,615. A woman on time is one in nine.
- **Addison Mizner**.

3,616. I've been on a calendar, but never on time.
- **Marilyn Monroe:** *Look, 5ᵗʰ March, 1957.*

3,617. Better late than never.
- *__English Proverb__*.

3,618. Punctuality is the virtue of the bored.
- **Evelyn Waugh:** *The Diaries of Evelyn Waugh* edited by Michael Davie, 1976.

3,619. He was always late on principle, his principle being that punctuality is the thief of time.
- **Oscar Wilde:** *The Picture of Dorian Gray*, 1891.

3,620. The early bird gets the worm, but the second mouse gets the cheese.
- **Steven Wright**.

QUARRELS

3,621. If it weren't for marriage, husbands and wives would have to quarrel with strangers.
- ***anon:*** *20,000 Quips and Quotes* by Evan Esar, 1968.

3.622. The worst thing about a domestic quarrel is that both husband and wife say what they think without thinking.
- ***anon, ibid.***

3,623. A smart husband knows just the right thing to say when he quarrels with his wife, but a smarter husband doesn't say it.
- ***anon, ibid.***

3,624. People generally quarrel because they cannot argue.
- **G. K. Chesterton.**

3,625. In most quarrels, there is fault on both sides. A quarrel may be compared to a spark, which cannot be produced without a flint, as well as a steel.
- **Charles Caleb Colton:** *Lacon,* or *Many Things in Few Words,* 1826, ed George J. Barbour, 2001.

3,626. The days are too short even for love; how can there be enough time for quarrelling?
- **Margaret Gatty**

3,627. Those who in quarrels interpose / Must often wipe a bloody nose.
- **John Gay:** *Fables,* 1727.

3,628. You can make up a quarrel, but it will always show where it was patched.
- **Edgar Watson Howe:** *Country Town Sayings,* 1911.

3,629. Family quarrels have a total bitterness unmatched by others. Yet it sometimes happens that they also have a kind of *tang*, a pleasantness beneath the unpleasantness, based on the tacit understanding that this is not for keeps; that any limb you climb out on will still be there later for you to climb back.
- **Mignon McLaughlin:** *The Neurotic's Notebook*, 1960.

3,630. When one will not, two cannot quarrel.
- *Spanish Proverb*.

3,631. Quarrels would not last long if the fault was only on one side.
- **Francois Duc de La Rochefoucauld:** *Maxims*, 1665.

3,632. In quarrelling the truth is always lost.
- **Publilius Syrus:** *Maxims*.

3,633. Lovers' quarrels are the renewal of love.
- **Terence:** *The Lady of Andros (Line 555)*, **circa** 166 BC.

QUOTATIONS

3,634. You can always depend upon children to quote you correctly, especially when it's something you shouldn't have said.
- **anon:** *20,000 Quips and Quotes* by Evan Esar, 1968.

3,635. QUOTATION. The act of repeating erroneously words of another.
- **Ambrose Bierce:** *The Devil's Dictionary*, 1911.

3,636. Collecting quotations is an insidious, even embarrassing habit, like rag-picking or hoarding rocks or trying on other people's laundry. I got into it originally while trying to break an addiction to candy. I kicked candy and now seem stuck with quotations, which are attacking my brain instead of my teeth.
- **Robert Byrne:** *The Other 637 Best Things Anybody Ever Said*, 1984.

3,637. The quotations, when engraved upon the memory, give you good thoughts. They make you anxious to read the authors and look for more.
- **Sir Winston Churchill:** *My Early Life: A Roving Commission*, 1930.

3,638. If we steal thoughts from the moderns, it will be cried down as plagiarism; if from the ancients, it will be cried up as erudition.
- **Charles Caleb Colton:** *Lacon*, or *Many Things in Few Words*, 1826 edited by George J. Barbour, 2001.

3,639. The wisdom of the wise, and the experience of the ages are perpetuated by quotations.
- **Isaac D'Israeli:** *Curiosities of Literature*, 1834.

3,640. Next to the originator of a good sentence is the first quoter of it.
- **Ralph Waldo Emerson:** *Letters and Social Aims*, 2005.
NB This is an unabridged facsimile of the first edition published in 1876.

3,641. Every quotation contributes something to the stability or enlargement of the language.
- **Samuel Johnson:** *A Dictionary of the English Language*, edited by David Crystal.

3,642. I love quotes. I find that quotes sometimes just make you stop in your tracks, and make you re-think the way you look at life.
- **Joan Lunden:** *Cable News Network Chat Show, 17th October, 2000.*

3,643. I quote others only in order to better express myself.
- **Michel de Montaigne:** *Essays*, 1580.

3,644. A facility for quotations covers the absence of original thought.
- **Dorothy L. Sayers:** *Gaudy Night*, 1936.

3,645. In fact, nothing is said that has not been said before.
- **Terence:** *The Eunuch*, **circa** 161 BC.

3,646. How lucky Adam was. He knew when he said a good thing, nobody had said it before.
- **Mark Twain:** *Notebook*. 1867, quoted in *The Wit and Wisdom of Mark Twain* edited by Alex Ayres, 1987.

READING

3,647. Reading is to the mind, what exercise is to the body. As by the one, health is preserved, strengthened, and invigorated: by the other virtue (which is the health of the mind) is kept alive, cherished, and confirmed.
- **Joseph Addison:** *The Tatler, No 147.*

3,648. Reading is a basic tool in the living of a good life.
- **Mortimer J. Adler.**

3,649. The man who can read a woman like a book probably likes to read in bed.
- **anon:** 20,000 *Quips and Quotes* by Evan Esar, 1968.

3,650. When I am dead, I hope it may be said:
"His sins were scarlet, but his books were read."
- **Hilaire Belloc:** *On His Books* in *Sonnets and Verse*, 1925.

3,651. Every person who knows how to read has it in their power to magnify themselves, to multiply the ways in which they exist, to make life full, significant, and interesting.
- **Aldous Huxley.**

3,652. Reading furnishes our mind only with materials of knowledge; it is thinking makes what we read ours.
- **John Locke:** *An Essay Concerning Human Understanding*, 1690.

3,653. It is like the rubbing of two sticks together to make a fire, the act of reading, an improbably pedestrian task that leads to heat and light.
- **Anna Quinlen:** *How Reading Changed My Life*, 1998.

REGRETS

3,654. The man who insists upon seeing with perfect clearness before he decides, never decides. Accept life and you must accept regret.
- **Henri Frederic Amiel:** *Journal Intime*, 1882.

3,655. The follies which a man regrets most are those which he didn't commit when he had the opportunity.
- *anon.*

3,656. A man is not old until his regrets take the place of dreams.
- **John Barrymore:** *Goodnight Sweet Prince: The Life and Times of John Barrymore* by Gene Fowler, 1943.

3,657. One of my chief regrets during my years in the theatre is that I couldn't sit in the audience and watch me.
- **John Barrymore:** *The Treasury of Humorous Quotations* edited by Evan Esar, 1951.

3,658. Regret for wasted time is more wasted time.
- **Mason Cooley:** *O Magazine, April, 2004*.

3,659. "Regrets," said Martin, "are the natural property of grey hairs; and I enjoy, in common with all other men, at least my share of such inheritance."
- **Charles Dickens:** *Martin Chuzzlewit*, 1844.

3,660 Regret is an appalling waste of energy; you can't build on it; it's only good for wallowing in.
- **Katherine Mansfield:** *20,000 Quips and Quotes* by Evan Esar, 1968.

3,661. We should regret our mistakes and learn from them, but never carry them forward into the future with us.
- **Lucy Maud Montgomery:** *Anne of Avonlea*, 1925.

3,662. Many of us crucify ourselves between two thieves – regret for the past and fear of the future.
- **Fulton Oursler**.

3,663. Regret for the things we did can be tempered by time; it is regret for the things we did not do that is inconsolable.
- **Sydney Smith**.

3,664. For of all sad words of tongue or pen,
The saddest are these: "It might have been!"
- **John Greenleaf Whittier:** *Maud Muller – A ballad,* 1856.

RELATIONSHIPS

3,665. The easiest kind of relationship for me is with ten thousand people. The hardest is with one.
- **Joan Baez**.

3,666. Learn to love, respect and enjoy other people.
- **Dale Carnegie**: *How to Win Friends and Influence People*, 1936.

3,667. Human relationships always help us to carry on because they always presuppose further development, a future - and also because we live as if our only task was precisely to have relationships with other people.
- **Albert Camus**: *Notebooks*, 1942 – 1951.

3.668. Treasure your relationships, not your possessions.
- **Anthony J. D'Angelo**: *The College Blue Book*, 1995.

3,669. I was born when she kissed me. I died when she left me. I lived a few days while she loved me.
- Humphrey Bogart in the role of Dixon Steele in the **1950 Film**: *In a Lonely Place*.

3.670. When you realize you want to spend the rest of your life with somebody, you want the rest of your life to start as soon as possible.
- Billy Crystal in the role of Harry Burns, playing opposite Meg Ryan as Sally Albright, in the **1989 Film**: *When Harry Met Sally* written by Nora Ephron.

3.671. Our only real hope for a more kindly and compassionate pattern of relationships is our willingness to look at the ways women and men collude in perpetuating the long-standing battle between the sexes and the warfare system.
- **Sam Keen**: *The Passionate Life: Stages of Loving*, 1993.

3,672. And I love you so,
The people ask me how,
How I've lived till now,
I tell them I don't know.
I guess they understand
How lonely life has been
But life began again
The day you took my hand.
- **Don McLean:** *And I Love You So,* from his first album *Tapestry,* 1970.

3,673. Come live with me and be my Love, and we will all the pleasures prove.
- **Christopher Marlowe:** *The Passionate Shepherd to His Love.* **circa** 1589.

3,674. The most important thing in any relationship is not what you get, but what you give.
 - **Eleanor Roosevelt:** *This is My Story,* 1937.

3,675. Sweet, ripe Golden Delicious seeks crisp, nutty Autumnal Russet quickly before Winter arrives and turns her into a crab-apple.
- **Saga Magazine:** *Connections, Women Seeking Men, November, 2008.*

3,676. Romance is about building trust, affection, and harmony between two caring people.
- **Mitch Thrower:** *The Attention Deficit Workplace,* 2005.

3,677. Many a girl is looking for an older man with a strong will - made out to her!
- **Henny Youngman:** *Henny Youngman's 400 Travelling Salesmen's Jokes,* 1966.

RELIGION

3,678. Faith brings people together; religion divides them.
- ***anon***.

3,679. Not all religion is to be found in the churches, any more than all knowledge is found in the classroom.
- ***anon***.

3,680. Genuine religion is a matter of feeling rather than a matter of opinion.
- **Christian Nestell Bovee**.

3,681. His religion, at best, is an anxious wish; like that of Rabelais.
Thomas Carlyle: *Burns* in *Critical and Miscellaneous Essays*, 1855.

3,682. Men will wrangle for religion, write for it, fight for it, die for it, any thing - but live for it.
- **Charles Caleb Colton:** *Lacon, or Many Things in a Few Words,* 1826 edited by George J. Barbour, 2001.

3,683. Religion is more like the response to a friend than it is like obedience to an expert.
- **Austin Farrer:** *Saving Belief: Discussion of Essentials*, 1964.

3,684. Religion is a crutch for people not strong enough to stand up to the unknown without help.
- **Robert A. Heinlein:** *Time Enough for Love*, 1987.

3,685. Religion . . . is a man's total reaction upon life.
- **William James:** *The Verities of Religious Experience*, 1902.

3,686. Religion. . . shall mean for us the feelings, acts and experiences of individual men in their solitude.
- ***ibid***.

3,687. There will be no peace among the nations without peace among the religions. There will be no peace among the religions without dialogue among the religions.
- **Hans Kung:** *from a talk given at the co-educational Catholic University of Santa Clara in California, 31ˢᵗ March, 2005.*

3,688. World peace depends upon inter-religious dialogue.
- **Hans Kung:** *publisher's blurb which gives this as Kung's motivation for writing his trilogy on the three great monotheistic faiths,* i.e. Judaism in 1991, Christianity in 1994, and Islam in 2004.

3,689. Religion is the opiate of the people.
- **Karl Marx:** *Critique of Hegel's Philosophy of Right,* 1843.

3,690. We define religion as the assumption that life has meaning. Religion, or lack of it, is shown not in some intellectual or verbal formulations, but in one's total orientation to life. Religion is whatever the individual takes to be his ultimate concern. One's religious attitude is to be found at that point where he has a conviction that there are values in human existence worth living and dying for.
- **Rollo May:** *Man's Search For Himself,* 1953.

3,691. True religion is the life we lead, not the creed we profess.
- **Louis Nizer.**

3,692. True religion does not draw men out of the world but enables them to live better in it and excites their endeavours to mend it.
- **William Penn:** *No Cross, No Crown,* 1682.

3,693. Religion is the best armour, but the worst cloak.
- *English Proverb.*

3,694. A man without religion is like a horse without a bridle.
- *Latin Proverb.*

3,695. There is no religion without love, and people may talk as they like about their religion, but if it does not teach them to be good and kind to men and beasts. At is all a sham.
- **Anna Sewell:** *Black Beauty,* 1877.

3,696. All religion relates to life, and the life of religion is to do good.
- **Emanuel Swedenborg:** *The Doctrine of the New Jerusalem Concerning Life,* 1758.

3,697. Religion is the state of being grasped by an ultimate concern… which itself contains the answer to the question of the meaning of our life.
- **Paul Tillich:** *Christianity and the Encounter of the World Religions,* 1961.

3,698. Being religious means asking passionately the question of the meaning of our existence and being willing to receive answers, even if the answers hurt.

REMEMBERING AND FORGETTING

3,699. "I can forgive, but I cannot forget," is only another way of saying, "I cannot forgive."
- **Henry Ward Beecher:** *Life Thoughts Gathered From the Extemporaneous Discourse of Henry Ward Beecher by One Of His Congregation*, 1859.

3,700. They went with songs to the battle, they were young.
Straight of limb, true of eye, steady and aglow.
They were staunch to the end against odds uncounted,
They fell with their faces to the foe.

They shall grow not old, as we that are left grow old;
Age shall not weary them, nor the years condemn.
At the going down of the sun and in the morning,
We will remember them.
- **Laurence Binyon**, verses 3 and 4 of his most famous poem *For the Fallen, 1914*. The full text of this poem is available on the Internet at: www.poemhunter.com under "poets", "Laurence Binyon", "For The Fallen".

3,701. A woman should never blame her husband for forgetting his mistakes; there's no need for both of them to remember the same things.
- **Evan Esar:** *20,000 Quips and Quotes*, 1968.

3,702. My wife has a terrible memory. She doesn't forget anything.
- **Leopold Fechtner:** *5,000 One-And-Two-Line Jokes*, 1979.

3,703. The more you say, the less people remember.
- **Francois Fenelon**

3,704. A retentive memory may be a good thing, but the ability to forget is the true token of greatness.
- **Elbert Hubbard:** *A Thousand And One Epigrams* by Elbert Hubbard and Fra Elbert Hubbard.

3,705. The tumult and the shouting dies -
The Captains and the Kings depart -
Still stands Thine ancient sacrifice,
An humble and a contrite heart.
Lord God of Hosts, be with us yet,
Lest we forget – lest we forget.

- **Rudyard Kipling:** verse 2 of the poem, *Recessional*, written on the occasion of Queen Victoria's Diamond Jubilee in 1897.

NB Since the end of the First World War this verse has often been incorporated into Remembrance Day Services as a plea never to forget past sacrifices. The full text of this poem is available on the Internet under: *Recessional (poem) - Wikipedia*

3,706. Consider this paradox: almost everything that is publicly said these days is recorded. Almost nothing of what is said is worth remembering.
- **Ted Koppel**.

3,707. The ability to forget and the inability to recall are altogether different skills.
- **Simon May:** quoted in *Geary's Guide to the World's Great Aphorists* by James Geary, 2007.

CP: "There's a difference between forgetting and not recalling" - the view expressed by **Alessandro Morandotty**, also quoted in *Geary's Guide to the World's Great Aphorists* by James Geary, 2007.

3,708. Marriage is the alliance of two people, one of whom never remembers birthdays, and the other never forgets them.
- **Ogden Nash**.

3,709. Yesterday ended last night. Every day is a new beginning. Learn the skill of forgetting, and move on.
- **Norman Vincent Peale:** *Have a Great Day – Every Day* (1984)

3,710. Forgetting a wrong is a mild revenge.
- *English Proverb*.

3,711. A beautiful maxim is that memory is like a piece of gold in the purse.
- *French Proverb*.

3,712. Remember me when I am gone away,
Gone far away into the silent land,
When you can no more hold me by the hand…

Yet if you should forget me for a while
And afterwards remember, do not grieve…

Better by far you should forget and smile,
Than that you should remember and be sad.
- **Christina Rossetti:** *Remember* in *Goblin Market and Other Poems*, 1862.

3,713. Sometimes it is expedient to forget even what we know.
- **Publilius Syrus**.

REMORSE

3,714. **A**. Now, there's no use crying over spoiled milk.
- **Jane Ace:** starred with her husband, Goodman Ace, in the long running American radio comedy show, *Easy Aces (1930-1945)*. Jane made great use of malaprops, such as the following :
B. "I'm his awfully wedded wife":
C. "I'm a member of the weeper sex":
D. "Home wasn't built in a day":
E. "I don't drink, I'm a totalitarian":
F. "I'm completely uninhabited":
G. "I've always wanted to see my name up in tights."

3,715. The water-wagon is the place for me; / It is no time for mirth and laughter,
The cold grey dawn of the morning after.
- **George Ade:** *The Sultan of Sula* – a satire in two acts, 1903.

3,716. Last night at twelve I felt immense. But now I feel like thirty cents.
- **George Ade**.

3,717. Remorse is the poison of life.
- **Charlotte Bronte:** *Jane Eyre*, 1847.

3,718. It isn't the experience of today that drives men mad. It is the remorse for something that happened yesterday, and the dread of what tomorrow may disclose.
- **Robert Jones Burdette**.

3,719. Regrets are the natural property of gray hairs.
- **Charles Dickens:** quoted in *The Treasury of Humorous Quotations* edited by Evan Esar, 1951.

3,720. True remorse is never just a regret over consequences: it is a regret over motive.
- **Mignon Mc Laughlin:** *The Neurotic's Notebook,* 1960.

3,721. There are some people who are very resourceful
At being remorseful,
And who apparently feel that the best way to make friends
Is to do something terrible and then make amends.
- **Ogden Nash:** *A Good Excuse is Worse Than None* in *Happy Days,* 1933.

3,722. The follies which a man regrets most in his life, are those he didn't commit when he had the opprtunity.
- **Helen Rowland:** *A Guide to Men,* 1922.

3,723. Sometimes I lie awake at night, and ask, "Where have I gone wrong?" Then a voice says to me, "This is going to take more than one night."
- Charlie Brown in **Charles Schulz's** Cartoon Strip, *Peanuts.*

3,724. For all sad words of tongue or pen,
The saddest are these: "I might have been!"
- **John Greenleaf Whittier:** *Maud Muller.* This poem, written in 1856, is quoted in full in *An American Anthology* edited by Edmund Clarence Stedman, 1900.

RESPONSIBILITY

3,725. Work while you have the light. You are responsible for the talent that has been entrusted to you.
- **Henri Frederic Amiel:** *Journal Intime*, 1882.

3,726. RESPONSIBILITY: n. A detachable burden easily shifted to the shoulders of God, Fate, Fortune,Luck or one's neighbour. In the days of astrology it was customary to unload it upon a star.
- **Ambrose Bierce**.

3,727. Crime is rampant. We even steal away from responsibility.
- **Andre Brie:** quoted in *Geary's Guide to the World's Great Aphorists* by James Geary, 2007.

3,728. We have learned a bit too late in the day that action springs not from thought, but from a readiness for responsibility.
- **Dietrich Bonhoeffer:** *Letters and Papers from Prison*, 1953.

3,729. Ultimately, man should not ask what the meaning of life is, but rather must recognize that it is he who is asked. In a word, each man is questioned by life; and he can only answer to life by answering for his own life; to life he can only respond by being responsible.
- **Victor Frankl:** *Man's Search for Meaning*, 1959.

3,730. Most people do not really want freedom, because freedom involves responsibility, and most people are frightened of responsibility.
- **Sigmund Freud:** *Civilization and its Discontents*, 1930.

3,731. The greatest day of your life and mine is when we take total responsibility for our attitudes. That's the day we truly grow up.
- **John Maxwell:** *Developing the Leader Within You*, 1993.

3,732. It is not only for what we do that we are held responsible, but also for what we do not do.
- **Moliere**.

3,733. Responsibility educates.
- **Wendell Phillips**.

3.734. You have to get beyond blaming others… give up your excuses… stand responsible for what you do… ultimately, ethics ends up as an individual exercise.
- **Price Pritchett:** *The Ethics of Excellence*, 1993.

3,735. We do not do what we want and yet we are responsible for what we are – that is the fact.
- **Jean-Paul Sarte:** *Situations,* 1939.

3,736. Man is condemned to be free, because once thrown into the world, he is responsible for everything he does.
- **Jean-Paul Sarte:** *Being and Nothingness,* 1943.

3,737. I don't think of myself as a poor deprived ghetto girl who made good. I think of myself as somebody who from an early age knew I was responsible for myself, and I had to make good.
Oprah Winfrey: *O Magazine, January, 2007.*

RETIREMENT

3,738. I will undoubtedly have to seek what is happily known as gainful employment on retiring from public office.
- **Dean Acheson**.
NB After the 1952 American presidential campaign Acheson's political career was over. Thereafter he returned to his law practice.

3,739. **A**. Retirement is the time in life when a woman has twice as much husband on half as much income.
B. Retirement is the period when you exchange the money in your wallet for snapshots of your grandchildren.
C. Retirement is the time in life when you stop lying about your age and start lying about the house.
D. Retirement is the period when you wake up in the morning with nothing to do, and go to bed at night with it still to be done.
- ***anon:*** quoted in *20,000 Quips and Quotes* by Evan Esar, 1968.

3,740. **A**. He elected to skip coffee breaks altogether and it enabled him to retire three years earlier.
B. He's always been an optimist. When he retired at sixty-five, he planted two acorns and bought himself a hammock.
C. This will be a big period of adjustment for him. He'll have to get used to taking his afternoon naps at home.
D. As a symbol of our gratitude, we have created this special gold watch to serve as a reminder of your many years with the company. It needs a lot of winding up, is always a little late, and every day at a quarter to five, it stops working.
- ***anon:*** quoted in *Winning With One-Liners* by Pat Williams, 2002

3,741. The hard part comes in choosing what to do and getting started making the first effort at something different. Once the initiative is taken we often find that we can do things we never thought we could.
- **Rosalyn and Jimmy Carter:** *Everything to Gain: Making the Most of the Rest of Your Life*, 1987.

NB *Library Journal* – a trade publication for librarians - has this to say about the Carter's book: "In this joint effort, the Carters present their formula for productive, happy, post-career living."

3,742. The worst part of doin' nothing is you never can take any time off.
- **Bennett Cerf:** *The Laugh's On Me,* quoting from Harry Oliver's *Desert Rat Scrap Book.*

3,743. When a man fell into his anecdotage it was a sign for him to retire.
- **Benjamin Disraeli:** *Lothair,* 1870.

3,744. It is time I stepped aside for a less experienced and less able man.
- **Scott Elledge:** on announcing his retirement from his post as the Goldwin Smith Professor of English Literature at Cornell University.

3,745. Many retired people live on a fixed income – fix the T.V., fix the car, fix the toilet, fix the...
- **Sam Ewing:** *The Sun, 25th May, 1999.*

3,746. People who refuse to rest honourably on their laurels when they reach "retirement" age seem very admirable to me.
Helen Hayes: *My Life in Three Acts,* 1990.
NB This was Helen Hayes' fourth book of memoirs.

3,747. Retirement is not about giving up, it's more about moving onto the next stage of your life.
- **Annie Hulley:** *How To Spend the Kid's Inheritance: All You Need to Know About a Successful Retirement,* 2006.

3,748. I have now the gloomy prospect of retiring from office loaded with serious debts, which will materially affect the tranquillity of my retirement.
- **Thomas Jefferson:** *in a letter to his daughter, dated 5th January, 1808,* quoted in *The Family Letters of Thomas Jefferson* edited by E.M .Betts **et al**, 1966.

3,749. Look before you leap. Before you retire, stay home for a week and watch daytime television.
- **Fred Metcalf:** *The Penguin Dictionary of Jokes,* 1993.

3,750. At his retirement ceremony the boss told him, "The way I see it, we're not so much losing a worker as gaining a parking space.
- ***ibid.***

3,751, I have considered retirement, but rejected it, one of the reasons being that my wife would go mad if I were around the house.
- **Warren Mitchell:** quoted in *The Press and Journal, Quotes of the Day, 4th December, 2007.*

3,752. Few men of action have been able to make a graceful exit at the appointed time.
- **Malcolm Muggeridge:** *The Most of Malcom Muggeridge,* 1966.

3,753. He lives well who lives retired, and keeps his wants within the limits of his means.
- **Ovid, circa** 17 AD.

3,754. Retirement needs careful planning in order to make it a fulfilling and rewarding phase of your life.
- **Publisher's blurb** on Jim Green's *"Your Retirement Masterplan",* 2004.

3,755. When men reach their sixties and retire, they go to pieces. Women go right on cooking.
- **Gail Sheehy:** quoted in *How to Retire , Happy, Wild and Free* by Ernie Zelinski, 2004.

3,756. When a man retires and time is no longer a matter of urgent importance, his colleagues generally present him with a watch.
- **R. C. Sherriff.**

3,757. I'm 65 and I guess that puts me in with the geriatrics. But if there were fifteen months in every year, I'd only be 48.
- **James Thurber:** *Time Magazine, 15th August, 1960.*

3,758. Retirement, we understand, is great if you are busy, rich and healthy. But then, under those conditions, work is great too.
- **Bill Vaughan:** *The Kansas City Star.*

3,759. The key to a happy retirement is to have enough money to live on, but not enough to worry about.
- **Ernie J. Zelinski:** *How to Retire, Happy, Wild and Free: Retirement Wisdom That You Won't Get From Your Financial Advisers,* 2004.

3,760. Retirement can be both exciting and demanding, bringing new challenges, new experiences, and new uncertainties. Regardless of how it turns out, retirement normally turns out far different from what people first envisage. For some, it is a big disappointment. For others it is

merely a big annoyance. And still for others – much to their delight – retirement becomes an opportunity to live life like never before.
- *ibid.*

3,761. The key to achieving an active and satisfying retirement involves a great deal more than having adequate financial resources; it also encompasses all other aspects of life – interesting leisure activities, creative pursuits, physical well-being, mental well-being, and solid social support.
- Publisher's blurp for **Ernie J. Zelinski's** book *How to Retire, Happy, Wild and Free.*

SCOTLAND AND THE SCOTS

3,762. When called on to pay for a round of drinks a Scotsman often has an impediment in his reach.
- ***anon***.

3,763. It's fine Scottish weather we're having. The rain is falling straight down.
- Mel Gibson in his role as William Wallace in the **1995 Film**: *Braveheart*, written by Randall Wallace and directed by Mel Gibson.

3,764. The Scots have been distinguished for humour, not for venomous wit, but for kindly, genial humour, which half loves what it laughs at.
- **James Anthony Froude**: *Inaugural Address Delivered at the University of St. Andrew's, 1869*. (NB Froude rhymes with "rood")

3,765. I have been trying all my life to like Scotchmen, and I am obliged to desist from the experiment in despair.
- **Charles Lamb:** *Essays of Elia*, 1823.

3,766. So this is your Scotland. It is rather nice, but dampish and northern and one shrinks a trifle inside one's skin. For these countries, one should be amphibian.
- **D. H. Lawrence:** *in a letter, 1926*.

3,767. Beautiful, glorious Scotland has spoilt me for every other country.
- **Mary Todd Lincoln:** wife of the 16th President of the US, *in a letter dated 21st August, 1869*, quoted in *The Mary Lincoln Letters* edited by Justin G. Turner, 1950.

3,768. When two taxis collided in Glasgow 48 people were injured.
- **Bernard Manning**.

3,769. My father was from Aberdeen, and a more generous man you couldn't wish to meet. I have a gold watch that belonged to him. He sold it to me on his death bed. I wrote him a cheque for it, postdated of course.
- **Chic Murray**.

3,770. The English are not happy unless they are miserable, the Irish are not at peace unless they are at war, and the Scots are not at home unless they are abroad.
- **George Orwell**.

3,771. That garret of the earth – that knuckle-end of England - that land of Calvin, oatcakes and sulphur.
- **Sydney Smith:** *Lady Holland's Memoir,* 1855.

3,772. It is never difficult to distinguish between a Scotsman with a grievance and a ray of sunshine.
- **P. G. Wodehouse:** *Blandings Castle,* 1935.

THE SEASONS

3,773. One swallow does not make a summer.
- **Aristotle:** *Nichomachean Ethics*, 4th century BC.

3,774. A perfect summer day is when the sun is shining, the breeze is blowing, the birds are singing, and the lawn mower is broken.
- ***anon***.

3,775. Spring being a tough act to follow, God created June.
- **Al Bernstein**.

3,776. The English winter - ending in July,
To recommence in August.
- **Lord Byron:** *Don Juan; Canto 13, Stanza* 42, 1821.

3,777. A haze on the far horizon, / The infinite, tender sky, /
The ripe, rich tint of the cornfields, / And the wild geese sailing high - /
And all over the upland and lowland / The charm of the golden rod, /
Some of us call it Autumn, / And others call it God.
- **William Herbert Carruth:** *Each in His Own Tongue, verse two*, in *The Little Book of American Poets, 1787 - 1900* edited by Jessie B.Rittenhouse, 1915.

3,778. Another damp day... I hope you won't pay the rheumatic penalties of a winter residence in England.
- **Wilkie Collins:** *The Black Robe*, 1881.

3,779. Season of mists and mellow fruitfulness...
- **John Keats:** *Ode to Autumn* in *The Golden Treasury of the Best Songs and Lyrical Poetry in the English Language*, 1875.

3,780. The only calendar I need is just outside my window. With eyes to see and ears to hear, nature keeps me posted.
- **Alfred A. Montapert**.

3,781. Never yet was a springtime, / Late though lingered the snow, / That the sap stirred not at the whisper / Of the south wind, sweet and low; /Never yet was a springtime / When the buds forgot to blow.
- **Margaret Elizabeth Sangster:** *Awakening* in *An American Anthology, 1787 – 1900* edited by Edmund Clarence Stedman, 1900.

3,782. If Winter comes, can Spring be far behind?
- **Percy Bysshe Shelley:** *Ode to the West Wind* in *The Golden Treasury* edited by Francis T. Palgrave, 1875.

THE SELF

3,783. Your only obligation in any lifetime is to be true to yourself.
- **Richard Bach:** *Illusions: The Adventures of a Reluctant Messiah*, 1977.

3,784. One who conquers himself is greater than another who conquers a thousand times a thousand on the battlefield.
- **Buddha:** *Dhammapada*. 6th century BC.

3,785. As soon as you trust yourself, you will know how to live.
- **Johann Wolfgang von Goethe:** *Faust*, 1808.

3,786. Love, cherish, and respect yourself. Become your own best friend and take care of yourself, for you are the only person with whom you will surely have a life long relationship.
- **Taro Gold:** *Open Your Mind, Open Your Heart.*

3,787. It is not the mountain we conquer, but ourselves.
- **Sir Edmund Hillary:** *Reader's Digest*. NB Hillary was the New Zealand mountaineer who, on 29th May, 1953, with the help of the Nepalese sherpa mountaineer, Tenzing Norgay, was the first to climb Mount Everest, the world's highest peak.

3,788. Everyone has imaginary ideas of himself as being this or that sort of person, and you can be sure that the images are highly complimentary. But since they are purely imaginary, they are highly sensitive to assault by reality.
- **Vernon Howard:** *Psycho-Pictography: The New Way to Use the Miracle Power of Your Mind*, 1976.

3,789. There's only one corner of the universe you can be certain of improving and that's your own self.
- **Aldous Huxley:** *Time Must Have a Stop*, 1944.

3,790. What ought a man to be? Well, my short answer is "himself".
- **Henrik Ibsen:** *Peer Gynt*, 1867.

3,791. Properly speaking, a man has as many social selves as there are individuals who recognise him.
- **William James:** *Principles of Psychology*, 1890.

3,792. Whenever two people meet there are really six people present. There is each man as he sees himself, each man as the other person sees him, and each man as he really is.
- ***ibid***.

3,793. This above all: to thine own self be true
And it must follow, as night the day,
Thou canst not then be false to any man.
- **William Shakespeare:** *Hamlet, Act 1, Sc 3*, 1601.

SELF-ESTEEM

3,794. Nothing splendid has ever been achieved except by those who dared to believe that something inside them was superior to circumstances.
- **Bruce Barton**.

3,795. He is a self-made man; and worships his creator.
- **John Bright**. NB Bright is here referring to Benjamin Disraeli.

3,796. An individual's self-concept is the core of his personality. It affects every aspect of human behaviour: the ability to learn, the capacity to grow and change. A strong, positive self-image is the best possible preparation for success in life.
- **Joyce Brother:** quoted in *Wisdom for the Soul: Five Millennia of Prescriptions for Spiritual Healing* by Larry Chang, 2006.

3,797. I am what I am; an individual, unique and different.
- **Sir Charles S. Chaplin:** *My Autobiography,* 1964.

3,798. To be nobody but yourself in a world which is doing its best, night and day, to make you everybody else, means to fight the hardest battle which any human being can fight, and never stop fighting.
- **E. E. Cumming:** *Selected Letters of E. E. Cumming,* 1969.

3,799. Nothing is easier than self-deceit. For what each man wishes, that he also believes to be true.
- **Demosthenes:** quoted in *Public Speeches* translated by J.H.Vince, 1930.

3,800. If you wish in this world to advance / Your merits you're bound to enhance:/You must stir it and stump it, / And blow your own trumpet, /Or, trust me, you haven't a chance.
- **Sir W. S. Gilbert:** *Ruddigore,* 1887.

3,801. You are your greatest asset. Put your time, effort, and money into training, grooming, and encouraging your greatest asset.
- **Tom Hopkins:** *How to Master the Art of Selling,* 1982.

3,802. Self-confidence is the first requisite to great undertakings.
- **Samuel Johnson:** *Lives of the English Poets,* 1781.

3,803. Believe in yourself! Have faith in your abilities! Without a humble but reasonable confidence in your own powers you cannot be successful or happy.
- **Norman Vincent Peale:** *The Power of Positive Thinking,* 1952.

3,804. Self-praise is no commendation.
- ***English Proverb***.

3,805. Until you have a proper sense of self-love, a healthy and wholesome self- esteem, you are not able freely and fully to love someone else. You don't give yourself to others or consider them valuable if you don't first of all consider yourself worthy.
- **Charles R. Swindoll:** *The Strong Family,* 1994.

3,806. In every aspect of our lives, we are always asking ourselves, "How am I of value? What is my worth?" Yet I believe that worthiness is our birthright.
- **Oprah Winfrey:** *O Magazine.*

3,807. To me, "successful" is getting to the point where you are absolutely comfort- able with yourself, and it does not matter how many things you have acquired.
- **Oprah Winfrey:** *in an interview, Chicago, 1991.*

SELF-KNOWLEDGE

3,808. "Know thyself" was the inscription over the Oracle of Delphi, and it is still the most difficult task any of us faces. But until you truly know yourself, strengths and weaknesses, know what you want to do and why you want to do it, you cannot succeed in any but the most superficial sense of the word.
- **Warren Bennis:** *Thoughts on Leadership: A Treasury of Quotations* compiled by William D. Hitt, 1991.

3,809. Let the world know you as you are, not as you think you should be. Because sooner or later, if you are posing, you will forget to pose, and then who are you?
- **Fanny Brice:** *The Fabulous Fanny* by Norman Katkov, 1952.

3,810. It is better to conquer yourself than win a thousand battles. Then the victory is yours, it cannot be taken from you.
- **Buddha:** *The Dhammapada*, 6th century BC.

3,811. O wad some Power the giftie gie us
To see oursels as ithers see us!
It wad frae mony a blunder free us
An' foolish notion.
- **Robert Burns:** *To A Louse, on seeing one on a lady's bonnet at church*, in *The Complete Illustrated Poems, Songs and Ballads of Robert Burns*, 1990. NB Scots: giftie" = *dim. of* gift: gie = give: frae = from
3,812. To know oneself, one should assert oneself... we continue to shape our personalities all our lives.
- **Albert Camus:** *Notebooks 1935 – 1942*, 1965.

3,813. It took me a long time and much painful boomeranging of my expectations to achieve a realization everyone else appears to have been born with: that I am nobody but myself.
- **Ralph Ellison:** *Invisible Man*, 1952.

3,814. Know and believe in yourself, and what others think won't disturb you.
- **William Feather:** *The Business of Life*, 1949.

3,815. How can one learn to know oneself? Never by introspection, rather by action. Try to do your duty, and you will know right away what you are like.
- **Johann Wolfgang von Goethe:** *Wilhelm Meister's Travels*, 1829.

3,816. Know yourself. Don't accept your dog's admiration as conclusive evidence that you are wonderful.
- **Ann Landers:** *Reader's Digest Quotable Quotes*, 1998.

3,817. If a man happens to find himself, he has a mansion which he can inhabit with dignity all the days of his life.
- **James A. Michener,** *attributed*

3,818. I own and operate a ferocious ego.
- **Bill Moyers:** *New York Times, 3/1/82.*

3.819. Heroes take journeys, confront dragons, and discover the treasure of their true selves.
- **Carol Pearson:** *The Hero Within*, 1986.

3,820. People often say that this or that person has not yet found himself. But the self is not something that one finds. It is something one creates.
- **Thomas Szasz:** *The Second Sin*, 1973.

3,821. Know thyself.
- **Thales:** *Lives and Opinions of Eminent Philosophers* by Diogenes Laertius, Classic Reprint, 2010.
NB This maxim was inscribed in the forecourt of the Temple of Apollo at Delphi.

3,822. Knowing others is intelligence; knowing yourself is true wisdom.
- **Lao Tzu:** *Tao Te Ching* interpreted by Stephen Mitchell, 1992.

SENSE OF HUMOUR

3,823. Men will take almost any kind of criticism except the observation that they have no sense of humour.
- **Steve Allen**.

3,824. Every survival kit should include a sense of humour.
- *anon*.

3,825. Our five senses are incomplete without the sixth - a sense of humour.
- *anon*.

3,826. Imagination was given to man to compensate him for what he is not, a sense of humour to console him for what he is.
- **Francis Bacon**: *Essays*, 1625.

3,827. A person without a sense of humour is like a wagon without springs – jolted by every pebble on the road.
- **Henry Ward Beecher**.

3,828. Total absence of humour renders life impossible.
- **Colette**: *Chance Acquaintances*, 1951.

3,829. Whenever I indulge my sense of humour, it gets me into trouble
- **Calvin Coolidge**: *20,000 Quips and Quotes* by Evan Esar, 1968.

3,830. A keen sense of humour helps us to overcome the unbecoming, understand the unconventional, tolerate the unpleasant, overcome the unexpected, and outlast the unbearable.
- **Billy Graham**: *Reader's Digest, March, 1993*.

3,831. If you could choose one characteristic that would get you through life, choose a sense of humour.
- **Jennifer James**.

3,832. Common sense and a sense of humour are the same thing, moving at different speeds. A sense of humour is just common sense, dancing.
- **William James:** quoted in *Geary's Guide to the World's Great Aphorists* by James Geary.

3,833. There are two insults which no human being will endure; the assertion that he hasn't a sense of humour. And the doubly impertinent assertion that he has never known trouble.
- **Sinclair Lewis:** *Main Street*, 1920.

3,834. A sense of humour is a major defence against minor troubles.
- **Mignon McLaughlan:** *The Second Neurotic's Notebook*, 1966.

3,835. I can imagine no more comfortable frame of mind for the conduct of life than a humorous resignation.
- **Somerset Maugham:** *A Writer's Notebook*, 1941.

3,836. Two consequences of a sense of humour contribute to the restoration of physical health. The first is the ability to laugh at yourself, and the other is the act of laughter itself. Humour is the miracle drug with no side effects.
- **Laurence J. Peter:** *The Laughter Prescription*, 1982.

3,837. A well developed sense of humour is the pole that adds balance to your steps as you walk the tightrope of life.
- **William Ward:** *Magazine, June, 2007*.

SEX

3,838. The battle of the sexes will never be won by either side – there's too much fraternizing with the enemy.
- ***anon.***

3,839. The nocturnal life / Of a man and his wife / This pattern quite often assumes / First two in a bed, / Then each in a bed, / Then sleeping in separate rooms.
- **Richard Armour:** *Sequence* in *An Armoury of Light Verse*, 1942.

3,840. The best after dinner speaker I have ever heard – Sir John Maude, Master of University College, Oxford... told us of the Luncheon Club where members' names were taken out of one receptacle, and the subject of the speech for the following week out of another. The member chosen on one occasion found he had to speak on Yachting – about which he knew very little. His wife helped him prepare a very poor paper, which in the event he discarded in favour of an impromptu talk on the subject of sex. He didn't tell his wife, who later heard complimentary things about the talk. She showed her astonishment by proclaiming her husband's near total lack of experience - occasions there had been but two: on the first he was violently sick, and on the second, his hat blew off!
- **Christopher Hamel Cooke:** quoted in *A Time to Laugh*, 1993.

3,841. The shortest speech ever made was on the subject of sex. The speaker stood up and said. "Ladies and Gentlemen it gives me great pleasure," and sat down again.
- ***ibid.***

3,842. Most of the so-called sexual incompatability in marriage springs from the delusion that sex is an *activity*, when it is primarily a *relationship*. If the relationship is faulty, the activity cannot long be self-sustaining, or truly satisfactory.
- **Sydney J. Harris:** *Pieces of Eight*, 1975.

3,843. Marriage has many pains, but celibacy has no pleassures.
- **Samuel Johnson:** *The History of Rasselas, Prince of Abyssinia,* 1769.

3,844. Contraceptives should be used on all conveivable occasions.
- **Spike Milligan:** *The Last Goon Show,* broadcast on 5th October, 1972.

3,845. A crusader's wife slipped from the garrison and had an affair with a Saracen/ She was not oversexed,/ Or jealous or vexed,/ She just wanted to make a comparison.
- **Ogden Nash:** *How Pleasant to Ape Mr Lear* in *There's Always Another. Windmill,* 1968.

3,846. Woman wants monogamy; / Man delights in novelty; / Love is woman's moon and sun; / Man has others forms of fun. / Woman lives but in her lord; / Count to ten, and man is bored. /
With this the gist and sum of it, / What earthly good will come of it?
- **Dorothy Parker:** *General Review of the Sex Situation.*

3,847. It's the only game that is never called off on account of darkness.
- **Laurence J. Peter:** *Quotations For Our Time,* 1977.

3,848. There is no greater or keener pleasure than that of bodily love – and which is more irrational.
- **Plato:** *The Republic,* **circa** 360 BC.

3,849. Civilized people cannot fully satisfy their sexual instinct without love.
- **Bertrand Russell:** *Marriage and Morals,* 1929.

3,850. Sex is a conversation carried on by other means. If you get on well out of bed, half the problems of the bed are solved.
- **Sir Peter Ustinov.**

3,851. Of children, as of procreation – the pleasure momentary, the posture ridiculous, the expense damnable.
- **Evelyn Waugh:** *in a letter to Nancy Mitford, dated 5th May, 1954,* quoted in *The Letters of Evelyn Waugh,* edited by Mark Amory, 1982.

SILENCE

3,852. Since long I've held silence a remedy for harm.
- **Aeschylus:** *Agamemnon* , 5th century BC.

3,853. Truth is not only violated by falsehood; it may be equally outraged by silence.
- **Henri Frederic Amiel:** *Journal Intime*, 1882.

3,854. The fact that silence is golden may explain why there is so little of it.
- *anon*.

3,855. The best time for you to hold your tongue is the time you feel you must say something or burst.
- **Josh Billings**.

3,856. Silence, when nothing need be said, is the eloquence of discretion.
- **Christian Nestell Bovee**.

3,857. Silences have a climax, when you have got to speak.
- **Elizabeth Bowen:** *The House in Paris*, 1935.

3,858. It is tact that is golden, not silence.
- **Samuel Butler:** *Notebooks*, 1912.

3,859. When you have nothing to say, say nothing.
- **Charles Caleb Colton:** *Lacon,* or *Many Things in Few Words*, 1826, edited by George J. Barbour, 2001.

3,860. As you go through life you are going to have many opportunities to keep your mouth shut. Take advantage of all of them.
- **James Dent:** *The Charleston Gazette.*

3,861. In silence a man can most readily preserve his integrity.
- **Meister Eckhart**.

3,862. Silence is safer than speech.
- **Epictetus:** *The Enchiridion.* 1st century BC.

3,863. Silence is not always a sign of wisdom, but babbling is ever a mark of folly.
- **Benjamin Franklin:** *Poor Richard's Almanack.*

3,864. Silence gives consent.
- **Oliver Goldsmith:** *The Good-Natured Man,* 1768.
CP: Charles Buxton's comment:"Silence is sometimes the severest criticism."

3,865. Silence, like a poultice, comes to heal the blows of sound.
- **Oliver Wendell Holmes:** *The Music Grinders* in *The Yale Book of American Verse* edited by Thomas R. Lounsbury, 1912.

3,866. It is easier not to speak a word at all than to speak more words than we should.
- **Thomas a Kempis:** *The Imitation of Christ, **circa** 1418.*

3,867. We will have to repent in this generation not merely for the vitriolic words and actions of the bad people, but for the appalling silence of the good people.
- **Martin Luther King:** *Why We Can't Wait,* 1964.

3,868. With the people I love most I can sit in silence indefinitely. We need both for our full development - the joy of the sense of sound, and the equally great joy of it's absence.
- **Madeleine L'Engle:** *A Circle of Quiet,* 1972.

3,869. Better to remain silent and be thought a fool than to speak out and remove all doubt.
- **Abraham Lincoln:** *The Wit and Wisdom of Abraham Lincoln* edited by Alex Ayres, 1992.

3,870. Silence is not only golden, it's seldom misquoted.
- **Bob Monkhouse:** *Just Say a Few Words,* 1988.

3,871. To save face, keep the lower half shut.
- *ibid.*

3,872. It is wise to be silent when occasion requires.
- **Plutarch:** *Matters Relating to Customs: On The Training of Children.*

3,873. Speech is silver, silence is golden.
- *German Proverb*.

3,874. If a word is worth one shekel, silence is worth two.
- *Hebrew Proverb*.

3,875. The cruellest lies are often told in silence. A man may have sat in a room for hours and not opened his mouth, and yet come out of that room a disloyal friend.
- **Robert Louis Stevenson:** *Virginibus Puerisque*, 1881.

3,876. Well-timed silence hath more eloquence than speech.
- **Martin Farquhar Tupper:** *Proverbial Philosophy*, 1838 - 1849

3,877. I have often regretted my speech, never my silence.
- **Publilius Syrus**.

3,878. To sin by silence, when we should protest, makes cowards out of men.
- **Ella Wheeler Wilcox:** *Protest* in *Poems of Problems*, 1914.

SLEEP

3,879. Next to a beautiful woman, sleep is the most wonderful thing in the world.
- ***anon:*** *20,000 Quips and Quotes* by Evan Esar, 1968.

3,880. The amount of sleep required by the average person is about half an hour more.
- ***anon. ibid.***

3,881. When at night you cannot sleep, talk to the Shepherd and stop counting sheep.
- ***anon.***

3,882. Sleep is a highly beneficial activity, yet, for some reason, many people frown on sleeping, especially during working hours.
- **Dave Barry:** *Dave Barry Turns Fifty*, 1998.

3,883. Blessed be the man who first invented sleep - a cloak to cover all human thoughts.
- **Miguel de Cervantes:** *Don Quixote*, 1605 and 1615.

3,884. While shepherds watch their flocks by night
 They sometimes fall asleep,
 That's one of the big dangers when
 Your job is counting sheep.
- **Richard Edwards:** *While Shepherds Watch* in *Nonsense Christmas Rhymes*, 2002.

3,885. Everything gets easier with practice – except getting up in the morning.
- **Leopold Fechtner:** *5,000 One-And-Two-Line Jokes*, 1979.

3,886. The best way to drive your wife crazy is to smile in your sleep.
- ***ibid.***

3,887. Sleeping at the wheel is a good way to keep from growing old.
- ***ibid***.

3,888. Sleep, rest of nature... at whose presence care disappears; who soothes hearts wearied with daily employment, and makes them strong again for labour.
- **Ovid:** *Metamorphoses, **circa** 2* AD.

3,889. All men whilst they are awake are in one common world; but each of them, when he is asleep, is in a world of his own.
 - **Plutarch:** *Moralia,* 2nd century AD

3,890. O sleep. O gentle sleep! Nature's soft nurse.
- **William Shakespeare:** *Henry 1V, Part One,* 1600.

3,891. Tir'd nature's sweet Restorer, balmy *sleep*!
- **Edward Young:** *Night Thoughts,* 1742 – 1745.

SMILES

3,892. Most smiles are started by another smile.
- *anon*.

3,893. Be your own florist – wreathe your face in smiles.
- *anon*.

3.894. We all learn from experience; no man wakes up his second baby just to see it smile.
- *anon: 20,000 Quips and Quotes* by Evan Esar, 1968.

3,895. To make a smile come, so they say, / Brings thirteen muscles into play; / While if you want a frown to thrive, / You've got to work up sixty-five.
- *anon: Jokes, Quotes and One-Liners, Volume One* by Herbert V. Prochnow and Herbert V. Prochnow Jr, 1983.

3,896. Some men smile in the evening, / Some men smile at dawn. / But the man worthwhile is the man who can smile / When his two front teeth are gone.
- *anon, ibid*.

3,897. Your good humour must be real, not simulated. Let your smiles come from the heart and they will become contagious.
- **Hugh B. Brown:** *An Abundant Life: The Memoirs of Hugh B. Brown* by E.B.Firmage, 1999.

3,898. Today, give a stranger one of your smiles, it might be the only sunshine he sees all day.
- **H. Jackson Brown Jr:** *P.S. I Love You*, 1990.

3,899. Life is made up, not of great sacrifices or duties, but of little things, in which smiles and kindnesses, and small obligations, given habitually, are what win and preserve the heart and secure comfort.
- **Sir Humphry Davy:** *Braude's Handbook of Stories for Toastmasters and Speakers* by Jacob M. Braude, 1979.

3,900. A smile is a curve that sets everything straight.
- **Phyllis Diller**.

3,901. A smile... is our natural expression of welcome to anything we like, and a happy laugh is only a more thorough going smile.
- **Max Eastman:** *Enjoyment of Laughter*, 1937.

3.902. You're never fully dressed without a smile.
- Part of the chorus of a song from the **1982 musical film**: *Annie*, based on the Little Orphan Annie comic strip.

3,903. They gave each other a smile with a future in it.
- **Ring Lardner:** *The Treasury of Humorous Quotations* edited by Evan Esar, 1955.

3,904. The teeth are smiling, but is the heart?
- *African Proverb*.

3,905. What sunshine is to the flowers, smiles are to humanity. These are but trifles, to be sure; but scattered along life's pathway, the good they do is inconceivable.
- *Anonymous Proverb:* first quoted in *Eliza Cook's Journal, Volume 2*. 1854 NB In recent years this has been incorrectly attributed to Joseph Addison.

3,906. I've learned that a smile is an inexpensive way to improve your looks.
- **Andy Rooney:** *CBS News Program: 60 Minutes*.

3,907. One may smile, and smile, and be a villain.
- **William Shakespeare:** *Hamlet, Act 1, Sc 5*, 1601.

3,908. Wrinkles should merely indicate where smiles have been.
- **Mark Twain:** *Following the Equator*, 1897.

SMOKING

3,909. Asthma doesn't seem to bother me any more unless I'm around cigars or dogs. The thing that would bother me most would be a dog smoking a cigar.
- **Steve Allen**.

3,910. Cigarettes are killers that travel in packs.
- *anon*.

3,911. I read in the *Reader's Digest* that cigarettes are bad for you. So I had to give up reading the *Reader's Digest*.
- *anon: The Penguin Dictionary of Modern Humorous Quotations* edited by Fred Metcalf, 1987.

3,912. People who give up smoking have the same problem as the newcomer in the nudist camp - they don't know what to do with their hands.
- *anon: Joey Adam's Encyclopaedia of Humour*, 1969.

3,913. WARNING: If you smoke in bed you could make an ash of yourself.
- *anon*.

3,914. "I don't care if you burn."
- **Sarah Bernhard** is reputed to have said this in reply to Oscar Wilde when he asked her, "Do you mind if I smoke?"

3,915. Smokers who blow smoke in my face will learn first hand (within minutes actually) how injurious smoking can be to their health.
- **Erma Bombeck:** *Aunt Erma's Cope Book*, 1985.

3,916. On one wall I saw written, "Smoking stunts your growth." Below it, about two feet off the groujnd, someone had written, "Now he tells me."
- **Tommuy Cooper:** *Just Like That*, 1975.

3,917. If you resolve to give up smoking, drinking and loving, you don't actually live longer; it just seems longer
- **Clement Freud:** *The Observer, December, 1964.*

3,918. Tobacco is a dirty weed, I like it.
It satisfies no normal need, I like it.
It makes you thin, it makes you lean,
It takes your hair right off your bean.
It's the worst darn stuff I've ever seen, I like it.
- **Graham Lee Hemminger:** *Froth Magazine, November, 1915.* NB *Froth Magazine* was the humour magazine published by the students at the Pennsylvania State University.

3,919. Thank heaven, I have given up smoking again! God! I feel fit. Homicidal but fit. A different man. Irritable, moody, depressed, rude, nervy, perhaps; but the lungs are fine.
- **Sir A. P. Herbert**..

3,920. What a weird thing smoking is and I can't stop it. I feel cosy, have a sense of well-being when I'm smoking, poisoning myself, killing myself slowly. Not slowly maybe. I have all kinds of pains I don't want to know about... But when I don't smoke, I scarcely feel as if I'm living. I don't feel I'm living unless I'm killing myself.
- **Russell Hoban:** *Turtle Diary,* 1975.

3,921. A custom loathsome to the eye, hateful to the nose, harmful to the brain, dangerous to the lungs, and in the black, stinking fume thereof nearest resembling the horrible stygian smoke of the pit that is bottomless.
- **King James 1 of England**, **V1 of Scotland:** *A Counterblast to Tobacco.*

3,922. It is now proved beyond doubt that smoking is one of the leading causes of statistics.
- **Fletcher Knebel:** *Reader's Digest, December, 1961.*

3.923. I'm glad I don't have to explain to a man from Mars why each day I set fire to dozens of little pieces of paper, and then put them in my mouth.
- **Mignon McLaughlin:** *The Second Neurotic's Notebook,* 1966.

3,924. Smoking helps you lose weight – one lung at a time.
- **MAD Magazine:** *The Half-Wit and Wisdom of Alfred E. Neuman,* 1997.

3,925. Much smoking kills live men and cures dead swine.
- **George D. Prentice**.

3,926. A chap in an Edinburgh bar having an after-work pint asked his colleagues: "Can I have a fag?" His mate with the ciggies quite reasonably pointed out to the chap that he had in fact just recently given up smoking. "Well, I'm in the process of quitting. I'm in the middle of phase one right now." When his pal asked what phase one was, he replied: "I've stopped buying."
- **Tom Shields:** *Tom Shields Takes The Fifth* with Ken Smith, 2002.

3,927. We all know that tobacco is extremely addictive, and that tobacco companies used to add chemicals to make their cigarettes even more addictive, until they got nailed for it, and that for several generations - again, until they got busted for it- the big tobacco companies aimed their marketing and advertising at kids and young people.
- **Morgan Spurlock:** *Don't Eat This Book: Fast Food and the Supersizing of America,* 2005.

3,928. Big tobacco companies spent billions of dollars to get people hooked as early as they could, and to have them "brand-loyal" slaves for the rest of their unnaturally shortened lives. Cigarettes were cool, cigarettes were hip, cigarettes were sexy. Smoking made you look like a cowboy or a movie starlet. And it worked... The change began in 1964, when the first surgeon general's warning about smoking and cancer scared the bejesus out of everybody.
- *ibid*.

3,929. I smoked my first cigarette and kissed my first women on the same day. I have never had time for tobacco since.
- **Arturo Toscanini:** *The Observer, 30th June, 1946,* quoted in *The Oxford Dictionary of Thematic Quotations* edited by Susan Ratcliffe, 2000.

3,930. There are some circles in America where it seems to be more socially acceptable to carry a hand-gun than a packet of cigarettes.
- **Katherine Whitehorn:** *The Observer, 30th October, 1988.*

SOLITUDE

3,931 Then stirs the feeling infinite, so felt in solitude, where we are least alone.
- **Lord Byron:** *Childe Harold's Pilgrimage, Canto 3, Stanza 90*, 1818.

3,932. I lived in that solitude which is painful in youth, but delicious in maturity.
- **Albert Einstein:** *The New Quotable Einstein* collected and edited by Alice Calaprice, 2005.

3,933. Better be alone than in bad company.
- **Thomas Fuller:** *Gnomologia, Adages and Proverbs*, 1732.

3,934. Conversation enriches the understanding, but solitude is the school of genius.
- **Edward Gibbon:** *Volume 5* of *The History of the Decline and Fall of the Roman Empire*, 1788.

3,935. Cultivate regular periods of silence and meditation. The best time to build judgement is in solitude, when you can think out things for yourself without the probability of interruption.
- **Grenville Kleiser**.

3,936. A solitude is the audience-chamber of God.
- **Walter Savage Landor:** *Imaginary Conversations and Poems*, 1829.

3.937. Solitude is as needful to the imagination as society is wholesome for the character.
 - **James Russell Lowel:** *Among My Books*, 1870.

3,938. Solitude terrifies the soul at twenty.
- **Moliere:** *The Misanthrope and Other Plays*, 1666.

3.939. We must reserve a back shop all our own entirely free, in which to establish our real liberty and our principle retreat and solitude.
 - **Michel Montaigne:** *Essays,* 1580.

3,940. Solitude is pleasant. Loneliness is not.
 - **Anna Neagle**.

3,941. I find it wholesome to be alone the greater part of the time. To live in company, even with the best, is soon wearisome and dissipating. I love to be alone. I never found the companion that was as companionable as solitude.
- **Henry David Thoreau:** *Walden; or, Life in the Woods,* 1854.

3,942. Our language has wisely sensed the two sides of being alone. It has created the word "loneliness" to express the pain of being alone. And it has created the word "solitude" to express the glory of being alone.
- **Paul Tillich:** *The Eternal Now.* 1997.

3,943. Only in solitude do we find ourselves.
- **Miguel De Unanumo:** *Essays and Soliloquijes,* 1924.

3,944. Loneliness is the ultimate poverty.
- **Abigail Van Buren:** *Dear Abby Column* quoted in *The Merriam-Webster Dictionary of Quotations, 1992.*

SPEAKERS

3,945. Accustomed as I am to public speaking, I know the futility of it.
- **Franklin Pierce Adams:** *The Treasury of Humorous Quotations* edited by Evan Esar, 1955.

3,946. Speakers ought never to forget the "Kiss Principle" – Keep It Simple, Stupid!
- *anon.*

3,947. I love a finished speaker, I really, truly do./ I don't mean one who's polished, / I just mean one whose through.
- **Richard Armour**.

3,948. I do not object to people looking at their watches when I am speaking. But I strongly object when they start shaking them to make certain they are still going.
- **Lord Birkett:** *The Observer, 30ᵗʰ October, 1960.*

3,949. Some speakers are like some gamblers - they don't have sense enough to quit while they're ahead.
- **Jacob M. Braude:** *Braude's Treasury of Wit and Humour for all Occasions* revised by Glenn Van Ekeren, 1991.

3,950. It is a very sad thing to have neither wisdom enough to speak well, nor sense enough to be silent.
- **Jean de LaBruyere:** *The Morals and Manners of the Seventeenth Century* translated by Helen Stott, 1890.

3,951. A good story teller is a person who has a good memory and hopes other people haven't.
- **Irvin S. Cobb:** *The Treasury of Humorous Quotations* edited by Evan Esar, 1955.

3,952. When you have nothing to say, say nothing.
- **Charles Caleb Colton:** *Lacon; or Many Things in Few Words,* 1826 edited by George J. Barbour, 2001

3,953. He adorned whatever subject he... spoke... upon by the most splendid eloquence.
- **Earl of Chesterfield:** commenting on his contemporary, Viscount Bolinbroke.

3,954. O speaker, O speaker,
Enough self-delusion -
What the crowd yearns to hear,
Are the words, "in conclusion."
- **Dale Dauten**.

3,955. A sophisticated rhetorician, inebriated with the exuberance of his own verbosity.
- **Benjamin Disraeli, 1ˢᵗ Earl of Beaconsfield:** *in a speech, 1828.* NB Disraeli was here referring to William Gladstone.

3,956. All the great speakers were bad speakers at first.
- **Ralph Waldo Emerson:** *The Conduct of Life.* 1860.

3,957. The more you say, the less people remember. The fewer the words, the greater the profit.
- **Francois Fenelon**.

3,958. Most speakers speak ten minutes too long
- **James C. Humes**.

3,959. The talkative man speaks from his mouth, the eloquent man speaks from the heart.
- **Joseph Joubert**.

3,960. The people only understand what they can feel; the only orators that affect them are those who move them.
- **Alphonse de Lamartine**.

3,961. I don't like to hear cut-and-dried sermons, no, when I hear a man preach, I like to see him act as if he was fighting bees.
- **Abraham Lincoln:** *The Words Lincoln Lived By,* by Gene Griessman, 1998.

3,962. He's a wonderful talker who has the art of telling you nothing in a great harangue
- **Moliere:** *Le Misanthrope,* 1666.

3,963. Every speaker has a mouth;
An arrangement rather neat.
Sometimes it's filled with wisdom;
Sometimes it's filled with feet.
- **Robert Orben**.

3,964. Speak little and to the purpose, and you will pass for somebody.
- *English Proverb*.

3,965. The tongue is to be feared more than the sword.
- *Japanese Proverb*

3,966. As it is the characteristic of great wits to say much in few words, so it is of small wits to talk much and say nothing.
- **Francois, Duc de la Rouchefoucauld:** *Maxims,* 1665.

3,967. People who know little are usually great talkers, while men who know much say little.
- **Jean Jacques Rousseau:** *Emile,* 1762.

3,968. Whatever your grade or position, if you know when and how to speak, and when to remain silent, your chances of real success are proportionately increased.
- **Ralph C. Smedley**.

3,969. The unprepared speaker has a right to be afraid.
- *ibid.*

3,970. Whales get killed only when they spout
- **Denis Thatcher:** *The Oxford Dictionary of Humorous Quotations, Second Edition,* edited by Ned Sherrin, 2005.

3,971. The man who can speak acceptably is usually given credit for an ability out of all proportion to what he really possesses.
- **Lowell Thomas:** *Quotable Business,* edited by Louis E. Boone.

3.972. Men of few words are the best men.
- **William Shakespeare:** *Henry V ,* 1599.

3,973. I disapprove of what you say, but I will defend to the death your right to say it.
- **Voltaire**, *attributed.*

SPEECHES AND SPEECHMAKING

3,974. Speeches are like babies - easy to conceive, but hard to deliver.
- **Joey Adams:** *Joey Adam's Encyclopedia of Humour*, 1968.

3,975. Of course it's very easy to be witty tomorrow, after you get a chance to do some research and rehearse your ad libs.
- *ibid*.

3,976. A good speech should have an attention riveting beginning and a climactic ending, and these should be as close together as possible.
- *anon*.

3,977. Out of the haze when one is dozing
 Comes the speaker's phrase, "And now, in closing."
- **Richard Armour:** *Happy Ending* in *An Armoury of Light Verse*, 1964.

3,978. Your speech should always be pleasant and interesting.
- **The Bible:** *Colossians* 4: 6, *Good News Bible*.

3,979. "Begin at the beginning," the King said, gravely, "and go on till you come to the end, then stop."
- **Lewis Carroll:** *Alice's Adventures in Wonderland*,1865.

3,980. A woman, upon her husband's return from a meeting one night asked, "How was your speech this evening?" "Which one?" he asked, "The one I was going to give, the one I did give, or the one I delivered so brilliantly on the way home in the car?"
- **Irvin S. Cobb:** *The Comic Encyclopedia*, 1978.

3,981. No speech can be entirely bad if it is short enough.
- *ibid*.

3,982. A moment of eloquence enthrals us, an hour's worth leaves us stupefied.
- **Mason Cooley**, *City Aphorisms, Second Selection*, 1985.

3,983. As a vessel is known by the sound, whether it be cracked or not; so men are proved by their speeches, whether they be wise or foolish.
- **Demosthenes**.

3,984. Blessed is the man who having nothing to say, abstains from giving wordy evidence of the fact.
 - **George Eliot**.

3,985. If you want to be seen, stand up. If you want to be heard, speak up. If you want to be praised, shut up.
- **Evan Esar:** *The Comic Encyclopedia,* 1978.

3,986. One thing I can guarantee you. You may not be a great deal wiser from my talk today, but you will be a great deal older.
- **Melvin Helitzer:** *Dick Enberg's Humorous Quotes For All Occasions,* 2000.

3,987. If you haven't struck oil in your first three minutes, stop boring!
- **Sir George Jessel:** *The Laugh's On Me* by Bennett Cerf, 1963.

3,988. Don't be nervous, / Don't be shy, /
 Clear your throat, / Straighten your tie. /
 Look your audience / In the eye, /
 Then smile with confidence / As you zip up your fly.
 - **Bruce Lansky:** *Before You Make a Speech* in *Lighten Up! Bk 2,* 1999.

3,989. I warned the Chairman that I wouldn't have time to prepare a speech and he told me to say something off the top of my head, so, here's a short talk on dandruff.
- **Bob Monkhouse:** *Just Say A Few Words,* 1988.

3,990. The unluckiest insolvent in the world is the man whose expenditure of speech is too great for his income of ideas.
- **Christopher Morley:** *Inward Ho!: Aphorisms Mainly on Literature,* 1923.

3,991. If you keep your mouth shut you will never put your foot in it.
- **Austin O'Malley**.

3,992. And 'tis remarkable that they
 Talk most who have least to say.
 - **Matthew Prior:** *Alma, or The Progress of the Mind,* 1718.

3,993. True eloquence consists in saying all that is necessary, and nothing but what is necessary.
   - **Francois, Duc de la Rochefoucauld:** *Maxims,* 1665.

3,994. My father gave me these hints on speech-making: "Be sincere... be brief ... be seated."
- **James Roosevelt**.

3,995. When you don't know what you're talking about it's hard to know when you're finished.
- **Tommy Smothers:** *Reader's Digest Quotable Quotes,* 2005.

SUCCESS

3,996. Success produces success, just as money produces money.
- **Diane Ackerman**.

3,997. Success! It's found in the soul of you,
And not in the realm of luck!
The world will furnish the work to do,
But you must provide the pluck.
You can do whatever you think you can,
It's all in the way you view it.
It's all in the start you make, young man;
You must feel that you're going to do it.
- **Franklin P. Adams**: *How Do You Tackle Your Work*.

3,998. If truth be known, most successes are built on a multitude of failures.
- *anon*

3,999. It is possible to fail in many ways; while to succeed is possible only in one.
- **Aristotle:** *Nicomachean Ethics*, 4th century BC.

4,000. Before anything else, preparation is the key to success.
- **Alexander Graham Bell**.

4,001. All that is necessary to break the spell of inertia and frustration is this: act as if it were impossible to fail.
- **Dorothea Brande**.

4,002. The person interested in success has to learn to view failure as a healthy, inevitable part of the process of getting to the top.
- **Joyce Brother:** *Business Class: Etiquette Essentials for Success at Work* by Jacqueline Whitmore, 2005.

4,003. Experience shows that success is due less to ability than to zeal. The winner is he who gives himself to his work body and soul.
- **Charles Buxton**.

4,004. Believe that you will succeed and you will.
- **Dale Carnegie:** *How to Win Friends and Influence People*, 1936.

4,005. My success just evolved from working hard at the business at hand each day.
- **Johnny Carson**.

4,006. There is no down side to winning. It feels forever fabulous.
- **Pat Conway:** *My Losing Season*, 2002

4,007. In order to succeed, your desire for success should be greater than your fear of failure.
- **Bill Cosby**.

4.008. Be persevering and keep digging. This is one of the most important rules. I've seen people within inches of success suddenly quit. By digging and digging you can turn failure into success. Don't give up.
- **E. Joseph Cossman:** *How I Made $1,000,000 in Mail Order*, 1964.

4,009. I am doomed to an eternity of compulsive work. No set goal achieved satisfies. Success only breeds a new goal.
- **Bette Davis:** *The Lonely Life*. 1962

4,010. The secret of success is constancy of purpose.
- **Benjamin Disraeli:** *in a speech, 24th June, 1872*.

4,011. Nothing succeeds like success.
- **Alexandre Dumas:** *Storming the Bastille or Six Years Later*, 1853. NB This was the third novel in the Marie Antoinette romances.

4,012. The first requisite for success is to develop the ability to focus and apply your mental and physical energies to the problem at hand- without growing weary. Because such thinking is often difficult, there seems to be no limit to which some people will go to avoid the effort and labour that is associated with it.
- **Thomas Edison**.

4,013. We succeed only as we identify in life... a single overriding objective, and make all other considerations bend to that one objective.
- **Dwight D. Eisenhower:** *in a speech, 2nd April, 1957.*

4,014. Along with success comes a reputation for wisdom.
- **Euripides:** *Hippolytus,* **circa** 428 BC.

4,015. Success is when your name is in everything but the telephone directory.
- **Sam Ewing:** *The Wall Street Journal, 11th April, 1997.*

4,016. Success seems to be largely a matter of hanging on after others have let go.
- **William Feather.**

4,017. History has demonstrated that the most notable winners usually encountered heartbreaking obstacles before they triumphed. They won because they refused to become discouraged by their defeats.
- **B. C. Forbes.**

4,018. How you start is important, but it is how you finish that counts. In the race forward speed is less important than stamina. The sticker outlasts the sprinter.
B.C. Forbes: *Readers' Digest, January, 1991.*

4,019. Madame Curie didn't stumble upon radium by accident. She searched and experimented and sweated and suffered for years before she found it. Success rarely is an accident.
- **B.C. Forbes.**

4,020. It is failure that is easy, success is always hard.
- **Henry Ford:** *My Life and Work: an Autobiography of Henry Ford,* in collaboration with Samuel Crowther, 1922.

4,021. Formula for success: rise early, work hard, strike oil.
- **J. Paul Getty.**

4,022. Success Begins in the Mind.
- **Jeff Keller:** title of Part One of *Attitude is Everything: Change Your Attitude and You Change Your Life,* 1999.

4,023. The only place success comes before work is in the dictionary.
- **Donald M. Kendall.**

4,024. I think success has no rules. But you can learn a lot from failure
- **Jean Kerr:** quoted in the satirical play :*Mary, Mary,* 1961.
.

4,025. The Lord gave us two ends – one to sit on and the other to think with. Success depends on which one you use the most.
- **Ann Landers**.

4,026. Successful people are successful because they are willing to do things that unsuccessful people are not willing to do.
- **Michael Le Boeuf:** *Insight – the lifestyle and leisure magazine, Dec,1986.*

4,027. Always bear in mind that your own resolution to succeed is more important than any other one thing.
- **Abraham Lincoln:** *The Words Lincoln Lived By* by Gene Griessman, 1998.

4,028. Remove failure as an option and your chances for success become infinitely better.
- **Joan Lunden:** *Answer to a question in a TV chat show held on 22nd October, 2,000.*

4,029. If you want to succeed in life you must pick three bones to carry with you at all times – a wish bone, a back bone, and a funny bone.
- **Reba McIntire**.

4,030. There is only one success... to be able to spend your life in your own way.
- **Christopher Morley:** *Where the Blue Begins,* 1922.

4,031. No matter how much you've done or how successful you've been, there's always more to do, always more to learn, and always more to achieve.
- **Barack Obama:** *in a speech, 2009.*

4,032. What exactly is success? For me it is to be found not in applause, but in the satisfaction of feeling that one is realizing one's idea.
- **Anna Pavlova:** *Pavlova: A Biography,* edited by A. H. Franks, 1979.

4,033. People become really quite remarkable when they start thinking that they can do things. When they believe in themselves they have the first secret of success.
- **Norman Vincent Peale:** *Positive Thinking Every Day: An Inspiration for Each Day of the Year,* 1993.

4,034. Success is a ladder you cannot climb with your hands in your pocket.
- *American Proverb*.

4,035. He who would climb the ladder must begin at the bottom.
- *English Proverb*.

4,036. Success makes a fool seem wise
- *English Proverb*.

4,037. If you want to be successful it's just this simple: Know what you are doing. Love what you are doing. And believe it what you are doing.
- **Will Rogers**.

4,038. Success is like winning the lottery or getting killed in a car crash. It always happens to somebody else.
- **Allan Sherman**: *A Gift of Laughter: The Autobiography of Allan Sherman*, 1965.

4,039. He has achieved success who has lived well, laughed often, and loved much.
- **Bessie Anderson Stanley**: *Success*. NB This poem appeared in *The Lincoln Sentinel*, November, 1905, as the prize winning entry in a contest for the best essay on "What Constitutes Success?"

4,040. What is success? I think it is a mixture of having a flair for the thing that you are doing, knowing that it is not enough, that you have got to have hard work and a certain sense of purpose.
- **Baroness Thatcher of Kesteven**: *Parade Magazine, July, 1986*.

TALENT

4,041. Talent isn't genius, and no amount of energy can make it so. I want to be great or nothing.
- Amy March's sentiments in **Louisa Alcott's** novel *Little Women*, 1869.

4,042. Doing easily what others find difficult is talent; doing what is impossible for talent is genius.
- **Henri Frederic Amiel:** *Journal Intime*, 1882.

4,043. Work while you have the light. You are responsible for the talent that has been entrusted to you.
- *ibid*.

4,044. Talent is like electricity. We don't understand electricity, (but) we use it.
- **Maya Angelou:** *Black Women Writers at Work*, by Claudia Tate, 1985.

4,045. Talent is like a faucet, while it is open, you have to write.
- **Jean Anouilh:** *New York Times, October, 1960*.

4,046. Those who are blessed with the most talent don't necessarily outperform everyone else. It's the people with follow-through who excel.
- **Mary Kay Ash**.

4.047. There are two kinds of talent, man-made talent and God-given talent. With man-made talent you have to work very hard. With God-given talent, you just touch it up once in a while.
- **Pearl Bailey:** *Newsweek, 4th December, 1967*.

4,048. When I stand before God at the end of my life, I would hope that I would not have a single bit of talent left, and could say, "I used everything you gave me."
- **Erma Bombeck**.

4,049. Hide not your talents, they for use were made. What's a sun-dial in the shade?
- **Benjamin Franklin**.

4,050. Great ability develops and reveals itself increasingly with every new assignment.
- **Baltasar Gracian**.

4,051. My gratitude and love to the higher power who gave me talent and to all those along my path who helped nourish it.
- The Ascription in **Allen Klein's** book *The Love & Kisses Quote Book*, 2006.

4,052. Use those talents you have...Take this tip from nature: The woods would be a very silent place if no birds sang except those who sang best.
- **Bernard Meltzer**.

4,053. No one can arrive from being talented alone. God gives talent, work transforms talent into genius.
- **Anna Pavlova:** *Pavlova* by A. H. Franks, 1978.

4,054. Work to make yourself remarkable by some talent or other.
- **Seneca**.

4,055. A great deal of talent is lost to the world for the want of a little courage. Every day sends to their graves a number of obscure men who have only remained obscure because their timidity has prevented them from making a first effort.
- **Sydney Smith:** *Elementary Sketches of Moral Philosophy*, 1850.

TAXES

4,056. An income tax form is like a laundry list – either way you lose your shirt.
- **Fred Allen:** *Quotable Business,* by Louis E. Boone, 1999.

4,057. Don't steal. The government hates competition.
- **American car bumper sticker**.

4,058. The following quotations are **Anonymous** statements about taxes:
A. A fine is a tax for doing wrong. A tax is a fine for doing something right.
B. Death and taxes may be certain, but we don't have to die every year.
C. In Britain today it takes more brains to figure out your tax than it does to earn the money to pay it.
D. Earning money would be a pleasure- if it wasn't so taxing.
E. I believe we should all pay our tax bill with a smile. I tried – but they wanted cash.
F. The government regards a citizen as one who has what it takes.
G. It has reached a point where taxes are a form of capital punishment
H. One of the great blessings about living in a democracy is that we have complete control over how we pay our taxes – cash, cheque or postal order.

4,059. Taxes are going up so fast that the government is likely to price itself right out of the market.
- **Dan Bennett:** *Quotations for Our Time,* by Laurence J. Peter

4,060. Taxation is based on supply and demand. We supply what the government demands.
- **Milton Berle:** *Milton Berle's Private Joke File,* 1989.

4,061. My son thinks "damn" and "taxes" are one word.
- *ibid*

4,062. Jesus said to them. "Give to Caesar what is Caesar's and to God what is God's."
- **The Bible:** *Mark 12: 17, NIV*.

4,063. A tax expert is anyone who can read five pages of the tax law without crying or ten pages without laughing.
- **James H. Borin**.

4,064. The collection of any taxes which are not absolutely required, which do not beyond reasonable doubt contribute to the public welfare, is only a species of legalized larceny.
- **Calvin Coolidge:** *Inaugural Address, 1923*.

4.065. The power to tax is the power to destroy. A government which lays taxes on the people not required by urgent public necessity and sound public policy is not a protector of liberty, but an instrument of tyranny.
- **Calvin Coolidge:** *Wit and Wisdom of the American Presidents: A Book of Quotations* edited by Joslyn Pine, 2001.

4,066. The art of taxation consists in so plucking the goose as to obtain the largest amount of feathers with the least amount of hissing.
- **Jean-Baptiste Colbert**.

4,067. In this world nothing can be said to be certain, except death and taxes.
- **Benjamin Franklin:** *in a letter to the French physicist, Jean-Baptiste Le Roy, 13ᵗʰ November, 1789*.

4,068. I am in favour of cutting taxes under any circumstance, and for any excuse, for any reason, whenever it's possible. The reason I am is because I believe the big problem is not taxes, the big problem is spending. The question is, "How do you hold down government spending? The only effective way I think of holding it down, is to hold down the amount of income the government has. The way to do that is to cut taxes.
- **Milton Friedman:** *Interview, 2002*.

4,069. The difference between tax avoidance and tax evasion is the thickness of a prison wall.
- **Denis Healy**.

4.070. The avoidance of taxes is the only intellectual pursuit that still carries any reward.
- **John Maynard Keynes: *attributed*,** as quoted in *A Dictionary of Scientific Quotations* by Alan L.McKay, 1977.

4,071. Indoors or out, no one relaxes / In March, that month of wind and taxes, / The wind will presently disappear, / The taxes last us all the year.
- **Ogden Nash:** *Thar She Blows* in *Verses*, 1949.

4,072. The two agencies that redistribute great fortunes are taxation and offspring.
- **Herbert V. Prochnow and Herbert V. Prochnow Jr:** *The Public Speaker's Source Book*, 1977.

4,073. The crime of taxation is not in the taking of it, it's the way that it's spent.
- **Will Rogers:** *The Best of Will Rogers* by Bryan Sterling, 1979.

4,074. There is no art which one government sooner learns of another than that of draining money from the pockets of the people.
- **Adam Smith:** *The Wealth of the Nations*, 1776.

4,075. What is the difference between a taxidermist and a tax collector? The taxidermist takes only your skin.
- **Mark Twain:** *Mark Twain's Notebook* by A.B.Paine, 1935.

4,076. A democratic government is one that will let you make all the money that you want. They just won't let you keep it.
- **Pat Williams:** *Winning With One-Liners.* 2002.

4,077. Income tax returns are the most imaginative fiction being written today.
- **Herman Wouk:** *The Penguin Dictionary of Modern Humorous Quotations* edited by Fred Matcalf, 1986.

TEACHERS AND TEACHING

4,078. Din it in, din it in.
Children's heads are hollow.
Din it in. din it in,
Still there's more to follow.
- **anon**. NB: Scots: <u>Din</u> = vb *Instil something to be learned by constant repetition*

4,079. A teacher affects eternity, he can never tell where his influence stops.
- **Henry Brooks Adams:** *The Education of Henry Adams*, 1907.

4,080. We all need someone who inspires us to do better than we know how.
- *anon*

4,081. School teachers are not fully appreciated by parents until it rains all day Saturday.
- *anon*

4,082. Teachers who educated children deserved more honour than parents who merely gave them birth; for bare life is furnished by the one, the other ensures a good life.
- **Aristotle:** *Lives of the Philosophers by Diogenes Laertius*. 4th century BC.

4,083. In teaching you cannot see the fruit of a day's work. It is invisible and remains so, maybe for twenty years.
- **Jacques Barzun:** *Teacher in America*, 1945.

4,084. Teaching is not a lost art, but the regard for it is a lost tradition.
- *ibid.*

4,085. Housework is a breeze. Cooking is a pleasant diversion. Putting up a retaining wall is a lark. But teaching is like climbing a mountain.
- **Fawn M. Brodie:** *The Los Angeles Times Magazine, February, 1977.*

4,086. Teaching is truth mediated by personality.
- **Phyllis Brooks:** *The Gigantic Book of Teachers' Wisdom* edited by Erin Gruwell, 2007.

4.087. A teacher is one who makes himself progressively unnecessary.
- **Thomas Carruthers**.

4,088. There are no miracles. There is nothing miraculous or magical about our successes. It took only love and determination.
- **Marva Collins:** *Ordinary Children, Extraordinary Teachers*, 1992.

4,089. It's important not to spend so much time being an adult that we forget what it is like to be a child.
- *ibid*.

4,090. If a man keeps cherishing his old knowledge so as continually to be acquiring new, he may be a teacher of others.
- **Confucius:** *Analects*, 6th century BC.

4,091. It's not what is poured into a student that counts, but what is planted.
- **Linda Conway**.

4,092. Who dares to teach must never cease to learn.
- **John Cotton Dana**. NB This statement was adopted as the motto of what was then called Kean College (pronounced 'Cane'), a teachers' training college now known as Kean University, New Jersey.

4,093. The whole art of teaching is only the art of awakening the natural curiosity of young minds for the purpose of satisfying it afterwards.
- **Anatole France:** *The Crime of Sylvestre Bonnard*, 1881.

4,094. I am not a teacher, but an awakener.
- **Robert Frost**.

4,095. You cannot teach a man anything, you can only help him to find it for himself.
- **Galileo**.

4,096. If he is indeed wise he does not bid you enter the house of wisdom, but rather leads you to the threshold of your own mind.
- **Kahlil Gibran:** *The Prophet, chapter 18: Teaching*. 1923.

4,097. Good teaching is one fourth preparation and three-fourths theatre.
- **Gail Godwin:** *The Odd Woman*, 1974.

4,098. The object of teaching a child is to enable him to get along without a teacher.
- **Elbert Hubbard**.

4,099. It must be remembered that the purpose of education is not to fill the minds of students with facts... it is to teach them to think, if that is possible, and always to think for themselves.
- **Robert Hutchins:** *The Gigantic Book of Teachers' Wisdom* edited by Erin Gruwell, 2007.

4,100. In teaching, you must simply work your pupil into such a state of interest in what you are going to teach him that every other object of attention is banished from his mind; then reveal it to him so impressively that he will remember the occasion to his dying day: and finally fill him with devouring curiosity to know what the next steps in connection with the subject are.
- **William James:** *Talks to Teachers on Psychology and to Students on Some of Life's Ideals*, 1899.

4,101. The child will always attend more to what a teacher does than to what the same teacher says.
- *ibid.*

4,102. To teach is to learn twice.
- **Joseph Joubert:** *Pensees*, 1842.

4,103. The teacher is the midwife of the pupil's thoughts.
- **Immanuel Kant:** *Metaphysics of Morals*, 1787.

4,104. The important thing is not so much that every child should be taught, as that every child should be given the wish to learn.
- **Sir John Lubbock**.

4,105. A teacher who is attempting to teach without inspiring the pupil with a desire to learn is hammering on cold iron.
- **Horace Mann**.

4,106. It goes without saying that no man can teach successfully who is not at the same time a student.
- **Sir William Osler:** *The Life of Sir William Osler* by Harvey Cushing, 1925.

4,107. Tell me and I'll forget, show me and I may remember , involve me and I'll understand.
- ***Chinese Proverb.***

4,108. More important than the curriculum is the question of the methods of teaching and the spirit in which teaching is given.
- **Bertrand Russell:** *Education and the Good Life*, 1926.

4,109. No one should teach who is not in love with teaching.
- **Margaret E. Sangster:** *An Autobiography From My Youth Up*, 1909.

4,110. For every person who wants to teach there are approximately thirty people who don't want to learn.
- **W. C. Sellar and R. J. Yeathman:** *And Now All This by the Authors of 1066 and All That*, 1932.

4,111. He who can, does. He who cannot, teaches.
- **George Bernard Shaw:** *Man and Superman*, 1903.

4,112. I cannot teach anybody anything, I can only make them think.
- **Socrates:** *The Gigantic Book of Teachers' Wisdom* edited by Erin Grunwell 2007.

4,113. Good teachers are costly, but bad teachers cost more.
- **Bob Talbert.**

 4,114. Teaching kids to count is fine, but teaching kids what counts is best.
- **Bob Talbert.**

4,115. If I were in charge of the universe, good teachers would earn far more than cabinet ministers; the latter are replaceable, the former are not.
 - **Phyllis Theroux:** *Bedtime Stories For Parents in the Dark.* 1988.

4,116. The art of teaching is the art of assisting discovery.
 Mark van Doren: *The Gigantic Book of Teachers' Wisdom* edited by Erin Gruwell, 2007.

4,117. The mediocre teacher tells. The good teacher explains. The superior teacher demonstrates. The great teacher inspires.
- **William Arthur Ward.**

4,118. Teaching is the greatest act of optimism.
- **Colleen Wilcox:** *The Gigantic Book of Teachers' Wisdom* edited by Erin Gruwell, 2007.

4.119. If tonight when you're in bed
You find it hard to sleep,
Then you should think of happy things
And then start counting sheep.

Then very soon your happy thoughts
Will gently calm your mind,
So when you fin'ly fall asleep
The sweetest dreams you'll find.

But never – ever – think of school.
Oh no ! For if you do,
You may start counting teachers
And have nightmares all night through.
- **Bob Woodruff**, *Some Bedtime Advice* in *If Kids Ruled the School Ruled The School* edited by Bruce Lansky, 2004.

TEARS

4,120. Tears are words the heart can't express.
- *anon*.

4,121. Tears are a form of feminine water power used to overcome masculine will power.
- *anon: 20,000 Quips and Quotes* by Evan Esar, 1968.

4,122. A woman generally resorts to tears when she wants to get something out of her system – or out of her husband.
- *ibid*.

4,123. Tears are nature's lotion for the eyes. The eyes see better for being washed by them.
- **Christian Nestell Bovee**.

4,124. "It opens the lungs, washes the countenance, exercises the eyes, and softens down the temper," said Mr Bumble, "so cry away."
- **Charles Dickens:** *Oliver Twist*, 1839.

4,125. Heaven knows we need never be ashamed of our tears, for they are rain upon the blinding dust of earth, overlaying our hard hearts.
- **Charles Dickens:** *Great Expectations*, 1860.

4,126. Every woman is wrong until she cries, and then she is right immediately.
- **Thomas Chandler Haliburton**.

4,127. Laugh and the World Laughs With You, Cry and You Simply Get Wet!
- **Barbara Johnson:** chapter title in her book, *Splashes of Joy*, 1992.

4,128. Women are never landlocked: they're always mere minutes away from the briny deep of tears.
- **Mignon McLaughlin:** *The Second Neurologist's Notebook*, 1966.

4,129. The most effective water power in the world – women's tears.
- **Wilson Mizner:** *The Treasury of Humorous Quotations* edited by Evan Esar, English Edition edited by Nicolas Bentley, 1955.

4,130. Tears at times have the weight of speech.
- **Ovid:** Roman poet, **circa** 17 AD.

4,131. What soap is for the body, tears are for the soul.
- *Jewish Proverb.*

4,132. O let not woman's weapons - water-drops - stain my manly cheeks.
- **William Shakespeare:** words spoken by Lear in *King Lear.*

4,133. Tears are the silent language of grief.
- **Voltaire:** *Candide,* 1759.

TELEPHONE

4,134. I've suffered from all the hang-ups known
And none is as bad as the telephone.
- **Richard Armour:** *Wall Street Journal, 11ᵗʰ July, 1985*.

4,135. Distinctly *not* known / As one of life's blisses / Is the voice on the phone / That demands, "Guess who this is!"
- **Richard Armour:** *When Long Distance Doesn't Lend Enchantment* in *An Armoury of Light Verse*, 1964.

4,136. Our house is a three-ring circus,
As all who have seen it have known.
And these are the rings I refer to:
The front door, the back door, the phone.
- **Richard Armour:** *Three-Ring Circus* in *An Armoury of Light Verse*, 1964.

4,137. "Mr Watson, come here, I want you."
- **Alexander Graham Bell**.
NB This was the first understandable sentence spoken over Bell's invention, the telephone, a patent for which was issued to Mr Bell on 7ᵗʰ March, 1876.

4,138, It is the opinion of the present reviewer that the weakness of plot is due to the great number of characters which clutter up the pages. The Russian School is responsible for this.
 - **Robert Benchley:** reviewing the New York Telephone Directory in *All Things New*, 1922.

4.139. Telephone: n. An invention of the devil which abrogates some of the advantages of making a disagreeable person keep his distance.
- **Ambrose Bierce:** *The Devil's Dictionary*, 1911.

4,140. The telephone gives us the happiness of being together yet safely apart.
- **Mason Cooley:** *City Aphorisms, Twelfth Selection*, 1993.

4,141. People who say, "Anything is possible", have never tried to complain to a recorded announcement.
- **Sam Ewing:** *National Enquirer.*

4,142. Uneasy lies the head that ignores a telephone call late at night.
- **William Feather:** *The Business of Life*, 1949.

4,143. It's no fun to kiss a girl over the phone unless you are in the booth with her.
- **Leopold Fechter:** *Encyclopedia of Ad-Libs, Crazy Jokes, Insults etc*, 1977.

4,144. Utility is when you have one telephone, luxury is when you have two, opulence is when you have three – and paradise is when you have none.
- **Doug Larson**.

4,145. The telephone is a good way to talk to people without having to offer them a drink.
- **Fran Lebowitz:** *An Uncommon Scold* by Abby Adams.

4,146. If you were going to die soon and had only one phone call you could make, who would you call and what would you say and why are you waiting?
- **Stephen Levine**.

4,147. If we discovered that we only had five minutes left to say all that we wanted to say, every telephone booth would be occupied by people calling other people to stammer that they loved them.
- **Christopher Morley**.

4,148. O misery, misery, mumble and moan!
Someone invented the telephone,
And interrupted a nation's slumbers,
Ringing wrong but similar numbers.
- **Ogden Nash:** *Look What You Did, Christopher!*

4,149. This telephone has too many shortcomings to be seriously considered as a means of communication. The devise is inherently of no value to us.
- **William Orton:** President of the Western Union Telegraph Company

is reputed to have said this in a *Company Memo, dated 1877.* The following year Alexander Graham Bell received a patent for his telephone.

THOUGHTS AND THINKING

4,150. As the physically weak man can make himself strong by careful and patient training, so the man of weak thoughts can make them strong by exercising himself in right thinking.
- **James Allen:** *As a Man Thinketh*, 1902.

4,151. As the plant springs from, and could not be without the seed, so every act of a man springs from the hidden seeds of thought, and could not appear without them. This applies equally to those acts called "spontaneous" and "unpremeditated" as to those which are deliberately executed.
- ***ibid.***

4.152. If you think you can, you can. And if you think you can't, you're right.
- **Mary Kay Ash:** *New York Times, 20ᵗʰ October, 1985.*

4,153. Our life is what our thoughts make it.
 - **Marcus Aurelius**

4,154. Whatever is true, whatever is noble, whatever is right, whatever is pure, whatever is lovely, whatever is admirable – if anything is excellent or praiseworthy - think about such things.
- **The Bible:** *Philippians 4: 8, NIV.*

4,155. It is the nature of thought to find its way into action.
- **Christian Nestell Bovee.**

4,156. What we are today comes from our thoughts of yesterday, and our present thoughts build our life of tomorrow. Our life is the creation of our mind.
- **Buddha:** *Dhammapada*, 5th century BC.

4,157. Not a hundredth part of the thoughts in my head have ever been or ever will be spoken or written - as long as I keep my senses, at least.
- **Jane Welsh Carlyle:** *Journal, 16th July, 1858.*

4,158. All great thoughts come from the heart.
- **Luc de Clapiers**, **marquis de Vauvenargues:** *Reflections and Maxims,* 1746.

4,159. Just because we increase the speed of information doesn't mean we can increase the speed of decisions. Pondering, reflecting and ruminating are undervalued skills in our culture.
- **Dale Dauten:** *The Arizona Republic Newspaper, 15th July, 1999.*

4,160. The ancestor of every action is a thought.
- **Ralph Waldo Emerson:** *Essays, First Series,* 1841.

4,161. In this world second thoughts, it seems, are best.
- **Euripides:** *Hippolytus,* **circa** 428 BC.

4,162. A man who cannot think is not an educated man however many college degrees he may have acquired. Thinking is the hardest work any one can do - which is probably the reason why we have so few thinkers.
- **Henry Ford:** *My Life and Work,* 1922.

4,163. All truly wise thoughts have been thoughts already thousands of times; but to make them truly ours, we must think them over again honestly, till they take root in our personal experience.
- **Johann Wolfgang von Goethe:** *Wilhelm Meister's Journeyman Years* 1829.

4,164. Positive thoughts (joy, happiness, fulfilment, achievement, worthiness) have positive results (enthusiasm, calm, well-being, ease, energy, love). Negative thoughts (judgement, unworthiness, mistrust, resentment, fear) produce negative results (tension, anxiety, alienation, anger, fatigue).
- **Peter McWilliams:** *You Can't Afford the Luxury of a Negative Thought.*

4,165. From a medical point of view, negative thinking suppresses the immune system, raises blood pressure, and creates a general level of stress and fatigue in the body.
- ***ibid:*** 1991.

4,166. Man's greatness lies in his power of thought
- **Blaise Pascal.**

4,167. A bookshop is one of the only pieces of evidence we have that people are still thinking.
- **Jerry Seinfeld**.

4,168. To find yourself, think for yourself.
- **Socrates**.

4,169. Ponder and deliberate before you make a move.
- **Sun Tzu:** *The Art of War*.

TIME

4,170. Time as he grows old teaches many lessons.
- **Aeschylus:** *Prometheus Bound.*

4,171. The bad news is time flies. The good news is you're the pilot.
- **Michael Altshuler**.

4,172. Time crumbles things; everything grows old under the power of time and is forgotten through the lapse of time.
- **Aristotle:** *Physics.* 4th century BC.

4,173. Let me tell you, time is a very precious gift of God; so precious that He only gives it to us moment by moment. He would not have you waste it.
- **Amelia Barr:** *Jan Vedder's Wife,* 1885.

4,174. One can only forget about time by making use of it.
- **Charles Baudelaire**.

4,175. I would I could stand on a busy corner, hat in hand, and beg people to throw me all their wasted hours.
- **Bernard Berenson**.

4,176. Lost time is time when we have not lived a full human life, time unenriched by experience, creative endeavour, enjoyment, and suffering.
 - **Dietrich Bonhoeffer:** *Letters and Papers From Prison,* 1953.

4,177. I definitely am going to take a course on time management... just as soon as I can work it into my schedule.
- **Louis E. Boone:** *Quotable Business.*

4,178. I commend you to take care of the minutes, for the hours will take care of themselves.
- **Lord Chesterfield:** *Letters to His Son,* 16th October, 1747.

4,179. Time is infinitely more precious than money, and there is nothing common between them. You cannot accumulate time; you cannot borrow time; you can never tell how much time you have left in the bank of life.
- **Israel Davidson**.

4,180. Time is a wonderful healer, but a poor beautician.
- **Sam Ewing:** *Mature Living, February, 1999.*

4,181. Unless you're serving time there's never enough of it.
- **Malcolm Forbes:** *The Forbes Book of Business Quotations* 1997.

4,182. Remember that time is money.
- **Benjamin Franklin:** *Advice to a Young Tradesman*, 1748.

4,183. Lost time is never found again.
- **Benjamin Franklin:** *Poor Richard's Almanack*, 1758.

4,184. The time is short, the opportunity is great, therefore crowd the hours with the best that is in you.
- **John G. Hibben:** *Graduation Address at Princeton University, 1913.*

4,185. If you can fill the unforgiving minute / With sixty second's worth of distance run / Yours is the earth and everything that's in it, / And – what is more - you'll be a man, my son!
- **Rudyard Kipling:** *Rewards and Fairies*, 1910.

4,186. Time is free, but it's priceless. You can't own it, but you can use it. You can't keep it, but you can spend it. Once you've lost it, you can never get it back.
- **Harvey Mackay:** *Harvey Mackay's United Features Syndicated Column.*

4,187. Lost, yesterday, somewhere between sunrise and sunset, two golden hours, each set with sixty diamond minutes. No reward is offered, for they are gone forever.
- **Horace Mann:** published as *A Beautiful Thought* in an American *Christian newspaper on 16th March, 1844.*

4,188. The first thing necessary for a constructive dealing with time is to learn to live in the reality of the present moment. For psychologically speaking, this present moment is all we have.
- **Rollo May:** *Man's Search for Himself,* 1953

4,189. Not the least of the torments which plague our existence is the constant pressure of *time*, which never lets us so much as draw breath but pursues us all like a taskmaster with a whip.
- **Arthur Schopenhauer:** *On the Suffering of the World* in *Studies in Pessimism* translated by T. Bailey Saunders, 1891.

4,190. A husband, returning in a terrible state at 4 am, so infuriated his wife that she threw the alarm clock at him. As his colleagues remarked the next day: "It's amazing how time flies when you're enjoying yourself."
- **Tom Shields:** *Tom Shields' Diary,* 1991.

4,191. Lost wealth may be replaced by industry, lost knowledge by study, lost health by temperance or medicine, but lost time is gone forever.
- **Samuel Smiles:** *Self Help,* 1859.

4,192. So little time do we have in this life that to waste any of it seems wanton. Every minute of every hour of every day is precious and should never be spent thoughtlessly.
- **Alan Taylor:** Scottish journalist. Quoted in *Life and Work, December, 2005.*

4,193. Time is / Too slow for those who wait, / Too swift for those who fear, / Too long for those who grieve, / Too short for those who rejoice, / But for those who love, / Time is eternity.
- **Henry van Dyke:** *Time Is.* NB This short poem was read at the Funeral Service of Diana, Princess of Wales, by her sister Lady Jane Fellowes.

4,194. One good way to extend one's lifespan is to not waste time.
- **Lu Xun:** considered one of the leading figures of modern Chinese. Literature. Quoted in *Geary's Guide to the World's Great Aphorists*, by James Geary, 2007.

TRAVEL AND TOURISM

4,195. Perhaps travel cannot prevent bigotry, but by demonstrating that all peoples cry, laugh, eat, worry and die, it can introduce the idea that if we try and understand each other, we may even become friends.
- **Maya Angelou:** *Wouldn't Take Nothing For My Journey Now*, 1993.

4,196. The saying, "Getting there is half the fun," became obsolete with the advent of commercial airlines.
- *anon.*

4,197. When you don't know where you're going, any road will take you there.
- *anon.*

4,198, When you come to look like you're passport photograph, you are too ill to travel.
- *anon.*

4,199. My feelings about temples is pretty much the same as my feelings about important cathedrals in Europe, which is that after you've seen a representative sample of them – say, two, it's time to move on to other major tourist activities such as lunch.
- **Dave Barry:** *Dave Barry Does Japan*, 1992.

4,200. There are two classes of travel - first class, and with children.
- **Robert Benchley:** *Pluck and Luck*, 1925.

4,201. In the South Pacific, because of their size, mosquitoes are required to file flight plans.
- **Erma Bombeck:** *When You Look Like You're Passport Photo, It's Time To Go Home*, 1991.

4,202. Yesterday we really assimilated the Spanish culture – we were a whole hour in Madrid.
- **Sid Caesar:** as a camera-festooned tourist to fellow traveller, Imogene Coca, in a sketch from the American TV Show *Your Show of Shows*.

4,203. The only way of catching a train I have ever discovered is to miss the train before.
- **G.K. Chesterton:** *Tremendous Triffles*, 1909.

4,204. Travel broadens a person. So do bedtime snacks.
- **Sam Ewing:** *Mature Living, May, 1997*.

4,205. Aunt Jane observed, the second time / She tumbled off a bus, / The step is short from the Sublime / To the Ridiculous.
- **Harry Graham:** *Equanimity* in *Ruthless Rhymes for Heartless Homes*, 1901.

4,206. Drake is going West, lads / So Tom is going East. / But tiny Fred / Just lies in bed, / The lazy little beast.
- **Spike Milligan:** *Go North, South, East and West, Young Man*.

4,207. The British tourist is always happy abroad as long as the natives are waiters.
- **Robert Morley:** *The Observer, 20th April, 1958*.

4,208. In the Middle Ages people were tourists because of their religion, where as now they are tourists because tourism is their religion.
- **Robert Runcie:** *The Independent Newspaper, 7th December,1988*.

4.209. For my part, I travel not to go anywhere, but to go. I travel for travel's sake.
- **Robert Louis Stevenson***: Travels With a Donkey*, 1879.

4,210. A pleasant travelling companion helps us on our journey as much as a carriage.
- **Publilius Syrus:** Roman epigrammatist. 1st century BC.

4,211. A journey of a thousand miles starts with a single step.
- **Lao Tzu:** *The Tao Te Ching*, translated by John H. McDonald, 1996.

4,212. Travel is glamorous only in retrospect.
- **Paul Theroux:** *The Observer, 7 th October, 1979*.

4,213. Travel is fatal to prejudice, bigotry, and narrow-mindedness, and many of our people need it sorely on these counts. Broad, wholesome, charitable views of men and things cannot be acquired by vegetating in one little corner of the earth all one's lifetime.
- **Mark Twain:** *Innocents Abroad.* 1869.

TROUBLE

4,214. People who invite trouble invariably complain when it accepts.
- *anon*.

4,215. In larger things we are convivial; / What causes trouble is the trivial.
- **Richard Armour:** *Armour's Armory – Syndicated Column*.

4,216. When I look back on all these worries I remember the story of the old man who said on his deathbed that he had had a lot of trouble in his life, most of which had never happened.
- **Winston Churchill:** *The Second World War, Volume 2: Their Finest Hour*, 1950.

4,217. I have learned in the great University of Hard Knocks a philosophy that no woman who has an easy life ever acquires. I have learned to live each day as it comes, and not to borrow trouble by dreading tomorrow. It is the dark menace of the future that makes cowards of us.
- **Dorothy Dix:** *Dorothy Dix. Her Book: Every-Day Helps for Every-Day People, 1926*.

4,218. People who try to drown their troubles never use water.
- **Sam Ewing:** *The Sun, 6th July, 1999*.

4,219. Troubles don't bother me. I'm too busy to worry in the daytime and too sleepy to worry at night.
- **Leopold Fechtner:** *5,000 One-And-Two-Line Jokes*, 1973.

4,220. If I had my life to live over I would have more actual troubles and fewer imaginary troubles.
- **Don Herold**.

4,221. Troubles are like babies; they only grow by nursing.
- **Douglas Jerrold**.

4,222. No drug, not even alcohol, causes the fundamental ills of society. If we're looking for the sources of our troubles, we shouldn't test people for drugs, we should test them for stupidity, ignorance, greed and love of power.
- **P. J. O'Rourke:** *Give War a Chance,* 1992.

4,223. The way I see it, if you want the rainbow, you gotta put up with the rain.
- **Dolly Parton**.

4,224. If you compared your troubles... with those of others, you would find that there are those whose troubles make yours look like minor inconveniences.
- **Catherine Pulsifer**.

4,225. It is a source of consolation to look back upon those great misfortunes which never happened.
- **Arthur Schopenhauer:** *The Essays of Arthur Schopenhauer: Counsels and Maxims* translated by T. Bailey Saunders, 1891.

4,226. Trouble is part of your life – if you don't share it, you don't give the person who loves you a chance to love you enough - **Dinah Shore**.

4,227. Anyone can hold the helm when the sea is calm.
- **Publilius Syrus:** *Moral Maxims,* 1st century BC.

TRUTH

4,228. The greatest friend of Truth is time, her greatest enemy is Prejudice.
- **Herbert Agar:** *A Time for Greatness: On Social and Political Problems of the Present Day*, 1942.

4,229. The camera never lies, and it takes a family album to convince some people that the truth is a terrible thing.
 - *anon.*

4,230. The man who says that he is the boss at home and in his office probably doesn't tell the truth in other matters either.
- *anon.*

4,231. Pretty much all the honest truth telling there is in the world today is done by small children.
- *anon.*

4232. Because a thing is eloquently expressed it should not be taken to be necessarily true; nor because it is uttered with stammering lips should it be supposed to be false.
 - **St Augustine of Hippo:** *Confessions,* ***circa*** 398 AD.

4,233. "What is truth?" said jesting Pilate, and would not stay for an answer.
 - **Francis Bacon:** *An Essay on Truth*, 1625.

4,234. No pleasure is comparable to the standing upon the vantage-ground of truth.
 - *ibid.*

4.235. If you hold to my teaching, you are really my disciples. Then you will know the truth, and the truth will set you free.
- **The Bible:** *John 8: 31– 32, NIV.*

4,236. As scarce as truth is, the supply has always been in excess of the demand.
- **Josh Billings:** *Affurisms* in *Josh Billings: Hiz Sayings*, 1865.

4,237. A truth that's told with bad intent / Beats all the lies you can invent.
- **William Blake:** *Auguries of Innocence*, 1863

4,238. 'Tis strange- but true; for truth is always strange; stranger than fiction.
- **Lord Byron:** *Don Juan*, 1824.

4,239. The truth is incontrovertible. Panic may resent it, ignorance may deride it, malice may destroy it, but there it is.
- **Sir Winston Churchill:** *The Wit and Wisdom of Winston Churchill* by James C. Humes, 1994.

4,240. We believe not a liar, even when he is speaking the truth.
- **Cicero:** *Proverbs*. 1st century BC.

4,241. The search for truth is more precious than its possession.
- **Albert Einstein**.

4,242. The truth is the hardest missile one can be pelted with.
- **George Eliot:** *Middlemarch*, 1872.

4,243. It's awfully easy to lie when you know that you're trusted implicitly.
- Celia Johnson in her role as a suburban housewife, playing opposite Trevor Howard, in the **1946 Film**: *Brief Encounter*, based on a Noel Coward play.

4,244. Half the truth is often a great lie.
- **Benjamin Franklin,:** *Almanack*, 1758.

4,245. The truth is more powerful than any weapon of mass destruction.
- **Mahatma Gandhi:** *Geary's Guide to the World's Great Aphorists*.

4,246. It is always the best policy to speak the truth, unless, of course, you are an exceptionally good liar.
- **Jerome K. Jerome:** *Idler Magazine, London, 1892.*

4,247. The naked truth is always better than the best dressed lie.
- **Ann Landers**.

4,248. Truth is generally the best vindication against slander.
- **Abraham Lincoln:** in a letter to Edwin Stanton, the Secretary of War, 18th July, 1864.

4,249. Who speaks the truth stabs Falsehood to the heart.
- **James Russell Lowell**.

4,250. The man who speaks the truth is always at ease.
- *Persian Proverb*.

- **4,251**. Son, always tell the truth, then you'll never have to remember what you said the last time.
- **Sam Rayburn:** *The Washingtonian Magazine, November, 1978.*

4,252. The truth is always the strongest argument.
- **Sophocles:** *Fragment 737.* 5th century BC.

4,253. Minor white lies permeate our daily lives, especially when we feel the need to protect someone else's feelings.
- **Mitch Thrower:** *The Attention Deficit Workplace,* 2005.

THE UNIVERSE

4,254. There is the cry that states: "If anyone finds out what the universe is for and why it is here, it will instantly disappear and be replaced by something more bizarrely inexplicable." There is another theory which states that this has already happened.
- **Douglas Adams:** *The Hitchhiker's Guide to the Galaxy,* 1979.

4,255. That's one small step for man, one giant leap for mankind.
- **Neil Armstrong** said this as he placed his left boot on the surface of the moon on 20th July, 1969.

4,256. I had rather believe all the Fables in the Legends, and the Talmud, and the Alcoran, than that this universe frame is without a Mind.
- **Francis Bacon:** *Essays: Of Atheism,* 1625.

4,257. I don't pretend to understand the Universe - it's a great deal bigger than I am.
- **Thomas Carlyle**.

4,258. The more clearly we can focus our attention on the wonders and realities of the universe about us, the less taste we shall have for destruction.
- **Rachel Carson,:** *Silent Spring,* 1962.

4,259. I'm sure the universe is full of intelligent life. It's just been too intelligent to come here.
- **Sir Arthur C. Clarke**.

4,260. It is impossible to conceive of this immense and wonderful universe as the result of blind chance or necessity.
- **Charles Darwin:** *The Origin of the Species,* 1859.

4,261. Two things are infinite; the universe and human stupidity, and I'm not sure about the universe.
- **Albert Einstein**.

4,262. If we find the answer to that, it would be the ultimate triumph of human reason - for then we would know the mind of God.
- **Stephen Hawking** referring to the question why we and the universe exist, as quoted in *A Brief History of Time*, in *Chambers Dictionary of Quotations*, 2005.

4,263. We are just an advanced breed of monkeys on a minor planet of a very average star. But we can understand the universe. That makes us something very special.
- **Stephen Hawking:** *Der Spiegel, 17th October, 1988.*

4,264. From the intrinsic evidence of his creation, the Great Architect of the Universe now appears as a pure mathematician.
- **James Jeans:** *The Mysterious Universe*, 1930.

4,265. The universe begins to look more like a great thought than like a great machine.
- *ibid.*

4,266. In my youth I regarded the universe as an open book, printed in the language of physical equations, whereas now it appears to me as a text written in invisible ink, of which in our rare moments of grace we are able to decipher a small fragment.
- **Arthur Koestler:** *Bricks to Babel* in *Encarta Book of Quotations,* edited by Bill Swainson, 2000.

4,267. Personally, I don't think there's intelligent life on other planets. Why should other planets be any different from this one?
- **Bob Monkhouse**.

4,268. The universe is full of magical things patiently waiting for our wits to grow sharper.
- **Eden Phillpots:** *A Shadow Passes*, 1918.

4,269. The distinguished preacher Dr Henry Ward Beecher and Colonel Robert Ingersoll, the vocal atheist, shared a common interest in astronomy. On one occasion, when Colonel Ingersoll visited Dr Beecher's home, he noticed a magnificent working model of the earth, sun and planets. After examining it closely, the Colonel inquired who had made it. 'Who made it?' replied Dr Beecher in simulated astonishment, 'Why nobody made it. It just happened!'
- **James A Simpson:** *The Laugh Shall be First*, 1998.

4,270. Our sun is one of 100 billion stars in our galaxy. Our galaxy is one of billions of galaxies populating the universe. It would be the height of presumption to think that we are the only living things in that enormous immensity.
- **Wernher von Braun:** *New York Times.*

4,271. For me, the idea of a creation is not conceivable without invoking the necessity of design. One cannot be exposed to the law and order of the universe without concluding that there must be design and purpose behind it all.
- **Wernher von Braun:** *in a letter to the California State Board of Education, 14th September, 1972.*

4,272. Sometimes I think the surest sign that intelligent life exists elsewhere in the universe is that it has never tried to contact us.
- **Bill Watterson:** *The Indispensable Calvin and Hobbes,* 1992.

VACATIONS

4,273. Vacations are easy to plan – your boss tells you when, and your wife tells you where.
- **Joey Adams:** *Joey Adams' Encyclopedia of Humour,* 1968.

4,274. A vacation is like love - anticipated with pleasure, experienced with discomfort, and remembered with nostalgia.
 - ***anon.***

4,275. A vacation is a two week holiday that makes you feel good enough to go back to work - and poor enough to have to.
- **Milton Berle:** *Private Joke File,*1989.

 4,276. Honolula – it's got everything. Sand for the children, sun for the wife, sharks for the wife's mother.
- **Ken Dodd:** *The Penguin Dictionary of Modern Humorous Quotations,* edited by Fred Metcalf, 1986.

 4,277. VACATION: Two weeks on the sunny sands and the rest of the year on the financial rocks.
- **Sam Ewing**.

4,278. As a member of an escorted tour, you don't even have to know the Matterhorn isn't a tuba.
- **Temple Fielding:** *Fielding's Travel Guide to Europe,* 1963.

4,279. A vacation is over when you begin to yearn for your work.
- **Morris Fishbein**.

4.280. When packing for a trip abroad, I know this may sound funny; pack half the clothes you think you need – and twice as much the money.
- **Charles Ghigna:** *Trip Tip,* quoted in *Lighten Up!* edited by Bruce Lansky.

4,281. No man needs a vacation so much as a man who has just had one.
- **Elbert Hubbard:** *Philistine: A Periodical of Protest*, 1905.

4,282. A women when on holiday, / A woman no longer young, / Was treated by a doctor, / For sunburn on her tongue.
- **Walter McCorrisken:** *Warning* in *A Wee Dribble of Dross*, 1993.

4,283. Whenever we start a vacation, it's the same thing. We get up at six o'clock in the morning to get an early start. First we eat breakfast; then we pack; then we notify the neighbours and police department; then we stop the milk, mail and newspaper deliveries; then we arrange for a kid to mow the lawn and water the garden; then we take the dog to the kennel; then the kids say good bye to their friends; then we set the lights that go on automatically, activate the burglar alarm system, lock all the doors and windows - and after all this is finally done, you know what we do? We go to bed because I hate night driving.
- **Robert Orben:** *Braude's Treasury of Wit and Humour for all Occasions, Revised Edition,* by Jacob M. Braude, 1991.

4,284. Those who say you can't take it with you never saw a car packed for a vacation trip.
- **Herbert V. Prochnow:** *The Toastmaster's Treasure Chest* by Herbert V. Prochnow and Herbert V. Prochnow, Jr, 1988.

4,285. The nicest thing about not going away on a vacation is that you don't have to come home to rest up from it.
- *ibid.*

4,286. No matter what happens, travel gives you a story to tell.
- *Jewish Proverb.*

4,287. Our vacation was great. My wife did all the driving, all I did was sit behind the wheel and steer.
- **Pat Williams:** *Winning With One-Liners*, 2002.

4,288. Nothing is quite so upsetting on a vacation as getting a call from the house sitter who asks, "Is it the custom to tip the firemen?"
- *ibid.*

VALUES

4,289. ... whatever is true, whatever is noble, whatever is right, whatever is pure, whatever is lovely, whatever is admirable – if anything is excellent or praiseworthy – think about such things.
- **The Bible:** *Philippians 4: 8, NIV*.

4,290. Personal leadership is the process of keeping your vision and values before you and aligning your life to be congruent with them.
- **Stephen Covey**.

4.291. Out of 5.8 billion people in the world, the majority of them are certainly not believers... realistically speaking, if the majority of humanity remain non-believers, it doesn't matter. No problem! The problem is that the majority have lost, or ignore, the deeper human values – compassion, a sense of responsibility. That is our big concern.
- **The Dalai Lama:** *Magazine, 1997*.

4,292. The hottest places in hell are reserved for those who, in a time of moral crisis, remain neutral.
- **Dante Alighieri:** *The Divine Comedy*, 1472.

4,293. It is not hard to make decisions when you know what your values are.
- **Roy Disney**.

4,294. Children are not casual guests in our home. They have been loaned to us temporarily for the purpose of loving them and instilling a foundation of values on which their future lives will be built.
- **James C. Dobson**.

4,295. The most important human endeavour is the striving for morality in our actions. Our inner balance and even our very existence depend on it. Only morality in our actions can give beauty and dignity to life.
- **Albert Einstein:** *in a letter to the Reverend C. Greenway of Brooklin, dated*

20th November, 1950. Quoted in *The New Quotable Einstein,* collected and edited by Alice Calaprice, 2005.

4,296. My family gave me values that have sustained me through situations that would challenge any person.
  - **Kathy Ireland**.

4,297. The individual increasingly comes to know who he is through the stand he takes when he expresses his ideas, values, beliefs and convictions.
- **Clark Moustakas**.

4,298. Our challenges may be new. The instruments with which we meet them may be new. But those values upon which our success depends - hard work and honesty, courage and fair play, tolerance and curiosity, loyalty and patriotism - these things are old. These things are true. They have been the quiet force of progress throughout our history... This is the price and the promise of citizenship.
- **Barack Obama:** *Inaugural Speech, 20th January, 2009.*

4,299. Virtue depends partly upon training and partly upon practice; you must learn first, and then strengthen your learning by action.
- **Seneca the Younger:** *Epistle on the Value of Advice,* 1st century, BC.

4,300. The Iron Lady of the Western World? Me! .... Well, yes – if that is how they wish to interpret my defense of the values and freedom fundamental to our way of life.
- **Margaret Thatcher:** referring to the Soviet magazine, *Red Star* which had called her the "Iron Lady".

4,301. Today we are afraid of simple words like goodness and mercy and kindness. We don't believe in the good old words because we don't believe in good old values, and that's why the world is sick.
- **Lin Yutang:** *The Importance of Living,* 1937.

VIOLENCE

4,302. Violence is the last refuge of the incompetent.
- **Isaac Asimov:** *Foundation*, 1951.

4,303. "Put your sword back in its place," Jesus said to him, "for all who draw the sword will die by the sword."
 - **The Bible:** *Matthew 26: 52, NIV*.

4,304. Violence is the repartee of the illiterate.
- **Alan Brien:** *Punch,February, 1973*.

4,305. All that is necessary for the triumph of evil is that good men do nothing.
 - **Edmund Burke:** *attributed*.

4,306. Victory attained by violence is tantamount to a defeat, for it is momentary.
- **Mahatma Gandhi:** *Leaflet, May, 1919*.

4,307. Non-violence is the first article of my faith. It is also the last article of my creed.
- **Mahatma Gandhi:** *Speech in which he defended himself against a charge of sedition, 23rd March, 1922*.

4,308. Non-violence is the answer to the crucial political and moral questions of our time; the need for man to overcome oppression and violence without resorting to oppression and violence.
Man must evolve for all human conflict a method which rejects revenge, aggression and retaliation. The foundation of such a method is love.
- **Martin Luther King:** *in a speech on accepting the Nobel Peace Prize, 11th December, 1964*. Quoted in *Bartlett's Familiar Quotations*, edited by Justin Kaplin, 16th Edition, 1992.

4,309. The ultimate weakness of violence is that it is a descending spiral, begetting the very thing is seeks to destroy. Instead of diminishing evil, it multiplies it. Through violence you may murder the liar, but you cannot murder the lie, nor establish the truth.
- **Martin Luther King:** *Strength to Love,* 1963

4,310. Nothing good ever comes from violence.
- **Martin Luther**.

4,311. Violence is a crime against humanity, for it destroys the very fabric of society. On my knees I beg you to turn away from the paths of violence.
- **Pope John Paul II:** *in a speech at Drogheda, Ireland, 29th September, 1979.* Quoted in *Chambers Dictionary of Quotations,* 1996.

WAR

4,312. In war, truth is the first casualty.
- **Aeschylus**.

4,313. Mine is the first generation able to contemplate the possibility that we may live our entire lives without going to war or sending our children to war. That is a prize beyond value.
- **Tony Blair:** *in a speech delivered at a NATO summit meeting in Paris on 27th May, 1997, reported in The Sun the next day.*

4,314. War may sometimes be a necessary evil. But no matter how necessary, it is always an evil.
- **Jimmy Carter:** *in a speech on accepting the Nobel Peace Prize, 10th December, 2002.*

4,315. War settles nothing. To win a war is as disastrous as to lose one.
- **Agatha Christie:** *An Autobiography*, 1977.

4,316. All wars are civil wars, because all men are brothers.
- **Francois Fenelon**.

4,317. If the mothers ruled the world there would be no goddamned wars.
- **Sally Field:** *Acceptance speech at the Emmy Award Ceremony, 2007.*

4,318. War is an unmitigated evil.
- **Mahatma Gandhi:** *Non-Violence in Peace and War*. 1948.

4,319. It is possible, barely possible, to have a just war, a war waged in self-defence only as a final desperate expedient. But this is a rare exception in history. Almost all have been avoidable, and were seen to have been so after they ended. They have been wars not of survival, but of pride, power, possession.
- **Sydney J. Harris:** *Pieces of Eight*, 1975.

4,320. Mankind must put an end to war or war will put an end to mankind.
- **John F. Kennedy:** *in a speech delivered at the United Nations General Assembly. 25th September, 1961.*

4,321. The most persistent sound which reverberates through man's history is the beating of war drums.
- **Arthur Koestler:** *Janus: A Summing Up,* 1978 .

4,322. I don't oppose all wars. What I am opposed to is a dumb war... a rash war. A war based not on reason but on passion, not on principle but on politics.
- **Barack Obama:** *in a speech at anti-Iraq war rally, Chicago, October, 2002.*

4,323. War does not determine who is right, only who is left.
- **Bertrand Russell.**

WEALTH AND POVERTY

4,324. If you want to be rich, just count all the things you have that money cannot buy.
- *anon*.

4,325. Poverty is the parent of revolution and crime.
- **Aristotle:** *Politics*.

4,326. I am a poor man, but I have this consolation: I am poor by accident, not by design.
- **Josh Billings**.

4,327. The wealth ov a person should be estimated, not bi the amount he haz, but bi the use he makes ov it.
- **Josh Billings:** *Josh Billings: His Complete Works*, 1873.

4,328. If we command our wealth, we shall be rich and free, if our wealth commands us, we are poor indeed.
- **Edmund Burke:** *Geary's Guide to the World's Great Aphorists* . by James Geary, 2007.

4,329. But I have learned a thing or two; I know as sure as fate, / When we lock up our lives for wealth, the gold key comes too late.
- **Will Carleton:** *The Ancient Miner's Story* in *Rhymes of our Planet*, 1895.

4,330. Wealth, after all, is a relative thing, since he that has little, and wants less, is richer than he that has much, but wants more.
- **Charles Caleb Colton:** *Lacon, or Many Things In Few Word*s, edited by George J. Barbour, 2001.

4,331. He is bound fast by his wealth, his money owns him rather than he owns it..
- **St. Cyprian**.

4,332. Wealth consists not in having great possessions, but in having few wants.
- **Epicurus**.

4,333. The Scriptures first taught the futility of riches, but it took an income tax to drive the lesson home.
- **Evan Esar:** *20,000 Quips and Quotes*, 1968.

4,334. Look at me. I worked myself up from nothing to a state of extreme poverty.
- Groucho Marx in his role as Groucho in the **1931 Film**: *Monkey Business*, written by S. J. Perelman and Will B. Johnstone.

4,335. He who has good health, good humour, and no debts is not poor.
- **B. C. Forbes:** *Forbes Epigrams or 1,000 Thoughts on Life*, 1922.

4,336. Wealth is nothing more or less than a tool to do things with.
- **Henry Ford:** *Theosophist Magazine, February, 1930*.

4,337. Wealth is not his that has it, but his that enjoys it.
- **Benjamin Franklin:** *Poor Richard's Almanack*, 1736.

4,338. He that is of the opinion Money will do everything, may well be suspected of doing everything for Money.
- **Benjamin Franklin:** *Poor Richard's Almanack*, 1753.

4,339. Wealth is not without its advantages, and the case to the contrary, although it has often been made, has never proved widely persuasive.
- **John Kenneth Galbraith:** *The Affluent Society*, 1958.

4,340. It is a herculean task to cope with the handicap of wealth.
- **Elbert Hubbard:** *A Thousand And One Epigrams,* extracted from: *Preachments: Elbert Hubbard's Selected Writings, Part 4, by Fra Hubbard*, 1922.

4,341. Poverty is a great enemy of human happiness; it certainly destroys liberty, and it makes some virtues impractical, and others extremely difficult.
- **Samuel Johnson:** *The Life of Johnson*, by James Boswell, 1791.

4,342.A decent provision for the poor is the true test of civilization.
- *ibid.*

4,343. Poverty is like punishment for a crime you didn't commit.
- **Eli Khamarov:** *Lives of the Cognoscenti.*

4,344. In our rich consumers' civilization we spin cocoons around ourselves and get possessed by our possessions.
- **Max Lerner:** *The Unfinished Country,* 1959.

4,345. Being poor has its advantages. Your car keys, for instance, are never in your other trousers.
- **Bob Monkhouse:** *Just Say a Few Words,* 1988.

4,346. The greatest wealth is contentment with a little.
- ***English Proverb.***

4,347. Who is the rich person? The one who is happy with what he has.
- ***Jewish Proverb.***

4,348. The only thing wealth does for some people is to make them worry about losing it.
- **Antoine de Rivarol.**

4,349. It is not the man who has too little, but the man who craves more, that is poor.
- **Seneca:** *Epistles,* 1st century BC.

4,350. For many men, the acquisition of wealth does not end their troubles, it only changes them.
- **Seneca:** *Letters to Lucilius,* 1st century BC.

4,351. The wretchedness of being rich is that you live with rich people. To suppose, as we all suppose, that we could be rich and not behave as the rich behave, is like supposing that we could drink all day and stay sober.
- **Logan Pearson Smith:** *Afterthoughts,* 1931.

4,352. Poverty is no disgrace to a man, but it is profoundly inconvenient.
- **Sydney Smith:** *The Wit and Wisdom of Sydney Smith,* 2010.

4,353. A man is rich in proportion to the number of things he can afford to let alone.
- **Henry David Thoreau:** *Walden; or Life in the Woods,* 1854.

4,354. How unfortunate and how narrowing a thing it is for a man to have wealth who makes a god of it instead of a servant.
- **Mark Twain:** *in a letter to Commodore Vanderbilt, 1869.*

4,355. Though I am grateful for the blessings of wealth, it hasn't changed who I am. My feet are still on the ground. I'm just wearing better shoes.
- **Oprah Winfrey**.

4,356. Those who know they have enough are truly wealthy.
- **Lao Tzu:** *The Tao Te Ching,* translated by John H. McDonald, 1996.

WEATHER

4,357. Bad weather always looks worse through a window.
- *anon*.

4,358. There is no such thing as inappropriate weather, just inappropriate dress.
- *anon*.

4,359. What dreadful hot weather we have! It keeps me in a continual state of inelegance.
- **Jane Austin:** *in a letter dated 18th September, 1796*.

4,360. The rain it raineth on the just / And also on the unjust fella; / But chiefly on the just, because / The unjust steals the just's umbrella.
- **Lord Bowen:** *The Fireside Book of Humorous Poetry*, William Cole, 1959.

4,361. A well known American writer said once that while everybody talked about the weather, nobody seemed to do anything about it.
- **Editorial** in *The Hartford Courant, 27th August, 1897*. NB It has been suggested that the writer referred to here may have been Mark Twain or Charles Dudley Warner.

4,362. In the coldest February, as in every other month.... the best thing to hold on to in this world is each other.
- **Linda Ellerbee:** *Move One*, 1992.

4,363. When all is said and done, the weather and love are the two elements about which one can never be sure.
- **Alice Hoffman:** *Here On Earth*, 1997.

4,364. Don't knock the weather. If it didn't change once in a while, nine out of ten people couldn't start a conversation.
- **Kin Hubbard**.

4,365. The weather is like the government, always in the wrong.
- **Jerome K. Jerome:** *Idle Thoughts of an Idle Fellow*, 1886.

4,366. On the Continent there is one topic which should be avoided – the weather. In England, if you do not repeat the phrase, "Lovely day, isn't it?" at least two hundred times a day, you are considered a bit dull.
- **George Mikes:** *How To Be An Alien: A Handbook For Beginners and Advanced Pupils* with Nicholas Bentley, 1946.

4,367. There are holes in the sky, / Where the rain gets in. / But they're ever so small, / That's why the rain is thin.
- **Spike Milligan:** *There Are Holes In The Sky*.

4,368. You aren't really old until nothing is fun enough to make you forget the weather.
- **Robert Quillen**.

4,369. It is best to read the weather forecast before we pray for rain.
- **Mark Twain:** *More Maxims of Mark*, 1927.

4,370. I just saw the first sign of Spring. There is a list on the refrigerator door of things to do.
- **Pat Williams:** *Winning With One-Liners*, 2002.

4,371. It was so cold I almost got married.
- **Shelley Winters:** *The New York Times, April, 1956*.

WEDDINGS

4,372. If it were not for the presents, an elopement would be preferable.
- **George Ade:** *Forty Modern Fables*, 1901.

4,373. Good luck on your wedding day, / I think you're bold and plucky, / And as the other two have failed, / Let's hope it's third time lucky!
- **Pam Ayres:** *With These Hands*. 1997.

4,374. Two aerials met on a roof, fell in love and got married. The ceremony was rubbish, but the reception was brilliant.
 - **Tommy Cooper**.

4,375. There are no words in the English language that lead to as many quarrels as "I do."
- **Evan Esar:** *20,000 Quips and Quotes*, 1968.

4,376. If you invite only married couples to your wedding, the presents are clear profit.
 - **Leopold Fechtner:** *Encyclopedia of Ad-Libs, Crazy Jokes, Insults And Wisecracks*, 1977.

4,377. After paying for the wedding, about all a father has left to give away is the bride.
- **Leopold Fechtner:** *5,000 One-And-Two-Line Jokes*, 1978.

4,378. Music played at weddings always reminds me of the music played for soldiers before they go into battle.
- **Heinrich Heine:** *Book Of Songs*, 1856.

4,379. I'm getting married in the morning, / Ding! Dong! The bells are gonna chime / Pull out the stopper; / Let's have a whopper; / But get me to the church on time.
- **Alan Jay Lerner:** *My Fair Lady*, 1956 stage musical adapted from George Bernard Shaw's play *Pygmalian*, made into an award-winning film in 1964.

4,380. To church in the morning, and there saw a wedding in the church which I have not seen many a day; and the young people so merry one with another, and strange to see what delight we married people have to see those poor fools decoyed into our condition.
- **Samuel Pepys:***Diary,* 25th December,1665.

4,381. Wedding: the point at which a man stops toasting a woman and begins roasting her.
- **Helen Rowland:** *A Guide To Men,* 1922.

4,382. When two people are under the influence of the most violent, most insane, most delusive, and most transient of passions, they are required to swear that they will remain in that excited, abnormal, and exhausting condition continuously until death do them part.
- **G. B. Shaw:** *Getting Married,* 1908.

WISDOM

4,383. Wisdom and penetration are the fruits of experience, not the lessons of retirement and leisure.
- **Abigail Adams:** *letter to her son, John Quincy Adams, 19th January, 1780.*

4,384 Wisdom lies in knowing how ignorant we are, and keeping the knowledge to ourselves.
- ***anon***.

4,385. Intelligence is when you spot a flaw in your boss's reasoning. Wisdom is when you refrain from pointing it out.
- **James Dent**.

4,386. The greatest wisdom not applied to action and behaviour is meaningless data.
- **Peter Drucker:** *The Effective Executive*, 1967.

4,387. He is a wise man who does not grieve for the things which he has not, but rejoices for those which he has.
- **Epictetus:** *Discourses*, 2nd century BC.

4,388. Knowledge can be communicated, but not wisdom. One can find it, live it, be fortified by it, do wonders through it, but one cannot communicate and teach it.
- **Herman Hesse:** *Siddhartha*, 1922.

4,389. The wisdom of the wise is an uncommon degree of common sense.
- **Dean Inge**.

4,390. The art of being wise is the art of knowing what to overlook.
- **William James:** *Principles of Psychology*, 1890.

4,391. Wisdom does not always come with age. Sometimes age comes by itself.
- **Ann Landers**.

4,392. Wisdom is the reward you get for a lifetime of listening when you'd have preferred to talk.
- **Doug Larson**.

4,393. It's so simple to be wise. Just think of something stupid to say and say the opposite.
- **Sam Levenson**.

4,394. The older I grow, the more I distrust the familiar doctrine that age brings wisdom.
 - **H. L. Mencken:** *Prejudices: Third Series,* 1922.

4,395. We can be knowledgeable with other men's knowledge, but we cannot be wise with other men's wisdom.
- **Michel de Montaigne:** *Essays,* 1580.

4,396. We don't receive wisdom; we must discover it for ourselves after a journey that no one can take for us or spare us.
- **Marcel Proust:** *Remembrance of Things Past,* 1927.

4,397. To acquire knowledge, one must study, but to acquire wisdom, one must observe.
- **Marilyn vos Savant**.

4,398. Practical wisdom is only to be learned in the school of experience. Precepts and instruction are useful so far as they go, but, without the discipline of real life, they remain of the nature of theory only.
- **Samuel Smiles:** *Self – Help,* 1859.

4,399. Wisdom is knowing how little we know.
- **Socrates**.

4,400. Wisdom is the daughter of experience.
 - **Leonardo da Vinci:** *The Notebooks of Leonardo da Vinci* translated by Jean Paul Richter, 1888.

4,401. Besides the noble art of getting things done, there is the noble art of leaving things undone. The wisdom of life consists in the elimination of non- essentials.
- **Lin Yutang,:** *O Magazine, 20th October, 2002*

WIVES

4,402. My wife is impossible. It is only safe to wake her from a distance, like Portugal.
- **Tim Allen:** *I'm Not Really Here,* 1996.

4,403. My wife possessively asserts / Her wifely right to pick my shirts / With steady hands and birdlike eyes./ She picks my hats and socks and ties / She picks, like other wives and mamas / My underware and my pyjamas. / She picks my coats, both sport and top, / And there I'd let the matter drop, / Except as I observe with rue, / She sometimes picks my pockets too.
- **Richard Armour:** *Taking Her Pick.*

4,404. It is a truth universally acknowledged, that a single man in possession of a good fortune, must be in want of a wife.
- **Jane Austin:** *Pride and Prejudice*

4,405. Wives are young men's mistresses, companions for middle age, and old men's nurses.
- **Francis Bacon:** *The Essays: Of Marriage & the Single Life,* 1597.

4,406. Every man who is high up loves to think that he has done it all by himself; and the wife smiles, and lets it go at that.
- **J. M. Barrie:** *What Every Woman Knows, Act 4,* 1908.

4,407. My wife is still as pretty as she used to be. It just takes her longer now!
- **Milton Berle.**

4,408. Helpmate: n. a wife, or bitter half.
- **Ambrose Bierce:** *The Devil's Dictionary,* 1911.

4,409. The most precious thing I have in life is your love for me.
- **Winston Churchill:** Written to his wife, Clementine, in 1920, quoted in *The Wit and Wisdom of Winston Churchill,* by James C. Humes, 1994.

4,410. My most brilliant achievement was my ability to be able to persuade my wife to marry me.
- **Winston Churchill:** *My Darling Clementine* by Jack Fishman, 1963.

4,411. I was in the attic the other day with the wife. Filthy, dirty and covered in cobwebs - but she's good with the kids.
- **Tommy Cooper:** *The Very Best Of Tommy Cooper, Vol 2,* 2005.

4,412. My wife said to me this morning, she said, "You'll drive me to my grave." I had the car out in two minutes.
- *ibid.*

4,413. Henry VIII had so many wives because his dynastic sense was very strong whenever he saw a maid of honour.
- **Will Cuppy:** *The Decline and Fall of Everybody,* 1950.

4,414. My wife and I were happy for twenty years. Then we met.
- **Rodney Dangerfield**.

4,415. My wife has a slight impediment in her speech – every now and then she stops to breathe.
- **Jimmy Durante**.

4,416. Man's best possession is a sympathetic wife.
- **Euripedes:** *Antigone, Frag. 164.* 5th century BC.

4,417. I'm a married man and I can't ask for a better wife – but I would like to.
- **Leopold Fechtner:** *5,000 One-And-Two-Line Jokes,* 1973.

4,418. The trouble with most men is they know all about women but nothing about wives.
- *ibid.*

4,419. There is one thing more exasperating than a wife who can cook and won't, and that's the wife who can't cook and will.
- **Robert Frost:** *The Treasury of Humorous Quotations* edited by Evan Esar, 1955.

4,420. I chose a wife, as she did her wedding gown, not for a fine glossy surface, but such qualities as would wear well.
- **Oliver Goldsmith:** *The Vicar of Wakefield*, 1766.

4,421. Of all blessings, no gift equals the gentle, trusting love and companionship of a good woman.
- **Elbert Hubbard**.

4,422. Any notion of a wife at forty is that a man should be able to change her, like a bank note, for two twenties.
- **Douglas Jerrold**.

4,423. Only two things are necessary to keep one's wife happy. One is to let her think she is having her own way, the other, to let her have it.
- **Lyndon B. Johnson:** *Wit and Wisdom of the American Presidents* edited by Joslyn Pine, 2001.

4,424. I say bless those wives that fill our lives with little bees and honey. They ease life's shocks, they mend our socks – but can't they spend the money.
- **Tom Lawrence:** *The Victorian Clown* by Jacky Bratten and Ann Featherstone. 2006.

4,425. If your wife wants to learn to drive, don't stand in her way.
- **Sam Levenson**.

4.426. I'm not saying my wife is a bad cook, but she uses a smoke alarm as a timer.
- **Bob Monkhouse**.

4,427. Wife swapping is never done in the best circles of society. Wives can rarely, if ever, be traded for anything useful like a set of golf clubs.
- **P. J. O'Rourke:** *Modern Manners: An Etiquette Book for Rude People*, 1989.

4,428. When a wife explores her husband's pockets, she generally gets what the average explorer does- enough material for a lecture!
- **Herbert V. Prochnow and Herbert V. Prochnow Jr:** *The Public Speaker' Source Book*, 1977.

4,429. There isn't a wife in the world who has not taken the exact measurement of her husband, weighed him and settled him in her own mind, and knows him as well as if she had ordered him after designs and specifications of her own.
- **Charles Dudley Warner**.

4,430. I could search the whole world over (and) you'd still be everything that I need.

- **Don Williams:** *You're My Best Friend,* lyrics by Ernest Tubb.

4.431. My wife is doing a better job of keeping her bills down. She bought a heavier paperweight.

- **Pat Williams:** *Winning With One-Liners,* 2002.

4,432. My wife used to be a guitar player. She got rid of the guitar and now just picks on me.

- **Henny Youngman:** *How Do You Like Me So Far?* 1963.

4,433. Can she talk! She was in Miami, and when she got home, her tongue was sunburned!

- *ibid.*

WOMEN

4,434. Women have a passion for mathematics. They divide their age by half, double the price of their clothes, and always add at least five years to the age of their best friend.
- **Marcel Achard**.

4,435. Women like silent men. They think they are listening.
- *ibid*.

4,436. Women are like cell phones. They like to be held and talked to, but push the wrong button, and you'll get disconnected.
- *anon*.

4,437. If it weren't for women, men would be wearing last week's socks.
- *anon*.

4,438. Liking their looks
But not their notions,
I view the sex
With mixed emotions.
- **Richard Armour:** *The Ladies* in *An Armoury of Light Verse*, 1964.

4,439. The true worth of a race must be measured by the character of its womanhood.
- **Mary McLeod Bethune:** *in a speech given in Chicago in the early 1930's*

4,440. WOMAN. n. an animal usually living in the vicinity of Man, and having a rudimentary susceptibility to domestication.
- **Ambrose Bierce:** *The Devil's Dictionary*, 1911.

4,441. Next to God, we are indebted to women, first for life itself, and then for making it worth having.
- **Christian Nestell Bovee:** *Thoughts, Feelings and Fancies*, 1857.

4,442. Auld nature swears, the lovely dears
Her noblest work she classes O.
Her prentice han' she tried on man,
An' then she made the lassies O.
- **Robert Burns:** *Green Grow the Rashes, O,* 1783.

4,443. Brigands demand your money or your life; women require both.
- **Samuel Butler:** *Further Extracts from Notebooks,* 1934.

4,444. Feminine logic is fallacious, shallow, inconsistent, irrelevant, capricious, transparent - and irrefutable.
- **Harold Coffin.**

4,445. Women are like tricks by sleight of hand,
Which, to admire, we should not understand.
- **William Congreve:** *Love For Love,* 1695.

4,446. But what is woman? - only one of nature's agreeable blunders.
- **Hannah Cowley:** *Whose The Dupe? Act II, Sc II,* 1779.

4,447. There are many things in life I will never understand – and they're all women.
- **Jim Davis.**

4,448 I'm not denying that women are foolish; God almighty made 'em match men.
- **George Eliot:** *Adan Bede,* 1859.

4,449. I should like to know what is the proper function of women, if it is not to make reasons for husbands to stay at home, and still stronger reasons for bachelors to go out.
 - **George Eliot:** *The Mill on the Floss,* 1860.

4,450. Only two kinds of people claim to understand women, one is a woman and the other is a liar.
- **Evan Esar:** *The Comic Encyclopedia,* 1978.

4,451. The great question that has never been answered, and which I have not yet been able to answer, despite my thirty years of research into the feminine soul, is "What does a woman want?"
- **Sigmund Freud:** *Sigmund Freud: Life and Work* by Ernest Jones, 1953.

4,452. If the heart of a man is depressed with cares,
The mist is dispelled when a woman appears.
- **John Gay:** *The Beggar's Opera, Act II, Sc I,* 1728.

4,453. The surest way to hit a woman's heart is to take aim kneeling.
- **Douglas Jerrold:** *Douglas Jerrold's Wit,* 1858.

4,454. A woman on time is one in nine.
 - **Addison Mizner:** *The Treasury of Humorous Quotations* edited by Evan Esar, 1955.

4,455. Be to her virtues very kind; / Be to her faults a little blind.
- **Matthew Prior:** *An English Padlock,* 1707.

4,456. An average woman's vocabulary is said to be about 500 words. Small inventory, but think of the turnover.
- **Herbert V. Prochnow and Herbert V, Prochnow Jr:** *The Public Speaker's Source Book,* 1977.

4,457. A woman is a man's solace, but if it wasn't for her, he wouldn't need any solace.
 - ***ibid.***

4,458. Once a girl gets past the age of eight, she knows her deadliest weapon is her tongue.
- **Publisher's blurb:** *Women's Wicked Wit* by Michelle Lovrie, 2001.

4,459. I'd much rather be a woman than a man. Women can cry, they wear cute clothes,and they are the first to be rescued off sinking ships.
- **Gilda Radner**.

4,460. A woman is like a tea bag. It's only when she's in hot water that you realize how strong she is.
- **Nancy Reagan:** *The Observer, 29th March, 1981.*

4,461. Money and women are the most sought after and the least known about of any two things we have.
- **Will Rogers**.

4,462. It takes one woman twenty years to make a man of her son – and another woman twenty minutes to make a fool of him.
- **Helen Rowland:** *A Guide To Men,* 1922.

4,463. Women are wiser than men because they know less and understand more.
- **James Stephens::** *The Crock Of Gold*, 1912.

4,464. In politics, if you want anything said, ask a man. If you want anything done, as a woman.
- **Margaret Thatcher:** *The People, September,1975.*

4,465. Somebody has said that woman's place is in the wrong. That's fine. What the wrong needs is a woman's presence and a woman's touch. She is far better equipped than men to set it right.
- **James Thurber:** *Lanterns and Lances*, 1961.

4,466. What, Sir, would the people of the earth be without women? They would be scarce , Sir, almighty scarce.
- **Mark Twain:** *"Woman – An Opinion,"* a speech delivered on 11th January, 1868. Quoted in *The Wit and Wisdom of Mark Twain: A Book of Quotations*, 1999.

4,467. Woman is ever fickle and changeable.
- **Virgil:** *The Aeneid, Bk IV*. 1st century BC.

4,468. When Venus said, "Spell 'no' for me" / "N-O," Dan Cupid wrote with glee, / And smiled at his success; / "Ah, child," said Venus, laughing low, / "We women do not spell it so, / We spell it 'Y-E-S.' "
- **Carolyn Wells**.

4,469. Whatever women do they must do twice as well as men to be thought half as good. Luckily, this is not difficult.
- **Charlotte Whitton:** Canadian feminist, quoted in *Canada Month, June, 1963*.

4,470. Women are meant to be loved, not understood.
- **Oscar Wilde:** quoted in *Lord Arthur Saville's Crime and Other Stories*, 1891.

WORDS

4,471. Let others, when the party's done
And they are home in bed,
Berate themselves for chances missed
And gems of wit unsaid.

I'm sleepless, taut. Beneath the sheets
My burning face is hid -
Not for the things I didn't say
But for the things I did.
- **Richard Armour:** *At Wit's End* in *An Armoury of Light Verse*, 1942.

4,472. A synonym is a word you use when you can't spell the word you first thought of.
- **Burt Bacharach**.

4,473. All words are pegs to hang ideas on.
- **Henry Ward Beecher:** *Proverbs From Plymouth Pulpit*, 1887.

4,474. To be fair, English is full of booby traps for the unwary foreigner. Any language where the unassuming word *fly* signifies an annoying insect, a means of travel, and a critical part of a gentleman's apparel is clearly asking to be mangled.
- **Bill Bryson:** *The Mother Tongue: English and How It Got That Way*, 1990.

4,475. A word in a dictionary is very much like a car in a mammoth motor show - full of potential, but temporarily inactive.
- **Anthony Burgess:** *A Mouthful of Air: Language and Languages, Especially English*, 1992.

4,476. A blow with a word strikes deeper than a blow with a sword.
- **Robert Burton:** *The Anatomy of Melancholy*, 1621.

4,477. Words are like money: there is nothing so useless, unless when in actual use.
- **Samuel Butler:** *The Note-books of Samuel Butler, Part VII,* 1912.

4,478. Words fascinate me. They always have. For me, browsing in a dictionary is like being turned loose in a bank.
- **Eddie Cantor:** *The Way I See It,* 1959.

4,479. "When I use a word," Humpty Dumpty said in a rather scornful tone, "it means just what I choose it to mean – neither more nor less."
- **Lewis Carrol:** *Through the Looking Glass.* 1872.

4,480. Words, which are the dress of thoughts, deserve surely more care than clothes, which are only the dress of the person.
- **Lord Chesterfield:** *Letters to His Son,* 20th November, 1753.

4,481. Short words are best and the old ones, when short, are best of all.
- **Winston Churchill:** *America* by Alistair Cooke, 1973.

4,482. Sticks and stones may break our bones, but words will break our hearts.
- **Robert Fulgham:** *All I Really Need to Know I learned in Kindergarden.*

4,483. Once a word has been allowed to escape, it cannot be recalled.
- **Horace:** Roman poet and satirist, 1st century BC.

4,484. Words are, of course, the most powerful drug used by mankind.
- **Rudyard Kipling:** *The Times, 15 February, 1923.*

4,485. When you put somethings into words, it leads to so many other thoughts.
- **Madeleine L'Engle:** *The Small Rain,* 1945.

4,486. He that uses his words loosely and unsteadily will either not be minded or not understood.
- **John Locke:** *An Essay Concerning Human Understanding,* 1689.

4,487. It's a good idea to keep your words soft and sweet because you never know when you'll have to eat them!
- **Mad Magazine:** *Alfred E. Neuman's View.*

4,488. People laugh at me because I use big words. But if you have big ideas you have to use big words to express them, haven't you?
- **Lucy Maud Montgomery:** *Anne of Green Gables*, 1908.

4,489. Words are like leaves. And where they most abound,
Much fruit of sense beneath are rarely found.
- **Alexander Pope:** *An Essay on Criticism*, 1711.

4,490. The scene is a classroom where the little darlings have been told to search the dictionary for an unteresting word around which to construct a sentence. One of the gems produced is: "My trousers yearn for me." The puzzled teacher seeks an explanation. The child opens the dictionary at the appropriate place and says :"There you are miss, yearn – to long for."
- **Tom Shields:** *Tom Shields Goes Forth*, 2,000.

4,491. Words are loaded pistols. You use them at your peril!
- **Tony Slattery:** *Halliwell's Who's Who in the Movies*, 1997.

4,492. I see that everywhere among the race of men it is the tongue that wins and not the deed.
- **Sophocles:** *Philoctetes*, 5th century BC.

4,493. Man does not live by words alone, despite the fact that sometimes he has to eat them.
 - **Adlai Stevenson:** *in a speech in Denver, Colorado, 5th September,1952*

4,494. When ever he spoke, which he did almost always, he took care to produce the very finest and longest words of which the vocabulary gave him the use, rightly judging that it was as cheap to employ a handsome, large, and sonorous epithet, as to use a little stingy one.
- **William Makepeace Thackery:** *Vanity Fair*, 1848.

4,495. No matter what anybody tells you, words and ideas can change the world.
- **Robin Williams**, in his role as the unorthodox teacher, Mr Keating, in the 1989 film: *Dead Poets' Society*, written by Tom Schulman.

WORK

4,496. Tell your boss what you really think about him and the truth will set you free!
- *anon.*

4,497. If a train station is where the train stops, what's a work station?
- *anon.*

4,498. Life is mostly froth and bubble,
Two things stand like stone:
Dodging duty at the double,
Leaving work alone.
- *anon.*

4,499. The more I want to get something done the less I call it work.
- **Richard Bach:** *Illusions: The Adventures of a Reluctant Messiah*, 1977.

4,500. It's not real work unless you would rather be doing something else.
- **James M. Barrie:** *Rectorial Address, St. Andrews University, 1922.*

4,501. I do most of my work sitting down, that's where I shine.
- **Robert Benchley:** *The Algonquin Wits* edited by Robert Drennan, 1968.

4,502. A man willing to work, and unable to find work, is perhaps the saddest sight that fortune's inequality exhibits under the sun.
- **Thomas Carlyle:** *Chartism – a pamphlet*, 1839.

4,503. Set me a task in which I can put something of my very self, and it is a task no longer, it is a joy.
- **Bliss Carman:** *The Forbes Book of Business Quotations*, 1991.

4,504. You seem to have no real purpose in life and won't realize at the age of twenty two that for a man life means work, and hard work if you mean to succeed.
- **Lady Randolph Spencer Churchill:** in a *letter to her son, Winston, dated 26th February, 1897,* quoted in *Jennie: The Life of Lady Randolph Churchill* by R.G. Martin, 1974.

4,505. Chose a job you love, and you will never have to work a day in your life.
- **Confucius** 5th century, BC.

4,506. Why delight in work? Fundamentally, I suppose, because there is a sense of relief and pleasure in getting something done – a satisfaction not unlike that which a hen enjoys on laying an egg.
- **Dale Dauten**.

4,507. I never did a day's work in my life. It was all fun.
- **Thomas Edison**.

4,508. Personally, I have nothing against work, particularly when performed quietly and unobtrusively by someone else.
- **Barbara Ehrenreich** *The Worst Years of Our Lives,* 1990.

4,509. Work is another unpleasant four letter word that many people avoid.
 - **Evan Esar** *The Comic Encyclopedia,* 1978.

4,510. Many a man works himself to death by burying himself in his work.
- **Evan Esar** *20.000 Quips and Quotes,* 1968.

 4,511. All work and no play makes Jack a dull boy – and Jill a wealthy widow.
- *ibid.*

4,512. Two things help to keep one's job. First, let the boss think he's getting his own way. Second, let him have it.
 - **Sam Ewing** *The Wall Street Journal, 4th December, 1996.*

4,513. Hard work spotslights the character of people. Some turn up their sleeves, some turn up their noses, and some don't turn up at all.
- **Sam Ewing** *Reader's Digest, November, 1996.*

4,514. Laziness may appear attractive, but work gives satisfaction. I can't understand people who don't like work.
- **Anne Frank:** *The Diary of a Young Girl,* 1947

4,515. The world is full of willing people; some willing to work, the rest willing to let them.
- **Robert Frost:** *The Treasury of Humorous Quotations* edited by Evan Esar, 1955.

4,516. From approximately the ages of 21 to 70, we will spend our lives working. We will not sleep as much, spend as much time with our families, eat as much, or recreate and rest as much as we will work. Whether we love our work, or hate it, succeed in it or fail, achieve fame or infamy through it, we are all, like sisyphus, condemned to push and chase that thing we call our job, our career, our work all of our days.
- **Al Gini:** *The Importance of Being Lazy: In Praise of Play. Leisure and Vacations,* 2003. NB In Greek mythology, Sisyphus, the evil king of Corinth, was condemned to spend all eternity in the underworld rolling a huge boulder uphill, which always fell back before he reached the summit.

4,517. When work is a pleasure, life is a joy! When work is a duty, life is slavery.
- **Maxim Gorky:** *How to Retire Happy, Wild and Free* by Ernie Zelinski, 2004.

4,518. Work is the greatest thing in the world, so we should always save some of it for tomorrow.
- **Don Herold:** *Reader's Digest, April, 1966.*

4,519. Working yourself to death is a highly regarded form of suicide.
- **Frans Hiddema:** *Geary's Guide to the World's Great Aphorists* by James Geary, 2007.

4,520. Life grants nothing to us without hard work.
- **Horace:** *Satires. **circa** 8 BC.*

4,521. Life without absorbing occupation is hell.
- **Elbert Hubbard:** *A Thousand and One Epigrams* – from Elbert Hubbard's *Selected Writings, Part 4.*

4,522. One way to make sure everyone gets to work on time would be to have 95 parking spaces for every 100 employees.
- **Michael Iapoce.**

4,523. I like work, it fascinates me. I can sit and look at it for hours. I love to keep it by me; the idea of getting rid of it nearly breaks my heart.
- **Jerome K. Jerome:** *Three Men in a Boat,* 1889.

4,524 I always wait for *The Times* each morning. I look at the obituary column, and, if I'm not in it, I go to work.
- **A. E. Matthews:** English stage and screen actor who continued to work well into his 80's.

4,525. A good rule of thumb is: if you get to be thirty five and your job involves wearing a name tag, you've probably made a serious vocational error.
- **Dennis Miller.**

4,526. The boss told me, "This is just a suggestion. You don't have to follow it unless you want to keep your job."
- **Bob Monkhouse:** *Just Say a Few Word,* 1988.

4,527. If we get fired, its not failure, it's a mid life vocational readjustment.
- **P. J. O'Rourke:** *Rolling Stone Magazine.*

4,528. I only go to work on days that don't end in 'Y'.
- **Robert Paul.**

4,529. The golden rule of work is that the boss's jokes are always funny.
- *ibid.*

4,530. You cannot be really first-rate at your work if your work is all you are. Don't ever confuse the two, your life and your work.
- **Anna Quindlen:** *A Short Guide to a Happy Life,* 2000.

4,531. It's true hard work never killed anyone, but I figure, why take the chance?
- **Ronald Reagan:** *in a speech delivered on 28th March, 1987.*

4,532. If work has taken over your life, finding a way to manage your time won't solve the problem. Instead, you'll need to manage yourself, get your priorities straight, and focus your attention on what really matters.
- **Cheryl Richardson:** *Take Time For Your Life,* 1999.

4,533. It took me better than a quarter century to learn, the hard way, that hard work at something you want to be doing is the most fun you can have out of bed.
- **Spider Robinson:** *It's Only Too Late if You don't Start Now* by Barbara Sher, 1998.

4,534. My experience has been that work is almost the best way to pull oneself out of the depths.
- **Eleanor Roosevelt:** *in a letter to Pauline Emmet dated 11th January,1939* in *Eleanor and Franklin* by Joseph P. Lash, 1971.

4,535. When you see what some girls marry, you realize how they must hate to work for a living.
- **Helen Rowland:** *A Guide to Men Being Encore Reflections of a Bachelor Girl.* 1922.

4,536. One of the symptoms of an approaching breakdown is the belief that one's work is terribly important.
- **Bertrand Russell:** *Conquest of Happiness,* 1930.

4,537. If I were a medical man, I should prescribe a holiday to any patient who considered his work important.
- ***ibid***

4,538. The man who does not work for the love of work, but only for money, is not likely to make money, nor to find much fun in life.
- **Charles Schwab:** *Quotable Business* by Louis E. Boone, 1999.

4,539. Perpetual devotion to what a man calls his business, is only to be sustained by perpetual neglect of many other things.
- **Robert Louis Stevenson:** *Virginibus Puerisque and Other Papers,* 1881.

4,540. We have become a generation of people who worship our work, who work at our play and who play at our work.
- **Charles Swindoll:** *Reader's Digest, September, 1994.*

4,541. I do not like work even when someone else does it.
- **Mark Twain:** *The Lost Napoleon* in *The Complete Essays of Mark Twain* edited by Charles Neider, 1963.

4,542. Work banishes those three great evils: boredom, vice and poverty.
- **Voltaire:** *Candide,* 1759.

4,543. No race can prosper till it learns that there is as much dignity in tilling a field as in writing a poem.
- **Booker T. Washington:** *Up From Slavery* (his autobiography), 1901.

4,544. There must be some truth in reincarnation. Just look at the way some office workers come back to life after quitting time.
- **Pat Williams:** *Winning With One-Liners*, 2002.

4,545. I don't have too large an office. People keep coming in and asking for brooms.
- *ibid.*

THE WORLD

4,545. There is no way in which to understand the world without first detecting it through the radar-net of our senses.
- **Diane Ackerman:** *A Natural History of Our Senses*, 1990.

4,546. It gets to seem as if way back in the Garden of Eden after the fall, Adam and Eve had begged the Lord to forgive them and he, in his boundless exasperation, had said, "All right, then, stay. Stay in the Garden. Get civilized. Procreate. Muck it up," and they did.
- **Diane Arbus:** *Diane Arbus: An Aperture Monogram*, 1972.

4,547. Until Eve arrived, this was a man's world.
- **Richard Armour:** *Sisterhood is Powerful: An Anthology of Writings from the Women's Liberation Movement*, 1970.

4,548. Try and leave this world a little better than you found it.
- **Robert Baden Powell:** *from a letter he had written to all Scouts, found in his desk after his death.*

4,549. I would rather live in a world where life is surrounded by mystery, than live in a world so small that my mind could comprehend it.
- **Harry Emerson Fosdick:** *Riverside Sermons*, 1958.

4,550. A world without love would be no world.
- **Johann Wolfgang von Goethe:** *Roman Elegies and Other Poems and Epigrams*, 1789.

4,551. We do not have to visit a madhouse to find disordered minds; our planet is the mental institution of the universe.
- **Johann Wolfgang von Goethe.**

4,552. This is my Father's world. O let me ne'er forget / That though the wrong seems oft so strong, God is the ruler yet.
- **Amy Grant:** *Legacy* (Audio CD), 2002.

4,553. If you think of this world as a place intended simply for our happiness, you will find it quite intolerable; think of it as a place of training and correction and it's not so bad.
- **C. S. Lewis:** *Answers to Questions on Christianity* in *God in the Dock: Essays on Theology and Ethics*, 1970.

4,554. The new electronic interdependence recreates the world in the image of a global village.
- **Marshall McLuhan:** *Gutenberg Galaxy*, 1962.

4,555. There are no passengers on Spaceship Earth. We are all crew.
- **Marshall McLuhan:** *Paradigms Lost: Learning From Environmental Mistakes, Mishaps and Misdeeds* by Daniel A. Vallero, 2006.

4,556. All the world's a stage and most of us are desperately unrehearsed.
- **Sean O'Casey:** *The Plough and the Stars*, 1926.

4,557. We do not inherit the earth from our ancestors, we borrow it from our children.
- *Native American Proverb.*

4,558. All the world's a stage,
 And all the men and women merely players;
 They have their exits and their entrances;
 And one man in his time plays many parts.
- **William Shakespeare:** *As You Like It, Act II, Sc VI1*, 1623.

WORRY

4,559. Blessed is the person who is too busy to worry in the daytime and too sleepy to worry at night.
- **Leo Aikman:** *The Atlanta Journal – Constitution.*

4,560. Don't tell me that worry doesn't do any good. I know better. The things I worry about don't happen.
- *anon.*

4,561. You do not get ulcers because of what you eat. You get ulcers from what is eating you.
- *anon.*

4,562. Worry is the interest paid by those who borrow trouble.
- *anon.*

4,563. Definition of worry: duress rehearsal.
- *anon.*

4,564. That worry is wrong and hard on your health / I haven't the slightest doubt, / But most of the people who tell me this / Have nothing to worry about.
- **Richard Armour:** *A Poem for Pollyannas* in *An Armoury of Light Verse.*

4,565. ... do not worry about tomorrow, for tomorrow will worry about itself. Each day has enough trouble of its own.
- **The Bible:** *Matthew 6: 34 NIV.*

4,566. Cast your cares on the Lord and he will sustain you.
- **The Bible:** *Psalm 55, verse 22a, NIV*

4,567. I've always worried a lot and frankly I'm good at it.
- **Erma Bombeck:** *If Life is a Bowl of Cherries – What Am I Doing in the Pits?* 1978.

4,568. That's the secret of life - replace one worry with another
- **Charlie Brown**, the Peanuts cartoon character created by Charles Schultz.

4,569. Worrying about worrying can be corrosive.
- **Jeremy Bullmore:** *Another Bad Day at the Office?* 2001.

4,570. There are two days in the week about which and upon which I never worry. Two careful days, kept sacredly free from fear and apprehension. One of these days is yesterday, and the other day I do not worry about is tomorrow.
- **Robert Jones Burdette:** *Robert Burdette: His Message,* 1922.

4,571. When I look back on all those worries, I remember the story of the old man who said... that he had a lot of issues in his life, but most of which never happened.
- **Sir Winston Churchill:** *The Wit and Wisdom of Winston Churchill* by James C. Humes, 1994.

4,572. Worrying is as futile as boredom, but harder work.
- **Mason Cooley:** *City Aphorisms, Fourth Selection,* 1987.

4,573. If you want to test your memory, try to recall what you were worrying about one year ago today.
- **E. Joseph Cossman**.

4,574. Some of your hurts you have cured,
And the sharpest you still have survived,
But what torments of grief you endured
From evils which never arrived!
- **Ralph Waldo Emerson:** *The Works of Ralph Waldo Emerson, Vol 9, Poems: Quatrains, Borrowing From the French,* 1909.

4,575. Worry is like a rocking chair: it gives you something to do, but it gets you nowhere.
- **Evan Esar:** *The Comic Encyclopedia,* 1978.

4,576. The reason why worry kills more people than work is that more people worry than work.
- **Robert Frost:** *The Treasury of Humorous Quotations* edited by Evan Esar and Nicolas Bentley, 1955.

4,577. To carry care to bed is to sleep with a pack on your back..
- **Thomas Chandler Haliburton**.

4,578. Worry is the interest paid on trouble before it falls due.
- **William Ralph Inge:** *Observer, Sayings of the Week, 14 February, 1932.*

4,579. If you believe that feeling bad or worrying long enough will change a past or future event, then you are residing on another planet with a different reality system.
- **William James.**

4,580. The sovereign cure for worry is prayer.
- *ibid.*

4,581. And the night shall be filled with music,
And the cares that infest the day,
Shall fold their tents, like the Arabs,
And as silently steal away.
- **Henry Wordsworth Longfellow:** final stanza of *The Day is Done* in *Yale Book of American Verse* edited by Thomas R. Lounsbury, 1912.

4,582. A day of worry is more exhausting than a week of work.
- **John Lubbock:** *The Use of Life*, 1895.

4,583. We often hear of people breaking down from overwork, but in nine out of ten (cases) they are really suffering from worry or anxiety.
- *ibid.*

4,584. Lord, save us from worrying, lest ulcers be our badge for our lack of faith.
- **Peter Marshal:** *The Prayers of Peter Marshall*, 1985.

4,585. Life wouldn't be worth living if I worry over the future as well as the present.
- **Somerset Maugham:** *Of Human Bondage*, 1915.

4,586. Worry affects circulation . . the heart . . the glands, the whole nervous system. I have never known a man to die from overwork, but many who died from worry.
- **Charles H. Mayo:** *The American Mercury.*

4,587. Happy the person who has broken the chains which hurt his mind, and has given up, once and for all.
- **Ovid:** Roman poet.

4,588. Action is worry's worst enemy.
- *American Proverb*.

4,589. Worry gives a small thing a big shadow.
- *Swedish Proverb*.

WRITERS AND WRITING

4,590. After being turned down by numerous publishers, he had decided to write for posterity.
- **George Ade:** *Fables in Slang,* 1899.

4,591. A professional writer is an amateur who didn't quit.
- **Richard Bach:** *A Gift of Wings,* 1974.

4,592. The free-lance writer is a man who is paid per piece or per word or perhaps.
- **Robert Benchley**.

4,593. It took me fifteen years to discover that I had no talent for writing, but I couldn't give it up because by that time I was too famous.
- **Robert Benchley:** *Robert Benchley: A Biography* by Nathaniel Benchley 1955.

4,594. The pen is mightier than the sword.
- **Edward Bulwer-Lytton:** *Richelieu,* 1839.

4,595. I figured I'd write a book of 250 or 300 pages. I knew I could do it, I had the paper.
- **George Burns:** *The Third Time Round* in *The Most of George Burns,* 1991.

4,596. If writers were good businessmen, they'd have too much sense to be writers.
- **Irvin S. Cobb**.

4,597. There are three reasons for becoming a writer. The first is that you need the money; the second, that you have something to say that you think the world should know, and the third is that you can't think what to do with the long winter evenings.
- **Quentin Crisp:** *The Naked Civil Servant,* 1968.

4,598. Manuscript: Something submitted in haste and returned at leisure.
- **Oliver Herford**.

4,599. No man but a blockhead ever wrote except for money.
- **Samuel Johnson:** *The Life of Samuel Johnson* by James Boswell, 1791.

4,600. Who casts to write a living line must sweat.
- **Ben Jonson:** *To the Memory of my Beloved, the Author, Mr William Shakespeare*, 1618.

4,601. One man is as good as another until he has written a book.
- **Benjamin Jowett:** *The Life and Letters of Benjamin Jowett, Master of Balliol College, Oxford* edited by Evelyn Abbott and Lewis Campbell, 1899.

4,602. I handed in a script last year and the studio didn't change one word. The word they didn't change was on page 87.
- **Steve Martin:** *when introducing the best adapted screenplay at the 2003 Oscar ceremony*.

4,603 Almost anyone can be an author; the business is to collect money and fame from that state of being.
- **A. A. Milne:** *Not That It Matters*, 1919.

4,604. If you steal from one author, it's plagiarism; if you steal from many, it's research.
- **Wilson Mizner:** *The Legendary Mizners* by Alva Johnston, 2003.

4,605. Writing, when properly managed, (as you may be sure I think mine is) is but a different name for conversation.
- **Laurence Sterne:** *Tristram Shandy* (Wordsworth Classics), 1996

YOUTH

4,606. You know your children have grown up when they stop asking you where they came from and refuse to tell you where they are going.
- *anon.*

4,607. Adolescence is the age at which children stop asking questions because they know all the answers.
- *anon.*

4,608. Young people are in a condition like permanent intoxication, because youth is sweet and they are growing.
- **Aristotle:** *Nichomachean Ethics.4th Cen. BC.*

4,609. Growing up is life's most unique experience.
- **James H. S. Bossard:** *The Large Family System: An Original Study of the Sociology of Family Behaviour,* 1956.

4,610. Youth is like Spring, an over praised season.
- **Samuel Butler:** *The Way of All Flesh,* 1903.

4,611. Young men are apt to think themselves wise enough, as drunken men are apt to think themselves sober enough.
- **Lord Chesterfield:** *Letters to His Son,* 20th November, 1753.

4,612. I do not regret the folly of my youth, but the timidity.
- **Mason Cooley:** *City Aphorisms.*

4,613. There's nothing wrong with the younger generation that 20 years won't cure.
- **Sam Ewing:** *Mature Living, March, 1999.*

4,614. This is a youth-orientated society, and the joke is on them because youth is a disease from which we all recover.
- **Dorothy Fuldheim:** *Treasury of Women's Quotations* edited by Carolyn

Warner, 1997.

4,615. I see no hope for the future of our people if they are dependent on the frivolous youth of today, for certainly all youth are reckless beyond words. When I was a boy, we were taught to be discrete and respectful of elders, but the present youth are exceedingly wise and impatient of restraint.
- **Hesiod**.

4,616. Remember that as a teenager you are at the last stage in your life when you will be happy that the phone is for you.
- **Fran Lebowitz:** *Social Studies*, 1981.

4,617. The turning point in the process of growing up is when you discover the core of strength within you that survives hurt.
- **Max Lerner:** *The Unfinished Country*, 1959.

4,618. Teenagers are people who act like babies if they're not treated like adults!
Mad Magazine: *The Wit and Wisdom of Alfred E. Neuman*.

4,619. It is an illusion that youth is happy, an illusion of those who have lost it.
- **Somerset Maugham:** *Of Human Bondage*, 1915.

4,620. If you are young and you drink a great deal it will spoil your health, slow your mind, make you fat – in other words, turn you into an adult.
- **P. J. O'Rourke:** *Modern Manners: An Etiquette Book for Rude People* 1983.

4,621. Adolescence is a border between childhood and adulthood. Like all borders, it's teeming with energy and fraught with danger.
- **Mary Pipher:** *Reviving Ophelia: Saving the Selves of Adolescent Girls* 1994.

4,622. Little children, headache; big children, heartache.
- ***Italian Proverb***.

4,623. I feel that adolescence has served its purpose when a person arrives at adulthood with a strong sense of self-esteem, the ability to relate intimately, to communicate congruently, to take responsibility, and to take risks.
- **Viginia Satir:** *The New Peoplemaking*, 1988.

4,624. Negotiating the adolescent stage is neither quick nor easy.... I have often said to parents, "If it isn't illegal, immoral, or fattening, give it your blessing."
- *ibid.*

4,625. Teenagers don't rebel against other teenagers, In fact, no other group watches its peers with more intensity, scrutinizing the latest convention so they can conform precisely to it.
- **Barbara Sher:** *It's Only Too Late If You Don't start Now,* 1998.

4,626. Don't laugh at a youth for his affectations; he is only trying out one face after another to find out his own.
- **Logan Pearsall Smith:** *Afterthoughts,* 1932.

4,627. Boys are perhaps beyond the range of anybody's sure understanding, at least when they are between the ages of eighteen months and ninety years.
- **James Thurber:** *Lanterns and Lances,* 1961.

4,628. The deepest definition of youth is life as yet untouched by tragedy.
- **Alfred North Whitehead:** *Adventures of Ideas,* 1933.

4,629. To get back my youth I would do anything in the world, except take exercise, get up early, or be respectable.
- **Oscar Wilde:** *The Picture of Dorian Grey,* 1891.

4,630. Boyhood, like measles, is one of those complaints which a man should catch young and have done with, for when it comes in middle life it is apt to be serious.
- **P. G. Wodehouse:** *Uneasy Money,* 1917.

YOUTH AND OLD AGE

4,631. When I was young my mind was on food, booze, and girls. Now I never think of food.
- **George Burns:** *The Third Time Around*, 1980.

4,632. When I was young I was called a rugged individualist. When I was in my fifties I was considered eccentric. Here I am doing and saying the same things I did then and I'm labelled senile.
- **George Burns:** in his role as Bill, the former vaudevillian, in the 1979 film: *Just You and Me, Kid*.

4,633. The dead might as well try to speak to the living as the old to the young.
- **Willa Cather:** *One of Ours*, 1922.

4,634. Youth is when you blame all your troubles on your parents; maturity is when you learn that everything is the fault of the younger generation.
- **Harold Coffin:** *The Associated Press*.

4,635. Rashness is the companion of youth, prudence of old age.
- **Marcus Tullius Cicero**.

4,636. As a youth, I sought out decadence; as an elder, I try to avoid decay.
- **Mason Cooley:** *City Aphorisms, Fourteenth Selection*, 1994.

4,637. If I tended towards frivolity as a boy, I am incorrigibly settled in it now.
- **Robertson Davies:** *The Diary of Samuel Marchbanks*, 1947.

4,638. Youth is a blunder; Manhood a struggle; Old Age a regret.
- **Benjamin Disraeli:** *Coningsby* or *The Younger Generation*, 1844.

4,639. In youth we learn; in age we understand.
- **Maria von Ebner-Eschenbach:** *Aphorisms*, 1905.

4,640. If we could be twice young and twice old, we could correct all our mistakes.
- **Euripedes**.

4,641. Young people exchange greetings; middle-aged people exchange civilities; old people exchange infirmities.
- **Sydney J. Harris:** *Clearing the Ground*, 1986.

4,642. Age is not an accomplishment, and youth is not a sin.
- **Robert A. Heinlein:** *Methuselah's Children*, 1958.

4,643. I don't regret a single "excess" of my responsive youth – I only regret, in my chilled age, certain occasions and possibilities I didn't embrace.
- **Henry James:** *in a letter to Hugh Walpole the English novelist.*

4,644. A boy's love comes from a full heart; a man's is more often the result of a full stomach.
- **Jerome K. Jerome:** *Idle Thoughts of an Idle Fellow*, 1886.

4,645. The surprising thing about young fools is how many survive to become old fools.
- **Doug Larson**.

4,646. Old age has its pleasures, which though different, are not less than the pleasures of youth.
- **Somerset Maugham**: *The Summing Up*, 1938.

4,647. The young have aspirations that never come to pass, the old have reminiscences of what never happened.
- **Saki:** *Reginald at the Carlton*, in *Reginald*, 1904.

4,648. When you are younger you get blamed for crimes you never committed and when you're older you begin to get credit for virtues you never had. It evens itself out.
- **I. F. Stone:** *International Herald Tribune, Paris, 16th March, 1988.*

4,649. If you live long enough, the venerability factor creeps in; you get accused of things you never did and praised for virtues you never had.
- **I. F. Stone:** *Quotations for Our Time* compiled by Laurence Peters, 1988.

4,650. It is the epitome of life. The first half of it consists of the capacity to enjoy without the chance; the second half consists of the chance without the capacity.

- **Mark Twain:** *in a letter to Edward Dimmitt, 19 July, 1901.* NB Edward Dimmitt formed a social club for men over the age of 60 in Kansas City. This opened in 1893 and disbanded 25 years later.

INDEX OF AUTHORS AND SOURCES

ABBEY, Edward (1927 – 89), American author, essayist and radical environmentalist.

ACE, Jane (1897 – 1974) American radio actress and comedienne.(See quote No 3,714)

ACHARD, Marcel (1899 – 1974) French playwright and screenwriter

ACHESON, Dean (1893 – 1971) American lawyer and democratic statesman.

ACKERMAN, Diane (1948 -) American author, poet, essayist and naturalist.

ACTON, Lord (1834 – 1902) English Catholic historian, politician and writer.

ADAMS, Abigail (1744 – 1818) Prolific letter writer, feminist and wife of John Adams.

ADAMS, Ansel (1902 – 84) American photographer and environmentalist.

ADAMS, Douglas (1952 – 2001) English author, playwright and humorist.

ADAMS, Franklin P (1881 – 1960) American columnist, poet, humorist & radio personality.

ADAMS, Henry Brooks (1838 – 1918) American historian, journalist and man of letters.

ADAMS, Hunter "Patch" (1945 -) American physician, social activist and author.

ADAMS, Jane. American social psychologist, consultant, postparent coach and author.

ADAMS, Joey (1911 – 99) American comedian, author and humour columnist.

ADAMS, John (1735 – 1826) 2nd US President (1797 – 1801), and Abigail's husband.

ADAMS, Scott (1957 -) Widely syndicated American cartoonist and non-fiction author.

ADDAMS, Jane (1860 – 1935) American feminist, social activist and author.

ADDISON, Joseph (1672 – 1719) English essayist, poet , playwright and politician.

ADE, George (1866 – 1944) American humorist, columnist, author and playwright

ADLER, Mortimer J (1902 – 2001) American philosopher, educator and popular author.

ADLER, Polly (1900 – 62) Russian-born American madam in New York in the 1920/30s.

AESCHYLUS (c. 524 BC – 455 BC) Greek playwright, regarded as the father of tragedy.

AESOP (c 620 – 564 BC) Writer of anecdotal stories with moral or practical lessons.

AGAR, Herbert (1897 – 1980) American journalist who won the Pulitzer Prize for history.

AGATE, James (1877 – 1947) English diarist, theatre critic, essayist and raconteur.

AHBEZ, Eden (1908 – 95) American song writer and recording artist.

AIKMAN. Leo (1908 – 78) American columnist , popular public speaker and humorist.

AIMEE, Anouk (1932 -) Award-winning French film actress

ALBRAN, Kehlog. The pseudonym for Martin Cohen and Sheldon Shacket, the authors of The Profit, a parody of Kahlil Gibran's The Prophet.

ALCOTT, Amos Bronson (1799 – 1888) American teacher and educational reformer.

ALCOTT, Louisa (1832-88) American author of novels and short stories for young people

ALDA, Alan (1936 -) American award-winning screenwriter, director, actor and author.

ALDRICH, Dean Henry (1647-1710) English cleric, theologian and philosopher.

ALEXANDER, Shana (1925-2005) American columnist, television personality and author.

AL-HALIF, Omar Ibn. Ancient Persian sage.

ALLEN, Fred (1894-1956) American Radio and TV comedian and master ad libber.

ALLEN, George (1918 – 90) American football coach.

ALLEN, Gracie (1902-1964) American comedienne who, with her husband George Burns, featured in vaudeville, radio, films and television for almost 40 years (1922 - 1958).

ALLEN, James (1864-1912) English poet and author of self-help and inspirational books.

ALLEN, Steve (1921-2000) American comedian, television personality and author.

ALLEN Tim (1953 -) American comedian and film and television actor.

ALLEN, Woody (1935 -) American actor, screenwriter and award-winning film director.

ALLPORT, Gordon (1897-1967) An American psychologist who focused on personality.

AL-SIQILLI, Ibn Zafar (1104-72) Distinguished Arab philosopher.

ALTSHULER, Michael. American motivational speaker on personal achievement.

AMHERST, Lord (1717-97) English army officer and first British Governor General in the territories that eventually became Canada.

AMIEL, Henri Frederic (1821-81) Swiss philosopher, poet and critic

AMIS, Sir Kingsley (1922-95) English novelist, poet, critic and teacher.

ANDERSON, Greg. Best selling American author, motivational speaker and cancer survivor.

ANDERSON, Karen (1958 -) American animal communicator, author and public speaker.

ANDERSON, Pamela (1967 -) Canadian model, actress and animal crusader.

ANDERSON, Robert Woodruff (1917-2009) American playwright, screenwriter, producer.

ANGELOU, Maya (1928 -) African-American poet, memoirist and civil rights activist.

ANOUILH, Jean (1910-87) Prolific prize-winning French playwright.

ANTISTHENES (c 445 – c 365 BC) Greek philosopher and accomplished orator.

ANTRIM, Doran. Author of *Teaching Music and Making it Pay*.

ANTRIM, Minna (1861 – 1950) American epigrammatist and author of books for children.

The APOCRYPHA. Those books of the Old Testament not accepted as Hebrew Scripture.

ARBUS, Diane (1923 – 71) Controversial American photographer and writer.

ARCHER, Lord Jeffrey (1940 -) English conservative politician and best-selling novelist.

ARCHIMEDES (c 287 - 212 BC) Greek mathematician, scientist and inventor.

ARETINO, Pietro (1492 – 1556) Italian poet, author, satirist and playwright.

ARISTOTLE (384 - 322 BC) Influential Greek philosopher

ARMOUR, Richard (1906 - 89) Prolific American whimsical and satirical poet.

ARMSTRONG, Cora Harvey. American gospel singer and musician.

ARMSTRONG, Neil(1930 - 2012) American astronaut, the first man to step on the moon.

ASH, Mary Kay (1918 – 2001) American entrepreneur, founder of Mary Kay Cosmetics.

ASIMOV, Isaac (1920 – 92) Russian-born American biochemist and science-fiction author.

ASTAIRE, Fred (1899 – 1987) American film and theatre dancer, singer and actor.

ATKINSON, Brooks (1894 – 1984) American journalist and highly esteemed theatre critic.

AUDEN, W. H. (1907 – 73) English-born American poet, prolific essayist and reviewer.

AUGUSTINE Saint (354 - 430 AD) Christian Bishop of Hippo, philosopher & theologian.

AURELIUS, Marcus (121-180 AD) Roman Emperor, stoic philosopher and aphorist.

AUSTEN, Jane (1775 – 1817) English romantic novelist.

AYRES, Pam (1947-) English comic poet, songwriter, stage, radio and

TV entertainer.

BACALL, Lauren (1924 -) American model and film actress.

BACH, Richard (1936 -) Avid American aviator author.

BACHARACH, Burt (1928 -) American pianist, composer and music producer.

BACON, Sir Francis (1561 – 1626) English philosopher, statesman, scientist and author.

BADEN-POWELL, Sir Robert (1857 – 1941) English general, founder of the Boy Scouts.

BAER, Arthur "Bugs" 1886 – 1969) American journalist and humorist.

BAEZ. Joan (1941-) American award-winning folk singer, songwriter and social activist.

BAGEHOT, Walter (1826 – 77) English economist, essayist, political analyst and journalist.

BAILEY, Pearl (1918 – 90) Award-winning American actress, singer and autobiographer.

BAKER, Russell (1925 -) Pulitzer prize-winning American columnist and humorist.

BALDWIN, James (1924 – 1987) American novelist, essayist and civil rights activist.

BALFOUR, Lady Frances (1858 – 1931) Woman's suffragette, biographer & church woman.

BALL, Lucille (1911 – 1989) American comedienne, actress, TV star and business woman.

BALZAC, Honore de(1799 – 1850) Prolific French novelist, short story writer and playwright.

BANCROFT, Anne (1931 - 2005) Award-winning American stage, film and TV actress.

BANGS, John Kendrick (1862 – 1922) American author, humorist, editor and satirist.

BANKHEAD, Tallulah (1903 – 1968) Flamboyant American stage and film actress.

BARBARA, Joseph (1911 – 2006) American film and television animator and director.

BARCLAY, William (1907 – 1978) Scottish clergyman, theologian, teacher and author.

BARDOT, Brigitte (1934 -) French fashion model, actress, singer and animal rights activist.

BARKER, Ronnie (1929 – 2005) English TV star and prolific writer of comedy sketches.

BARR, Amelia (1831 – 1919) English-born American journalist and novelist.

BARRIE, Sir J. M (1860 – 1937) Scottish novelist and playwright.

BARRY, Dave (1947 -) American humour columnist, writer and musician.

BARRYMORE, John (1882 – 1942) American stage and film actor.

BARTH, Karl (1886 – 1968) Swiss Protestant theologian, educator.and prolific author.

BARTON, Bruce (1886 – 1967) American Congressman, advertising executive and author.

BARZUN, Jacques (1907 - 2012) American historian, philosopher of education and author.

BAUDELAIRE, Charles (1821 – 1867) French poet, essayist, art critic and translator.

BAUM, L. Frank (1856 – 1919) American journalist and author of children's books.

BAYLY, Thomas Haynes (1797 – 1839) English poet, songwriter and dramatist.

BEAUVOIR, Simone de (1908 – 1986) French philosopher, feminist and political activist.

BEECHER, Henry Ward (1813 – 1887) American clergyman, preacher and social reformer.

BEERBOHM, Sir Henry "Max"(1872 – 1956) English caricaturist, essayist and critic.

BEHAN, Brendan (1923 – 1964) Irish poet, short story writer, novelist and playwright.

BELL, Alexander Graham (1847 – 1922) Scots-born American scientist and inventor.

BELLOC, Hilaire (1870 – 1953) French-born English author of funny poems for children.

BELLOW, Saul (1915 – 2005) Canadian-born American Nobel Prize-winning novelist.

BENCHLEY, Peter (1940 – 2006) American novelist and non-fiction author.

BENCHLEY, Robert (1889 – 1945) American humorist, columnist, drama critic and actor.

BENDER, Texas Bix. American author of humorous books about cowboys and the west.

BENN, Tony (1925 -) English Labour politician and diarist.

BENNETT, Alan (1934 -) English playwright, screenwriter, actor and author.

BENNETT, Arnold (1867 – 1931) English journalist, novelist, essayist and critic.

BENNETT, Dan (1962 -) American prize-winning juggler, comedian and public speaker.

BENNETT, Robert (1933 -) Republican Senator from Utah..

BENNIS, Warren (1925 -) American economist and author. A pioneer in leadership studies.

BENNY, Jack (1894 – 1974) One of the top American entertainers of the 20th century.

BENSON, Ezra Taft (1899 – 1994) 13th President of the Mormon Church.

BENTHAM, Jeremy (1748 – 1832) English philosopher, economist, and social reformer.

BENTLEY, Nicolas (1907 – 78) English illustrator, cartoonist, editor and author.

BERENSON, Bernard (1865 – 1959) Lithuanian-born American art historian and critic.

BERESFORD, Lord Charles (1846 – 1919) English admiral and Member of Parliament.

BERGAMIN, Jose (1895 – 1983) Spanish writer, essayist, poet and playwright.

BERGMAN, Ingrid (1915 - 82) Award-winning Swedish actress.

BERGSON, Henri (1859 – 1941) A major and influential French philosopher.

BERLE, Milton (1908 – 2002) American award-winning comedian and early TV star.

BERNBACH, William "Bill"(1911 – 82) American advertising executive and copywriter.

BERNERS-LEE, Sir Tim (1955-) English computer scientist who invented the Web.

BERNHARDT, Sarah (1844 – 1923) Highly acclaimed French stage and silent film actress.

BERNSTEIN, Al. American Journalist, sportscaster and boxing analyst.

BERRA, Yogi (1925 -) Former major baseball league player, coach and manager.

BETHUNE, Mary McLeod(1875 – 1955) African-American educator & civil rights activist.

BIBESCO, Elizabeth (1897 – 1945) English writer, poet and deviser of aphorisms.

The BIBLE. The Christian scriptures consisting of the Old and the New Testament.

BIERCE, Ambrose (1842 - 1914 ?) American journalist, short story writer and satirist.

BILLINGS, Josh (1818 – 85) American humorist, lecturer and author.

BINYON, Laurence (1869 – 1943) English poet and art historian.

BIRKETT. Lord (1883 – 1962) English barrister, judge, politician and Methodist preacher.

BISHOP, Jim (1907 – 87) American syndicated columnist and author.

BISSET, Jacqueline (1944 -) English international film star and television actress.

BLACKWELL, Lawana.Prolific and popular American novelist.

BLAIR, Tony (1953 -) Scottish barrister, Labour politician, PM from 1997 till 2007.

BLAKE, William (1757 - 1827) English poet, painter, printmaker and mystic.

BLESSINGTON, Marguerite, the Countess of (1789 – 1849) Irish novelist.

BLITZER, Roy. American authority on human resources and business management.

BLUNKETT, David (1947 -) English Labour politician, blind from birth.

BLY, Mary E. American Shakespearian scholar and prolific romantic novelist.

BOGART, Humphrey (1899 – 1957) Academy award-winning American film star.

BOHR, Niels (1885 – 1962) Danish Nobel Prize-winning physicist.

BOLTON, Robert. American expert on ways to improve human performance.

BOMBECK, Erma (1927 – 96) American humorist, author and syndicated columnist.

BONHOEFFER, Dietrich (1906 – 45) German Lutheran pastor, theologian and martyr.

BONNELL, John. Pastor of the NY Fifth Avenue Presbyterian Church from 1935 till 1962.

BONO, Edward de (1933 -) A leading authority in the field of creative thinking.

BONSTETTEN, Karl von (1745 – 1833) Swiss deist with cosmopolitan interests.

BOONE, Louis E (1941-) American academic who writes on business and economics.

BOORSTIN, Daniel (1914 – 2004) American social historian, professor and prolific author.

BOREN, James H. American humorist, satirist, public speaker, educator and author.

BOSSARD, James (1888 – 1960) American social historian and prolific author.

BOSWELL, James (1740 – 95) Scottish lawyer and biographer of Dr Samuel Johnston.

BOVEE, Christian Nestell (1820 – 1904) American author of widely circulated epigrams.

BOWEN, Lord Charles (1835 – 94) English judge, translator and wit.

BOWEN, Elizabeth (1899 – 1973) Anglo-Irish novelist and short story writer.

BOYDE, Major Malcolm. Infantry officer killed in action, June, 1944.

BOYLE, Hal. (1911 - 74) American Pulitzer-winning journalist for *The Associated Press*.

BRADSTREET, Anne (1612 – 72) English-born American writer and puritan poet.

BRANDE, Dorothea (1893 – 1948) Well respected American writer and editor.

BRANDO, Marlon (1924-2004) Oscar Award-winning American stage and film star.

BRAUDE, Jacob. American raconteur and author of books of wit and wisdom.

BRAULT, Robert. American free-lance writer for over forty years.

BRAUN, Wernher von (1912 – 77) German-born American rocket scientist and engineer.

BREATHNACH, Sarah Ban. American author of best-selling inspirational books.

BRENT, Charles Henry (1862 – 1929) Canadian-born American Episcopalian Bishop.

BRICE, Fanny (1891 – 1951) American comedienne, singer, stage, radio and film actress.

BRIE, Andre (1950 -) German left wing politician. Member of the European Parliament.

BRIEN, Alan (1925 – 2008) English newspaper columnist, foreign correspondent and critic.

BRIGGS, Dorothy. American school psychologist and family counsellor.

BRIGHT, John (1811 – 89) English quaker, MP, radical statesman, orator and reformer.

BRITT, Steuart Henderson (1907 – 79) American advertising and marketing consultant.

BRODIE, Fawn M. (1915 – 81) American biographer and Professor of History at ACLA.

BRON, Eleanor (1938 -) English stage, film and television actress and author.

BRONTE, Charlotte (1816-55) English novelist and poet.

BROOKS, Phyllis. American teacher.

BROTHERS, Joyce (1927 -) American psychologist and syndicated advice columnist.

BROUN, Heywood C (1888 – 1939) American columnist who wrote on social issues.

BROWN, Alan Whitney (1952 -) American comedian and Emmy Award-winning writer.

BROWN, Gordon (1951 -) Scottish Labour MP since 1983. PM from 2007 till 2010.

BROWN, Hugh (1883 – 1975) Highly regarded Mormon leader, teacher and speaker.

BROWN, H. Jackson. American author of best-selling inspirational books.

BROWN, Pam (1948 -) Australian poet, librarian and editor.

BROWN, Rita Mae (1944 -) Prolific American novelist, screenwriter and feminist.

BROWN, Ronald (1926 -) Bishop of Birkenhead from 1974 till 1992.

BROWNING, Elizabeth Barrett (1806 – 61) English poet; wife of Robert Browning.

BROWNING, Robert (1812 – 89) English poet.

BRUCE, Lenny (1925 – 66) American comedian, satirist and social critic.

BRUDZINSKI, Wieslaw (1920 - 96) Polish satirist and aphorist.

BRUYERE, Jean de la (1645 – 96) French moralist and philosopher.

BRYSON, Bill (1951 -) American best-selling author of serious and humorous books.

BUCHAN, John, Baron Tweedsmuir (1875 – 1940) Scottish author and statesman.

BUCK, Pearl (1892 – 1973) Prolific American Nobel Prize-winning novelist.

BUCHWALD, Art (1925 – 2007) American humorist and Pulitzer Prize-winning columnist.

BUDDHA, Gautama, (c.563 - 483 BC) Spiritual teacher who founded Buddhism.

BULLMORE, Jeremy,(1929 -) Highly respected figure in the UK advertising scene.

BULWER-LYTTON, Edward (1803 – 1873) English politician, novelist, poet & playwright.

BUNUEL, Luis (1900 – 1983) Spanish screenwriter and film director.

BURDETTE, Robert Jones (1844 – 1914) American Baptist minister, columnist & humorist.

BURGESS, Anthony (1917 – 1993) Influential English novelist, libretist and translator.

BURGESS, Gelett (1866 – 1951) American artist, art critic, poet, author and humorist.

BURKE, Billie (1884 – 1970) Early Broadway musical comedy star and film actress.

BURKE, Edmund (1729 – 1797) Irish philosopher, political theorist., MP, and author.

BURNS, George (1896 – 1996) American comedian, writer and Oscar-awarded actor.

BURNS, Robert (1759 – 1796) Scottish poet & lyricist regarded as Scotland's national poet.

BURROUGHS, John (1837 – 1921) American conservationist and essayist.

BURTON, Robert (1577 – 1640) English Anglican clergyman, scholar and writer.

BUSCAGLIA, Leo F. (1924 - 1998) American academic, motivational speaker and author.

BUTLER, Nicholas Murray (1862 – 1947) American academic, philosopher and educator.

BUTLER, Samuel (1835 – 1902) English scholar,novelist, essayist and satirist.

BUXTON, Charles (1823 – 1871) English writer, philanthropist, MP and social reformer.

BUXTON, Sir Thomas Fowell (1786 – 1845) English social reformer, abolitionist and MP.

BYRNE, Robert (1928 -) American novelist and collector of wise and witty quotations.

BYRON, Lord George (1788 – 1824) Influential English romantic poet.

CAEN, Herb (1916 – 1997) Pulitzer Prize-winning *San Francisco Examiner* columnist.

CAESAR, Julius (c. 100 BC – 44 BC) Roman statesman and military leader.

CAESAR, Sid (1922 -) Emmy Award-winning American comic actor and TV personality.

CAINE, Sir Michael (1933 -) Accomplished Oscar-awarded English film star.

CALDWELL, Janet Taylor (1900 – 1986) English-born American author of popular fiction.

CALHOUN, John (1782 – 1850) American statesman, political theorist,orator and writer.

CAMPBELL, Joseph (1904 – 1987) American mythologist, writer and lecturer.

CAMPBELL, Thomas (1777 – 1844) Scottish poet and tutor..

CAMPOLO, Tony. Prolific American Christian author and highly regarded speaker.

CAMUS, Albert (1913 – 60) French Nobel Prize-winning author, journalist and philosopher.

CAMUTI, Louis (1893 – 1981) American vet who devote his practice solely to cats.

CANTOR, Eddie (1892 – 1964) American comedian, dancer, singer, actor and songwriter.

CAPP, AL (1909 – 1979) American humorist, prize-winning cartoonist, creator of *Li'l Abner*

CARAS, Roger A (1928 – 2001) American wildlife photographer and preservationist.

CARLETON, Will (1845 – 1912) American poet who wrote mainly about rural life.

CARLIN, George (1937 – 2008) American award-winning comedian and social critic.

CARLYLE, Jane Welsh (1801 – 1866) Scottish letter-writer, diarist and wife of Thomas.

CARLYLE Thomas (1795 – 1881) Scottish essayist, historian and political philosopher.

CARMAN, William Bliss (1861 – 1929) Canadian poet widely recognised internationally.

CARNEGIE, Andrew (1835 – 1919) Scots-born American entrepreneur and philanthropist.

CARNEGIE, Dale (1888 – 1955) American lecturer & writer of books on self-improvement.

CARPENTER, John (1948-) American film director, screenwriter and producer.

CARROL, Lewis (1832 – 1898) English poet and children's novelist.

CARRUTH, William Herbert (1859 – 1924) American poet, and linguistic scholar.

CARRUTHERS, Thomas. Possibly a teacher or involved in education administration.

CARSON, Frank (1926 -) Irish comedian and television personality.

CARSON, Johnny (1925 – 2005) American television host, monologist and comedian.

CARSON, Rachel (1907 – 1964) American marine biologist, ecologist and prolific author.

CARTER, "Jimmy" (1924 -) Democratic politician and 39th President of USA (1977- 81).

CARVER, George Washington (1864 – 1943) African-American scientist and educator.

CASEY, Karen. American speaker and author of best-selling inspirational books.

CASSIDY, David (1950 -) American songwriter, singer and actor.

CATHER, Willa (1873 – 1947) American Pulitzer prize-winning novelist, essayist and poet.

CATO the Elder (234 – 149 BC) Roman statesman, militery tribune and orator.

CAVANAUGH, Frank (1876 – 1933) American football player and coach.

CERF, Bennett (1898 - 1971) American raconteur and author of humour books.

CERVANTES, Miguel de (1547 – 1616) Spanish novelist, poet and playwright.

CHALMERS, Irena (1935 -) American award-winning author of cook books.

CHAMFORT, Nicholas (1741 – 1794) French writer best known for his witty aphorisms.

CHANDLER, Raymond (1888 – 1959) Anglo-American author of detective novels.

CHAPLIN, Sir Charles (1889 – 1977) English comic film actor and director.

CHARLES, Prince of Wales (1948 -) Eldest son of Queen Elizabeth and Prince Philip.

CHASE, Stuart (1888 – 1985) American economist, accountant and advertising executive.

CHATEAUBRIAND, Francois Rene de (1768 – 1848) French writer, politician & diplomat.

CHER (1946 -) Award-winning American singer-songwriter, actress and record producer.

CHESTER, Henry (1870 – 1942) Australian politician.

CHESTERFIELD, Lord (1694 – 1773) English politician, diplomat and letter writer.

CHESTERTON, Gilbert Keith (1874 - !936) English journalist, poet, essayist and novelist.

CHEVALIER, Maurice (1888 – 1972) French vaudeville entertainer, actor and singer.

CHILD, Julia (1912 – 2004) American chef, television personality and author.

CHILDS, George W (1829 – 1894) American publisher, businessman and philanthropist.

CHILRE, Doc Lew. Founder of an Institute to harness the power of the heart's intelligence.

CHING, Tao Te. Ancient Chinese collection of epigrammatic reflections on human life.

CHRISTIE, Agatha (1890 - 1976) English crime writer, author of short stories and plays.

CHURCHILL, Lady Randolph (1854 – 1921) American mother of Sir Winston Churchill.

CHURCHILL, Lord Randolph (1849 – 1895) English statesman and father of Winston.

CHURCHILL, Sir Winston (1874 – 1965) English politician, PM, brilliant orator & author.

CICERO, Marcus Tullius (106 BC – 43 BC) Roman politician, philosopher and orator.

CLAPIERS, Luc de, Marquis de Vauvenargues (1715 – 1747) French moralist and essayist.

CLARKE, Sir Arthur C (1917 – 2008) English science fiction writer.

CLARKE, Kenneth (1940 -) Conservative MP for Rushcliffe since 1970.

CLARKSON, Jeremy (1960 -) English broadcaster and motoring journalist.

CLAY, Henry (1777 – 1852) American statesman and orator.

CLEMENTS, Jonathan. Anglo-American award-winning personal finance columnist.

COATS, Carolyn. American author of children's books and cookery books.

COBB, Irvin S (1876 – 1944) Prolific American author, journalist and humorist.

COCKS, Sir Barnet, Clerk to the House of Commons.

COFFEE, Captain Gerald. American naval officer who spent 7 years as a Vietnam POW

COFFIN, Harold (1905 – 1981) One time humour columnist for *The Associated Press*.

COFFIN, William Sloane (1924 – 2006) American Presbyterian minister.and peace activist.

COGGAN, Donald (1909 – 2000) Anglican scholar and 101st Archbishop of Canterbury

COHEN, Alan. American lecturer and author of best selling inspirational books.

COLBERT, Jean-Baptiste (1619 – 1683) French politician and financial reformer.

COLERIDGE, Samuel Taylor (1772 – 1834) English poet, literary critic and philosopher.

COLETTE (1873 – 1954) Award-winning French novelist.

COLLINS, Jim. (1958 -) American business consultant, management expert and lecturer.

COLLINS, Joan (1933 -) English film and television star.

COLLINS, Marva (1936 -) American educator, author and speaker.

COLLINS, Wilkie (1824 – 1889) Prolific English novelist, short story writer, and essayist.

COLSON, Charles (1931 -) American Christian writer and speaker.

COLTON, Charles Caleb (1780 – 1832) English clergyman, poet, essayist and aphorist.

CONFUCIUS (551 - 479 BC) Chinese thinker, social philosopher and moral teacher.

CONGREVE, William (1670 – 1729) English poet and author of witty plays.

CONNOLLY, Billy (1942 -) Scottish comedian, musician, actor, TV presenter and author.

CONRAD, Joseph (1857 – 1924) Polish-born English novelist.

CONWAY, Linda. American compiler of quotations about teachers.

CONWAY, Pat (1945 -) Best selling American novelist.

COOK, Peter (1937 – 1995) English comedian and author of witty reviews.

COOKE, Alistair (1908 – 2004) English-born American journalist and broadcaster.

COOKE, Christopher Hamel (1921 – 2002) Outstanding Anglican clergyman.

COOLEY, Mason (1929 – 2002) American author of many books of aphorisms.

COOLIDGE, Calvin (1872 – 1933) Republican politician and 30th President of the USA.

COOPER, Jilly (1937 -) English columnist and prolific author of romantic novels.

COOPER, Tommy (1921 – 1984) Anglo-Welsh magician and comedian.

COPE, Wendy (1945 -) Award-winning English poet and television critic.

CORBETT, Ronnie (1930 -) Scottish comedian and television personality.

CORNEILLE, Pierre (1606 – 1684) French playwright , the founder of French tragedy.

CORTES, Hernando (1485 – 1547) The first of the Spanish conquistadors.

COSBY, Bill (1937 -) Award-winning American actor, comedian, author and TV producer.

COSSMAN, E. Joseph. Self-made American multi-millionaire and marketing specialist.

COUSINS, Norman (1915 – 90) American journalist, editor and writer.

COVEY, Stephen R (1932 -) American author of best selling time management books.

COWARD, Sir Noel (1899 – 1973) Witty English playwright, songwriter and singer.

COWLEY, Hannah (1743 – 1809) English poet and playwright.

COWPER, William (1731 – 1800) English poet and hymn writer.

COX, Marcelene. American humorist and author of parenting and inspirational books.

CRANE, Frank (1861 – 1928) Presbyterian minister, scholar, essayist, writer and speaker.

CRASHAW, Richard (1613 – 1649) English poet who converted to Roman Catholicism.

CRAWFORD, Joan (1905 – 1977) American film, television and theatre actress.

CRISP, Quentin (1908 – 1999) English writer, model and raconteur.

CRYSTAL, Billy (1948 -) American actor, writer, producer, comedian and film director.

CUMMINGS, E. E (1894 – 1962) American poet, essayist, author and playwright.

CUMMINGS, William Thomas. (1903 – 1945) American army chaplain in World War Two.

CUPPY, Will (1884 – 1949) American literary critic, humorist and satirical author.

CURTIS, Charles. American author of books on the law and public affairs.

CYPRIAN, St. (c. 210 – 258) Bishop of Carthage, theologian and martyr.

DAHL, Arlene (1928 -) American film actress, beauty columnist and business woman.

DALAI, Lama (1935 -) The spiritual leader of the Tibetan people.

DAMON, Bertha. American humorist, author, lecturer, editor and wit.

DANA, Charles Anderson (1819 – 1897) American journalist, newspaper editor and author.

DANA, John Cotton (1856 – 1929) Influential American librarian and museum director.

D'ANGELO, Anthony J. American creator of *The Inspirational Book Series*.

DANGERFIELD, Rodney (1921 – 2004) American comedian, actor and TV personality.

DANTE ALIGHIERI (1265 – 1321) Italian poet.

DARROW, Clarence (1857 – 1938) American defence counsel, champion of the underdog.

DARWIN, Charles (1809 – 1882) English naturalist who developed the theory of evolution.

DAUTEN, Dale. (1950 -) Widely syndicated American columnist and humorist.

DAVID, Elizabeth (1913 – 1992) Acclaimed and influential English cookery writer

DAVID, Harold "Hal" (1921 -) American lyricist who worked closely with Burt Bacharach.

DAVIDSON, Israel (1870 – 1939) American scholar, the leading Hebrew writer of his day.

DAVIES, Robertson (1913 – 955) Canadian academic, critic, novelist and playwright.

DAVIES, W. H. (1871 – 1940) Welsh "super tramp" poet and writer.

DAVIS, Bette (1908 – 1989) Academy award-winning American film star.

DAVIS, Jim (1945 -) American cartoonist, creator of the widely popular *Garfield*.

DAVY, Sir Humphry (1778 – 1829) English chemist, inventor of the Davy safety lamp.

DAWSON, Les (1931 – 1993) English television comedian.

DAY, Doris (1922 -) Award-winning American actress, singer and animal rights activist.

DAY, Dorothy (1897 – 1980) American journalist, social activist & devout Catholic convert.

DELILLE, Jacques (1738 – 1813) French poet and translator.

DEMING,W. Edwards (1900 – 1993) American statistician, professor, consultant & author.

DEMOSTHENES (c. 384 BC – 322 BC) Greek statesman and orator of ancient Athens.

DENT, James (1928 – 1992) American humorist, columnist and political cartoonist.

DESCARTES, Rene (1596 – 1650) French scholar dubbed "father of modern philosophy."

DE VRIES, Peter (1910 – 1993) American magazine editor and author of uproarious novels.

DEWER, Sir Thomas (1864 – 1930) Charismatic Scottish whisky distiller and aphorist.

DEWEY, John (1859 – 1952) American philosopher, teacher and educational reformer.

DIBDEN, Charles (1745 – 1814) English playwright, musician, songwriter and actor.

DICKENS, Charles (1812 – 1870) Prolific English novelist and social critic.

DIETRICH, Marlene (1901 – 1992) German-born American actress, singer and entertainer.

DILLARD, Annie (1945 -) Pulitzer prize-winning author, poet and environmentalist.

DILLER, Phyllis (1917 - 74) Award-winning American stand-up comedienne and actress.

DIPHILUS (4th century BC) Greek poet and writer of comedies.

DISNEY, Roy (1930 – 2009) Senior executive of the Walt Disney Company.

DISNEY, Walt (1901 – 1966) American animator, film producer, director and entrepreneur.

D'ISRAEL, Isaac (1766 – 1848) English man of letters and father of Benjamin Disraeli.

DISRAELI, Benjamin (1804 – 1881) English statesman, PM, brilliant debater and novelist.

DIX, Dorothy (1861 – 1951) Pen name of a highly paid American advice columnist.

DIXON, Norma. American comic poet.

DIXON, William Mac Neile (1866 – 1946) Irish academic and Professor of English.

DOANE, William Croswell (1832 – 1913) American Episcopalian Bishop.

DOBSON, James (1936 -) American Christian psychologist and author.

DOCHERTY, Tommy (1928 -) Scottish professional footballer and football manager.

DODD, Ken (1927 -) English comedian, songwriter and singer.

DONNE, John (c 1572 – 1631) English poet and Dean of St. Paul's Cathedral.

DORMANN, Henry. O. An American collector of quotations from people of influence.

DOSTOEVSKY, Fyodor(1821 – 1881) Russian novelist, essayist and author of short stories.

DOUGLAS, Kirk (1916) American film star and producer.

DRUCKER, Peter (1909 – 2005) American management consultant, teacher and writer.

DRYDEN, John (1631 – 1700) English poet laureate, literary critic and playwright.

DUKAKIS, Olympia (1831 -) Award-winning American stage, film and television actress.

DUMAS, Alexander (1802 – 1870) French novelist, essayist and playwright.

DUNNE, Finley Peter (1867 – 1936) American humorist and newspaper columnist.

DURANT, Will (1885 – 1981) Prolific American writer, historian, philosopher and teacher.

DURANTE, Jimmy (1893 – 1980) American singer, comedian and actor.

DURRELL, Lawrence (1912 – 1990) English novelist, poet and travel writer.

DURST, Will (1952 -) American political satirist and radio talk show host.

DYER, Wayne (1940 -) American author and lecturer in the field of self-development.

DYLAN, Bob (1941 -) Award-winning American singer songwriter and musician.

DYSON, Esther (1951 -) American entrepreneur and authority on digital technology.

EARHART, Amelia (1897 – 1939) American record breaking aviation pioneer.

EASTMAN, Max (1883 – 1969) American writer, poet and political activist.

EBAN, Abba (1915 – 2002) Israeli diplomat, politician and orator.

EBNER-ESCHENBACH, Marie von (1830 – 1916) Austrian novelist, dramatist & aphorist.

ECKHART, Meister (1260 – 1327) German theologian, philosopher and mystic.

EDDISON, Sydney. Lecturer and author of award-winning gardening books.

EDISON, Thomas A (1847 – 1931) American inventor with over 1,000 patents in his name.

EDWARD VII (1841 – 1910) Son of Queen Victoria. King of UK from 1901 till his death.

EDWARD VIII (1894 – 1972) Abdicated in order to marry Mrs Wallis Simpson

EDWARDS, Richard. American children's poet and author.

EHRENREICH, Barbara (1941 -) American feminist, author, columnist and political activist

EINSTEIN, Albert (1878 – 1955) German-born American theoretical physicist and author.

EISENHOWER, Dwight (1890 – 1969) Five-star American General who served as Supreme Commander in Europe in WW2. Was the 34th President of USA (1953 – 60).

ELDREDGE, Niles (1943 -) American paleontologist.

ELIOT, Charles (1834 – 1926) American academic who transformed Harvard University.

ELIOT, George (1819 – 1880) The pen name of the English novelist Mary Anne Evans.

ELIOT, T.S (1888 – 1965) American-born English poet, playwright and literary critic.

QUEEN ELIZABETH 2nd (1926 -) Queen of Great Britain since 1952.

ELLEDGE, Scott (1943 -) Professor of English Literature at Cornell University.

ELLERBEE, Linda (1944 -) American television journalist.

ELLISON, Ralph Waldo (1914 – 1994) American novelist, literary critic, scholar and writer.

ELTON, Ben (1959 -) English comedian, novelist, playwright and television director.

EMERSON, Ralph Waldo (1803 – 1882) American philosopher, essayist and poet.

ENBERG, Dick (1935 -) Award-winning American radio and TV

sportscaster and speaker.

EPHRON, Nora (1941 - 2012) American novelist, screenwriter, playwright and director.

EPICTETUS (Epic-TEE-tus) (c.55 – 135 AD) Greek sage and Stoic philosopher.

EPICURUS (341 BC – 270 BC) Greek philosopher, founder of Epicureanism.

ERNST, Morris L. (1888 – 1976) American lawyer who dealt primarily with civil liberties.

ESAR, Evan (1899 – 1995) American humorist, author of books of wise and witty quotes.

EURIPES (c. 480 – 406 BC) Prolific Greek dramatist of ancient Athens.

EVANS, Richard L (1906 – 1971) Mormon leader responsible for a weekly radio program.

EVANS, William R. American author.

EWING, Sam (1920 – 2001) American free lance writer and humorist.

FALKLAND, Lord (1610 – 1643) English politician, soldier and author.

FARRER, Austin (1904 – 1968) An English theologian, philosopher and author.

FAULKNER, William (1897 – 1962) Nobel Prize-winning American novelist.

FEATHER, William (1889 – 1981) Magazine editor and master epigrammatist.

FECHTNER, Leopold. American author of books of jokes and epigrams.

FEINSTEIN, Brett. American political advertising executive.

FELLINI, Federico (1920 – 1993) Award-winning Italian film director and screenwriter.

FENELON, Francois (1651 – 1715) French Roman Catholic Archbishop and theologian.

FENWICK, Cathy. Canadian humour therapist, educator and international speaker.

FERGUSON, Marilyn (1938 – 2008) American psychologist, author and public speaker.

FERGUSON, Ron. Widely experienced Church of Scotland minister, journalist and author.

FIELD, Eugene (1850 – 95) American humour columnist and writer of children'a poetry.

FIELD, Sally (1946 -) Award-winning American actress, screenwriter and director.

FIELDING, Henry (1707 – 54) English novelist, humorist, satirist and playwright.

FIELDING, Temple. (1913 – 83) American author of travel guide books.

FIELDS, W.C. (1880 – 1946) American vaudevillian, comedian, film actor and screenwriter.

FISHBEIN, Morris (1889 – 1976) American physician and medical journal editor.

FISHER, John. American advertising executive, author of *The Plot to Make You Buy*.

FITCH, James Marston (1907 - 2000) American architect, preservationist and author.

FITZGERALD, Edward (1809 – 83) English scholar, poet and translator.
FLYNN, Errol (1909 – 59) Flamboyant Australian-born American film star.

FOGLE, Bruce (1944 -) Canadian veterinarian and prolific author, resides in London.

FORBES, B. C. (1880 – 1954) Scottish financier who founded *The Forbes Magazine.*

FORBES, Malcolm (1919 – 1990) B.C's son who expanded and diversified the magazine.

FORD, Anna (1943 -) English journalist, television presenter and news reader.

FORD, Corey (1902 – 1969) American humorist, author, outdoors man and screenwriter.

FORD, Gerald (1913 – 2006) Republican politician and 38th President of the USA(1974-77).

FORD, Harrison (1942 -) American film star and producer.

FORD, Henry (1863 – 1947) American car manufacturer, devised the modern assembly line.

FORSTER, E. M. (1879 – 1970) English novelist and short story writer and literary critic.

FORSYTH, Frederick (1938 -) Prolific best selling English novelist.

FOSDICK, Harry Emerson (1878 – 1969) American Baptist clergyman and noted preacher.

FOSS, Sam Walter (1858 – 1911) American librarian, poet, journalist and humorist.

FOWLER, Gene (1890 – 1960) American journalist, author and screenwriter.

FRANCE, Anatole (1844 – 1924) French Nobel Prize-winning novelist.

FRANK, Anne (1929 – 1945) German Jewish diarist, died in Belsen concentration camp.

FRANKL, Victor (1905 – 1997) Austrian neurologist, psychiatrist and holocaust survivor.

FRANKLIN, Benjamin (1706 – 90) American scientist, inventor, statesman and author.

FREDERICK, "The Great" (1712 – 86) Enlightened King of Prussia from 1740 till 1786.

FREUD, Sir Clement (1924 – 2009) English chef, journalist, politician and TV personality.

FREUD, Sigmund (1856 – 1939) Austrian neurologist and psychiatrist.

FRIEDMAN, Milton (1912 – 2006) American Nobel Prize-winning economist.

FROMM, Erich (1900 – 80) German-born American psychologist and social philosopher.

FROMME, Allan (1916 – 2003) American psychologist.

FROST, Robert (1874 – 1963) Highly regarded Pulitzer prize-winning American poet.

FROTHINGHAM, Andrew. American author of books of quotations for speakers.

FROUDE, ("Frood") James, (1818 – 94) Controversial English historian and biographer.

FRY, Christopher (1907 – 2005) English award-winning playwright and screenwriter.

FRY, Stephen (1957 -) English actor, comedian, writer, TV presenter and film director.

FRY, William. American pioneer in the field of humour research.

FULDHEIM, Dorothy (1893 – 1984) American television journalist and television host.

FULGHUM, Robert (1937 -) American author and essayist.

FULLER, Thomas (1654 – 1734) English physician and collector of epigrams.

FUNSETH, Rod (1933 – 85) American professional golfer, one of the games long hitters.

GABLE, Clark (1901 – 60) American film star dubbed "The King of Hollywood"

GABOR, Zsa Zsa (1917 -) Hungarian-born American beauty queen, actress and socialite.

GALBRAITH, John Kenneth (1908 – 2006) Canadian-born American economist and author.

GALILEO (1564 – 1642) Italian physicist. One of the founders of modern science.

GALLOZZI, Chuck. American author of many personal development articles available on the internet. See: "Counterpoint Article Library – Chuck Gallozzi trans4mind"

GANDHI, Mahatma (1869 – 1948) India's political & spiritual leader prior to independence

GARBO, Greta (1905 – 90) Swedish-born American actress.

GARDNER, John W (1912 – 2002) American author of books on achieving excellence.

GARY, Romain (1914 – 1980) Popular French novelist, film director and screenwriter.

GASKELL, Elizabeth (1810 – 1865) English novelist who wrote about social issues.

GATES, Bill (1955 -) American computer entrepreneur, co-founder of Microsoft.

GATTY, Margaret (1809 – 1873) English author of books for children.

GAY, John (1685 - 1732) English poet and dramatist.

GAY, Peter (1923 -) German-born American author and history professor.

GERVASO, Roberto (1937 -) Italian political comentator and epigrammatist.

GETTY, J. Paul (1892 – 1976) American industrialist.Founder of the Getty Oil Company.

GHIGNA, Charles (1946 -) American award-winning author of children's books and poems.

GIBBON, Edward (1737 – 94) English author of *The Decline & Fall of the Roman Empire.*

GIBRAN, Khalil (1883 – 1931) Lebanese-born American artist, poet,essayist & philosopher.

GIBSON, Mel (1956 -) American-born Australian film star, screenwriter and director.

GILBERT, Sir W.S. (1836 – 1911) English dramatist, poet and librettist.

GINI, Al. American Professor of Business Ethics.

GLASGOW, Arnold (1905 – 98) American editor of a humour magazine.

GLASGOW, Ellen (1873 – 1945) American Pulitzer Prize-winning novelist.

GLIDEWELL, Jan. American humour columnist on *The St. Peterburg Times.*

GOAR, Carol. Widely experienced Canadian columnist on *The Toronto Star.*

GODWIN, Gail (1937 -) Award-winning American novelist and short story writer.

GOETHE, Johann Wolfgang von (1749 – 1832) German scholar, author and polymath.

GOLD, Taro. American author of books of inspirational quotes and poems.

GOLDSMITH, Oliver (1730 – 1774) Irish journalist,poet, essayist, novelist and playwright.

GOLDTHWART, Bobcat (1962 -) American actor, comedian, screenwriter and director.

GOLDWYN, Samuel (1879 – 1974) Polish-born American film producer.

GOODHEART, Annette. Internationally recognized therapist and laughter coach.

GORDON, Adam Lindsay (1823 – 1870) Australian poet, jockey and politician.

GORDON, Caroline (1895 – 1981) Acclaimed American novelist and literary critic.

GORKY, Maxim (1868 – 1936) Russian novelist, writer of short stories and plays.

GOSMAN, Fred G. American author of books on parenting.

GRACIAN, Baltasar (1601 – 1658) Spanish Jesuit scholar, moralist and philosopher.

GRAFFITI. Generally unauthorized writing or drawing on a flat surface in a public place.

GRAFTON, Sue (1940 -) American author of detective novels and TV screenwriter.

GRAHAM, Harry (1874 – 1936) English writer of humorous verses.

GRAHAM, William (Billy) (1918 -) American Baptist minister, evangelist and author.

GRAMMER, Kelsey (1955 -) American actor, producer, writer and comedian.

GRANT, Amy (1960 -) American singer-songwriter best known for her Christian music.

GRANT, Ulysses (1822 – 85) Union officer who became the 18th President of the USA.

GRAVINA, Giovanni (1664 – 1718) Italian scholar and man of letters.

GRAY, John. American author of books on relationships and personal growth.

GREELY, Horace (1811 – 72) Influential American newspaper editor and politician.

GREEN, Jim. Best-selling author with over 40 published titles.

GREENE, Graham (1904 – 91) Prolific English novelist and essayist.

GREENLEAF, Robert (1904 – 90) American consultant on business management.

GRELLET, Stephen (1773 – 1855) French Quaker missionary to North America.

GRENFELL, Joyce (1910 – 79) English TV and film actress, comedienne and monologist.

GRETZKY, Wayne (1961 -) Canadian high scoring professional ice hockey player.

GRIZZARD, Lewis (1946 – 94) Humour columnist, comedian and lecturer.

GROENING, Matt (1954 -) American cartoonist who created *The Simpsons*.

GROSS, Milton (1895 – 1953) American comic book writer, illustrator and animator.

GRUFFUDD, Loan (1973 -) Welsh film and television actor and musician.

GUEDALLA, Philip (1889 – 1944) English barrister, historian and biographer.

GUEST, Edgar Albert (1881 – 1959) American poet widely read in his day.

GURNEY, Dorothy Frances (1858 – 1932) English poet and hymn writer.

GYATSO, Tenzin (1935 -) The 14th Dalai Lama, the spiritual leader of Tibetan Buddhists.

HAAN, Charles (1920 – 2012) Harvard Law School Professor.

HAIG, Alexander (1924 – 2010) American General who served in WW2, Korea & Vietnam.

HAILE Selassie (1892 – 1975) Emperor of Ethiopia from 1930 till 1974.

HAJDUSIEWICZ, Babs Bell. American poet, educator and best-selling children's author.

HALIBURTON, Thomas Chandler (1796 – 1865) Nova Scotian judge & best selling author.

HALL, Doug. American inventor, author and marketing expert.

HAMILTON, Christine (1949 -) English public speaker, author and television personality.

MAMMARSKJOLD, Dag (1905 – 1961) Swedish diplomat, 2nd Secretary-General of UN.

HAMMERSTEIN, Oscar (1895 – 1960) Very prolific award-winning American lyricist.

HANCOCK, Tony (1924 – 1968) English situation comedy actor on radio and television.

HANLEY, Victoria. American author of fantasy novels for young people.

HANSOME, Rhonda. American stand up comedienne and actress.

HARBURG, E.Y. (1896 – 1981) Popular award-winning American song writer.

HARDIMAN, Larry. See Politics No 3,425.

HARKINS, David. English painter and poet, best known for his poem *Remember Me.*

HARKNESS, Richard (1907 – 77) American radio and TV journalist with NBC.

HARRIS, Sydney (1917 – 86) English-born American syndicated columnist and author.

HARVEY, Paul (1918 – 2009) Popular American radio broadcaster.

HASKINS, Minnie Louise (1875 – 1957) American poet and social science lecturer.

HAVEL, Vaclav (1936 - 2011) Czech playwright, essayist, poet and statesman.

HAYES, Helen (1900 – 93) Award-winning American actress.

HAYES, Rutherford B.(1822 – 93) Republican politician and 19th President of the USA.

HAYS, Brooks (1898 – 1981) American lawyer and Democratic politician.

HAYWORTH, Rita (1918 – 87) American dancer and film actress.

HAWKING, Stephen (1942 -) English theoretical physicist and Professor of Mathematics.

HAWTHORNE, Nathaniel (1804 – 64) American novelist and short story writer.

HAZLITT, William (1778 – 1830) English philosopher, essayist and literary critic.

HEALEY, Denis (1917 -) English MP, briefly deputy leader of the Labour party.

HECHT, Ben (1894 – 1964) American novelist, playwright, screenwriter and film producer.

HEFFER, Eric (1922 – 91) English Labour MP from 1964 till his death.

HEGEL, Georg Wilhelm Friederich (1770 – 1831) German philosopher.

HEILBRUN, Carolyn (1926 – 2003) American author of novels and scholarly studies.

HEINE, Heinrich (1797 – 1856) German poet, essayist and literary critic.

HEINLEIN, Robert (1907 – 1988) Popular and influential American science fiction writer.

HEINSIUS, Daniel (1580 – 1655) Dutch classical scholar and poet.

HELITZER, Melvin. Advertising executive, Professor of Journalism, author and humorist.

HELLER, Joseph (1923 – 1999) American novelist best known as author of *Catch-22*, 1961.

HEMMINGER, Graham Lee (1895 – 1950) American authority on advertising.

HENNESSY, Val. English journalist and chief book reviewer for *The Daily Mail*.

HEPBURN, Audrey (1929 – 93) Belgium-born English film star and humanitarian.

HERBERT, Sir Alan P. (1890 – 1971) English humorist, novelist, librettist and politician.

HERBERT, Frank (1920 – 86) Prolific and popular American science fiction writer.

HERBERT, George (1593 – 1633) Welsh Anglican clergyman, poet and author.

HERFORD, Oliver (1863 – 1935) English-born American poet, author and humorist.

HEROLD, Don (1889 – 1966) American illustrator, cartoonist, author and humorist.

HERRIOT, James (1916 – 1995) Scots trained veterinary surgeon and short story writer.

HESIOD (8th century BC) One of the earliest known Greek poets.

HESSE, Hermann(1877 – 1962) German-born Swiss Nobel Prize-winning poet and novelist.

HEYWOOD, John (c 1497 – c 1518 AD) English poet, playwright and epigrammatist.

HIBBEN, John (1861 – 1933) American Professor of Logic and President of Princeton.

HICKSON, William Edward (1803 – 70) English educational writer and editor.

HIDDEMA, Frans (1923 – 1997) Dutch psychoanalyst, poet and aphorist.

HIGGINSON, Thomas (1823 – 1911) American clergyman, author and abolitionist.

HILL, Gene (1941 - 2010) Columnist for *Field & Stream Magazine* & author of dog books.

HILL, Napoleon (1883 – 1970) American author of books on personal success.

HILL, Sir Rowland (1795 – 1879) English teacher and campaigner for postal reform.

HILLARY, Sir Edmund (1919 – 2008) New Zealand explorer and mountaineer.

HILLIS, Burton (1915 – 1977) American columnist on *The Kansas City Star*.

HILTON A (1851 – 1877) Anglican curate, the author of a collection of verse parodies.

HIPPOCRATES (c. 460 BC – 377 BC) Greek physician called "The Father of Medicine."

HIRSCH, Mary. American humour columnist and teacher of humorous writing.

HITCHCOCK, Sir Alfred (1899 – 1981) English film director and producer.

HITLER, Adolph (1889 – 1945) Absolute dictator of Germany from 1933 – 1945.

HOBAN, Russell (1926 -) American writer of fiction, poetry and children's books.

HOCH, Edward (1930 – 2008) American writer of short stories and detective novels.

HOFFENSTEIN, Samuel (1890 – 1947) American screenwriter and humorous poet.

HOFFER, Eric (1902 – 83) American aphorist, philosopher and writer on social issues.

HOFFMAN, Alice (1952 -) American novelist and author of books for youung adults.

HOFFMAN, Dustin (1937 -) Award-winning American film star.

HOLLANDER, Nicole (1939 -) Widely syndicated American newspaper cartoonist.

HOLLER, William. General Sales Manager of Chevrolet from 1933 till 1945.

HOLMES, John Andrew (1812 – 99) American lawyer and writer.

HOLMES, Oliver Wendell. Snr (1809 – 94) American physician, poet, lecturer and essayist.

HOLMES, Oliver Wendell Jnr (1841 – 1935) American judge on the Supreme Court.

HOLTZ. Lou (1937 -) American football coach, sportscaster, motivational speaker & author.

HOPE, Bob (1903 - 2003) English-born American vaudevillian, comedian and actor.

HOPKINS, Tom. American authority on selling, public speaker and prolific author.

HORACE (65 – 8 BC) The leading Roman poet during the time of Augustus.

HORNE, Harriet Van (1920 – 98) American newspaper columnist, film and TV critic.

HOWARD, Sandra (1940 -) English model, novelist and wife of a Conservative politician.

HOWARD, Vernon (1918 – 92) American philosopher, spiritual teacher and author.

HOWE, Edgar Watson (1853 – 1937) American editor, novelist and aphorist.

HOWE, Julia Ward (1819 – 1910) American feminist, social activist, suffragette and poet.

HUBBARD, Elbert (1856 – 1915) American artist, publisher, philosopher and essayist.

HUBBARD, Kin (1868 – 1930) American humorist, cartoonist and journalist.

HUFELAND, Christoph Wilhelm (1762 – 1836) German physician and author.

HUGEL, Friedrich von(1852 – 1925) Austrian RC layman, theologian & Christian apologist.

HUGHES,Langston (1902 – 67) African-American poet, novelist and social activist..

HUGO, Victor (1802 – 85) French novelist, playwright, poet and human rights activist.

HULLEY, Annie. English TV star, voice over artist, property invester and author.

HUME, David (1711 – 76) Scottish philosopher, economist, essayist and historian.

HUMES, James. American presidential speech writer and author of humour books.

HUNGERFORD, Margaret Wolfe (1855 - 97), Prolific Irish author of romantic novels.

HURLOCK, Elizabeth. American psychologist and author.

HURT, John (1940 -) Award-winning English actor.

HUTCHESON, Francis (1694 – 1746) Scottish philosopher.

HUTCHINS, Robert Maynard (1899 – 1977) American educational philosopher.

HUTCHINSON, Horace G (1859 – 1932) English author.

HUXLEY, Aldous (1894 – 1963) English intellectual,novelist, essayist, humanist & pacifist.

HUXLEY, Thomas Henry (1825 – 1895) English marine biologist and agnostic.

IACOCCA, Lee. Successful American businessman.

IAPOCE, Michael. American comedy writer who stresses the use of humour in business.

IBSEN, Henrik (1828 – 1906) Norwegian playwright second in popularity to Shakespeare.

INGE, Dean William Ralph (1860 – 1954) English Anglican prelate and Cambridge don.

INGELOW, Jean (1820 – 1897) English poet and novelist.

INGERSOLL, Robert G (1833 – 1899) American orator, lecturer and agnostic author.

IRELAND, Kathy (1963 -) American model, entrepreneur and marketing guru.

JACKS, L. P (1860 – 1955) English Unitarian minister, educator, philosopher and author.

JACKSON, Glenda (1936 -) English award-winning actress and Labour MP since 1992.

JAMES, Henry (1843 – 1916) American novelist who spent the last 40 years of his life in England, becoming a British subject in 1915.

JAMES, Jennifer. American writer and international speaker on change and thinking skills.

JAMES, Dame Phyllis Dorothy(1920 -) English crime writer known as P. D. James.

JAMES, William (1842 – 1910) American psychologist, philosopher and prolific author.

JAMES , King of the United Kingdom (1566 – 1625) During his reign the King James (Authorized) Version of the Bible was published.

JAY, Sir Anthony (1930 -) Co-author of two English television political comedies.

JEANS, Sir James (1877 – 1946) English physicist, astronomer and mathematician.

JEFFERSON. Thomas (1743 – 1826) Principal author of the Declaration of Independence.

JENKINS. Katherine (1980 -) Welsh Mezzo-soprana.

JEROME, Jerome (1859 – 1927) English playwright and author of humorous novels.

JERROLD, Douglas (1803 – 59) English writer, playwright and wit.

JESSE, Edward (1780 – 1868) English author of popular books on natural history.

JESSEL, Sir George (1824 – 83) Influential English trial judge and soliciter general.

JOHNSON, Barbara (1947 – 2009) American literary critic and Professor of English

JOHNSON, Dame Celia (1908 – 82) English stage and screen actress.

JOHNSON, Lyndon B. (1908 – 73) Democratic statesman, 36th President of the USA.

JOHNSON. Samuel (1709 – 84) Prolific English author, lexicographer and wit.

JONES, Bobby (1902 – 71) One of the greatest golfers of all time,.retired at the age of 28.

JONES, Franklin P. (1908 – 80) Philadelphia journalist and humorist.

JONG, Erica (1942-) American feminist writer, poet and novelist.

JONSON, Ben (1572 - 1637) English actor, poet and dramatist.

JORDAN, William George (1864 - 1928) American editor and author of self-help books.

JOUBERT, Joseph (1754 - 1824) French moralist and essayist.

JOWETT, Benjamin (1817 - 93) English classicist, theologian and Professor of Greek.

JUNG, Carl G (1875 - 1961) Swiss psychiatrist who founded analytical psychology.

JUVENAL (c. AD 60 - 140) Roman poet and satirist.

KANT, Immanuel (1724 - 1804) Influential German philosopher.

KARR, Alphonse (1808 - 90) French critic, journalist, editor and novelist.

KAUFMAN, George S (1889 - 1961) American playwright, drama critic and humorist.

KEATS, John (1795 - 1821) English romantic poet considered the best poet of his day.

KEEN, Sam (1931 -) Noted American professor, philosopher and author.

KEILLOR, Garrison (1942 -) American humorist, radio personality and writer.

KELLER, Helen (1880 - 1968) American author, public speaker, campaigner for the blind.

KELLER, Father James (1900 - 1977) American Roman Catholic priest and TV presenter.

KELLER, Jeff. American speaker, seminar leader and writer on human potential.

KELLY, Gene (1912 -) American dancer, actor, choreographer, film director and producer.

KELSEY, Linda. English free lance magazine writer, journalist and novelist.

KEMP, Penny. English writer who has published books on environmental issues.

KEMPIS. Thomas a (1380 - 1471) German Catholic monk and religious writer.

KEN, Thomas (1637 – 1711) English cleric, hymnwriter and bishop.

KENDAL, Felicity (1946 -) English stage and television actress.

KENDALL, Donald (1921 -) American businessman and political adviser.

KENNEDY, John F. (1917 – 63) The first Roman Catholic elected President of the USA.

KENNEDY, Marge. American author of books on parenting and education of children.

KERR, Deborah (1921 – 2007) Scottish film and television actress.

KERR, Jean (1922 – 2003) American playwright, screenwriter and humorist.

KETTERING, Charles (1876 – 1959) American engineer and inventor with 140 patents.

KEYNES, John Maynard (1883 – 1946) Influential English economist.

KHAMAROV, Eli (1948 -) English-born American philosopher..

KIERKEGAARD, Soren (1813-55) Danish philosopher and theologian.

KING, Martin Luther, (1929 – 68) American Baptist minister and civil rights leader.

KING, Stephen (1946 -) American author of best-selling horror novels.

KIPLING, Rudyard (1865 – 1936) English short story writer, poet and novelist.

KISSINGER, Henry (1923-) German-born American academic and diplomat.

KLEIN, Allen. American professional speaker, author of inspirational books of quotations.

KLEISER, Grenville (1868 – 1935) American author of guides to oratorical success.

KNEBEL,Fletcher (1911 - 93) American columnist, author of works of political fiction.

KOESTLER, Arthur (1905 – 83) Hungarian novelist, essayist and biographer.

KONNER, Joan. American TV documentary and news producer & Professor of Journalism.

KOPPEL, Ted. English-born American broadcast journalist and news analyst.

The KORAN (or Qur'an) The sacred book of Islam.

KUBLER-ROSS, Elizabeth (1926 – 2004) Swiss-born American psychiatrist.

KUNDERA, Milan (1929-) Czech-born French essayist, poet, novelist and playwright.

KUNG, Hans (1928-) Swiss Roman Catholic theologian.

LA BRUYERE, Jean de (1645 – 96) French satirist.

LAMARTINE, Alphonse de (1790 – 1869) French writer, poet and statesman.

LAMB, Charles (1775-1834) English essayist and critic.

LANDERS, Ann. The pen name of a widely syndicated American advice columnist.

LANDON, Michael (1936-91) American actor, writer, director and producer.

LANDOR, Walter Savage (1775-1864) English writer, poet and essayist.

LANESE, Janet. American contributing editor for parenting and religious magazines.

LANSKY, Bruce (1941-) Internationally acclaimed American poet and anthologist.

LARDNER, Ring Jr (1915 – 2000) American journalist and Oscar-winning screenwriter.

LA ROCHEFOUCAULD Francois de(1613 – 80) French writer, moralist and epigrammatist

LARSON, Doug. American syndicated columnist and epigrammatist.

LAWRENCE, D. H. (1885 – 1930) English novelist, poet and short story writer.

LAWRENCE, Tom . 19th century English circus clown and comedian.

LEACOCK, Stephen (1869 - 1944) English-born Canadian economist, writer and humorist.

LEAR, Edward (1812 – 88) English author of humorous and nonsense poetry for children.

LEARY, Timothy (1920 – 1996) American writer, psychologist, philosopher and teacher.

Le BOEUF, Michael. American business consultant, author and speaker.

LEBOWITZ, Fran (1950 -) American author, essayist and social columnist.

Le GUIN, Ursula (1929) American novelist, children's author in fantasy & science fiction.

LEHRER, Tom (1928 -) American singer-songwriter known for pithy and humorous songs.

LEIGH, Henry S (1837 – 1883) American poet.

LEMONS, Abe (1922 – 2002) American major league basketball coach.

L'ENGLE, Madeleine (1918–2007) American writer best known for her young adult fiction.

LENNON, John (1940 – 1980) English singer-songwriter, one of the Beatles.

LENO, Jay. (1950 -) American stand-up comedian and television host.

LEONARDO da Vinci (1452 – 1519) Italian painter, sculptor, engineer, inventor & writer.

LERMONTOV, Mikhail (1814 – 18 41) Russian novelist and poet killed in a duel.

LERNER, Alan Jay (1918 – 1986) American lyricist and songwriter for musicals.

LERNER, Harriet (1944 -) American authority on the psychology of women and families.

LERNER, Max (1902 – 1992) American journalist and columnist with *The New York Post.*

LESSING, Doris (1919 -) English novelist awarded the Nobel Prize for literature aged 87.

LEVENSON, Sam (1911 – 1980) American journalist, humorist, writer and television host.

LEVINE, Joseph E (1905 – 1987) American film producer and distributor.

LEVINE, Stephen (1937 -) American author known for his work on death and dying.

LEVITT, Ellis. American financier and philanthropist.

LEWIS,Clive Staples (1898 – 1963) Lay theologian and Oxford professor.

LEWIS. J. Patrick. American children's poet, author and speaker.

LEWIS, Sinclair(1885 – 1951) Nobel prize-winning American novelist & short story writer.

LI AO (1935 -) One of the most important modern Chinese essayists today.

LICHTENBERG, Georg Christoph (1742 – 1799) German scientist, philosopher & aphorist.

LIEBMANN, Joshua Loth (1907 – 1948) American Rabbi, author and public speaker.

LINCOLN, Abraham (1809 – 1865) Republican politician and 16th President of the USA.

LINCOLN, Mary Todd (1818 – 1862) Wife of Abraham Lincoln.

LINDBERG, Anne Morrow (1906 – 2001) A pioneering American aviator, author and poet.

LINKLETTER, Art (1912 – 2010) Canadian-born American radio and TV personality.

LIN YUTANG (1895 – 1976) Chinese philologist, essayist and translator.

LITTLE Mary Wilson. Late 19th century American writer.

LIVINGSTON, Irene. American author of books and poems for children.

LOCKE, John (1632 – 1704) English philosopher.

LOEB Evelyn. Prolific American author of inspirational books.

LOMBARDY, Vince (1913 – 1970) American football player, coach and executive.

LONGFELLOW, Henry Wadsworth (1807 – 1882) American poet and scholar.

LOOS, Anita (1888 – 1981) American author, screenwriter and playwright.

LOREN, Sophia (1934 -) Award-winning Italian film actress.

LORENZ, Konrad (1903 – 1989) Austrian zoologist, ornithologist and prolific author.

LORIMER, George Horace (1867 – 1937) Editor-in-Chief of *The Saturday Evening Post*.

LOUIS. Joe (1914 – 81) American world heavyweight boxing champian from 1937 till 1948.

LOWELL, James Russell (1814 – 1891) American poet, editor, critic and diplomat.

LU, XUN (1881 – 1936) Pen name of one of the major Chinese writers of the 20th century.

LUBBOCK, Sir John (1834 – 1913) English naturalist, biologist and politician.

LUCANO, Max (1955 -) Prolific and best-selling American author and pastor.

LUCAS, Edward Vernall (1868 -1938) Prolific English author and humorist.

LUCE, Clare Boothe (1903 – 1987) American playwright, journalist and Congresswoman.

LUNDEN, Joan (1950 -) American journalist, author and popular television host.

LUTHER, Martin (1483 – 1546) German priest who initiated the Protestant Reformation.

LYONS, Kim (1973 -) American personal trainer, nutritionist and fitness model.

LYNN, Jonathan. English comedy writer, actor and director.

McCABE, Charles (1915 – 1983) Columnist for *The San Francisco Chronicle.*

McCARTHY, Eugene (1916 – 2005) American poet and politician.

McCORRISKEN, Walter. Scottish "semi-skilled" poet, winner of a bad poetry competition.

McCULLOUGH, Coleen (1937 -) Internationally acclaimed Australian novelist.

McCULLOUGH, David (1933 -) American social historian and prize-winning author.

MACDONALD, Lord Angus (1940 -) Member of the House of Lords.

MACHALE, "Des", Irish academic and author of books of humorous quotations.

McINTIRE, Reba (1955 -) Award-winning American country singer, actress and producer

McGee, Paul. An international speaker and best-selling author of motivational books.

McGINLEY, Phyllis (1905 - 78) American poet, essayist and writer of children's books.

McGINNIS, Kim. American free-lance writer and entrepreneur.

McKAY, David (1873 – 1970) Highly esteemed 9th President of the Mormon Church.

MACKAY, Harvey. American public speaker and best-selling author of inspirational books.

McKENTY, Bob. American author of perceptive and humorous poems.

McLAUGHAN, Mignon (1913 - 83) American journalist, editor and author.

McLEAN, Don (1945 -) American singer-songwriter.

MACLEISH, Archibald (1892 - 1982) Prize-winning American poet and Congress librarian.

McLUHAN, Marshall (1911 - 80) Canadian author and Professor of English.

McMANUS, Patrick (1933 -) American columnist and outdoor humour writer.

McMORRIS, Kristina. American award-winning novelsit.

McWILLIAMS, Peter (1949 - 2000) American author of best-selling self-help books.

MACHIAVELLI, Nicola (1469 - 1527) Italian political philosopher, playwright and writer.

MACY, John Jr (1917 - 86) American government administrator and civil servant.

MAD MAGAZINE. Satirical American humour magazine which parodies current culture.

MADISON, James (1751 - 1836) 4th President of USA (1809 – 1817).

MAETERLINCK, Maurice (1862 - 1949) Belgian playwright, poet and essayist.

MAGEE, John Gillespie (1922 - 41) Anglo-American pilot, author of poem *High Flight*.

MAIMONIDES (1135 - 1204) Jewish Rabbi and the greatest Torah scholar of his day.

MANDELA, Nelson (1918 -) South African lawyer and politician.

MANDINO, Og (1923 - 96) American author of best-selling books on success.

MANN, Horace (1796 - 1859) American education reformer.

MANNING, Bernard (1930 - 2007) English comedian and night club owner.

MANSFIELD, Katherine (1883 – 1923) Talented English writer of short stories.

MARABOLI, Steve. American academic, inspirational author and speaker.

MARDEN, Orison Swett (1850 - 1924) Prolific American author of inspirational books.

MARGOYLES, Mariam (1941 -) English-born Australian award-winning actress.

MARKOE, Merrill (1948 -) American television writer and comedian.

MARLOWE, Christopher (1564 – 93) English playwright and poet.

MARQUIS, Don (1878 – 1937) American journalist, humorist and writer.

MARSHALL, Peter (1902 – 49) Scots-born American clergyman and Senate Chaplain.

MARSTON, Stephanie. American best-selling author and family therapist.

MARTIAL (c. 49 – 104 AD) Roman poet considered the creator of the modern epigram.

MARTIN, Joe. Noted as "the world's most prolific cartoonist" in Guinness Book of Records.

MARTIN, Steve. (1945 -) American actor, comedian, playwright, musician and composer.

MARX, Groucho (1890 – 1977) American comedian, film actor and wit.

MARX, Karl (1818 – 1883) German philosopher, historian, communist and revolutionary.

MARX, Zeppo (1901 – 1979) The youngest of the 5 Marx brothers, was a theatrical agent.

MASLOW, Abraham (1908 – 1970) American founder of Humanistic Psychology.

MASON, Jackie (1936 -) American stand-up comedian, featured on TV, films and radio.

MATTHEWS A.E. (1868 – 1960) English stage and film character actor.

MAUGHAM, W. Somerset (1874 – 1965) English playwright, novelist & short story writer.

MAUROIS, Andre (1885 – 1967)Prolific French author of novels, biography, science fiction.

MAXWELL, John C (1947 -) American pastor, speaker and author of books on leadership.

MAY, Rollo (1909 – 1994) American existentialist psychologist.

MAY, Simon (1956 -) English philosopher, author and aphorist.

MAYO, Charles H. (1865 – 1939) American physician, co-founder of the Mayo Clinic.

MAYS, Benjamin (1894 – 1984) American minister,educator, scholar and social activist.

MEAD, Margaret (1901 – 1978) American anthropologist and social psychologist.

MELTZER, Bernard (1916 – 1998) American host on a radio advice call-in show.

MENCKEN, H. L. (1880 – 1956) American journalist, essayist, satirist and critic.

MENNINGER,William (1899 – 1966) American psychiatrist.

MEREDITH, George (1828 – 1909) English novelist and poet.

MEREDITH, Owen. The pen name used by Robert Bulwer-Lytton for his books of poetry.

MERRITT, Dixon Lanire (1879 - 1972) American newspaper editor, poet and humorist.

MESTRUM, Theo (1956 -) Dutch author of aphorisms.

METCALF, Fred. English author of books of quotations and jokes.

MEURER, Dave.. American author of humorous books.

MICHELANGELO (1475 – 1564) Italian painter, sculptor, architect and poet.

MICHENER, James (1907 – 97)American author of many meticulously researched novels.

MIEDER, Wolfgang (1944 -) Professor of German and an authority on proverbs.

MIKES, George (1912 – 1987) Author of books which poke fun at people in foreign lands.

MILL, John Stuart (1806 – 73) English philosopher, economist and social reformer.

MILLE, Agnes de (1905 – 1993) American dancer and choreographer.

MILLER, Dennis. Award-winning American comedian, television talk show host and actor.

MILLER, John (1947 -) Former professional golfer on the PGA tour.

MILLER, Michael .American clinical and public health microbiologist.

MILLIGAN, Spike (1918 – 2002) English comedian, novelist, poet and jazz musician.

MILLMAN, Dan (1946 -) World trampoline champion and author of self-help books.

MILNE, A. A. (1882–1956) English playwright, novelist, poet & author of children's stories.

MILTON, John (1608 – 1674) English poet and outspoken pamphleteer.

MISS PIGGY. The voluptuous and love-lorn star of the Muppet Show.

MITCHARD, Jacquelyn (1957 -) American journalist, essayist and novelist.

MITCHELL, Warren (1926 -) English stage and television actor.

MITCHUM, Robert (1917 – 1997) American film actor.

MIZNER, Addison (1872 – 1933) American architect, entrepreneur, writer and wit.

MIZNER, Wilson (1876 – 1933) American playwright, raconteur and entrepreneur.

MOLIERE (1622 – 1673) French playwright – a master of comedy.

MONKHOUSE, Bob (1928 – 2003) English comedy writer, comedian, TV host and author.

MONKHOUSE, William Cosmo (1840 – 1901) English poet and art critic.

MONROE, Marilyn (1926 – 1962) American model, actress and singer.

MONTAIGNE, Michel de (1533 – 1592) French essayist and statesman.

MONTALVO, Juan (1832 – 1889) Ecuadorian author, essayist and anti-cleric.

MONTAPERT, Alfred Armand. American author of inspirational books.

MONTESQUIE, Charles de Secondat, Baron de (1689 – 1755) French political philosopher.

MONTGOMERY, Lucy Maud (1874 – 1942) Prolific Canadian novelist.

MOORE, Thomas (1779 – 1853) Irish poet, singer, songwriter and entertainer.

MOORE, Sir Thomas (1478 – 1535) English social philosopher, author and statesman.

MORANDOTTY, Alessandro (1909 – 79) Italian art collector and dealer.

MORDILLO, Guillermo (1932 -) Argentinian cartoonist.

MORECAMBE, Eric (1926 – 1984) English TV comedian with partner Ernie Wise..

MORELL, Thomas (1703 – 84) English librettist and classical scholar.

MORLEY, Christopher (1890 – 1957) American journalist, novelist, essayist and poet.

MORLEY, Robert (1908 - 1992) English theatre and film actor.

MORRIS, Desmond (1928 -) English zoologist, ethologist, painter and author.

MOUSTAKAS, Clark. American clinical psychologist.

MOYERS, Bill (1934 -) American journalist, TV news commentator, producer and author.

MUGGERIDGE, Malcolm (1903 – 90) English journalist, author and media personality.

MULLEN, Tom (1934 -) American quaker, author of *A Very Good Marriage*.

MURDOCH, Dame Iris (1918 – 99) Irish-born English novelist, playwright and poet.

MURRAY, Chic (1919 - 85) Scots comedian, stage and film actor.

MURRAY, Mitch (1940 -) English songwriter, speech maker, record producer and author.

NASH, Ogden (1902 – 71) American comic poet best know for his outrageous rhymes.

NEAGLE, Anna (1908 – 86) English actress.

NEAL, Patricia (1926 – 2010) American Oscar-winning screen and stage actress.

NEESON, Liam (1952 -) Irish actor who has been the recipient of many awards.

NELSON, Horatio (1759 – 1805) English flag officer in the Royal Navy.

NERBURN, Kent. American sculptor, theologian and writer.

NEVILL, Lady Dorothy (1826 – 1913) English author of a number of volumes of memoirs.

NICKLAUS, Jack (1940 -) Highly successful American professional golfer.

NIEBUHR, Reinhold (1892 – 1971) American theologian, professor, editor and writer.

NIGHTINGALE, Florence (1820 – 1910) English founder of nursing as a profession.

NIMMO, Derek (1930 – 99) English character actor, after-dinner speaker and writer.

NIN, Anais (1903 – 77) French diarist and one of the finest writers of female erotica.

NIZER, Louis (1902 – 94) Noted American trial lawyer.

NOLTE, Dorothy (1924 – 2005) American columnist and writer on family matters.

NOONAN, Peggy (1959 -) Columnist on *The Wall Street Journal* and best-selling author.

NORDEN, Denis (1922 -) English comedy writer and television presenter.

NORTON, Eleanor Holmes (1937 -) African-American lawyer, professor and politician.

NUESE, Josephine. American author of *The Country Garden*.

OATES, Joyce Carol (1938 -) American novelist, poet and Professor at Princeton.

OBAMA, Barack (1961 -) The first African-American to be elected President of the USA.

O'BRIEN, Conan (1963 -) American comedian, television host and writer.

O'CASEY, Sean (1880 - 1964) Major Irish playwright and memoirist.

O'HUIGINN, Sean. Appointed Ambassador of Ireland to Germany in 2002.
OLATUNJI, Babatunde (1927 – 2003) Nigerian drummer, recording artist & social activist.

OLIVER, Mary (1935 -) Prolific American Pulitzer Prize-winning poet.

OLSON, Tillie (1912 – 2007) American novelist and author of short stories and essays.

O'MALLEY, Austin (1858 – 1932) American physician, writer and humorist.

O'MARA, Peggy. American public speaker and publisher, editor and owner of *Mothering*.

ONO, Joko (1933 -) Japanese-born American artist, author, musician and peace activist.

ORBEN, Robert (1927 -) Prolific American author of books of quips and jokes.

O'ROUKE, P. J (1947 -) American political satirist.

ORTMAN, Mark. American author.

ORTON, William (1948 – 2009) American businessman.

ORWELL, George (1903 – 1950) English satirist, novelist and political essayist.

OSLER, Sir William (1849 – 1919) Canadian physician, pathologist, educator and author.

OUIDA.(1839 - 1908) The pen name of Marie Loiuse de la Ramee, an English novelist.

OURSLER, Fulton (1893 – 1952) American journalist, playwright, editor and author.

OVID (43 BC – AD 17) Roman poet, author of three major collections of erotic poetry.

OWENS, Gary (1936 -) American disc-jockey and voice actor.

OXENHAM, John (1852 – 1941) English journalist, novelist, poet and hymn-writer.

PADDISON, Sara, American author of *The Hidden Power of the Heart*.

PAIGE, Leroy R. "Satchel".(1906 – 82) Accomplished African-American baseball player.

PAINE, Thomas (1737 – 1809) English-American pamphleteer and political activist.

PALMER, Arnold (1929 -) Highly successful American professional golfer.

PARACHIN, Victor. American clergyman, freelance journalist and author of inspiring books.

PARKE, Ross American child psychologist, authority on family life and father's role therein.

PARKER, Dorothy (1893 – 1967) American poet, essayist, cynic and wit.

PARKER, Sarah Jessica (1965 -) American actress and producer.

PARSONS, Tony (1953 -) English journalist, columnist, broadcaster and novelist.

PARTON, Dolly (1946 -) American singer-songwriter, actress and philanthropist.

PASCAL, Blaise (1623 – 1662) French physicist, religious philosopher and theologian.

PATTON, George S (1885 – 1949) The most successful US field commander of any war.

PAUL, Robert. English computer scientist and humorist.

PAVAROTTI, Luciano (1935 – 2007) One of the most successful tenors of all time.

PAVLOVA, Anna (1881 – 1931) One of the finest classical ballet dancers of all time.

PEACOCK, Thomas Love (1785 – 1866) English novelist , essayist and poet.

PEALE, Norman Vincent (1898 – 1993) American preacher and author of self-help books.

PEARSON, Carol.Best-selling American author and Professor of Leadership Studies.

PECK, M. Scott (1936 – 2005) American psychiatrist and best-selling author.

PENN, William (1644 – 1718) English Quaker who established the colony of Pennsylvania.

PEPYS, Samuel (1633 – 1703) English civil servant and diarist.

PERKINS, Leslie Danford. American author of humorous poems mainly for children.

PETER, Laurence (1919 – 90) Canadian educator, management theorist and humorist.

PHILLIPS, Stephen (1864 – 1915) English poet and dramatist.

PHILLIPS, Wendell (1811 – 84) American abolitionist, outstanding orator and writer.

PHILLPOTS, Eden (1863 – 1960) English author, poet and dramatist.

PIPHER, Mary (1947 -) American clinical psychologist, author and international speaker.

PITT, William, 1st Earl of Chatham (1708 – 78) Senior English statesman and orator.

PITZER, Gloria. American author of over 39 recipe books.

PLATO (c. 427 – 347 BC) Greek philosopher taught by Socrates and teacher of Aristotle.

PLAUTUS (c. 254 – 184 BC) Roman auther of comedies. 21 of his plays survive.

PLINY THE YOUNGER (61 – 112 AD) Roman Lawyer, magistrate and letter writer

PLUTARCH (c. 46 – 120 AD) Greek historian, biographer and essayist.

POGREBIN, Letty Cotton (1939 -) American journalist, writer and feminist advocate.

POOLE, Mary Pettibone. American author and deviser of epigrams.

POPE, Alexander (1688 – 1744) English poet, satirist and wit.

POPE John 23rd (1881 – 1963) Enlightened Catholic churchman, elected Pope in 1958.

POPE John Paul 2nd (1920 – 2005) Polish-born Pope acclaimed an influential world leader.

PORTER, Cole (1892 – 1964) American composer and lyricist, mainly of musical comedies.

POST, Emily (1872 - 1960) American author and columnist on etiquette.

PRATCHETT, Sir Terry (1948 -) English best-selling science fiction writer.

PRENTICE, George (1802 - 70) American newspaper editor and poet.

PRESLEY, Elvis (1935 - 77) American singer referred to as "The King of Rock and Roll".

PRIESTLEY, J.B. (1894 -1984) English novelist, playwright and critic.

PRIOR, Matthew (1664 - 1721) English poet, satirist and diplomat.

PRITCHARD, Michael. Acclaimed American keynote speaker, humorist and author.

PRITCHETT. Price (1941 -) American business adviser, speaker and author.

PRITCHETT, Sir Victor Sawdon (1900 - 97) Prolific English short story writer and critic.

PROCHNOW, Herbert (1897 - 1998) American author of books of anecdotes and epigrams.

PROUST, Marcel (1871 - 1922) French novelist, critic and essayist.

PROVERB. A short pithy saying in general use, held to embody an accepted truth.

PUBLILIUS SYRUS. A Latin writer of maxims who flourished in the 1st century BC.

PULSIFER, Catherine (1957 -) American author who contributes words of wisdom and inspiration to the website on: www.stresslesscountry.com.

PUZO, Mario (1920 - 99) American novelist and screenwriter who wrote about the mafia.

QUANT, Mary (1934 -) English fashion designer who introduced the miniskirt in 1966.

QUIDA (1839 – 1908) The pseudonym of the prolific English novelist Maria Louise Rame.

QUILLEN, Robert (1887 - 1948) American journalist, syndicated columnist and humorist.

QUINDLEN, Anna (1953 -) American Pulitzer Prize-winning columnist and novelist.

RADNER, Gilda (1946 - 89) American comedienne, television and film actress.

RAND, Ayn (1909 - 82) American philosopher, novelist, screenwriter and playwright.

RATTINER, Susan. American editor of books of quotations.

RAY, John (1627 – 1705) English author of important works on botany, zoology & proverbs.

RAY, Ted (1905 – 77) English comedian who played comedy rolls on radio and films.

RAYBURN, Sam (1882 – 1961) American politician.

REAGAN, Nancy (1921 -) Widow of former United States President, Ronald Reagan.

REAGAN, Ronald (1911 – 2004) Republican politician, 40th president of US. (1981 – 1989).

REARD, Louis (1897 – 1984) French automobile engineer who invented the bikini in 1946.

REES, Nigel (1944 -) English writer of fiction and humour, radio host for panel games.

REEVE, Christopher (1952 - 2004) American actor, screenwriter, film director and author.

REILLY, Rick (1958 -) American sports writer, columnist and author.

REVSON, Charles (1906 - 75) American business tycoon, co-founder of Revlon Cosmetics.

RHODES, Cecil (1853 - 1902) English-born South African politician and businessman.

RICHARDSON, Cheryl. Best-selling American author, speaker and life coach.

RICKOVER, Admiral Hyman (1900 – 86) Four-star admiral in the American navy.

RINEHART, Mary Roberts (1876 – 1958) American crime writer.

RIVAROL, Antoine de (1753 – 1801) French writer and witty epigrammatist.

RIVERS Joan (1933 -) American comedienne, actress, television personality and author.

ROBINSON, Spider (1948 -) Canadian award-winning science fiction writer.

ROCHEFOUCAULD, Francois de (1613 - 80) French author of maxims and memoirs.

ROCKEFELLER, John. (1839 – 1937) American industrialist and philanthropist.

RODDICK, Dame Anita (1942 – 2007) Successful and enlightened English businesswoman.

RODREGUEZ, Paul (1955 -) Mexican-born American comedian and actor.

ROGERS,Will (1879 – 1935) American columnist, lecturer, humorist and actor.

ROHN, Jim (1930 – 2009) American entrepreneur, motivational coach, speaker and author.

ROMULA, Carlos (1899 - 1985) Filipino diplomat, politician, journalist, and author.

ROONEY, Andy (1919 -) American TV commentator, syndicated columnist and author.

ROOSEVELT, Eleanor (1884 – 1962) Wrote a daily newspaper column from 1935 – 1962.

ROOSEVELT, Franklin D (1882 – 1945) Democratic politician, 32nd President of the USA.

ROOSEVELT, James (1907 – 1991) Democratic party activist and businessman.

ROOSEVELT, "Teddy" (1858 – 1919) Republican politician, 26th President of the USA.

ROSSETTI, Christina (1830 – 94) English poet and devout high Anglican.

ROSTEN, Leo (1918 – 97) Polish-born American teacher, scriptwriter, author and humorist.

ROTH, Philip (1933 -) Prolific American award-winning novelist.and short story writer.

ROUSSEAU, Jean Jacques (1712 – 78) Swiss-born French social philosopher and writer.

ROWLAND, Helen (1875 – 1950) American journalist, author and humorist.

ROWLAND, J. K. (1965 -) Scottish author of the Harry Potter fantasy novels.

RUBINSTEIN, Helena (1870 – 1965) Polish-born American beautician & cosmetics tycoon.

RUDNER, Rita (1953 -) American comedienne, screenwriter and actress.

RUDOLPH, Wilma (1940-94) American Olympic prize-winning athlete.

RUNBECK, Margaret Lee (1905-56) Prolific American author.

RUNCIE, Robert (1921-2000) English cleric, archbishop of Canterbury from 1980 – 1991.

RUSHDIE, Salman (1947 -) Indian-born English novelist.

RUSSELL, Bertrand (1872 - 1970) English philosopher and social reformer.

RUSSELL, Mark (1932 -) American political comedian and satirist.

RUSSELL, Rosalind (1907 – 76) American stage and screen actress.

SABIN, Louis. American author.of books for young adults and children.

SAGA MAGAZINE. UK's top selling subscription magazine for today's over 50s.

SAGAN, Carl (1934 - 96) Highly successful American author of popular science books.
SAINT-EXUPERY, Antoine de (1900 – 44) French aviator and author.

SAKI (1870 - 1916) Pen name of Hector Hugh Munro, satirist and witty short story writer.

SALLUST (86 – c.34 BC) Roman historian.and politician.

SAMALIN, Nancy. A leading keynote speaker and author on parenting issues.

SANDBURG, Carl (1878 – 1967) American Pulitzer Prize-winning poet, editor and author.

SANGSTER, Margaret Elizabeth (1838 – 1912) American poet, editor and author.

SANTAYANA, George (1863 – 1952) American philosopher, poet, essayist and novelist.

SARTON, May (1912 – 95) American poet, novelist and memoirist.

SARTRE, Jean-Paul (1905 – 80) French philosopher, playwright and novelist.

SATIR, Virginia (1916 – 88) American author and family therapist.

SAVAGE, Robert C. American pastor and editor of *Life Lessons: An Inspirational Book.*

SAVANT, Marilyn vos (1946 -) American magazine columnist, author and playwright.

SAYERS, Dorothy L.(1893 – 1957) English crime writer, essayist and playwright.

SCARR, Sandra (1936 -) Author and Professor of Psychology at University of Virginia.

SCHACHTEL, Rabbi Hyman Judah (1907 – 90) American theologian, educator and author.

SCHAEF, Anne Wilson (1934 -) American psychotherapist, consultant, lecturer and author.
SCHIAPARELLI, Elsa(1896 – 1973) Italian-born Parisian fashion designer.

SCHILLER, Johann Christoph Frederich (1759 – 1805) German poet, historian, playwright.

SCHOPENHAUR, Arthur (1788 – 1860) German atheistic philosopher.

SCHREIBER, Brad. American playwright, screenwriter, journalist and writer.

SCHULLER, Robert (1926-) American pastor, televangelist and author.

SCHULMAN, Michael. American academic, author of books on ethics and morality.

SCHULTZ,Charles (1922 – 2000) American cartoonist, creator of *The Peanuts Comic Strip.*

SCHWAB, Charles (1862 – 1939) American steel magnate.

SCHWEITZER, Albert (1875 – 1965) Protestant theologian, organist & missionary surgeon.

SCOTT-HOLLAND, Henry (1847 – 1918) English churchman, author and professor.

SCOTT-MAXWELL, Florida (1883 – 1979) American playwright, author and psychologist.

SEABEES. From the initials of "CONSTRUCTION BATTALION" (CB) of US navy.

SEEGER, Pete (1919 -) American folk singer-songwriter of anti-war protest songs.

SEINFIELD, Jerry (1954 – 2009) American stand up comedian, actor and writer.

SELASSIE, Haile (1892 – 1975) Emperor of Ethiopia from 1930 till 1974.

SELDON, John (1584 – 1654) English jurist and scholar of England's ancient laws.

SELIGMAN, Martin (1942 -) American psychologist and author of self-help books.

SELLAR, W.C.(1898 – 1951) Scottish humorist who wrote for *Punch*

SELLERS, Peter (1925 – 80) English film actor, radio personality and comedian.

SENECA (c. 4 BC – 65 AD) Roman stoic philosopher, statesman, dramatist and humorist.

SERVICE, Robert (1874 - 1958), English-born Canadian poet, "The Bard of the Yukon".

SEWELL, Anna (1820 – 78) English novelist, best known as the author of *Black Beauty*.

SHAKESPEARE, William (1564 – 1616) English poet and the world's greatest dramatist.

SHAW, George Bernard (1856 – 1950) Irish playwright, novelist and author of short stories.

SHEEHY, Gail (1937 -) Award-winning literary journalist and prolific best-selling author.

SHEEN, Fulton (1895 - 1979), American RC archbishop and able TV preacher.

SHELLEY, Percy Bysshe (1792 - 1822) One of the major English romantic poets.

SHER, Barbara. American career counsellor, best-selling author of books on achievement.

SHERIDAN, Richard Brinsley (1751 – 1816) Irish playwright, poet and MP for 32 years.

SHERMAN, Allan (1924 – 73) American comedy writer and television producer.

SHERMAN, James. Best-selling American author.

SHERO, Fred (1925 – 90) Canadian ice hockey player and coach.

SHERRIFF, R.C. (1896 – 1975) English novelist, playwright and screenwriter.

SHIELDS, Tom. Scottish journalist with *he Glasgow Herald*.

SHORE, Dinah (1916 – 94) American singer, actress and television personality.

SHRINER, Herb (1918 – 70) American humorist, radio and TV personality and monologist.

SIDNEY, Sir Philip (1554 – 86) English poet, courtier and soldier.

SIEGEL, Bernie. American physician, lecturer and author.

SILCOCK, Arnold. Edited *Verse and Worse* – a collection of humorous verse (1952).

SILESIUS, Angelus (1624 – 77) German mystic and poet.

SIMON, Carly (1945 -).American award-winning singer-songwriter, musician and author.

SIMPSON, James. A former Moderator of the General Assembly of the Church of Scotland and an able and popular after-dinner speaker and author.

SKINNER, B.F. (1904 – 90) American psychologist, taught at Harvard from 1947 till 1974.

SLATTERY, Tony (1959 -) English comedian and television and film actor.

SMEDES, Lewis (1921 – 2002) American theologian and prolific author.

SMEDLEY, Ralph (1878 – 1965) The American founder of Toastmasters International.

SMILES, Samuel (1812 – 1904) Scottish author of *Self Help* (1859)

SMITH, Adam (1723 – 90) Scottish moral philosopher and pioneer of political economics

SMITH, Dave (1940 -) American librarian and archivist for the Walt Disney Company.

SMITH, Francis Marion (1846 – 1931) American business magnate.

SMITH, Ken. Scottish journalist on *The Glasgow Herald*.

SMITH, Lilian (1897 - 1966) American writer and social critic.

SMITH, Logan Pearsall (1865 – 1946) American essayist, aphorist and critic.

SMITH, Sydney (1771 – 1845) English Anglican cleric, essayist and wit.

SMITH, Will (1969 -) American award-winning actor and film producer.

SMOTHERS, Tommy (1937 -) American comedian, composer and musician.

SOCRATES (c. 469 – 399 BC) Classical Greek philosopher.

SOLON (c. 638 – 558 BC) Athenian statesman, law maker and poet.

SOMERS, Suzanne (1946 -)American actress, singer, business woman and self-help author.

SOPHOCLES (495 – 406 BC) Greek dramatist, one of the three great tragedians.

SOUTHEY, Robert (1774 – 1843) English poet, essayist, historian and prolific letter writer.

SPARK, Dame Muriel (1918 – 2006) Award-winning Scottish novelist.

SPENCER, Herbert (1820 – 1903) English philosopher, sociologist and political theorist.

SPOCK, Benjamin (1903 – 98) Americam paediatrician, author of *Baby & Child Care*.1946.

SPRINGSTEEN, Bruce (1949 -) American rock singer-songwriter and guitarist.

SPURGEON, Charles (1834 – 92) Influential English Baptist preacher and prolific author.

SPURLOCK, Morgan (1970 -) American television producer, journalist and screenwriter.

SAINT FRANCIS of ASSISI (1181 – 1226) Italian Catholic friar, mystic and preacher.

STANLEY, Bessie Anderson (1879 - 1952) Known only for her poem *Success*.

STANLEY, Edward, 15th Earl of Derby (1826 – 1893) Senior English Statesman.

STANTON, Elizabeth Cady (1815 - 1902) American advocate for women's rights.

STANTON, Will (1918 – 96) American humorist, author of books and short stories.

STEELE, Sir Richard (1672 – 1729) English essayist, dramatist, journalist and politician.

STEPHENS, James (1882 - 1950) Irish poet. and novelist.

STERN, Gladys (1890 – 1973) English novelist, author of short stories, plays and memoirs.

STERNE, Laurence (1713 – 68) Irish novelist and Anglican clergyman.

STEVENSON, Adlai (1900 – 65) Articulate American democratic politician and diplomat.

STEVENSON, Robert Louis (1850 – 94) Scottish novelist, poet, essayist and travel writer.

STOLL, Clifford. American astonomer, computer system administrator and Internet guru.

STONE, I. F (1907 – 89) Iconoclastic American investigative journalist.

STOPPARD, Sir Tom (1937 -) Award-winning English playwright and screenwriter.

STOWE, Harriet Beecher (1811 – 1896) American abolitionist, social reformer and novelist.

STRICKLAND, Gillian (1869 – 1954) American journalist, humorist, poet and speaker.

STRONG, Anna Louisa, (1885 - 1970) American left-wing journalist.

STUBBS, Una (1937 -) English stage and television actress.

SULTANOFF, Steve. American clinical psychologist, therapeutic humorist and speaker.

SUNDAY, W.A. "Billy" (1862 – 1935) American evangelist.

SUTTON, "Willie" (1901 – 80) American bank robber and author.

SWANSON, Gloria (1899 – 1983) American film actress from the silent days.

SWEDENBORG, Emmanuel (1688 – 1772) Swedish theologian and Christian mystic.

SWIFT, Jonathan (1667 – 1745) Anglo-Irish cleric, satirist, essayist and author.

SWINDOLL, Charles (1934 -) American pastor, author and radio preacher.

SYKES, Eric (1923 – 2012) English radio, TV and film writer, actor and director.

SYRUS, Publilius (1st century BC) Latin author of wise and moral maxims.

SZASZ ("SAAS"), Thomas (1920 -) American academic and psychiatrist.

TACITUS (56 – 117 AD) Roman senator, orator and historian.

TAGORE. Rabindranath (1861 – 1941) Bengali Nobel Prize-winning poet and novelist.

TALBERT, Bob (1936 – 1999) For 31 years a daily columnist with *The Detroit Free Press*.

TAO TE CHING. Chinese text, the main book of Taoism, written by the sage Lao Tzu.

TARKINGTON, Booth (1869 – 1946)American Pulitzer Prize-winning novelist & dramatist.

TAYLOR, Alan. Journalist and columnist with *The Herald* and *Sunday Herald*.

TAYLOR, Alan (1959 -) American television and film producer and screenwriter.

TAYLOR, Ann (1782 – 1866) English poet and literary critic.

TAYLOR, Bert Leston (1866 – 1921) American columnist, humorist, poet and author.

TAYLOR, Ida Scott. 19th century English author.

TEASDALE, Sara (1884 – 1933) American lyrical poet.

TENNYSON, Alfred, Lord (1809 – 1892) English poet and Poet Laureate (1859 – 1892).

TERENCE (c. 190 BC – 159 BC) Playwright of the Roman Republic.

THACKERAY, William Makepeace (1811 – 1863) English satirical novelist.

THALES (c. 624 BC – 546 BC) Regarded as the first philosopher in the Greek tradition.

THATCHER, Major Sir Denis. English businessman and husband of former prime minister.

THATCHER, Margaret (1925 – 2013) English Conservative PM from 1979 till 1990)

THAVES, Bob (1924 – 2006) American award-winning cartoonist.

THEROUX, Paul (1941 -) American award-winning travel writer and novelist.

THEROUX, Phyllis. American essayist, columnist, teacher and author.

THOMAS, Lowell (1892 – 1981) American writer, broadcaster and traveller.

THOREAU, Henry David (1817 – 62) American author, poet and naturalist.

THROWER, Mitch. American author, financier, entrepreneur and triathlete.

THURBER, James (1894 – 1961) American author, cartoonist and celebrated wit.

THURMAN, Howard (1899 – 1981) American philosopher, theologian, educator and auther.

TILL, Antonia American editor and author of cookery books.

TILLICH, Paul (1886 – 1965) German-born American theologian and philosopher.

TIRUVALLUVAR. Celebrated Tamil poet.

TOFFLER, Alvin (1928 -) American writer and futurist.

TOLLE, Eckhart (1948 -) German-born Canadian resident. Author and spiritual teacher.

TOLSTOY, Leo (1821 - 1910), Russian novelist, essayist, dramatist and reformer.

TOMLIN, Lily (1939 -) American actress, comedienne, writer and producer.

TOSCANINI, Arturo (1868 – 1957) Italian conductor and accomplished musician.

TOYNBEE, Arnold (1889 – 1975) English historian who wrote a 12 volume analysis of the
  rise and fall of civilisation entitled *A Study of History* (1934 – 1963)

TRACY, Brian (1944 -) Canadian self-help author.

TREVELYAN,G.M, (1876 – 1962) English historian, pioneered the study of social history.

TRUMAN, Harry (1884 – 1972) Democratic statesman, the 33rd President of the USA.

TUPPER, Martin Farquhar (1810 – 89) English writer and poet.

TWAIN, Mark (1835 – 1910) American author, lecturer and humorist.

TWITTY, Conway (1933 – 93) One of America's most successful country music artists.

TYGER, Frank. An aphorist frequently quoted on the Internet. Little is known about him.

TZU LAO (6th century BC) A Chinese philosopher, a central figure in Taoism.

TZU SUN. Ancient Chinese military general and strategist.

ULLMAN, Samuel (1840 – 1924) American businessman, best known for his poem *Youth*.

UNAMUNO. Miguel de (1864 – 1936) Spanish essayist, novelist and poet of Basque origin.

UPDYKE, John (1932 – 2009) American novelist, short story writer, poet and critic.

USTINOV, Sir Peter (1921 – 2004) English actor, writer and noted wit and raconteur.

VALERY, Paul (1871 – 1945) French poet, essayist, philosopher and aphorist.

VAN BUREN, Abigail. The pen name of a widely syndicated advice column begun in 1956.

VAN DOREN, Mark (1894 – 1972) Pulitzer Prize-winning author, poet and critic.

VAN DYKE, Henry (1852 – 1933) American clergyman, educator and author.

VAUGHAN, Bill (1915 – 77) American author, aphorist and syndicated columnist

VIORST, Judith (1931 -) American journalist, author of advice books and children's books.

VIRGIL (1ˢᵗ century BC) Roman poet.

VOLTAIRE (1694 – 1778) French historian, political philosopher, essayist and novelist.

WAGNER, Richard (1813 – 83) German opera composer, conductor and essayist.

WAITLEY, Denis (1933 -) American motivational speaker, consultant and writer.

WALKOWICZ, Chris. Award-winning American author on dog related subjects.

WALLACE, Susan. American author of *Love and War:250 Years of Wartime Love Letters*.

WALTERS, Julie (1950 -) Award-winning English actress and novelist.

WALTON, Izaac (1593 - 1683) English author of *The Compleat Angler* (1653)

WANAMAKER, John (1838 - 1922) American businessman who pioneered advertising.

WARD, Artemus (1834 - 67) American humorist, lecturer and author of short stories.

WARD, Thomas (1652 – 1708) English Catholic author of *The English Reformation* (1710).

WARD,William Arthur(1921 – 94) American columnist and author of inspirational maxims.

WARNER, Charles Dudley (1829 – 1900) American essayist and novelist.

WASHINGTON, Booker (1856 – 1915) American educator, author and civil rights leader.

WASHINGTON, George (1732 – 99) The first President of the USA (1789 – 1797).

WATTERSON, Bill (1958 -) American syndicated cartoonist, creator of *Calvin & Hobbes*.

WATSON, Thomas (1874 – 1956) President of International Business Machines.

WAUGH, Evelyn (1903 – 66) English novelist, short story writer, biographer and diarist.

WAYNE, John (1907 – 79) American film actor, director and producer.

WEBSTER, Paul Francis (1907 – 84) Highly successful American lyricist.

WEIL, Simone (1909 – 43) French philosopher, political activist and Christian mystic.

WELLES, Orson (1915 – 85) American writer, actor and producer

WELLS, Carolyn (1862 – 1942) American novelist and poet noted for he nonsense verses.

WESLEY, John (1703 – 1791) English founder of Methodism.

WEST, Dame Rebecca (1892 – 1983) English author, literary critic and travel writer.

WHARTON, Edith (1862 – 1937) Pulitzer Prize-winning novelist and short story writer.

WHITE, E. B (1899 – 1985) American author and long time contributer to *The New Yorker*.

WHITE, Gail. Award-winning and widely published American poet.

WHITEHEAD, Alfred North (1861 – 1947) English mathematician, educator and author.

WHITEHORN, Katherine (1928 -) English journalist, columnist, writer and wit.

WHITTIER, James Greenleaf (1807 – 92) Influential American Quaker poet and abolitionist.

WHITTON. Charlotte (1896 – 1975) Canadian feminist and mayor of Ottawa.

WIESEL, Elie (1928 -), American professor, political activist, author & holocaust survivor

WILCOX, Bonnie. American author of books about dogs.

WILCOX, Colleen. American senior schools administrator.

WILCOX, Ella Wheeler (1850 - 1919) American author and poet.

WILDE, Oscar (1854 – 1900) Irish writer, dramatist and wit.

WILLIAMS, Don (1939 -) American country singer and songwriter.

WILLIAMS, Pat (1940 -) American motivational and inspirational speaker and writer.

WILLIAMS, Robin (1951 -) Award-winning American actor and comedian.

WILLIAMS, Tennessee (1911 – 1983) American playwright, screenwriter, essayist and poet.

WILLIAMSON, Marianne (1952 -) American spiritual activist, author and lecturer.

WILMOT, John, 2nd Earl of Rochester (1647 – 60) English poet, wit and libertine.

WILSON, Earl (1907 – 87) American journalist, gossip columnist and author.

WINFREY, Oprah (1954 -) American television host, producer and philanthropist.

WINTERS, Shelley (1920 – 2006) American actress.

WISE, Ernie (1925 - 99) English comedian and television entertainer.

WODEHOUSE, P.G (1881 - 1975) English novelist, lyricist and writer of screenplays.

WOGAN, Sir Terry (1938 -), Irish radio and television broadcaster.

WOODEN, John (1910 – 2010) Highly successful American college basketball coach.

WOODRUFF, Robert "Bob". American children's poet.

WOODRUFF, Julia Louisa. American writer.

WOODS, Tiger (1975 -) World class American professional golfer.

WOOLCOTT, Alexander (1887 – 1943) Wittty American columnist for *The New Yorker*.

WOOTEN, Patty. American author of books related to humour.

WORDSWORTH, William (1770 – 1850) English poet.

WOUK, Herman (1915 -) Pulitzer Prize-winning American novelist

WRIGHT Clarissa (1947 -) English celebrity chef and television personality.

WRIGHT, Stephen (1955 -) American comedian.

WYNDHAM-LEWIS, Dominic Bevan (1891 – 1969) English columnist, wit and humorist.

YEATHMAN, R. J. (1897 – 1968) English humorist who wrote for *Punch*.

YEATS, W.B. (1865 – 1939) Irish poet and dramatist. The foremost literary figure of his day.

YOUNG, Edward (1681 – 1765) English poet best remembered for *Night Thoughts*.

YOUNGMAN, Henry "Henny" (1906 – 98) English-born American comedian.

YUTANG, Lin (1895 – 1976) Chinese- American writer, translater and linguist.

ZIGLAR, "Zig" (1926 - 2012)) American author, salesman and motivational speaker.

ZELINSKI, Ernie. Best-selling American author and unconventional career expert.

ZENO of Citium (c. 334 – c. 262 BC) Greek founder of the stoic school of philosophy.

ZUNIN, Leonard. American psychiatric consultant, distinguished researcher and lecturer.

ZUNIN Hilary Stanton. Co-author with her husband, Leonard, of *The Art of Consolation*.

ABOUT THE AUTHOR

John Andrew has had a varied, eventful and highly accomplished life. To condense it into its essence, he spent eleven years as a Church of Scotland minister in Peterculter, Aberdeenshire, followed by twenty five years as Principal Teacher of Religious and Moral Education at Kincorth Academy, Aberdeen.

He holds an MA and a BD from Edinburgh University and a Dip Ed and a Dip RE from Aberdeen College of Education.

The author has had three books published: From Abraham to David, published by Hultons/Stanley Thornes in 1985, The Life and Work of Jesus, by the same publisher, also in 1985 and A Puzzle Pack of Bible Knowledge, published by Stanley Thornes in 1989.

These three books are interesting because they were all published during his teaching career and were completely innovative at that time because they comprised a set of puzzles and word games and crosswords long before any puzzle magazines came into existence. Perhaps more amazing is that, although the books were withdrawn from publication in 1993, they continue to sell and it is obviously great testimony to the books and the author that, 28 years after being withdrawn, he still receives a royalty cheque every single year.

A further string to his bow is that he is an accomplished and highly skilled public speaker whose talents are always in demand. From his rather (and unnecessarily so) nervous first address at a Burns Supper he developed into a highly respected speaker at Various events throughout the year, including Rotary and Probus Club meetings, Kirk soirees and village concerts. It is, in part, because of his incorporation of wise and witty quotations into these talks that this latest book emerged.

25596528R00401

Printed in Great Britain
by Amazon